NAVIGATING THE AS/400

2ND EDITION

JOHN ENCK
MICHAEL RYAN

To join a Prentice Hall PTR Internet Mailing list, point to:
http://www.prenhall.com/mail_lists/

Prentice Hall PTR
Upper Saddle River, New Jersey 07458

ISBN 0-13-862551-4

90000

9 780138 625511

Library of Congress Cataloging-in-Publication Data

Enck, John, 1956-
    Navigating the AS/400: A Hands-On Guide / John Enck and Michael Ryan -- 2nd ed.
    p.   cm.
    Includes bibliographical references and index.
    ISBN 0-13-862558-1
    1. IBM AS/400 (Computer)I. Ryan, Michael, 1957- .   II. Title.
    QA76.8.I25919E531997
    004. 1'45--dc21   97-25872
                                            CIP

Editorial/production supervision: *Dawn Speth White*
Cover designer: *Jayne Conte*
Cover Art Photograph: *Carribean Map - Still Life by Garry Gay*
Manufacturing manager: *Alexis R. Heydt*
Marketing manager: *Stephen Solomon*
Acquisitions editor: *Michael Meehan*
Editorial assistant: *Barbara Alfieri*

©1998 by Prentice Hall PTR
Prentice-Hall, Inc.
A Simon & Schuster Company
Upper Saddle River, NJ 07458

Prentice Hall books are widely used by corporations and government agencies
for training, marketing, and resale.

The publisher offers discounts on this book when ordered in bulk quantities.
For more information, contact: Corporate Sales Department, Phone: 800-382-3419;
Fax: 201-236-7141; E-mail: corpsales@prenhall.com; or write: Prentice Hall PTR,
Corp. Sales Dept., One Lake Street, Upper Saddle River, NJ 07458.

Printed in the United States of America
10 9 8 7 6 5 4 3 2 1

ISBN   0-13-862558-1

Prentice-Hall International (UK) Limited, *London*
Prentice-Hall of Australia Pty. Limited, *Sydney*
Prentice-Hall Canada Inc., *Toronto*
Prentice-Hall Hispanoamericana, S.A., *Mexico*
Prentice-Hall of India Private Limited, *New Delhi*
Prentice-Hall of Japan, Inc., *Tokyo*
Simon & Schuster Asia Pte. Ltd., *Singapore*
Editora Prentice-Hall do Brasil, Ltda., *Rio de Janeiro*

Contents

Notices

ACKNOWLEDGEMENTS

John Enck: As always, thanks to Marlene, Leanne, and Sean Enck for their patience and tolerance.

Michael Ryan: Thanks to Donna and Tommy for their caring and support.

TRADEMARKS

The following terms are trademarks of the IBM Corporation:

    Application System/400, AS/400, C/400, COBOL/400, FORTRAN/400, IBM, OfficeVision, OfficeVision/400, Operating System/400, OS/2, OS/400, PC AT, PC XT, Personal Computer AT, Personal Computer XT, Personal System/2, PL/I, PS/2, RPG III, RPG/400, SAA, SQL/400, Systems Application Architecture, 400

Introduction

0.1 THE AS/400 LEGACY

In the early part of 1988 the computer industry was buzzing with rumors of the "Silverlake" project. Although most of the technical details were kept under wraps, the industry knew "Silverlake" was the next generation of IBM midrange processors—the heir apparent to the throne room where the System/38 ruled from one chair and the System/36 from another. In many minds "Silverlake" was to usher in a new generation of midrange computing which would shore up the position of midrange processors in the face of the encroaching hordes of PCs, LANs, and the crumbling bastions of mainframes.

The name "Silverlake" was borrowed from a body of water located near the IBM Rochester, Minnesota center responsible for the development of the system. Although several analysts predicated the final system would bear the "Silverlake" moniker, the final product was released to the world in June of 1988 as the AS/400, the "AS" standing for "Application System," and the "400" rumored to represent the number of users the high-end system would handle.

The AS/400 was heralded into the data processing community with great vigor and much hoopla. In the months preceding the announcement IBM allowed software companies to load and test their software applications on the AS/400. The payoff for this effort was that the AS/400 was released with thousands of ready-to-run commercial application programs from both IBM and other companies. At the time of the announcement current IBM customers, prospective buyers, independent consultants, and many others were invited to view the announcement over IBM's nationwide video-link. The audience was introduced to the architecture of the AS/400 and its operating system, OS/400.

At that time in June of 1988, the AS/400 was presented as the single point of migration for the aging IBM System/38 and System/36. The System/38 was originally introduced in 1978 and was followed by the System/36 in 1983. A look at the AS/400 showed that it possessed major attributes of both systems: the processing power and database capabilities of the System/38, and the user-friendly menu structures and communications capabilities of the System/36. (In the first year after the announcement it became clear that the AS/400 was more similar to the System/38 than the System/36 when it came to porting applications.)

But what, exactly, was so great about the AS/400? Was it a precursor of things to come, or simply a rehash of things past?

0.2 THE OS/400 OPERATING SYSTEM

In truth, the AS/400 is a mixture of both old and new. On one hand, the contemporary hardware design and fresh operating system implementation clearly make the AS/400 a new breed of machine. On the other hand, the OS/400 operating system retains many core concepts of the System/38 operating system (CPF). In particular, two significant System/38 concepts have now become distinctive earmarks of the AS/400.

- Single-level storage—The operating system controls all access to memory storage and the physical disk media through the implementation of a logical storage "pool." Because the pool contains memory and can span multiple physical drives, users and applications are isolated from the specific details of the number of drives, the characteristics of an individual drive, or the distinctions between items stored in memory and items stored on disk.
- Object orientation—All information and structures on the AS/400 are organized into objects. Additional information is associated with each object to record creation, size, and access information. Virtually every item on the AS/400 is regarded as an object. For example, AS/400 objects include users, output queues, documents, folders, files, libraries, programs, menus, communication lines, controllers and devices, and many other entities.

Above and beyond these two capabilities are a number of OS/400 features that bring depth to the AS/400. Although none of these features are as newsworthy as single-level storage and an object-oriented architecture, they deliver the "meat and potatoes" capabilities required by the midrange market. Some of the more important features include

- simple-to-use menu structures for entry-level users and command line structures for advanced users. This allows users to gain familiarity with OS/400 through a series of menus, but once the functions are understood, the menus can be bypassed through the use of command line directives.
- a number of predefined libraries (for example, QSYS, QDOC, and QUSRSYS) and support of user-defined libraries. Files are a type of object contained in libraries and may contain program source code, screens, database information, and more.
- the use of folders to manage word processing documents. Folders can contain documents and also other folders. This provides a hierarchical structure similar to the directory structures used by other operating systems. All folders are stored in the IBM-supplied QDOC library.
- built-in database functions. Specifically, logical file definitions can be overlaid on top of physical data files to facilitate simple random access, indexed retrieval, or even complex relational retrieval. A logical file can be confined to a single physical file, or it can span multiple physical files.

- Distributed Data Management (DDM), SNA Distribution Services (SNADS), and Display Station Pass-through (DSPT) facilities. DDM allows one AS/400 to access files on another AS/400 in real time. SNADS provides a "store and forward" facility for transferring data and print files. Display Station Pass-through permits a user to access a second AS/400 as if he or she were a locally attached user.

- message queues at the user, workstation, and program level. These queues allow programs to interact with other programs or with users, permit users to communicate with other users, and let both users and programs interact with OS/400 tasks and resources.

Of course, OS/400 also provides functions to handle user security, print spooling, device operations, job accounting, and other "normal" operating system functions.

Accompanying the OS/400 operating system are a number of IBM and third-party applications. Although the wide variety of line-of-business applications has clearly been a major factor in the acceptance and popularity of the AS/400 product line, a second factor has been the availability of two products that handle difficult, but often critical, functions.

- OfficeVision/400—The original AS/400 implementation of OfficeVision was supposed to be part of IBM's multiplatform approach to office automation using IBM's System Application Architecture (SAA). Although the SAA-based project failed, the AS/400 product survived and has since gone on to provide basic office automation— word processing, document filing, electronic mail, and calendar management—to AS/400 users. OfficeVision is also capable of interfacing with mainframe-based office automation packages (such as PROFS and NOTES), allowing it to be an active participant in large corporate networks.

- Client Access—Client Access provides a means of integrating PCs and PS/2s with the AS/400 environment. Client Access is a product that operates in both the PCs and the AS/400(s) and provides workstation emulation, reciprocal printing, shared folder access (network-based disks), and file transfer, as well as other integration functions. Client Access can be run in both LAN and nonLAN environments, allowing it to serve as a solution in virtually any type of network.

Several versions of OS/400 have been released since its introduction in 1988. In the period between 1988 and 1991, the initial release, formally called Version 1 Release 1, was replaced by Version 1 Release 2, which was, in turn replaced by Version 1 Release 3. In 1991, a new version, Version 2 Release 1, was introduced and then succeeded by Version 2 Release 2 in 1992. IBM released Version 3 Release 1 in 1994. This version has been dubbed "The Foundation for The Future" by IBM as an indication of the future direction for OS/400. The operating system was fundamentally rewritten for V3R1 with the use of object-oriented tools and languages. Version 3 Release 2 (for CISC systems) and Version 3 Release 7 (for RISC systems) succeeded Version 3 Release 1 in 1996. Although each version has had its own pros and cons, each has faithfully adhered to the fundamental architecture of the AS/400 presented in 1988.

0.3 THE AS/400 HARDWARE

As in the case of the operating system, the hardware packaging of the AS/400 has gone through several evolutions. At the time of the announcement, the major AS/400 models were the B10, B20, B30, B40, B50, and B60 systems.

AS/400 models are grouped according to "system units," which refer to the enclosure and cabinetry associated with the model. The B10 and B20 used the model 9404 system unit, while the B30 through B60 used the model 9406 cabinet. These initial models also varied greatly in range and price; the entry level B10 was priced at $19,000, while the B60, which offered 5.5 times the performance (and perhaps even greater productivity) of a B10, was priced at $229,500. All of the models also had different levels of support for memory, disk storage, and communication capabilities.

The B-series models were eventually joined by C-series, D-series, and E-series models, some of which were packaged in a small new 9402 system unit. With the release of the E-series models, the price and performance range of the AS/400 models was greatly expanded. The low-end E02 offers 1.5 times the performance of the B10 for a basic unit price of $10,200, while the high-end E95 offers 42.1 times the performance of the B10 for a basic unit price of $973,000.

This increased growth in performance has been matched by increased storage capability. For example, the E02 can be configured with a maximum of 24 MB of memory and 1.976 GB of disk while the E95 can be configured with up to 512 MB of memory and 124.68 GB of disk storage. Again, this is in sharp contrast to the original B10/B60 line where the B10 could be configured with a maximum of 8 MB of memory and 945 MB of disk, and the B60 could handle a maximum of 96 MB of memory and 27.3 GB of disk. The newer "black box" AS/400 Systems have even greater processing capabilities and are discussed in Chapter 15 ("Advanced Topics").

Another capability of the AS/400 hardware that has contributed to its success is the wide range of communication options it supports. An AS/400 can be outfitted with a number of communication adapters that can operate concurrently. For example, a single AS/400 can be configured to communicate with workstations using twin-axial links, with a mainframe using a high-speed SDLC link, with PCs on an Ethernet LAN, and with other AS/400s on a token-ring LAN—and all interactions can be concurrent. Other types of connections are available and can also operate concurrently.

The performance advantages offered by the AS/400 architecture are achieved through the use of multiple processors. A main system processor handles core OS/400 functions, while a multifunction input/output processor oversees the activities of the storage devices and communications adapters. Performance is further enhanced through the use of intelligent communication adapters which contain their own microprocessors. Overall, this multiple processor approach allows the AS/400 to apply the best processor resources for a particular task—communications tasks are handled by the adapter, the multifunction processor regulates the flow of data between storage and communications devices and the system processor, and the system processor handles the mainstream computing activities.

0.4 THE AS/400 MARKET

The streamlined hardware architecture combined with the fully featured OS/400 operating system and the thousands of applications it hosts has made the AS/400 what it is today.

But what does that mean? After all, if the AS/400 is so "hot," why isn't it selling like hotcakes?

As a matter of fact, it is selling like hotcakes. At the time of this writing, more than 450,000 AS/400s are in place across the world. Although this may seem like a trivial number when compared to PC sales, it is actually quite dramatic when put in perspective to the midrange and mainframe market. For example

- The IBM mainframe was introduced to the market in 1964; at this time there are only approximately 24,000 in place.
- The Digital VAX computer was introduced in 1977; there are now approximately 500,000 in place.

With these figures in mind, obtaining a base of over 450,000 units over the course of nine years is quite impressive.

Where are these AS/400s being placed?

Unquestionably, the majority of AS/400 units are placed in medium-size businesses or at the departmental level of large corporations to handle line-of-business data processing chores. This includes the classic applications such as payroll, accounts receivable, accounts payable, order processing, and billing, but it also includes new, specialized applications such as manufacturing management and medical administration. In these areas the database capabilities inherent to the AS/400 make it a natural selection for data-intensive operations.

Beyond the line-of-business role, AS/400 systems have also been playing a significant role in the "right-sizing" evolution many companies have been going through. In this capacity, multiple AS/400 systems represent an ideal solution for a corporation that is moving away from a large centralized mainframe, but whose data processing load is too large or complex to be distributed on a PC LAN.

Where isn't the AS/400 being placed?

The AS/400 is rarely (never say never) used as a shop floor or laboratory controller for analog devices or as a graphics workstation. This type of technical processing remains the domain of Digital VAX machines, UNIX machines, and other specialized computer systems. But even though AS/400 systems are rarely seen in these technical environments, they may very well be just around the corner, collecting and analyzing data from the technical computers, or simply handling another aspect of the business.

Finally, note that a key element that has allowed the AS/400 to penetrate into new accounts is its communications and networking capabilities. An AS/400 can easily communicate with other AS/400s, with larger IBM mainframes, with Digital VAX and UNIX systems, and with PC LANs—and these interactions can all occur at the same time over a variety of communication links. This flexibility in the area of networking makes the AS/400 a strong contender for the role of an application or database server in any size or style of network.

0.5 THIS AS/400 BOOK

When you put all of the adjectives aside, a computer is basically a tool kit. Unfortunately, the tools in the kit are not simple and obvious like a hammer and saw; computer tools are sophisticated and intricate and they require training and practice to use effectively. With this in mind, this book is intended to serve as a guide. As such, it does not teach you how to build anything, rather it shows you how to use the tools at your disposal to support your own creative efforts.

Every effort has been made to make this reference book valuable on a day-to-day basis. To accomplish this goal, the book is logically organized along the following lines

- Chapters 1 through 4 discuss the basic aspects of the AS/400 of interest to all categories of users. This includes workstation usage, sign-on and sign-off procedures, help facilities, command language, the user environment, and information on libraries, files, and members.

- Chapters 5 through 8 explain operational and programmer-oriented structures and facilities. These chapters explain the queues and writers, messages, the Source Entry Utility (SEU), the AS/400 Command Language (CL), and operations.

- Chapters 9 through 12 describe significant utilities available for the OS/400 operating system. These include OfficeVision, the Data File Utility (DFU), the Screen Design Aid (SDA), and the Programming Development Manager (PDM).

- Chapter 13 explains the System/36 environment on the AS/400, including management, performance improvement, and saving and restoring information in the environment. Chapter 14 describes AS/400 communications, including Client Access, Display Station Passthrough, and AS/400 networking and data communications considerations. Chapter 15 describes a variety of advanced subjects, including AS/400 SQL and the new RISC systems.

- Appendices A through E provide reference material on commands, objects, keyboard functions, devices, and special programming operators.

Screen images and example commands are shown wherever possible. Please note, however, that the AS/400 supports two styles of screens (basic and intermediate) on some commands. For the sake of manageability, this book shows intermediate screens [you can change screen styles by using the <F21> (select assistance level) key].

Is this book for you?

The intended audience of this book is data processing amateurs and professionals who are currently having, or are anticipating having, hands-on encounters with an AS/400. And these days, that includes just about everyone.

1

Getting Started

Your first exposure to an AS/400 is gained by using a workstation to sign onto an AS/400 and interact with the OS/400 operating system and the applications it sponsors. Once you have successfully signed on an AS/400, you can then access several built-in help facilities to obtain help and usage information directly from the AS/400. In this chapter you will learn how to

- utilize a 5250 workstation
- sign on and sign off an AS/400
- access OS/400 help information
- use the Tutorial System Support (TSS) facility.

1.1 THE 5250 WORKSTATION

The family of workstations used in conjunction with the AS/400 is called the "5250" family, although, in fact, many of the actual workstations have model numbers that bear no resemblance to "5250." For example, members of the 5250 family include the 5251, 5291, 3196, and 3197 workstations. The 5250 family also includes a line of output devices that range from low-end dot matrix printers to high-end laser printers.

All 5250 workstations are "block mode" devices. This means that information you type into the screen is not sent to the application until you press the <ENTER> key. The term "block mode" comes from the fact that you can enter and edit all your information on the workstation screen and then transmit it to the AS/400 as a block of data. The usable area of the screen has twenty-four lines with each line being eighty characters wide. Below this data entry area is a status line.

Most AS/400 programs and applications take advantage of the workstation's block mode operation by using menus and formatted data entry screens to send and receive information to the workstation. For example, when a program gives you information, it typically presents the information one screen at a time. If more than one screen's worth of information is available, you can review the information by using special workstation keys to advance to the next screen or go backward to the previous screen. When a program wants to receive information from you, it will present a data entry template on the screen. This template, often referred to as a "menu" or a "form," is divided into areas that you cannot change and areas that you can change. The areas that you cannot change are used by the program to provide you with instructions and prompts. The areas that you can change are termed "fields." These fields are your data entry areas and may be any size, ranging from one or two characters in width to the size of the entire screen. Fields may be defined for alphanumeric data, supporting the entry of letters, numbers, or symbols, or fields may be numeric-only, allowing the entry of only numeric data.

When you are working with a menu or a form, you simply enter the information you desire into the appropriate fields. The four most important keys you will use for data entry are

- The <FIELD ADVANCE> key. This key moves the cursor from the current input field to the next input field and looks and acts like a "tab" key.
- The <FIELD EXIT> key. This key is used after you have entered information into a field and you want to move on to the next field. The <FIELD EXIT> key clears any remaining characters in a field (or right-aligns the information if the field is numeric) then moves the cursor to the next input field.
- The <RESET> key. This key is used to clear error conditions caused by improper data entry (for example, an attempt to enter data in a protected area of the screen) or by the application program.
- The <ENTER> key. This key transmits the information you have entered to the program.

Although you can also use the cursor keys to move from field to field, they may land the cursor in a protected area of the screen. If you attempt to enter data in a protected area, you will receive an error indication and you will then have to press the <RESET> key before continuing.

REMEMBER: After you complete your data entry operations, press the <ENTER> key to send the information to the program.

1.1.1 The 5250 Keyboard

The keyboard is the primary input and control mechanism for interacting with the AS/400. The 5250 family of workstations has several variations on keyboard layout. The two most prevalent layouts are shown in the following diagrams (see Diagrams 1–1 and 1–2).

Diagram 1–1: IBM 5251 Workstation Keyboard Layout

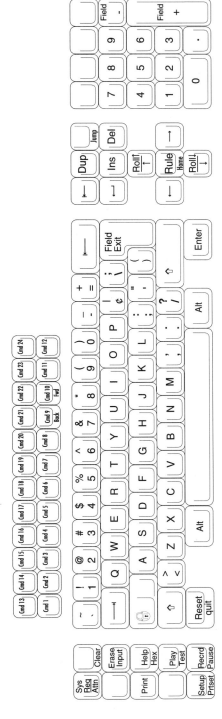

Diagram 1–2: IBM 3197 Workstation Keyboard Layout

3

Despite the seeming differences between the two layouts shown, both keyboards support the same set of base functions. Since the 5251 layout has less keys available, many of the functions available on the 3197 layout as a single key must be performed on the 5251 keyboard using multiple keystrokes. For example, to invoke function key <F10> on the 3197 keyboard you simply press the <Cmd10> key. On the 5251 keyboard, however, you must press the <CMD> key and then press the "0" key to perform the equivalent operation. Or to invoke <F13> on a 5251 keyboard, you press the <CMD> key, then the <SHIFT> key and the "1" key.

The issue of keyboard layout is often further complicated by having PCs and PS/2s emulate 5250 workstations. This is because the PC and PS/2 keyboard layouts differ from the 5250 workstation layouts. In the case of PCs and PS/2s, however, the workstation emulation software actually "maps" the PC or PS/2 keys to the equivalent 5250 keys. For example, to generate an <F10> on a PC 101-style keyboard, you might press the <F10> key. But to generate the <F13> key, you might need to press <SHIFT> and the <F1> key.

For the sake of simplicity, this chapter will assume that you are using the modern 3197 keyboard layout. If, in reality, you are using an older 5251 workstation or a PC or PS/2, you will still be able to access the same key functions, but you may need to refer to your workstation or workstation emulation documentation to find the equivalent key or key combination to press.

As shown in the diagram, the 3197 keyboard contains 122 keys that are divided into five major key groupings. The top set of keys—keys <Cmd1> through <Cmd24>—are function keys normally referred to as <F1> through <F24>. The left set of keys—<SYSRQ>, <PRINT>, <HELP>, and so forth—are special system keys.

The main keypad contains the standard alphanumeric characters and special keys that are used during most data entry activities. To the right of the main keypad are the cursor/page positioning keypad and the numeric keypad. The cursor/page positioning keypad is used for cursor movement, screen movement, and local editing. The numeric keypad contains the numbers 0 through 9 and the special field operators <FIELD+> and <FIELD-> which are used in conjunction with numeric-only data entry fields (see Diagram 1–3).

NOTE: Because 5250 workstations were designed to support a number of international languages, keys are often left blank for a particular language. Blank keys have no meaning and generate an error condition if pressed.

1.1.2 The Function Keypad

The twenty-four function keys located on the top of the keyboard may be labeled <Cmd1> through <Cmd24> or <F1> through <F24>; in both cases they correspond with functions <F1> through <F24>. The use and meaning of the twenty-four function keys is entirely dependent on the program you are interacting with. Because the meaning can vary from application to application, most programs show a list of valid function keys and their meaning on the lower part of the display (see Diagram 1–4 and Figure 1–1).

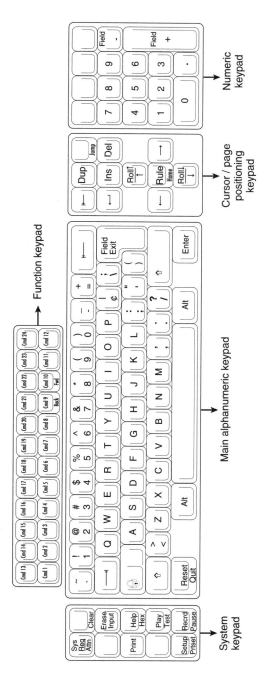

Diagram 1–3: Key Grouping of the IBM 3197 Keyboard

Diagram 1–4: IBM 3197 Function Keypad

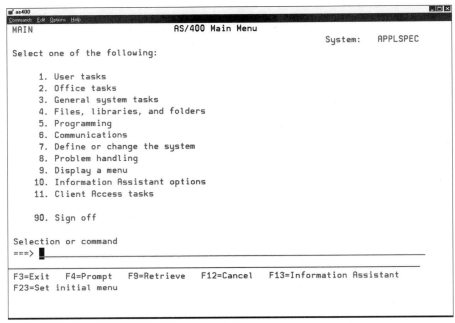

Figure 1–1: AS/400 Main Menu with Valid Function Keys

The AS/400 operating system, OS/400, also relies on the use of several specific function keys. For example, the <F3> key cancels the current operation, the <F9> key recalls the last command, and the <F12> key cancels the current operation and returns to the previous screen. Please refer to Chapter 2 ("The AS/400 Command Language") for a complete description of function key use by OS/400 itself.

1.1.3 The System Keypad

The keys located on the left side of the keyboard perform a variety of AS/400 and local workstation operations. The keys and their associated functions are as follows (see Diagram 1–5):

<SYSRQ>—A System Request is invoked by pressing and holding the <SHIFT> key and then pressing the <SYSRQ> key. Once pressed, a data entry line appears on the bottom of the screen. If you then press <ENTER>, the System Request menu will appear. This menu allows you to view information about your AS/400 session, to invoke a secondary session, or to switch between a primary and secondary AS/400 session. More information on the <SYSRQ> key is provided in Chapter 15 ("Advanced Topics"). The System Request function is normally only available when you are signed on the AS/400.

Diagram 1–5: IBM 3197 System Keypad

<ATTN>—The Attention function can be used to suspend the current operation and activate the default attention program defined in your user profile. You must be signed on to use the <ATTN> key. Also note that the purpose of the attention program may change from application to application. Finally, this function may be disabled by your AS/400 administrator. Please consult Chapter 4 ("The AS/400 User Environment") for more information on user profiles.

<CLEAR>—The Clear function is activated by pressing and holding the <ALT> key and then pressing the <CLEAR> key. Once pressed, all input fields in the current screen are erased and the cursor is relocated to the first field on the display.

<ERASE INPUT>—The Erase Input function is invoked by pressing the <SHIFT> and <ERASE INPUT> keys together. When the Erase Input function is selected, the current input field is erased and the cursor moves to the beginning of that same field.

<PRINT>—The Print function sends a copy of the current screen to the default print output queue for your current session. This key may, however, be used by application programs for other purposes. You must be signed on to use this function.

<HELP>—The Help function brings up information about the current screen or the current field. The context (menu-level or field-level) for the help information is dependent on the application program. You must be signed on to use this function. See the *AS/400 Help Facility* section of this chapter for more information on the help function.

<HEX>—The Hex function is activated by pressing <ALT> and <HEX> together. Once these keys are pressed, a two-digit hexadecimal value can be entered into an input field.

<PLAY>—The Play function allows you to play keystrokes that you have associated with function keys through the <RECRD> key. To activate the function key, press <PLAY> and then the desired function key.

<TEST>—The Test function is used for advanced diagnostics. It has no value for normal operations.

<SETUP>—The Setup function allows you to define some of the operating characteristics for your workstation. Please refer to the *Workstation Configuration* section of this chapter for more information.

<PRTSET>—The Printer Setup function is activated by pressing the <ALT> and <PRTSET> keys. This is an advanced function that allows you to define the attributes for a printer directly attached to your workstation.

<RECRD>—The Record function allows you to associate keystrokes with function keys. These keystrokes are activated through the <PLAY> key. A maximum of 1500 keystrokes may be recorded in total. To make an assignment for a function key, first press the <RECRD> key, then press the function key you want to use, and then enter the keystrokes. When you have finished entering keystrokes, press <RECRD> again to finish the recording. Other Record operations of note are as follows:

- When you press <RECRD> a small "map" of the function keys appears on the status line. The keys that appear solid have a definition associated with them and the keys that are hollow do not. Also note that an "R" is present in the status line, followed by the remaining number of keystrokes you may use.

- If you accidentally start the Record function you can immediately press <RECRD> again to terminate its operation.

- If you attempt to re-record an assigned key, you will hear an alarm when you press that function key. You can press <RECRD> to leave the assignment intact. If you want to delete the existing assignment, press the <DELETE> key.

- To abandon a recording session after you have assigned a function key, press the <ALT> and <QUIT> keys. This action will delete your current input and the existing definition as well.

- If you want to have a pause in the replay of keystrokes during the <PLAY> function, press the <PAUSE> key twice. During playback, the function will pause until the <PLAY> key is pressed again.

<PAUSE>—The Pause function is activated by pressing <ALT> and <PAUSE> together. This function is used with the <RECRD> key to insert a pause in a keystroke sequence.

1.1.4 The Main Alphanumeric Keypad

The main keypad contains the letters and numbers used for normal typing and data entry operations. The 5250 family of workstations is available in a wide variety of languages, so the keys and their placement is dependent on the language in use.

NOTE: For U.S. English users, the keyboard follows the standard "QWERTY" layout. One unusual aspect of the keyboard, however, is the absence of square brackets ("[" and "]").

In addition to the standard typing keys, the following special purpose keys are located on the main keypad for the indicated function (see Diagram 1–6):

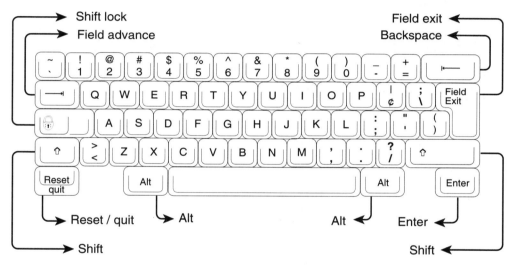

Diagram 1–6: IBM 3197 Main Keyboard

<FIELD ADVANCE>—The Field Advance function moves the cursor from the current field to the next field.

<SHIFT LOCK>—The Shift Lock function locks the alphanumeric keys into their shifted states. When shift lock is in effect, letters appear in uppercase and the special symbols appear when the numeric keys are pressed (for example "!" instead of "1," "@" instead of "2," and so on). Shift lock remains in effect until one of the standard <SHIFT> keys is pressed.

<SHIFT>—Two <SHIFT> keys are located on the main keypad, and both keys perform the same function. The Shift function is activated by pressing and holding either <SHIFT> key. Once activated, letters appear in uppercase and symbols appear instead of numbers. The Shift function also releases the Shift Lock function.

<RESET>—The Reset function is used to clear the workstation of error conditions and to terminate Help, Insert, and System Request functions. Error conditions are normally the result of improper data entry activities. For example, attempting to input data in a protected area of the screen, or attempting to input alphabetic data in a numeric field causes an error condition. When an error occurs, all workstation functions are suspended until the <RESET> key is pressed. Although many error codes appear as a highlighted number on the workstation, programs may also set the error condition and send a text message to the screen. Please refer to Table 1-A for a list of common errors.

Table 1-A: Common Error Codes and Their Meanings

Code	Meaning
0000—	<HELP> key pressed, but no help is available
0001—	The AS/400 lost the last character you entered
0002—	You input an invalid character code
0003—	<ALT> key used with an invalid key
0004—	You attempted to input data in a protected area
0007—	Failure to input data in a mandatory-enter field (**)
0010—	You tried to input alphabetic data in a numeric field
0011—	Attempt to input data in the sign area of a numeric field
0012—	You tried to insert data at the end of a field
0013—	You tried to exit a field after pressing <INSERT>
0014—	You attempted to exit a mandatory-fill (*) field
0015—	Failure to enter a self-check field correctly
0016—	You pressed <FIELD-> but the field is not numeric
0017—	Attempt to Field Exit out of a mandatory-fill (*) field
0018—	You pressed an illegal key to exit the field
0019—	You pressed <DUP> key in a field that does not support it
0020—	You pressed an illegal key for the field
0021—	You attempted to skip a mandatory-enter field (**)
0022—	Miscellaneous system error
0023—	Illegal use of the Hex function
0026—	You pressed <FIELD-> but the last character is not numeric

Table 1-A: (continued)

Code	Meaning
0027—	You pressed an unsupported key
0028—	You pressed an unsupported key
0029—	Illegal key in a multikey sequence
0040—	0054—Data communications failure
0099—	Attempt to use a function that requires you to be signed on
9001—	9010—Invalid operation during Record or Play function
9012—	Invalid key used during Setup function
9015—	Illegal use of the Quit function
9016—	You pressed an illegal combination of several keys
9019—	Invalid key used during Record or Play function
9030—	Jump function not available for your workstation
9051—	Illegal key pressing during Printer Setup function
9052—	Printer not ready (or out of paper)

(*)   A mandatory fill field must be completely filled or left entirely blank.
(**)   A mandatory enter field must receive data input (but it does not have to be completely filled).

<QUIT>—The Quit function is activated by pressing <ALT> and <QUIT> together. This function is used in conjunction with the Record and Play functions previously discussed in the *System Keys* section of this chapter.

<ALT>—The <ALT> key is used in conjunction with other keys to select functions. The keys available for use with <ALT> bear labels on the front of key caps (as opposed to the top). For example, the <HELP> key is also the <HEX> key and the <SETUP> key is also the <PRTSET> key. To use the <ALT> key, press and hold it down, and then press the desired function.

<ENTER>—The Enter function transmits the information contained in the data entry fields to the AS/400 program. When you press <ENTER>, an "X" appears in the status line indicating that further input is prohibited. Once the "X" appears, you must wait for a response from the AS/400 before you perform any new activity. The "X" disappears when a response is received.

<FIELD EXIT>—The Field Exit function may be used in alphanumeric fields to erase information in the current field that is behind and to the right of the cursor, and then advance the cursor to the next field. The <FIELD EXIT> key is one of several keys available to operate on fields; however, the <FIELD EXIT> key is the most frequently used. The other keys that perform field-level operations are as follows:

- The <FIELD ADVANCE> key on the main keypad moves the cursor to the next field without affecting the contents of the current field.
- The <FIELD BACK> key on the cursor/page positioning keypad moves the cursor to the beginning of the current field or to the beginning of the previous field without affecting the contents of the current field.
- The <FIELD+> key on the numeric keypad is used in numeric fields to right-justify the field contents and clear the sign position of the field. In reality, the <FIELD EXIT> key and the <FIELD+> key perform the exact same functions and are therefore interchangeable.
- The <FIELD-> key on the numeric keypad is used in numeric fields to right-justify the field contents and add a negative sign to the field. The <FIELD-> key cannot be used in alphanumeric fields.
- Pressing both the <CLEAR> key on the system keypad and the <ALT> key on the main keypad erases the contents of all fields on the display.
- Pressing the <ERASE INPUT> key on the system keypad and the <SHIFT> key on the main keypad erases the contents of the current field, with the cursor remaining in the same field.

<BACKSPACE>—The Backspace function performs a destructive backspace and eliminates the character to the left of the cursor. If the backspace occurs at the beginning of a field, the cursor moves to the last character of the previous field and that character is deleted.

1.1.5 The Cursor and Page Positioning Keypad

The cursor/page positioning keypad contains positioning keys and editing keys. This keypad, the main alphanumeric keypad, and the function keypad are the three most used keypads for general operations. The specific key functions on the cursor/page positioning keypad are as follows (see Diagram 1–7):

<FIELD BACK>—The Field Back function moves the cursor to the beginning of the current field or to the beginning of the previous field if it is already at the beginning of the current field. Any information in the current field is unaffected.

<DUP>—Activating the Duplicate function requests the program to use the data from the last record entered in the current field. When <DUP> is pressed, an asterisk with a line above it appears in the field. NOTE: This is not a system-wide function; the application program must support the use of the <DUP> key.

<JUMP>—The Jump function is only available on 5250 workstations that contain dual addresses. For these models (for example, the 3197) pressing <ALT>

and <JUMP> changes the display to show the activity for the alternate address. In more general terms, the dual address capability allows a single workstation to appear to the AS/400 as two workstations, and the Jump function allows you to move back and forth between the two. Also note that you can use the Jump function even if you are waiting for a response on your current session.

<NEW LINE>—The New Line function moves the cursor to the beginning of the first input field on the next line of the display.

<INS>—The Insert function allows you to enter new characters at the cursor position. When you press <INSERT>, the insert mode symbol ("^") appears on the status line of the display, and the Insert function will remain on until you press the <RESET> key. When the insert mode is enabled, existing characters behind or to the right of the cursor are moved over to the right as you type new characters. If you attempt to insert more characters than will fit in a field, the "X" will appear on the status line and the keyboard will lock. Pressing <RESET> will clear this error condition.

<DEL>—The Delete function deletes the character at the current cursor location.

<CURSOR UP>—Pressing this key moves the cursor up one row. If the cursor is on the top row, it will reappear on the bottom row.

<CURSOR DOWN>—Pressing this key moves the cursor down one row. If the cursor is on the bottom row, it will reappear on the top row.

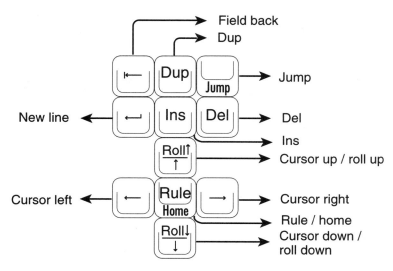

Diagram 1–7: IBM 3197 Cursor/Page Positioning Keypad

<CURSOR LEFT>—Pressing this key moves the cursor left one character position. If the cursor is in the left-most position, it will reappear at the right-most position.

<CURSOR RIGHT>—Pressing this key moves the cursor right one character position. If the cursor is in the right-most position, it will reappear at the left-most position.

<ROLL UP>—The <ROLL UP> function requests the next screen in a multiscreen series. You can tell if you have multiple screens available by the presence of the highlighted keywords "More" or "Bottom" on the lower right portion of the screen. If you press the <ROLL UP> key when you are at the last ("Bottom") screen of the multiscreen series, you will receive the message "Already at bottom of area."

<ROLL DOWN>—The <ROLL DOWN> function requests the previous screen in a multiscreen series. You can tell if you have multiple screens available by the presence of the highlighted keywords "More" or "Bottom" on the lower right portion of the screen. If you press the <ROLL DOWN> key when you are at the first screen of the multiscreen series, you will receive the message "Already at top of area" (see Diagram 1–8).

NOTE: The direction of movement for the <ROLL UP> and <ROLL DOWN> keys can be changed by the system administrator.

<HOME>—The Home function is activated by pressing <ALT> and <HOME> together. Once triggered, the Home function moves the cursor to the beginning of the first input field on the screen.

<RULE>—The Rule function turns the ruler on or off. The appearance of the ruler is defined in the workstation configuration. Please see the *Workstation Configuration* section in this chapter for more information.

1.1.6 The Numeric Keypad

The numeric keypad contains the standard number set (0 through 9), and a period (.) in a calculator-style arrangement. The purpose of this keypad is to facilitate the fast entry of numbers for those typists who are accustomed to this layout. In addition to the number keys, the numeric keypad contains the <FIELD+> and <FIELD-> keys to operate on numeric input fields (see Diagram 1–9).

Numeric fields contain a reserved space for a sign. This space is the right-most position in the field. When you press <FIELD+> or <FIELD EXIT> in a numeric field, the number is right-justified and the sign position is cleared (it appears as a blank in the field) to signify a positive number. When you press <FIELD-> in a numeric field, the number is right-justified and a minus is placed in the sign position to designate a negative number.

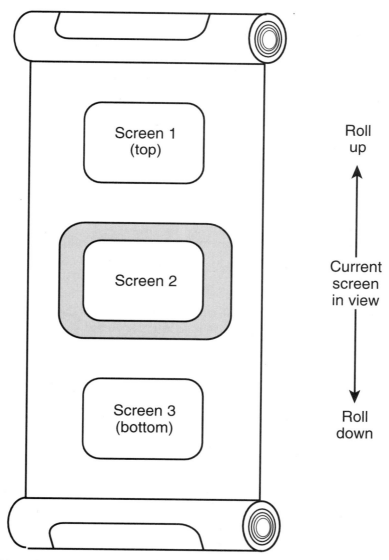

Diagram 1–8: Illustration of the Roll Up/Roll Down Function

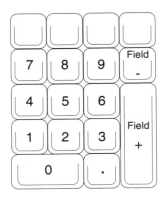

Diagram 1–9: IBM 3197 Numeric Keypad

If you do not use the <FIELD EXIT>, <FIELD+>, or <FIELD-> in a partially filled numeric field, the left-justified number will be treated as an input error. Unfortunately, the workstation does not indicate if the cursor is currently positioned in a numeric field or alphanumeric field. To avoid confusion, you should get in the habit of always using the <FIELD EXIT> key to exit partially filled fields. Because <FIELD EXIT> works on both types of fields (numeric and alphanumeric), it is an excellent all-purpose "tool."

1.1.7 Status Line

The bottom line of the workstation display contains indicators that show the current status of communications with the AS/400 and the status of local workstation options. The significance of each indicator is as follows (see Diagram 1–10):

> System Available—A block character in this position indicates that the AS/400 is connected and available for communications.

> Logical Display—A number in this position indicates the logical display you are currently using. If your workstation supports two addresses, this number will change between "1" and "2" as you use the <JUMP> key to switch between logical displays.

> Message Waiting (1)—The presence of a symbol in this position indicates that one or more messages are waiting on the message queue associated with logical display 1. If the symbol is hollow, you are currently accessing the first logical display. If the symbol is solid, you are currently accessing the second logical display.

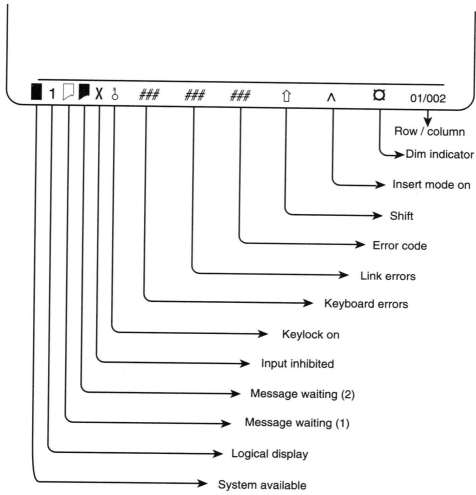

Diagram 1–10: Display of the IBM 3197 Status Line

Message Waiting (2)—The presence of a symbol in this position indicates that one or more messages are waiting on the message queue associated with logical display 2. If the symbol is hollow, you are currently accessing the second logical display. If the symbol is solid, you are currently accessing the first logical display.

Input Inhibited—An "X" in this position indicates that the workstation will not accept any new input from you. This condition results when you transmit information to the AS/400 and clears when you receive a response. This condition will also occur if you make a data entry or keyboard error. An error will be noted by the presence of a highlighted error number or message, and can be cleared by pressing the <RESET> key.

Keylock On—If this symbol is present, the physical lock on the workstation has been engaged and no keyboard input is allowed. Turn the key to unlock the keyboard.

Keyboard Errors—The number in this position is a cumulative count of the number of keyboard errors that have occurred since the workstation was powered on. This information will only appear when the Extended Codes function has been enabled. Please see the *Workstation Configuration* section of this chapter for more information.

Link Errors—The number in this position is a cumulative count of the number of communications errors that have occurred since the workstation was powered on. This information will only appear when the Extended Codes function has been enabled. Please see the *Workstation Configuration* section of this chapter for more information.

Error Code—This position is one of several screen locations used to display codes indicating an operational or communications error. Press <RESET> to clear the error.

Shift—The shift symbol appears whenever either the <SHIFT> key or the <SHIFT LOCK> key has been pressed. When this indicator is present, all alphabetic letters will appear in uppercase and symbols will appear instead of numbers when the main alphanumeric keypad is used.

Insert Mode On—The presence of the "^" symbol indicates the insert mode is on. When the insert is on, new characters are inserted into the field at the current cursor locations. When the insert is off, new characters overwrite any existing information in the field.

Dim Indicator—The dim indicator symbol will appear when the workstation automatically blanks the screen to protect it from phosphor burn. The screen can be restored by pressing any key. This feature can be disabled as described in the *Workstation Configuration* section of this chapter.

Row/Column—The numbers in this position indicate the current row and column positions where the cursor is located. The display of row/column information may be suppressed. Please see the *Workstation Configuration* section of this chapter for more details.

Additional indicators are available for international operations. Also note that if you activate the <SETUP> or <PRTSET> keys, the normal status line will be replaced by one of the setup status lines. Please consult the *Workstation Configuration* section of this chapter for additional information.

1.1.8 Workstation Configuration

Workstation options are configured through the <SETUP> key. This function allows you to define your personal preferences for various workstation options. When you press the <SETUP> key, the standard status line changes to the setup status line. The indicators shown on the setup status line have the following meanings (see Diagram 1–11):

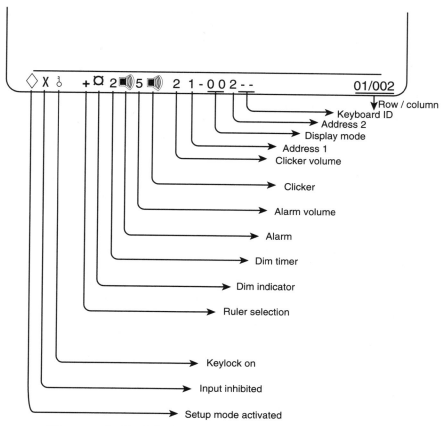

Diagram 1–11: Display of the IBM 3197 Setup Status Line

Setup Mode Activated—A diamond symbol in this position indicates that the Setup function has been activated.

Input Inhibited—The "X" symbol will only appear if the key lock for the workstation has been enabled after you have entered the setup mode. If an "X" is present, you are prevented from making any configuration changes until you unlock the workstation.

Keylock On—The presence of this symbol means the workstation key is engaged. Also note that the Input Inhibited symbol will be present.

Ruler Selection—Three styles of rulers are supported by the workstation: crosshair ruler line, a vertical ruler line, and a horizontal ruler line. This position in the status line will show as "+," "l," or "-" to indicate the current selection as crosshair, vertical, or horizontal. To change the current selection, press the <F2> key. Each time you press <F2>, the next option will appear.

Dim Indicator—The dim indicator symbol is the same symbol used in the standard status line. The symbol is shown as a reference for the Dim Timer adjustment.

Dim Timer—Immediately to the right of the Dim Indicator is a number that specifies the amount of inactive time, in minutes, before the workstation will automatically blank the screen (except for the status line). The choices are 0, 2, 5, 10, and 20, and can be selected by pressing the <F3> key. Selecting 0 minutes disables the automatic blanking.

Alarm—The alarm symbol is shown to provide reference for the Alarm Volume adjustment.

Alarm Volume—Immediately to the right of the Alarm symbol is a number that determines the volume of the audible alarm. This alarm is sounded by the workstation in the event of an operational or communications error; it can also be activated by an application program. The range of permissible settings is from 0 to 5. A level of 0 means the alarm is disabled. Use the <F4> key to rotate through the values until you reach the desired setting.

Clicker—The clicker symbol is shown to provide reference for the Clicker Volume adjustment.

Clicker Volume—Immediately to the right of the Clicker symbol is a number that determines the volume of the "click" sounded for each keystroke. The volume may be set between 0 and 5, with the value of 0 disabling the clicker. Choose the setting you want by pressing the <F5> key until the desired value appears. Also note that you can use the <F6> key to disable or enable the clicker function.

Address 1—This position in the setup status line shows the communications address assigned for your first logical display. This information is defined during the initial setup and configuration of the workstation and cannot be changed through the standard <SETUP> key.

Display Mode—The display mode indicators show if the workstation is configured as one logical display, two logical displays, or one logical display and an attached printer. The display mode is defined during the initial setup and configuration of the workstation and cannot be changed through the standard <SETUP> key (see Diagram 1–12).

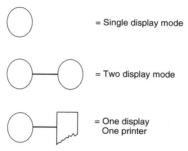

Diagram 1–12: Illustration of the Setup Status Line Display Mode

Address 2—This position in the setup status line shows the communications address assigned for your second logical display or printer, if one is defined. This information is defined during the initial setup and configuration of the workstation and cannot be changed through the standard <SETUP> key.

Keyboard ID—This position in the setup status line should show—unless you are using a custom keyboard. The keyboard definition is defined during the initial setup and configuration of the workstation and cannot be changed through the standard <SETUP> key.

Row/Column—The current row and column position of the cursor can be displayed in this position in the standard status line. To enable or disable the row/column display, press the <F11> key and the cursor location information will appear or disappear.

Additional functions that can be configured through the <SETUP> key include:

Cursor appearance—Pressing <F7> changes the cursor from nonblinking to blinking or vice versa. Pressing <F8> allows you to toggle between an underline and block cursor.

Extended Display—The <F10> key switches the display between normal and extended modes. While in extended mode, nondisplayable screen characters appear as special symbols and the communications and keyboard error counters appear on the status line.

Color Mode—Pressing <F12> toggles between color and limited color mode.

If your workstation is configured to support one logical display and an attached printer, the <PRTSET> key sequence may be used to control the output characteristics of the printer. The selection and configuration of an attached printer must be performed in conjunction with the selection and configuration of the workstation. In short, this is an advanced topic.

1.2 SIGNING ON TO THE AS/400

Your first exposure to the AS/400 will be the Sign On menu. The AS/400 is a secure system, so you must sign on to it before you can perform any commands or access any applications. The Sign On menu shows your current system, workstation, and subsystem assignments. For the most part, these assignments should have no great personal importance to you. More important are the five data entry fields, with the first two fields being of extreme importance to the sign on process (see Figure 1–2).

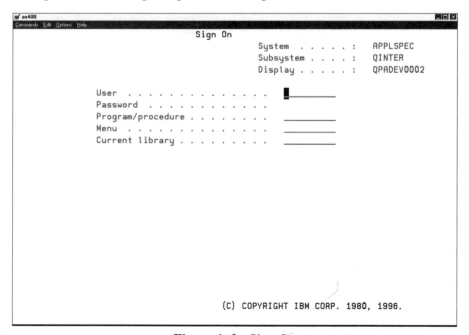

Figure 1–2: Sign On

The "User" and "Password" fields allow you to enter your assigned user identification and password. You could, for example, type "ENCK" into the "User" field, press <FIELD EXIT> to advance to the "Password" field, type "JOHN," and then press the <ENTER> key to transmit. Note that you cannot see the information you type into the "Password" field.

When you are initially assigned a user name, your password is normally set to that same name. Passwords are not required by the AS/400, so you may only need to enter a user name. Finally, note that a proper user name and password entitles you to sign on to the AS/400 on one or more workstations.

The AS/400 has several predefined user names. The two most frequently used names are 'QSECOFR' and 'QSYSOPR.' These users are supplied as the default user names used to manage and operate the AS/400, respectively. Because these users are quite powerful, they are normally protected by a password. A third user name "QUSER" is the opposite case. 'QUSER' is a default user name with limited capabilities that is often used by batch jobs and network-based programs that access the AS/400.

After you input your user name, your password, and press the <ENTER> key, an "X" will appear in your workstation status line. The "X" indicates that you are inhibited from further input while the AS/400 verifies your user name and password.

When the AS/400 completes the verification, you may be presented with up to two optional information-only screens. Specifically, you may see a display showing you the date and time of your last sign on access, and you may be presented with a message indicating that your "queue is already allocated." If either of these screens appear, press <ENTER> to move on to the next display. Once these optional screens have been displayed, you will be presented with a new menu.

The exact menu that each user receives after signing on is a user-level option. By default, the AS/400 Main Menu is sent to the user. This menu definition can be changed in the user's profile definition as discussed in Chapter 4 ("The AS/400 User Environment") (see Figure 1–3).

The AS/400 Main Menu contains a list of options and a data entry area at the bottom of the screen to allow the entry of an option. In most cases the menu will also have a command line to facilitate the free-form entry of commands; however, this capability may be restricted in your user profile as described in Chapter 4.

1.2.1 The Program, Menu, and Library Options

The final three fields in the Sign On menu can be used as a shortcut to access a particular menu or program when your sign on is complete. As in the case of entering commands on a command line, your ability to use these fields is dependent on how your user profile is set up. The specific operations these three fields control are as follows:

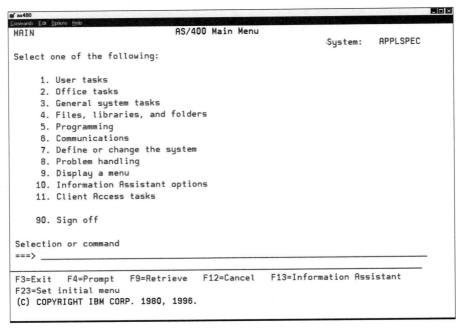

Figure 1–3: Main Menu

If you want to run a specific program or procedure, you can specify its name in this "Program/Procedure" field. The AS/400 will invoke that program or procedure after it processes your sign on information. Also note that if you want to run a program out of a library that is not in your default library list, you should also specify the library name in the "Current library" field.

If you want to go to a specific menu, enter the menu name in the "Menu" field when you are signing on. The AS/400 will take you to that menu after processing your sign on name and password.

Finally, if you want to use a specific library as your default library when creating and locating objects, you can declare a library name in the "Current library" field. As mentioned, this can be used in conjunction with the "Program/Procedure" field to run a program or procedure from a specific library.

NOTE: If you specify an invalid menu name or program/procedure name, your sign on will be aborted and you will receive an error message. Press <ENTER> to clear the message and return to the Sign On display.

Please refer to Chapter 2 ("The AS/400 Command Language") and Chapter 3 ("Libraries, Files, and Members") for additional information on menus, programs, and procedures. You may also refer to Chapter 4 ("The AS/400 User Environment") for more detailed information on user attributes and options.

1.3 THE AS/400 HELP FACILITY

Basic information on most AS/400 menus and field items is available through the <HELP> key. The <HELP> key may also be available when you are working with application programs, but that is a guideline and not a strict rule. When in doubt, try <HELP>.

The <HELP> key is context-sensitive. If you are currently viewing a standard menu and press the <HELP> key, you will see information about that menu. If, however, your cursor is located in a field on a data entry screen and you press <HELP>, you should see information about that specific field.

For example, assume you are viewing the Main Menu and you press the <HELP> key. You will see help information about the main menu (see Figure 1–4).

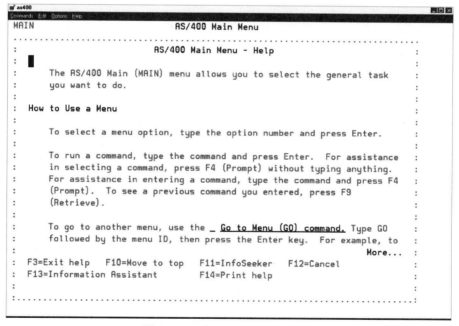

Figure 1–4: Main Menu help

In a different case, assume you are in the Work With File display (as discussed in Chapter 3 ("Libraries, Files, and Members")). If your cursor is located in the "File" field and you press <HELP>, you will see information about the "File" field (see Figure 1–5).

```
as400                                                              _ □ ×
Commands  Edit  Options  Help
                          Work with Files (WRKF)

  Type choices, press Enter.

  File . . . . . . . . . . . . . .   _____      Name, generic*, *ALL
    Library  . ...........................................................
  File attribut :                    File (FILE) - Help                  :
              : █                                                        :
              : Specifies the name and library of the files to be listed :
              : on the Work with Files display.  Only those files to which :
              : you have authority are shown.                            :
              :                                                          :
              : This is a required parameter.                            :
              :                                                          :
              : The possible values are:                                 :
              :                                                          :
              : *ALL                                                     :
              :      All files are listed.                               :
              :                                                          :
              :                                                 More...  :
              : F2=Extended help   F10=Move to top   F11=InfoSeeker      :
  F3=Exit   F4= : F12=Cancel        F20=Enlarge       F24=More keys      :
  F24=More keys :                                                        :
              :...........................................................:
```

Figure 1–5: Work with Files field-level help

Both types of help displays allow you to use the <ROLL UP> and <ROLL DOWN> keys to move forward and backward through the information. Other function keys supported by the help displays will be listed on the bottom of the help area. The primary set of function keys used by help displays include:

<F2> Extended Help—If additional help is available above and beyond the information currently being displayed, the <F2> key will be listed. Normally this key is used when displaying field-level help information. By pressing <F2>, you can access the help information for all of the fields on the display, including the current field.

<F3> Exit Help—Pressing <F3> terminates the help display and returns you to your system screen.

<F10> Move to Top—You can force the display to begin at a specific line by moving the cursor to a line on the display and pressing the <F10> key. That line will then move up to the top of the display.

<F11> Search Index—The <F11> key invokes a search index function to scan for keywords. Please see the *User Support and Education* section of this chapter for more information.

<F12> Cancel—Pressing <F12> terminates the help display and returns you to your previous screen.

<F13> User Support—The <F13> key takes you to the User Support and Education menu. The functions available on that menu are explained in the next section of this chapter.

<F20> Expand—The <F20> key is available on help displays that only take up a portion of the workstation screen. Pressing <F20> enlarges the display area to consume more of the workstation screen.

<F24> More Keys—If more function keys are available for use than can be displayed in the help area, the <F24> key will be available to rotate through the available key functions.

1.4 USER SUPPORT AND EDUCATION

The User Support and Education menu contains a number of functions that are extremely useful for obtaining additional information on AS/400 topics. Access to the User Support and Education menu can be gained in one of three ways

- by entering 10 (User Support and Education) on the AS/400 Main Menu.
- by pressing <F13> when a help display is on the workstation screen.
- by entering the command "GO SUPPORT" on a command line (see Figure 1–6).

The User Support and Education menu features nine options. Each option has the following purpose:

1. How to use Help—This option displays narrative text on how to use the <HELP> key to obtain help information. While the text is being displayed, you can use the <ROLL UP> and <ROLL DOWN> keys to page through the information, or the <F3> or <F12> keys to exit.
2. Search System Help Index—This option allows you to obtain help information based on keywords or phrases. Please see the Search Help Index section of this chapter for details.

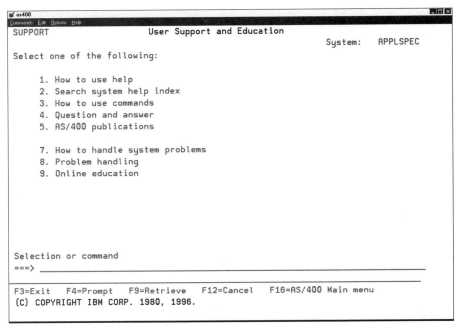

Figure 1–6: User Support and Education

3. How to use Commands—This option displays narrative text on how to use AS/400 commands. You can use the <ROLL UP> and <ROLL DOWN> keys to page through the information, or the <F3> or <F12> keys to exit.

4. Question and Answer—This option allows you to access a special question and answer database that has been customized for your site. This is an advanced function.

5. AS/400 Publications—This option shows a list of the standard IBM documents associated with the AS/400 and its optional programs. You can use the <ROLL UP> and <ROLL DOWN> keys to move through the list, or <F3> or <F12> to exit.

6. IBM Product Information—This option initiates a communications link to a remote IBM system that allows you to look up information on new or existing IBM products and services. This is an advanced function.

7. How to Handle System Problems—This option presents narrative text that explains the basic procedures used for handling problems. You can use the <ROLL UP> and <ROLL DOWN> keys to page through the information, or <F3> or <F12> to exit.

8. Problem Handling—This option brings up a secondary menu that can be used to analyze and resolve operational problems with the system. This is an advanced function.

9. Online Education—This option starts the online education module. This module is discussed in the *Online Education* section of this chapter.

Please note that all of these options may not be present on your display. In particular, option 6 (IBM Product Information) is often restricted to avoid unnecessary use of the communications link.

1.4.1 Search System Help Index

The search help facility allows you to look for help information based on a keyword or phrase. Alternately, you can use the search help facility to browse through its entire list of entries. Access to the search help facility can be gained in one of three ways

- by pressing <F11> (Search Index) from one of the information displays generated by the <HELP> key.
- by selecting option 2 (Search System Help Index) from the User Support and Education menu.
- by entering the STRIDXSCH command on a command line.

The Search System Help Index menu provides a data entry area for you to enter your keyword or phrase. Alternatively, you may leave the data entry area blank and press <ENTER> to view the complete list of index entries. The following function keys may be used with the Search System Help Index:

<F3> Exit, and <F12> Cancel—Exit (or cancel) the search index function. You will either leave the search index function (<F3>) or return to the previous screen (<F12>).

<F5> All Topics—Pressing this function key displays a list of all index entries. This is the equivalent of not specifying a keyword or phrase on the Search System Help Index menu and pressing <ENTER>.

<F13> User Support—This option takes you to the User Support and Education menu.

Once you have made your selection from the Search System Help Index menu, the Main Help Index for AS/400 menu appears. This menu lists the entries relevant to the selection criteria (if any) you supplied. The Main Help Index for AS/400 menu supports the same function keys as the Search System Help Index menu. In addition, you can use the input field to the left of each entry to select one of two options

5 Display Topic—Selecting option 5 presents the narrative text associated with the topic on your screen. You can use the <ROLL UP> and <ROLL DOWN> keys to move forward and backward through the information. You can also use any of the following function keys:

<F3> Exit Help—Pressing <F3> terminates the current display and returns you to your last main menu (for example, the User Support and Education menu if you selected the search function from that menu).

<F10> Move to Top—You can force the display to begin at a specific line by moving the cursor to a line on the display and pressing the <F10> key. That line will then move up to the top of the display.

<F12> Cancel—Pressing <F12> terminates the current display and returns you to your previous screen.

<F13> User Support—The <F13> key takes you to the User Support and Education menu.

6 Print Topic—This option sends the narrative text associated with the topic to your default print queue.

1.4.2 Online Education

The online education facility provides intermediate and advanced training on a number of AS/400 topics. Each topic is presented in an electronic "course," and each course is further broken down into a series of "modules." The number of courses you have to choose from will vary from system to system, but all systems have a course entitled "Tutorial System Support." This course is worth a look for all new AS/400 users.

Access to the online education facility can be gained by selecting option 9 (Online Education) from the User Support and Education menu, or by entering the STREDU command from a command line.

NOTE: If you are logged on as a security manager (for example, 'QSECOFR'), you will receive the Start Education Administration menu. To continue on into the online education facility, select the option called "Work as a student."

If you are using the online education for the first time, you will receive the Specify Your Name menu which asks for your first and last name. After supplying your name, you will then be presented with the Select Course menu to select a specific course you want to access.

If more courses are available than can fit on your display, you can use the <ROLL UP> and <ROLL DOWN> keys to move through the list. To obtain more information on a course, enter option 8 (Display Description) next to the title to obtain additional information on the course. Additional function keys supported by this menu include

<F3> Exit, and <F12> Cancel—Press <F3> or <F12> to terminate this menu operation.

<F17> Top, and <F18> Bottom—Pressing <F18> displays the last (bottom) entries on the list of options. Pressing <F17> returns you to the top of the list. You may accomplish the same results with the <ROLL UP> and <ROLL DOWN> keys.

<F9> Print list—Press <F9> to send the list to your default print queue.

If you are a new user, you should type a 1 (Select) next to the "Tutorial System Support" course and press <ENTER>.

After you select a course, the Select Audience Path menu appears. This menu allows you to identify yourself as a specific type of user. Specifying a type of user allows the online education facility to present only the modules within a course that are appropriate to your audience level.

You can use <ROLL UP> and <ROLL DOWN> to review your choices and use option 8 (Display Description) for clarification of an audience level or option 5 (Display Modules) for the list of topics included in the course for that type of user. The additional function keys available at this menu are the same keys available in the Select Course menu.

Once you identify an appropriate level, type a 1 next to the description that best suits your needs and press <ENTER>.

NOTE: Once you define your audience and course the first time you will bypass these menus on subsequent access to the online education facility.

The Select Course Option menu is the normal starting point for the online education facility. All access after the first one begins at this menu.

The upper portion of the Select Course Option menu displays the audience and course assignments currently in effect. The rest of the menu presents the following options available for selection:

1. Start next module—Selecting this option begins the next module associated with your audience level.

2. Resume bookmark module—Selecting this option allows you to return to a point in a module where you left a "bookmark." You may set a bookmark when you exit online education while in the middle of a module. This option will not be present if a bookmark has not been previously set.

3. Select module in audience path—Selecting this option allows you to review the modules associated with your audience level and select a particular module.

4. Select audience path—Entering this option takes you to the Select Audience Path menu so you can review or change your course selection as previously discussed.

5. Select course—Entering this option takes you to the Select Course menu so you can review or change your course selection as previously discussed.

Making a selection through option 1, 2, or 3 starts the module presentation process. As the first step in this process, the message "Initialization in progress" will appear on your workstation. When initialization is complete, the online education facility will display the contents of the module on your workstation one screen at a time.

To move from the current screen to the next screen, press the <ENTER> key. The <ENTER> key is the sole means of advancing through the contents of a module. When you complete a module, the online education facility then moves on to the next module in your course.

To exit the course, press the <F3> (Exit) or the <F12> (Cancel) key. In response, you will receive the Exit Module menu.

The three options available on the Exit Module menu are as follows:

1. Exit this module—This option terminates the current module but does not mark it complete. The next time you use the online education facility you will start at the beginning of this module.

2. Exit this module and set bookmark—This option terminates the module but saves your current location in the module. When you subsequently use the online education facility you can select option 2 (Resume bookmark module) on the Select Course Option menu to return to the same location.

3. Exit this module and mark it complete—This option closes the current module so that next time you use the online facility you will start at the beginning of the next module in the course.

Once you have terminated the module using one of the exit options, you will return to the Select Course Option module.

1.5 SIGNING OFF THE AS/400

When you are finished interacting with the AS/400, you should sign off the system. Signing off can be accomplished by selecting option 90 (Signoff) from the AS/400 Main Menu. Other menus (such as AS/400 Office) also have a signoff option, or by entering the SIGNOFF command from a command line.

If you use the command line method, you can also use the command syntax SIGNOFF LOG(*LIST) to have a copy of your AS/400 work log sent to your default print queue.

After you have successfully signed off the AS/400, the Sign On screen reappears on your workstation.

2

The AS/400 Command Language

The two type of interfaces used by OS/400 that enable you to perform work are commands and menus. This chapter will describe command structure, parameters and defaults, menus, and menu navigation.

2.1 COMMAND STRUCTURE

Commands used by OS/400 follow a common format. This format is fairly consistent, but there are a few exceptions. Some commands are easy to remember, such as GO, which displays a menu. Others such as STRIDXSRC (Start Index Search) are a bit more difficult. IBM (and most programmers) use a standard convention for the naming of commands.

The format for command names is *vrbqualobj*, where *vrb* is the verb that indicates the action to take, *qual* is a qualifier to further identify the object, and *obj* is the object on which to perform that action.

The verbs used by OS/400 and their meanings are

- STR Start
- END End
- DSP Display
- CRT Create
- DLT Delete
- ADD Add
- WRK Work with
- VRY Vary
- SLT Select

The object portion of a standard command name is similar for all commands that perform operations on an object. For example, DSPOBJD (Display Object Description) and WRKOBJ (Work with Objects) share the "OBJ" object type. A complete list of all OS/400 object types is located in Appendix B, but here are some of the more common object types that you may encounter

- OUTQ   Output Queue
- MSGQ   Message Queue
- F   File
- LIND   Line Description
- CTLD   Controller Description
- DEVD   Device Description
- JOBD   Job Description

The qualifier portion of a standard command name is a bit more difficult to define. The qualifiers are only used in the command name; you will not see them elsewhere on the system. Some of the different qualifiers are

- D   Description
- STS   Status
- PRD   Products
- SRC   Search
- CFG   Configuration

The naming convention for OS/400 commands is easy to remember and allows you to easily come up with the correct command name. For example, if you wanted to display a line description, you would select the correct verb (DSP for DiSPlay), the correct object (LIN for LINe), and the correct qualifier (D for Description). Putting these together would give you DSPLIND–Display Line Description!

However, entering DSPLIND on the command line and pressing <ENTER> causes the error "Parameter LINE Required" to appear. This error indicates that the command DSPLIND needs a required parameter, and that the parameter name is LINE. A prompted command display (see below) will be shown for the command with the missing parameter highlighted.

Commands usually require additional information in the form of parameters. Parameters indicate the object to which the action of the command is directed. Most commands have parameters that are known as required parameters. These parameters must be included in order for the command to function. Other parameters may be optional; the command does not need optional parameters in order to function, but you may need to specify these parameters to produce the desired result.

Many commands allow the use of generic values. The generic values are represented by ending an object name with an * (asterisk). This indicates that the command should use any object that begins with the characters specified, and to disregard any characters after the asterisk in the object name. This is known as using a wild card character. This type of processing is often used with "work with" commands.

Most commands provide default values for parameters. These defaults may be common responses to parameters, or they may be responses that you entered the last time you used that command. A common response may be to use *LIBL where the command requires a library. This tells the command to search the library list for the library needed.

An example of a default response resulting from the last time you used a command would be with the STRSEU (Start Source Entry Utility) command. This command "remembers" the values that you entered when you last used the command. If STRSEU is entered on the command line with no additional parameters, the command will use the library, source file, member, and editing option that you had entered from the previous time you used the STRSEU command. Several of the STR (Start) commands will remember the values you entered the previous time you used the command.

2.2 TYPES OF COMMANDS

There are basically two types of commands: informational commands and action commands. Action commands are also divided into direct action commands and "work with" commands. Commands that are informational in nature are often display (DSP) commands. Direct action commands use command verbs such as ADD (Add), DLT (Delete), or STR (Start). "Work with" commands use the command verb WRK. The following section will examine these types of commands.

2.2.1 Informational Commands

Informational commands do not change the content, value, or characteristics of an object. They merely provide some information concerning the object. Common examples of informational commands are DSPOBJD (Display Object Description), DSPSYSVAL (Display System Value), or DSPNETA (Display Network Attributes). These commands also have parameters that you may want to specify to narrow the scope of the commands.

For instance, the DSPOBJD command has required parameters of Object and Type. You need to specify these parameters so that the DSPOBJD command can locate the correct object, both by its name and type. The DSPOBJD command defaults the library parameter to *LIBL, meaning the library list will be searched for the object. The Library parameter is required, but has a default value. Optional parameters for this command are Detail and Output. The Detail parameter refers to the level of information that will be displayed. The levels with this command are *BASIC and *SERVICE. They produce a different type of information from the DSPOBJD command. The Output parameter will determine where the information will be output. The Output parameter defaults to a value of * (asterisk), meaning the information will be displayed at the terminal. Another possible value for the Output parameter is *PRINT, meaning the information will be printed and placed in a spooled file on an output queue.

Other informational commands have the same type of structure. Usually some parameters will be required and others will be optional. Most informational commands allow the command's output to be directed to a print file. Some informational commands allow the output to be directed to a file on disk. This is very helpful when using CL (Command Language) programs that process the command's output. More will be explained about this technique in Chapter 7 ("Command Language Programs").

2.2.2 Direct Action Commands

Direct action commands are used to change the content, value, or characteristics of an object. They are usually single-purpose, meaning that you cannot process more than one operation at a time with direct action commands. Note this singleness of purpose versus "work with" commands, which allow multiple operations to multiple objects at one time.

An example of a direct action command is STRPRTWTR (Start Print Writer). This command starts a printer writer to allow spooled output files on an output queue to be printed to a physical printer. This command has many parameters; only the required entry WTR (Writer) does not have a default value. The STRPRTWTR command has only one purpose: to associate a print writer job with an output queue.

2.2.3 "Work with" Commands

The "Work with" commands always use the WRK verb. A "work with" command will present a list of objects upon which you may perform various operations. The list concept is important in OS/400 processing since it allows you to see a list of objects rather than only one object. A commonly used "work with" command is the WRKF (Work with Files) command. Entering this command on a command line and pressing <ENTER> without specifying any parameters will produce a list of all files in all libraries in your library list.

When the list is presented, you may perform multiple operations. You may specify option 4 to delete a file, option 5 to display a file, and so on. You may specify more than one option at a time. You may delete a file and display another file with the same operation. OS/400 will perform the operation on the first file encountered in the list, then perform the operation on the next file in the list until all operations have been performed. List processing with "work with" commands is a very powerful tool.

You may also specify optional parameters with a command such as WRKF. For instance, you can specify a particular library to search for files, or group the files by using a generic object name such as ACCT*. This means that the command provides a list of all files in all libraries in your library list that begin with the letters "ACCT". You can further qualify the list by including a library name with the generic qualifier. This produces a list of all files that begin with the letters "ACCT" that were in a specific library.

2.3 COMMAND USAGE

2.3.1 Finding the Right Command

Understanding the naming convention for commands helps you to find the right command. By knowing the correct verb, object type, and qualifier, you can often "sound out" the correct command name.

OS/400 also provides a command to help you search for commands. This command is SLTCMD (Select Command). Entering SLTCMD with a partial or generic command name produces a list of all commands that begin with those characters.

For instance, entering the command SLTCMD WRKC* produces a list of commands such as

- WRKCOSD   (Work with Class of Service Descriptions)
- WRKCTLD   (Work with Controller Descriptions)
- WRKCFGSTS   (Work with Configuration Status)

You can read the description of the commands in the list and then enter the correct command name. You may make the selection criteria as narrow or as broad as you wish, but be aware that OS/400 has over 700 commands in the command set!

2.3.2 Prompting Commands

As mentioned earlier, commands use parameters to determine the correct object upon which to perform an action, or to narrow the scope of a list of objects that would be presented with a "work with" command. You may enter the parameters in keyword format on a command line shown with the following WRKOBJ (Work with Objects) command:

```
WRKOBJ OBJ(PUBLIC/ACCT*) OBJTYPE(*FILE).
```

You can also prompt for the command parameters. To do this, enter the command on the command line (and any parameters in correct order) and press the <F4>, which is the prompt key. Entering the command and prompting produces the following display (see Figure 2–1):

Enter the object name, the library, and the object type. Pressing <ENTER> after this entry causes the command to execute, just as if you had entered all the information on the command line. All OS/400 commands allow prompting for the required and optional parameters. Some commands have no parameters, such as STRPDM (Start Programming Development Manager). Prompting a command without parameters causes the following display (see Figure 2–2):

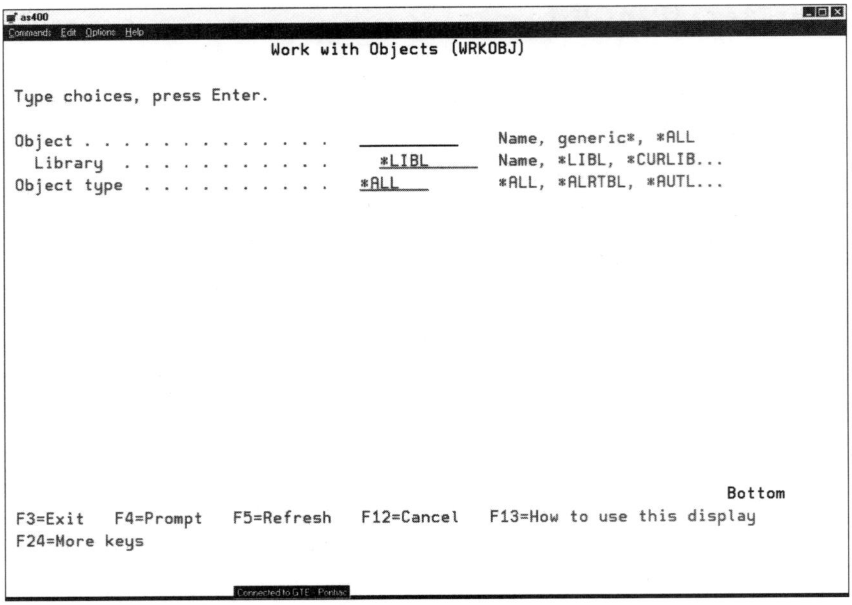

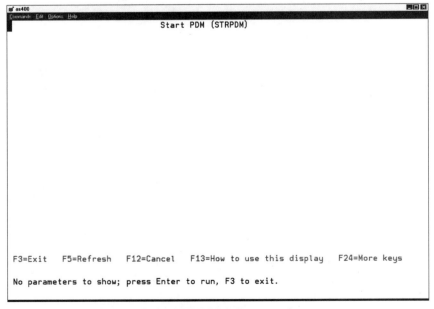

Figure 2–1: WRKOBJ Command screen

Figure 2–2: STRPDM Command screen

In this case, press <ENTER> to execute the command.

2.3.3 The Prompted Command Display

The display for a prompted command uses special characters and highlights to indicate certain information. A highlighted field is a required field. The command will not execute unless a value is entered for this parameter. The > symbol next to a parameter means that this information has been supplied by OS/400 via a menu option, or from parameters specified when the command was prompted.

Special prompting characters you can use within fields are the ? character, which will display a list of allowable values; the & character, which will increase the length of an entry field (if allowed); the + character, which allows more entries to be added to the list; the > character, which allows additional entries to be entered ahead of the current value (with lists); and the < character, which deletes the entry in a list.

The concept of lists within commands bears more explanation. Many commands have parameters that may use or require additional entries. A command that uses this technique is the Start Pass-through (STRPASTHR) command. This command allows a workstation attached to an AS/400 to connect to another AS/400 appearing as a local device [see Chapter 15 ("Advanced Topics") for additional information on STRPASTHR]. Entering the STRPASTHR command and prompting will produce the following display (see Figure 2–3):

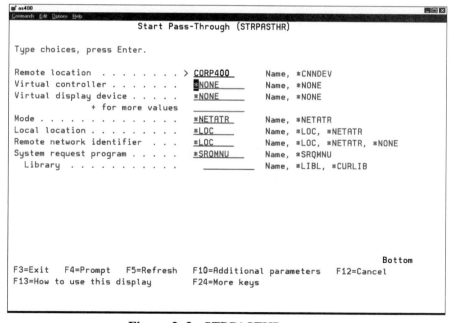

Figure 2–3: STRPASTHR screen

This command requires a "Remote location name" entry and either a "Virtual controller" or "Virtual display device" entry. Note the legend for the entry beneath "Virtual display device." This legend, + for more values, indicates that multiple values can be entered into a list. Enter the first value for "Virtual display device," and enter a + sign for the next value. Press <ENTER> to provide an entry list for more values; this is shown with the following screen (see Figure 2–4):

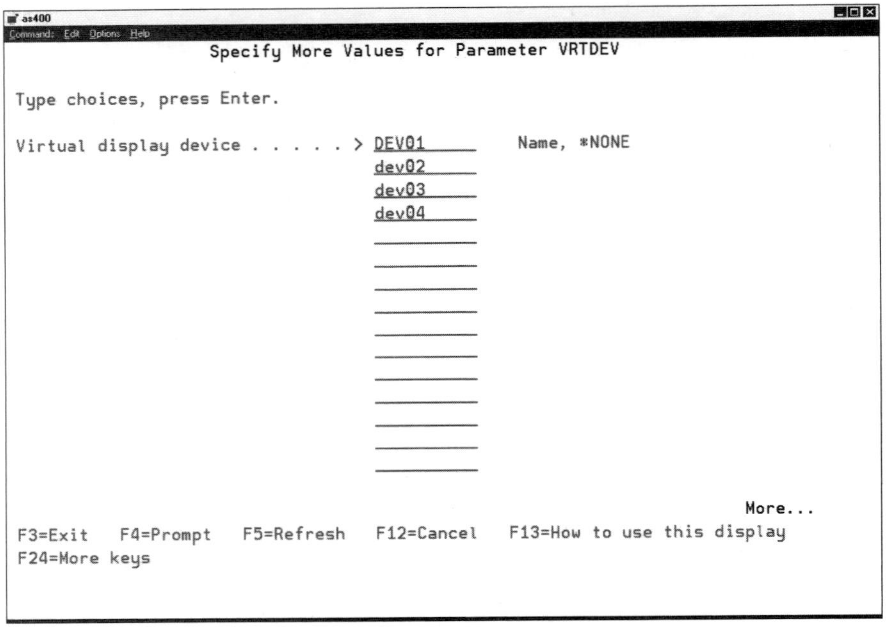

```
 as400                                                                  _ □ ×
Command: Edit Options Help
                    Specify More Values for Parameter VRTDEV

 Type choices, press Enter.

 Virtual display device . . . . . >  DEV01          Name, *NONE
                                     dev02
                                     dev03
                                     dev04
                                     _____
                                     _____
                                     _____
                                     _____
                                     _____
                                     _____
                                     _____
                                     _____
                                     _____
                                     _____
                                     _____

                                                                     More...
 F3=Exit   F4=Prompt   F5=Refresh   F12=Cancel   F13=How to use this display
 F24=More keys
```

Figure 2–4: Specify More Values for Parameter VRTDEV screen

Enter the additional values for this parameter, pressing the <ENTER> key when complete. Remember, the <ENTER> key will either execute the command, or return from entering list values. Pressing <ENTER> will return you to the command display (see Figure 2–5).

The list of values entered for the VRTDEV parameter has been returned to the command prompt. Note that the legend "+ for more values" is still on the screen. This means that you may still enter more values if needed by simply typing a + over the first character in the last value, and pressing the <ENTER> key. You are then at the additional values prompt where you can specify more values at the end of the list. Other prompt characters will allow you to specify the new value anywhere in the list.

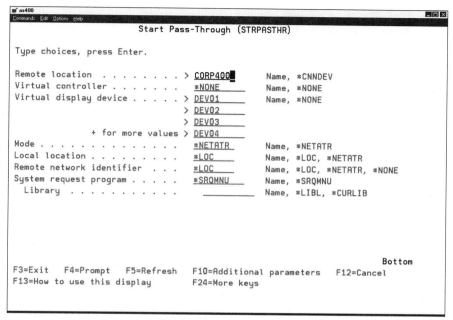

Figure 2–5: STRPASTHR continued screen

2.3.4 Prompted Command Keys

The keys that are used in command prompting are the <ENTER> key, which will execute the command (or return to the prompt if a list of values for a parameter were being entered; the <HELP> key, which provides help for the command (as does the <F1> key); and the <ROLL UP> and <ROLL DOWN> keys, which will roll through the entered values for a parameter.

The command prompting process can use many function keys. All of the function keys that can be used with command prompting will be explained in this section, but please note that not all commands will use all function keys.

The <F1> key shows the available help for the command. This key is very helpful to explain how and why the command should be used. The <F1> key also explains all the function keys available for the command.

The <F3> key is the Exit key. Pressing <F3> at any point when completing the parameters will exit the command and display the major screen from which the command was invoked. Note that the major screen may not be the screen where the command was entered and prompted; it may be an earlier screen. This is especially common when prompting a command from a list of objects. To cancel a command and return to the immediate prior screen, use the <F12> (Cancel) key. This key cancels the command and returns immediately to the screen where the command was entered and prompted.

The <F5> key refreshes the screen. This is useful for status commands such as Work with Active Jobs (WRKACTJOB), or Work with System Status (WRKSYSSTS). The <F5> key retrieves the information requested again and redisplays the screen.

The <F9> key shows all the parameters possible for this command. The <F10> key will show additional parameters. The <F10> display may differ from the <F9> key display since the command will do conditional prompting, meaning that the command will only show the parameters that are reasonable for that command with the information that has been entered.

For instance, the CRTLINSDLC (Create SDLC Line) command needs to know if the line will be a dial-up line or a leased line. When you have entered the value for the "SWITCHED" keyword (*YES means a dial-up line, *NO means a leased line), the command will no longer prompt you for dial-up parameters and instead will provide prompts for leased line characteristics.

Another function key used with command prompting is the <F11> key. This shows keywords rather than the allowable choices. An example of this display, again using the WRKOBJ command, looks like this (see Figure 2–6):

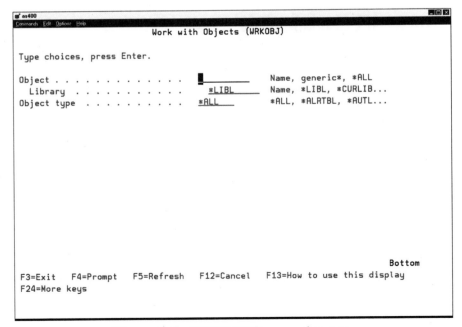

Figure 2–6: WRKOBJ Command screen

This allows you to see the keywords rather than the list of allowable values.

The <F13> key shows how to use the display. Pressing <F13> displays the IBM command help text. This help text (which runs to many screens) explains how to use command prompting.

The <F14> key allows you to see the command string as it would be constructed and passed to the OS/400 command processor. This is valuable in two ways: to examine the command and its parameters before it is executed, and to view the command string in order to key it in at a command line or to use it in a Command Language program. You could use the <PRINT> key to print the completed command string for later inclusion in a CL program.

The <F15> key displays error messages from the command. This is helpful when you enter an invalid value for a parameter. You can press <F15> to display the error message, place your cursor on the error message, then press the <HELP> key (or <F1>). This shows the second level text associated with the error message, which provides you with more information to determine and correct the error.

The <F16> key executes the command at that point and will not show any further screens that may be associated with other command parameters. For example, the CPYF (Copy File) command has seven screens upon which you would need to press <ENTER> to continue. If you have entered all the parameters that you require for the command execution and can accept all the other default values, use the <F16> key to bypass the remaining screens and execute the command. By the way, OS/400 places all required and commonly used parameters on the first or second screen to allow you to bypass the more often unused screens when prompting.

The <F18> key provides Double Byte Character Set (DBCS) conversion.

The <F24> key shows the other keys available for this command. Since more function keys are available than will fit on the last two lines of the display, the <F24> key will cycle through the available function keys. Function keys that are not shown on the screen are still available to be used.

2.3.5 Command Recall

Occasionally, you want to execute a command again. You may need to execute the command repeatedly (with a slight parameter change), or you may have made an error on the command. You can, of course, enter the command on the command line, prompt the command, and reenter the parameters. OS/400 offers an alternative called command recall. Command recall allows you to retrieve previously entered commands. The command recall key is the <F9> key. Pressing the <F9> key will retrieve the previously entered command, pressing the <F9> key again will retrieve the command before that, and so on.

After you press the <ENTER> key, and the command executes, you are returned to the screen from which you entered and prompted the command. If you wish to execute the command again, or if you wish to change a parameter and rerun the command, you can recall the command with the <F9> key. This key places the command, the keywords, and the parameter values on the command line. You can change a value on the command line and press <ENTER> to execute the command. Alternatively, after pressing <F9>, you can press the <F4> key to prompt the command again. All the values that have been entered will be placed in the appropriate parameter, and the command can be executed after any changes.

2.3.6 Summary of Prompt Characters

A highlighted field is a required entry: The command will not execute without a value for this parameter.

The > character indicates the value for this parameter was supplied from the command line, a menu, or a previous command.

?   Displays a list of allowable values.

&   Increases the length of an entry field (if allowed).

+   Allows more entries to be added to the list.

>   Enables additional entries to be entered ahead of the current value in a list.

<   Deletes the entry in a list.

2.3.7 Summary of Prompt Function Keys

<F1>   Shows the available help for the command and the function keys available for the command.

<F3>   Exits the command without execution.

<F5>   Refreshes the screen.

<F9>   Shows all parameters possible for this command.

<F10>   Shows additional parameters (conditional prompting).

<F11>   Displays keywords rather than a description of the allowable choices.

<F12>   Cancels the command and returns to the previous screen.

<F13>   Shows how to use command prompting.

<F14>   Displays the command string.

<F15>   Displays error messages from the command.

<F16>   Executes the command immediately without showing further screens associated with other command parameters.

<F18>   Provides Double Byte Character Set (DBCS) conversion.

<F24>   Shows the other keys available for this command.

2.4 OS/400 MENUS

OS/400 offers two methods to accomplish tasks: commands and menus. Menus are actually a different way of running commands. Each menu option eventually executes a command that could be executed by specifying the command itself.

Menus display their name in the upper left corner of the screen. You may directly access these menus rather than proceeding through any previous menus. In addition, when the menu option executes a command to be executed, the name of the command is shown (exactly as if the command were being prompted). This is helpful since you could note the command being used, and then use that command directly in the future.

Menus are a "user-friendlier" method of command execution. A user does not need to remember all the commands to perform the job; he or she can use the more understandable menus. While the menus execute commands, they also provide the important function of grouping similar commands together. This provides a common point for command execution.

There are two types of menus: user menus and OS/400 menus. This chapter will explain the OS/400 menus. The creation and use of user menus is explained in Chapter 11 ("Screen Design Aid").

2.4.1 The Main Menu

The OS/400 "Main Menu" is an optional menu that can be displayed upon signing on to the AS/400. Your installation may have a custom menu, in which case you would be presented with the options for that menu. The OS/400 "Main Menu" contains several options. Your user class and security access determine the options that will be shown. The OS/400 "Main Menu" is as follows (see Figure 2–7):

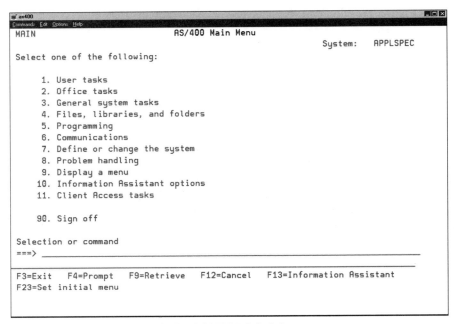

Figure 2–7: OS/400 Main Menu screen

2.4.2 Main Menu Options

Option 1 (User tasks) from the OS/400 main menu shows the USER menu. This displays a menu that allows you to change characteristics of your interactive session, display or send a message, submit or work with batch jobs, change your password or user profile, and other tasks. These options relate to your job; you cannot access other users' jobs, profiles, or messages.

Option 2 (Office tasks) displays the OFCTSK menu. This allows access to OfficeVision/400 (explained in Chapter 9), the system directory (used for routing messages), documents, and folders.

Option 3 (General system tasks) shows the SYSTEM menu. This enables you to work with different types of functions, such as jobs, the save and restore process, messages, devices, and security. Generally only system operators and managers have access to these functions.

Option 4 (Files, libraries, and folders) displays the DATA menu. The Data File Utility, Structured Query Utility, and other functions are available from this menu option. Saving and restoring files, libraries, and folder processes are available through this menu option.

Option 5 (Programming) shows the PROGRAM menu. This menu allows access to programming activities such as debugging, utilities, and a special programmer's menu.

Option 6 (Communications) displays the CMN Menu. This menu enables the user to access communications activities. Processes such as network management, communications configuration, and sending and receiving files are accessible from this menu.

Option 7 (Define or change the system) shows the DEFINE menu. This menu provides access to system configuration, security, operating system changes and fixes, and system values. Generally, only system operators and managers have access to these functions.

Option 8 (Problem handling) displays the PROBLEM menu. This menu helps the system operator or manager to resolve system problems and to work with network management. It contacts IBM with questions (and receives answers), and displays logs such as the system history log and error log.

Option 9 (Display a menu) executes the GO command to display a menu. The GO command will be explained later in this chapter.

Option 10 (Information Assistant option) shows the SUPPORT menu. This allows access to the OS/400 online education, the system help index, a reference of publications available from IBM, and problem handling.

Option 11 (Client Access tasks) displays the PCSTSK menu. This menu is divided into two areas: a user area and an administrator area. The user area allows you to copy a PC document to and from an AS/400 database, work with documents and folders, and use Personal Computer Organizer functions. The administrator area allows you to initialize Client Access, enroll new users, and to configure connections from the PC to the AS/400.

Option 90 (Sign off) executes the SIGNOFF command.

2.4.3 Invoking a Menu

Menus are invoked through the use of the GO command. Entering the GO command and a menu name on a command line and pressing <ENTER> will display that menu. You can also specify the name of the library that contains the menu if the menu is not in your library list. Another option for the GO command is the "Return point" (RTNPNT) parameter. Specifying *YES for this parameter (the default) will cause control to be returned to the screen where the GO command was entered. An example of the GO command is GO MAIN. This displays the AS/400 main menu. If the menu is not in your library list, enter the library name, such as GO USERLIB/USERMENU.

2.4.4 Major Command Groups

There are many commands on an AS/400. Remember that one purpose of menus is to group like commands. These commands can be further grouped into major command groups. Each of the major command groups provide a menu where commands can be selected for execution. You can display the major command groups by displaying the MAJOR menu with the GO MAJOR command. You can also display the major command groups by pressing the prompt key (F4) with nothing on the command line.

The MAJOR menu displays the following screen (see Figure 2–8):

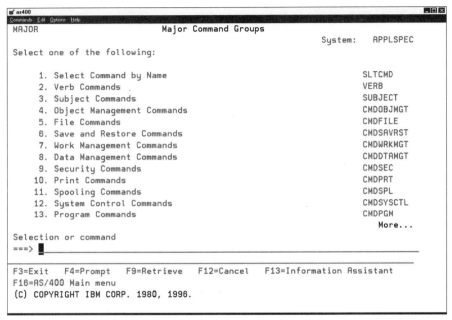

Figure 2–8: Major Command Groups

This menu displays more than 20 major command groups. Note that all the commands represented are accessible through the use of the command and are also available as menu options from another menu. This menu merely provides a convenient grouping of the major commands.

The SLTCMD option has been discussed in the section on commands. This allows you to enter a portion of a command name (a generic name) suffixed with an asterisk (*). OS/400 will search for and display a list of all commands that begin with those characters. This is very helpful when you need to add or change an object and are not quite sure of the object type or the qualifier, but you know the operation you need to perform. You can simply enter the command verb with an asterisk (for example, ADD* or CHG*) (see Figure 2–9).

Pressing <ENTER> would provide a list of all commands that begin with the characters you had entered. You could then scan the descriptions of the commands and select the correct command.

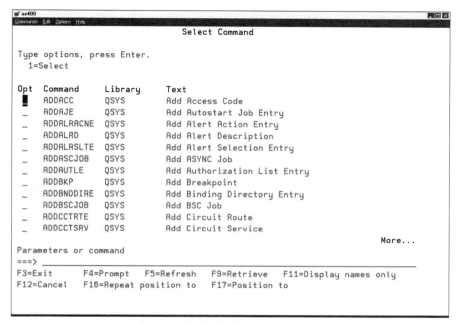

Figure 2-9: SLTCMD screen

The VERB menu group commands use a different technique which group the commands by the verb used. The menu will display options such as Add Commands, Allocate Commands, Answer Commands, and so on. There are more than 80 different command groupings available through the VERB menu. The VERB menu is helpful for the same reason as the SLTCMD command: It provides a method of accessing a command without knowing the complete command name. The SLTCMD access a command based on a partial command name. The VERB menu accesses commands based on the type of action the command performs. The following display shows a portion of the VERB menu (see Figure 2-10).

The SUBJECT menu groups commands are based on the subject. The subject could be an object (CMDFILE for file commands) or an action (CMDDWN for down commands). The subject could also be a condition such as an error (CMDERR). There are almost three hundred subjects that can be accessed through the SUBJECT menu. The following display shows a portion of the SUBJECT menu (see Figure 2-11).

The commands that are available through the different major command groups are all available from other menus or from executing the command directly. The major command groups provide an alternative method for identifying and executing commands.

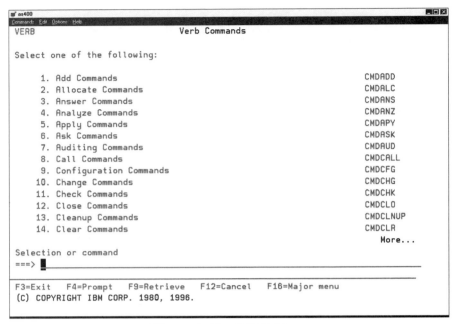

Figure 2–10: VERB Menu

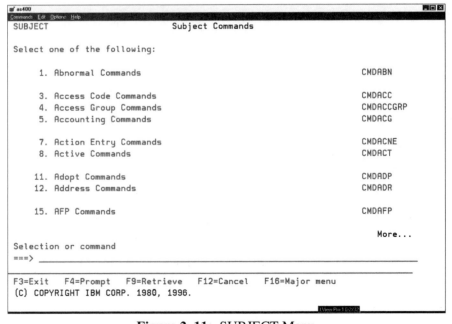

Figure 2–11: SUBJECT Menu

2.5 ERROR HANDLING

Occasionally, an error occurs when executing a command. While this is a rare occurrence (we are sure that you have entered the command correctly), you need to be able to recover from error conditions.

2.5.1 Types of Errors

Different types of errors can occur when using OS/400 services. One type of error is a command language error. This type of error occurs when you enter a parameter incorrectly (possibly a spelling error), or when the command needs a different type of information than you are providing. The example shows the type of error message received when a parameter is misspelled (see Figure 2–12).

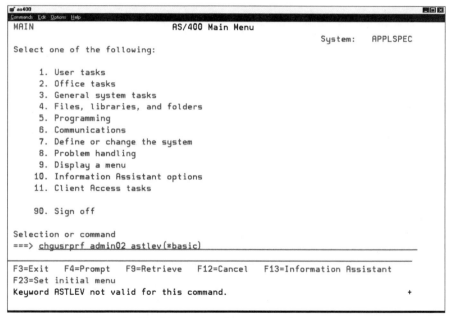

Figure 2–12: Example of command language error

Programming errors will be shown in different formats depending on the program. A program will be able to handle data entry errors or errors that are within the purview of the program. These errors should cause an error message to be displayed, with some type of instructions on how to correct the error. A program may not be able to handle certain critical errors. These critical errors may then cause a system error.

System errors, caused when the system encounters a problem from which it cannot recover, need immediate attention as they stop any further processing of the offending program or command. System errors cause an error message to "break" into the current screen. This means that the screen will clear and the error message will be displayed. A command line will display at the bottom of the screen to provide the options to recover from the error.

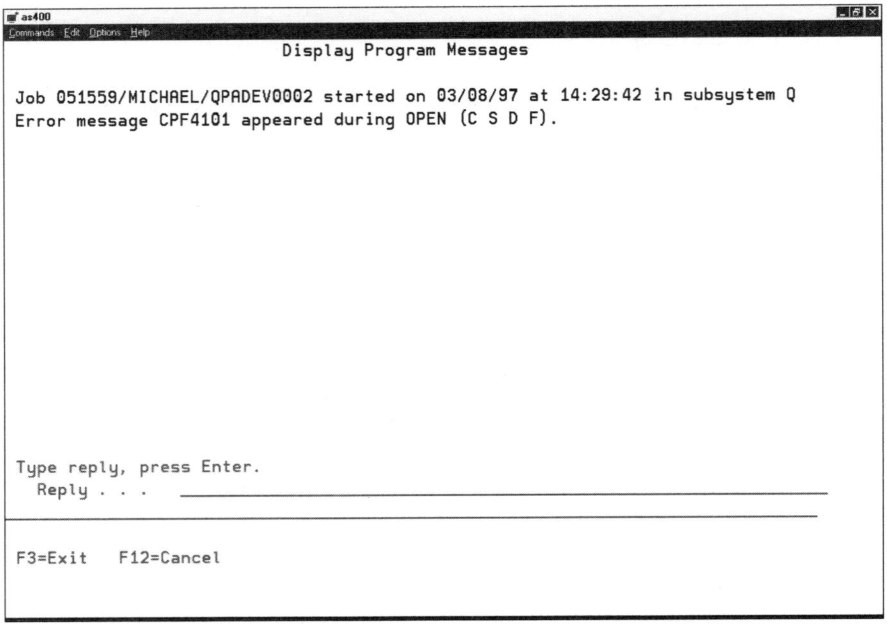

```
as400                                                              _ 8 x
Commands Edit Options Help
                         Display Program Messages

 Job 051559/MICHAEL/QPADEV0002 started on 03/08/97 at 14:29:42 in subsystem Q
 Error message CPF4101 appeared during OPEN (C S D F).













 Type reply, press Enter.
   Reply . . .   _____
                 _____


 F3=Exit    F12=Cancel

```

Figure 2-13: Example of system error message

2.5.2 Error Recovery

An error message will be displayed when a system error occurs. The error message will be in the form of an error message ID and the error message itself. The error message is in what is known as the "first level" message format. This means that the error message is only showing the first level of message text.

Position your cursor on the error message and press the <HELP> key. This will display the second-level message text. This will provide (at least for OS/400 error messages) additional information with which you can make the decision on how the error should be handled. The following example shows second level message text.

```
ai400                                                                    _ 回 ×
Commands  Edit  Options  Help
                        Additional Message Information

Message ID . . . . . . :    RPG1216      Severity . . . . . . . :   99
Message type . . . . . :    Inquiry
Date sent . . . . . . :     03/08/97     Time sent . . . . . . :    14:29:56

Message . . . . :    Error message CPF4101 appeared during OPEN (C S D F).
Cause . . . . . :    The RPG program SL0700R in library MINITE received the
  message CPF4101 while doing an implicit OPEN to file N1XTAP. See the job log
  for a complete description of message CPF4101. If the file has a device type
  of SPECIAL, there may be no message in the job log.
Recovery . . . :    Enter C to cancel, S to obtain a printout of system
  storage, D to obtain an RPG formatted printout of system storage, or F to
  obtain a full formatted printout of system storage.
Possible choices for replying to message . . . . . . . . . . . . . . . :
  D -- Obtain RPG formatted printout of system storage.
  S -- Obtain printout of system storage.
  F -- Obtain full formatted printout of system storage.
                                                               More...
Press Enter to continue.

F3=Exit   F6=Print   F9=Display message details
F10=Display messages in job log   F12=Cancel   F21=Select assistance level
```

Figure 2-14: Example of second-level help

Activity cannot continue until the error message receives a response. System error messages are inquiry messages and require a response. A system error message may use different options, but several options are common. Each of these common options will be discussed. Your installation may have certain requirements for system error recovery. The system error message options can cause damage to the system or to data. If you are unsure about using the options, contact your system manager.

The C option will cancel the process causing the error. This will abruptly cancel the program or command.

The D option will dump the offending program. This option will cause a printout of the status of the program and may aid support personnel to determine the cause of the error. The program will also be cancelled.

The F option will provide a full formatted dump of the offending program. This option will cause a printout of the status of the program as with the D option, and includes formatting to help support personnel to determine the cause of the error. The program will also be cancelled.

The G option signals OS/400 to continue (or go). This is often used for recoverable "errors" such as inserting the next diskette in series for a save operation.

The I option will ignore the error. This option may be exactly what is required. An appropriate example of using the Ignore option is when changing forms on the printer. The print writer will display a message indicating that a new type of form is required. The proper response in this case would be to change the forms and the message with an I, meaning ignore the error condition and continue processing. Certain error conditions can be ignored and others must be responded to differently. Be certain you know what the error condition is referring to before you respond with an I.

The R option will cause OS/400 to retry the command that caused the error. This may be an appropriate response depending on the error condition. If you are trying to display a diskette and the diskette is not in the diskette drive, you will receive an error message. After placing the diskette in the diskette drive, you can respond to the error with an R. This causes the command to be tried again, and then displays the diskette. Again, be sure you know what the error condition is referring to before you respond with an R.

The S option will provide a system dump of the offending program and the system values. This option will cause a printout of the status of the program as with the D option. In addition, the S option includes system information to enable support personnel to determine the state of the system at the time of the error. The program will also be cancelled.

3

Libraries, Files, and Members

OS/400 uses libraries, files, and members as components to organize data. Libraries can also contain other objects used by the system and programs. This chapter will describe the organizational structure and related commands for accessing and manipulating libraries, files, and members.

3.1 WHAT IS A LIBRARY?

A library contains objects. All objects that exist on the system must reside in a library. In fact, if an object is not in a library (due to a system error), the object cannot be accessed or manipulated. Libraries contain files, but they also contain many other types of objects. It is important to remember that all objects reside in a library.

There are three types of libraries: system libraries, user libraries, and product libraries. There is no difference in the actual format of the library; the difference is in their attributes.

System libraries (libraries with an attribute of *SYS) are considered part of OS/400. System library names usually begin with the letter "Q" (QSYS, QUSRSYS, and so on). They are handled separately for operations such as saves and restores. They cannot usually be manipulated by users or user programs. System libraries are saved with the SAVSYS command.

User libraries are all libraries that are owned or created by users and user programs. They are usually the largest number of libraries on a system. The application systems running on an AS/400 are contained in user libraries. User libraries are saved with the SAVLIB LIB(*NONSYS) command.

Product libraries are libraries used for specific application systems. Product libraries are essentially user libraries since they are handled similar to a user library for access and manipulation. The main reason for OS/400 to support product libraries is to allow the application to be located in a specific library and to be able to access them through the library list in a certain location.

3.2 WHAT ARE FILES AND MEMBERS?

There are two kinds of files on an AS/400: a database file and a device file. In brief, a database file can be a "physical file" that contains data records or source statements, or a "logical file" that contains access information for data. In contrast, a device file describes the operational characteristics of a physical hardware device (for example, a tape, printer, or diskette).

Members are separate entities within a database file. Every database file that contains information has at least one member. When a user or user program accesses a file, they are actually accessing a member in the file. A database file may contain multiple members. A file usually has a member with the same name as the file. This member is accessed when only a file name is specified for a command or a program. A member may also be specified with most commands that access a file.

Members can be used to subdivide similar information in a file. For instance, you may have a physical file that contains sales information. You can use members to segregate data by month with each member containing sales records for a given month along with a program to produce a sales report. Using this technique, you can provide an override (OVRDBF—Override Database File) to direct the program to the correct member for the month you wish to report.

Source physical files also use members. Since source physical files contain program source statements, each member would contain the source statements for a different program. In fact, IBM has certain default files that it will search to find program source statements. These default file names will be discussed in Chapter 12 ["Programming Development Manager (PDM)"].

A file is logically subdivided into records, which are subdivided into fields. A record format describes a record and is a description of the fields in a file and the order of the fields. A field is a unit of information that cannot be subdivided and still contains meaningful information. One of the more interesting aspects of the OS/400 file structure is that the data elements (files, record formats, and fields) are externally described. While it is not a requirement to externally describe the data elements, almost all AS/400 installations provide an external data description of files.

3.3 LIBRARY AND FILE WILDCARDS

You may specify some special values to reference files and libraries. One special value is *ALL. This means that all files within a library (or a library list) should be accessed or made available for access in a list. Another special value is a generic file name, which ends with an asterisk (*). A generic file name is used with command list processing. To use a generic file name, specify the first few characters of the filenames and end the filenames with an asterisk. This would make all files that have the same leading characters available for processing. Both libraries and files can use the special value *ALL and a generic name for some commands.

3.4 EXTERNAL VERSUS INTERNAL DATA DESCRIPTIONS

Internal data description is the traditional approach to data description. This means that the data attributes are described internally to application programs. Maintaining data format descriptions in multiple programs is cumbersome, costly, and can be incomplete or inaccurate. Program-described data results in data redundancy, inefficient use of storage, multiple descriptions of storage formats and access views, data that is program-dependent, and duplication of maintenance efforts.

Externally described data results in permanent data storage, reduction or elimination of data redundancy, and more efficient use of storage. External data descriptions also allow data to be accessible to multiple programs for varying purposes, provides more up-to-date access of current data, and enables data to be described once to the system for storage, access, and presentation. In addition, file format changes are known to all programs and data is program-independent.

Another important effect of externally described files is the way they are accessed by programs. The description of the file is accessed during program compilation. The compiler will read the file descriptions for files declared in the program and will transfer the descriptions of the record formats and fields to the program. In this way, the program and data independence is maintained. The description of the data and the program accessing the data are kept apart.

Since the program accesses the file description at compilation, the file cannot be changed after the program is compiled. If this were to happen, the program would attempt to access fields or records that were different or even missing. Therefore, OS/400 provides a mechanism to avoid this problem. Record format level checking prevents a program from accessing a file that has been changed since the program was compiled.

A record format level identifier is created as part of the file description when the file is created. The compiled program contains the record format level identifier for each file in the program. If the program attempts to access a file and the program level identifier is different than the file's level identifier (indicating that the file has been recreated), the program will signal a system error.

The procedure for creating programs is to create the files required (data is not needed at this point), and then compile the programs. If a file is changed, the program will need to be recompiled. While it is possible (and sometimes necessary) to override this level checking, it is the usual practice to use this procedure. The record format level checking can be disabled by specifying *NO for the "Level check" (LVLCHK) parameter when creating a physical database file.

3.5 TYPES OF FILES

As previously noted, an AS/400 supports both database files and device files. Database files are then further broken down into physical files and logical files. Both physical and logical files may contain multiple members. The difference between the two is that a physical file contains the actual data; the logical file contains a view of that data.

3.5.1 Access Paths

Both physical and logical files use access paths to access records in the file. An access path describes how records may be presented to programs. An access path may either be in arrival sequence or in keyed sequence. An arrival sequence access path indicates that records will be presented in the order in which they were added to the file; in other words, the first record added to the file will be the first record presented to a program. A keyed sequence access path means that records will be accessed based on the value of certain fields in the file. These fields, known as key fields, would allow access to the records in any order, not just the order in which they were added to the file.

3.5.2 Physical Files

A physical file contains data and has only one record format. Data is stored in fixed length records in physical files. Physical files can be accessed by an arrival or keyed sequence access path. Physical files have an attribute of PF.

Physical files contain either data records with an attribute of *DTA, or source statements with an attribute of *SRC (usually referred to as source physical files). Both types may be accessed by many of the same commands; however, each file type has specific commands that only work with that type of physical file.

3.5.3 Logical Files

A logical file contains a view of the data contained in one or more physical files. Logical files do not contain any actual data. There can be a maximum of 32 record formats for nonjoin logical files, and a maximum of one record format for join logical files. Logical files can be accessed by an arrival or keyed sequence access path. Logical files have an attribute of LF.

Logical files can show the data in a physical file in different ways. For example, a logical file can be constructed to omit certain fields or records from a file. The data still remains in the file, but that information is not presented to the program. This ensures that someone not authorized to certain data could not see the data. For example, a clerk responsible for mailing birthday cards to employees would not be able to see another employee's salary, even if the salary was in the same record as the name and address information.

Another important function of logical files is the ability to join data from two or more physical files into one logical record. This provides access to multiple files based on matching key values and encourages normalization of the data.

There are four types of logical files: simple logical file, join logical file, multiple format logical file (also known as a union file), and a view (used for SQL processing). The SQL view logical files will be discussed in Chapter 15 ("Advanced AS/400 Topics").

A simple logical file is based on only one physical file, and is used to provide a different access path, select and/or omit criteria, or field attribute changes. Records may be read, updated, and deleted with a simple logical file. The primary use for a simple logical file is to provide a different method of access to a physical file.

For example, when using a physical file that had an access path based on a key value such as customer number, a simple logical file can be built over the physical file to provide access by customer name. Records can then be accessed and manipulated by name.

A join logical file combines information from two or more physical files into one record format. A join logical is a powerful construct; you can access more than one physical file with a single read. The physical file records are joined together, creating a logical record, based on one or more matching fields in both files. A program can only read from a join logical file. Updating existing records, writing new records, or deleting records is not allowed. Only one record format is allowed with join logical files.

An example of a join logical file is a situation where the database is normalized. The customer name and address information is in one physical file, while the customer sales information is in a different file. A join logical file can be built over the two physical files, with the physical files "joined" by a common key value, such as the customer number. When the customer number is input into a program, the program can read the join logical file, providing both name and address information and sales information in a single record format. While the record cannot be updated, it is available for read access.

A multiple format logical file (also known as a union file) uses multiple record formats. Like a join logical, it is based on two or more physical files. However, a union logical file has a record format for each physical file on which it is based.

An example of where a union logical file can be used is in invoice printing. A physical file may exist that contains the invoice header information (address, shipping instructions, and so on) and another physical file that contains the invoice detail information (part ordered, quantity shipped, and so on). A union file can first access the invoice header file, then process the invoice detail file until the end of that invoice. The common key in this example could be the invoice number.

3.5.4 Device Files

Device files in OS/400 provide information regarding the characteristics of physical devices on the system. Device files can provide information to OS/400 such as lines-per-inch or font (printer files), volume name (tape or diskette files), or communication characteristics (communication files).

The five types of device files are: printer device files (*PRTF), tape device files (*TAPF), diskette device files (*DKTF), communication files (*ICFF—Inter System Communication or *DDMF—Distributed Data Management), and display files (*DSPF). This last file type describes the characteristics of a display screen used for interactive programs. A display file contains the literals, field definitions, and some editing for the screen. Display files will be explained in detail in Chapter 11 ("Screen Design Aid (SDA)").

3.6 FILE AND MEMBER OPERATIONS

An important point to understand regarding file and member operations on an AS/400 is that the file structure is very sophisticated. This sophistication has both advantages and disadvantages. An advantage is that the relational database manager provides many different options for accessing files. Physical and logical file access paths can be constructed to provide exactly the access needed for a file. Record access is very fast on an AS/400.

A disadvantage to the file structure is that creating new file objects can be very slow. This is also true for opening and closing files. While the record access is very fast once the file is open, the AS/400 is noticeably slower than other systems in opening and closing files.

This necessitates that file operations be handled differently than on other systems. One technique that is often used is called "preopening" files. Preopening files calls for a driver program to open the files that are to be used by the other programs in the jobstream. This will allow the other programs to immediately access the records in the file without a delay due to file open time. In addition, the next program in the jobstream can begin execution quicker, as it does not have to wait for the previous program to close the files. The driver program should close all files after the jobstream has completed.

Another technique to maximize speed with AS/400 file operations is to avoid creating and deleting temporary files. Efficiency can be realized by having permanent work files. This is a stark contrast to the nonAS/400 practice of having a program create a temporary work file, manipulate the work file during the execution of the program, and then delete the file after the program has completed. The key to using permanent work files is clearing the data from the file (this is explained later in this chapter with the Clear Physical File Member (CLRPFM) command).

3.6.1 Creating a File

Creating a new database file on an AS/400 is more complicated than on many systems because most AS/400 systems have database files that are externally defined. While files are not required to be defined externally, most are defined externally for the reasons mentioned earlier.

The first step in externally defining a file is to determine the requirements of the file. This means that the usage, fields, and (in the case of display or printer files) literals to be contained in the file must be determined. While external file definition provides many advantages, poor file design can still occur with a lack of requirements.

The next step in defining files externally requires creating the Data Description Specifications for the file. These specifications, known as DDS, describe the file to OS/400. Actually, DDS is like a language in itself. Included in the description are field names, lengths and attributes, access path information, select and omit criteria, and other attributes. The following will describe DDS, required entries, and discuss file creation. Both physical and logical file creation will be explained.

3.6.2 Data Description Specifications (DDS)

The DDS are entered into members of source physical files through the Source Entry Utility (SEU). SEU is fully explained in Chapter 6 ["Basic Editing with the Source Entry Utility (SEU)"].

3.6.3 DDS Syntax

Columns 1 through 44 of the source record contain the DDS positional entries, and columns 45 through 80 contain the keyword entries. The source statements are in fixed format and their use varies somewhat depending on the type of file being created. All DDS records should contain the letter A in column 6. This indicates that the statements are DDS statements.

The positional entries define the most common attributes of records and fields (names, length, and so on). One of the most common entries is the Specification Type in column 17. The Specification Type indicates whether the source record contains information about a record format, a field name, a key field, a select or omit field, or a join field.

Positions 19 through 28 contain the name of the field or record format. Positions 30 through 37 describe the type, length, and number of decimal positions for a field, while position 38 determines the field usage. The usage of a field determines if the field is input, output, both input and output, or a different usage for the field. In addition, if the file being described is a printer file or a display file, positions 39 through 44 define the location on the display or on the report.

Positions 45 through 80 of the source record contain the keyword entries. Keyword entries define the less common attributes such as edit masks for output numeric fields, color and highlighting information for fields and literals in display files, input editing for fields, and many other attributes.

3.6.4 Data Description Specification Examples

The following is an example of DDS that could be used for a simple physical file. The file will contain a customer number, a name field, an address field, city, state, and zip code fields, and a beginning balance field. The customer number will be a key field, meaning the access path for this file will be in keyed sequence. Note the positional entries.

```
   0    1    2    3    4    5    6
   1234567890123456789012345678901234567890123456789012345678901234 5
    *
    *  Record format REC01
    *
   A       R REC01
    *
    *  Field layouts follow
    *
   A          CUSTNO      5S 0
   A          NAME       15A
   A          ADDR       20A
   A          CITY       15A
   A          STATE       2A
   A          ZIP         9S 0
   A          BALANC     11S 2
    *
    *  Key Field
    *
   A       K CUSTNO
```

These Data Description Specifications indicate the following:

The record format name is REC01. This is determined by the R in column 17, followed by the record format name beginning in column 19.

CUSTNO is a 5 position numeric field with 0 decimal places. This is indicated by the decimal places entry ending in column 34.

NAME, ADDR, CITY, and STATE are all character fields. Position 35 contains an A, meaning character field.

ZIP is a 9 position numeric field with 0 decimal positions, and BALANC is an 11 position numeric field with 2 decimal positions.

CUSTNO is a key field. This is indicated by the K in column 17, following all other field definitions.

The following is an example of DDS that could be used for a simple logical file. The file, built over the preceding physical file, exists to provide a keyed access path based on name and to limit access to the physical file data. This will allow a program to access the records in the physical file in name order. Remember, logical files contain no data, only a view of the physical file data. An important point to note with logical file DDS is that no fields need to be specified—all fields in the physical file are accessible through the logical file. Alternatively, if the logical file defines fields, then those fields are the only fields that can be accessed through the logical file. This logical file will contain the customer number, the name, the address, city, state, and zip code fields, but will not provide the beginning balance field. The name will be the key field for this file.

```
0     1     2     3     4     5     6
1234567890123456789012345678901234567890123456789012345678901234 5
   *
   *  Record format REC01
   *
A       R LFREC
   *
   *  Field layouts follow
   *
A           CUSTNO
A           NAME
A           ADDR
A           CITY
A           STATE
A           ZIP
   *
   *  Key Field
   *
A       K NAME
```

These Data Description Specifications indicate the following:

The record format name is LFREC. Note that the length and data type of fields do not need to be defined—the definition of the fields is done in the physical file DDS.

The BALANC field is not defined in the logical file. This indicates that the BALANC will not be accessible to the program that accesses this file.

The NAME is the key field.

Creating the Data Description Specifications does not create the file. A file is created with an appropriate Create command. The Create command will invoke the DDS processor, which will check the DDS source statements for correct syntax and produce a listing of the file layout and any errors encountered in the validation.

If the Data Description Specifications contain no errors (or at most minor warnings), the file will be created. Note that when the file is created, it will, by default, first delete an existing file of the same name if one exists. This will of course also delete any data in the file. Exercise caution before creating a new file so that you are not unknowingly deleting an existing file.

The Create command for a physical file is the Create Physical File (CRTPF) command. The following is a CRTPF command that would create the physical file shown previously.

```
CRTPF FILE(*CURLIB/PHYFILE) SRCFILE(*LIBL/QDDSSRC) +
SRCMBR(*FILE) TEXT('Customer physical file').
```

The "File" and "Library" (FILE) parameter determines the name of the physical file to be created. The "Source file" and "Library" (SRCFILE) parameter determines the location of the member containing the DDS source. The "Source member" (SRCMBR) parameter is the member in the source file where the DDS statements are located. The "Text description" (TEXT) parameter is up to 50 characters of descriptive text.

The Create command for a logical file is the Create Logical File (CRTLF) command. The following is a CRTLF command that would create the logical file shown previously.

```
CRTLF FILE(*CURLIB/LOGFILE) SRCFILE(*LIBL/QDDSSRC) +
SRCMBR(*FILE) TEXT('Logical file with no balance field').
```

The "File" and "Library" (FILE) parameter determines the name of the logical file to be created. The "Source file" and "Library" (SRCFILE) parameter determine the location of the member containing the DDS source. The "Source member" (SRCMBR) parameter is the member in the source file where the DDS statements are located. The "Text description" (TEXT) parameter is up to 50 characters of descriptive text.

In summary, creating a physical or logical file requires the following steps: (1) Define the requirements of the file. (2) Create the Data Description Specifications. (3) Create the file using the DDS and the appropriate CRT command.

The above description for creating files was oriented toward creating a physical or logical database file. Remember another type of file: the source physical file. Source physical files contain source members, which in turn contain source statements for programs.

A source physical file is created using the Create Source Physical File (CRTSRCPF) command. This command is very similar to the Create Physical File command, with the exception of some of the defaults. A source physical file is usually created with no existing members, so the Member option is set to *NONE. In addition, Data Description Specifications are not required or used when creating source physical files. The record length defaults to 92 characters, which is what is needed for a source physical file. The following is an example of the CRTSRCPF command:

```
CRTSRCPF FILE(WRKLIB/QRPGSRC) TEXT('Source file').
```

The "File" and "Library" (FILE) parameter determines the resulting location of the source file to be created. The "Text description" (TEXT) parameter is up to 50 characters of descriptive text.

3.6.5 Renaming Files

Files are renamed in OS/400 with the Rename Object (RNMOBJ) command. The following shows the RNMOBJ command:

```
RNMOBJ OBJ(*LIBL/MONTHSALES) OBJTYPE(*FILE) NEWOBJ(LASTSALES).
```

The "Object" (OBJ) parameter is the name of the object to be renamed. The "Object type" (OBJTYPE) parameter determines the type of the object. The "New object" (NEWOBJ) parameter will the new name of the object.

Note that with the RNMOBJ command you are able to rename any object, not just a file. OS/400 has no command to rename a file specifically.

More often, you will need to rename members within a file. The file name will remain the same, while the member name within the file will change. The command to rename a member within a database file is Rename Member (RNMM). The RNMM command is as follows:

```
RNMM FILE(WRKLIB/PROSPECT) MBR(CURRENT) NEWMBR(BASELINE).
```

The RNMM command requires the name of the file that contains the member ("Database file" and "Library" (FILE)), the member name ["Member" (MBR)], and the new name that you wish to call the member ["New member" (NEWMBR)]. Entering appropriate values for the prompts will result in renaming a member in a file.

3.6.6 Copying Files

Files are copied in OS/400 with the Copy File (CPYF) command. This command will result in actually copying members in a file to a new file. You may also create a new file with the CPYF command. The following is an example of the CPYF command:

```
CPYF FROMFILE(PRODLIB/PRODDATA) TOFILE(PRODLIB/SAVEDATA) +
FROMMBR(PAYROLL) TOMBR(*FROMMBR) CRTFILE(*YES).
```

The CPYF command will default to copying the first member of a file to the first member of another file. Remember that a Create Physical File or Create Logical File command will default to creating a file containing one member, with that member name being the name of the file being created. You may specify a different member, if desired, or copy all members. The parameters for the CPYF command are the "From file" and "Library" (fromfile), the "To file" and "Library" (TOFILE), and the "From member" (FROMMBR) and "To member" (TOMBR) parameters.

The "From member" (FROMMBR) parameter can be the first member in the file (*FIRST), a generic member (any members whose names begin with the letters specified, a specific member, or all members (*ALL).

The "To member" (TOMBR) name can be the first member (*FIRST), a specific member name, or the special value *FROMMBR. The *FROMMBR value indicates that the target member name should be the same as the source member name. This is especially helpful when copying all the members in a file. You could specify *ALL for the "From member" name, and *FROMMMBR for the "To member" name. This would copy all members from one file to another and name the copied members the same as the member from which they were copied.

The CPYF command can also be used to print a file. Specify *PRINT for the "To file" name and the source file will be printed to your default print device. The printout will be formatted, with column numbers and record numbers.

Another parameter that can be specified with the CPYF command is "Replace or add records" (MBROPT). This parameter refers to the disposition of the target member if it exists in the target file. The *REPLACE parameter means that the records copied from the source member should replace any records in the target member. In other words, the contents of the existing target member will be removed, then the new contents of the source member will be placed in the target member. Another value for the "Replace or add records" parameter is *ADD. Specifying *ADD will add or concatenate the records from the source member to the end of the records in the target member.

The "Create file" (CRTFILE) parameter will allow you to create a new file as part of the CPYF command. Specifying *YES will create a new file, assuming the file does not already exist. The newly created file will have the same format (record and field layout) as the original file.

The "Print format" (OUTFMT) parameter is only used if the "To file" parameter contains a value of *PRINT. The two choices for the "Print format" parameter are *CHAR and *HEX. Specifying *CHAR means that the records will print in character format, while a value of *HEX means that the information will be printed in hexadecimal format. The *HEX value is helpful to use if you need to inspect the contents of a database file.

There are many other options for the CPYF command. Some of these options allow you to specify beginning and ending records to copy, allow you to select or omit records to copy based on a key or field value, and allow you to convert the format of the file. Converting the format of a file is especially useful when copying a database file to or from a source physical file. You can use the "Format option" (FMTOPT) parameter with a value of *CVTSRC when copying a data physical file to or from a source physical file.

Another CPYF "Format option" parameter value, *NOCHK, allows you to copy records from one member to another without OS/400 checking the field layout of the file. Remember that most files on an AS/400 are externally described. The record formats, field names and sizes, and other information are part of the file. Occasionally, you may need to copy data that is not divided into the same fields. Perhaps the file was created on another system, or was created with an internal description. The CPYF command with a value of *NOCHK for the "Format option' parameter will copy data from a member to another member, placing the data from left to right in the new record.

3.6.7 Deleting Files

Files can be deleted from the system with the Delete File (DLTF) command. This command will erase a file permanently and you will not be able to recover the file except by restoring from backup. The DLTF command is straightforward; the following example command removes a file from the system:

```
DLTF FILE(PRODLIB/SAVEDATA).
```

Enter the name of the "File" (FILE) to be deleted, and the "Library" name if required. Note that the DLTF command will use the library list to find the file if the library name is not specified. OS/400 will delete the first occurrence of the file that it finds as it searches the library list. This may not be what you have in mind, so be careful when using the library list. You can also specify the library that contains the file to be deleted.

The DLTF command will delete an entire file, including all the members in the file. You may need only to remove a specific member from the file and not delete the entire file. Of course, OS/400 provides a command to remove a member from a file, the Remove Member (RMVM) command.

The Remove Member command requires entries for the name of the "Database file" (FILE) that contains the member and the "Library" name if desired. The default for the library name is again *LIBL, meaning search the library list for the file containing the member. Use caution when not fully qualifying an object name as in this case; you may remove a member from the wrong file. The following shows an example RMVM command:

```
RMVM FILE(WRKLIB/PROSPECT) MBR(BASELINE).
```

The RMVM command also requires the name of the "Member" (MBR) to remove. You may specify a specific name or *ALL, which means all members in the file. You may also specify a generic name by entering some characters and ending the generic name with an asterisk (*). Using a generic name will remove all members from the file that begin with the characters entered.

You may need only to clear the data from a member in a file rather than deleting the file or removing a member. Remember that while AS/400 record access is very fast, creating, deleting, opening, and closing files is comparatively slow. An AS/400 technique to avoid this problem is to use permanent work files. This increases the overall efficiency of the system because OS/400 does not need to create and delete the files.

The Clear Physical File Member (CLRPFM) command clears the data from a member in a file. As noted, this is much faster than the creation and deletion process. The CLRPFM command is displayed below here.

```
CLRPFM FILE(WRKLIB/PROSPECT) MBR(CURRENT).
```

The parameters for the CLRPFM member are the "File" name (FILE) (and "Library" name if required), and the "Member" (MBR) name.

The "Library name" defaults to *LIBL, meaning OS/400 will search your library list to find the file indicated in the "File name" prompt.

The "Member name" parameter defaults to *FIRST, which may be appropriate. Remember that data files on an AS/400 are usually created with only one member, and the member has the same name as the file. You may also enter a specific member name or another special value. Entering *LAST for the "Member name" prompt will clear the last member in a file.

3.6.8 Displaying Files

The members of a file may be displayed by using the Display Physical File Member (DSPPFM) command. This command will display the contents of a member in a file. When physical files are created they usually have a member with the same name as the file name; this is the default of the Create Physical File (CRTPF) command. This way, the only member in a file (the usual case for a data physical file) can be accessed through several file-related commands where the command "File" name parameter defaults to *FIRST or *FILE. Note that creating a file with a member having the file name is not the default for the Create Source Physical File (CRTSRCPF) command.

The DSPPFM command will display the contents of a member in a file. The display can be "panned" right and left through the use of function keys enabling the entire record to be viewed. The following is an example of a DSPPFM command:

```
DSPPFM FILE(PRODLIB/PRODDATA) MBR(*FIRST) FROMRCD(*END).
```

The "File" and "Library" parameter (FILE) needs to be completed. The "Member" prompt defaults to *FIRST; again, that default is probably appropriate for data files.

The "From record" parameter determines where the display of the member will begin. The default for this parameter is 1, which means that records will be displayed beginning with the first record in the member. You may also specify a specific record number to begin the display or the special value *END. Entering *END for the "From record" parameter will display the last record in a member. This can be useful when testing a program that is adding records to the file. The last record will be displayed, allowing you to roll through the data from the end of the member toward the beginning.

When you have entered the appropriate parameters and pressed the <ENTER> key, you will be presented with the following display (see Figure 3–1):

The heading of the display shows the file name, library name, member name, the record number (shown at the top of the display), and the column number (shown in the left-most position). Note that there are two input areas on the display: "Control" and "Find." The "Control" field allows you to maneuver around the file to display records. The "Find" field allows you to enter a string of characters that OS/400 will use to search for a match.

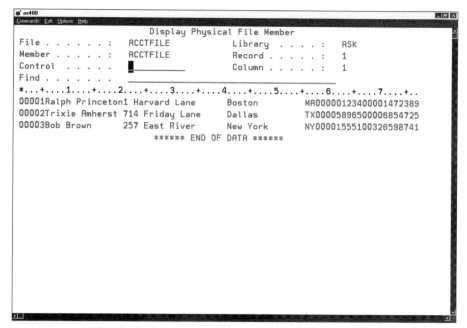

Figure 3–1: DSPPFM display

The "Control" field allows you to enter certain commands that will move the viewing window. This allows you to view different parts of the file. If the move places the viewing window before the beginning or after the end of the file, the first or last record (depending on the move direction) will be displayed and a message will indicate that the end of the file has been reached. The "Control" field has the following allowable values:

TOP	Move the viewing window to the top of the file.
BOT	Move the viewing window to the bottom of the file.
num	A number entry will display the data beginning with the record specified.
+num	Move the viewing window forward in the file the number of records specified.
–num	Move the viewing window backward in the file the number of records specified.
W	Move the viewing window one character to the right. The W+ entry may also be used.
W–	Move the viewing window one character to the left.
W+num	Move the viewing window to the right the number of characters specified.
W–num	Move the viewing window to the left the number of characters specified.
Wnum	Move the viewing window to the column specified.

The "Find" field allows you to search the file for a specific character string. Entering a value in the "Find" field and pressing the <F16> key will cause OS/400 to find the value specified. If the string for which you are searching contains embedded blanks (such as "embedded blanks"), surround the string with apostrophes or quotation marks. You may also search for a hexadecimal value (useful for data files with packed numeric data) by entering an x prior to the hex string. You must enter an even number of hex digits. For instance, to search for the packed decimal number 123, enter x123f in the "Find" field and press the <F16> key to begin the search.

Pressing the <F16> key again will repeat the search for the same value. If you wish to further qualify the search, you may press the <F14> key. This will display a screen where you may specify options such as columns to search. This can narrow down the search and make the search faster.

Another function key that is used with the DSPPFM command is the <F10> key. Pressing the <F10> will display the data in hexadecimal format. The data will be displayed in hexadecimal format on the left of the screen and in character format on the right side of the screen.

The <F19> and <F20> keys will move the viewing window to the left and right, respectively. While the windowing commands entered in the "Control" field will also provide this function, it is simpler to move the viewing area with the <F19> and <F20> keys.

3.6.9 Listing a File Description

Every file on an AS/400 has a file description. This file description contains a great deal of information regarding the file. Some of the information contained in a file description includes the characteristics of the file. These characteristics include the name of the file, the library that contains the file, the number of members in the file, the maximum number of members, and other information. The Display File Description (DSPFD) command has a variety of options that can be chosen to provide exactly the information you need.

The following display shows the format of the DSPFD command:

```
DSPFD FILE(PRODLIB/PRODDATA) TYPE(*MBRLIST).
```

The "File" (FILE) parameter requires an entry. The entry may be a specific file name, a generic name (one that ends with *), or the special value *ALL. The special value *ALL will display the file descriptions of all the files within the "Library" parameter's constraints in succession.

The "Library" portion of the FILE parameter defaults to *LIBL, meaning the library list will be searched for the file or files specified in the "File" prompt. Another special value for the "Library" prompt is *CURLIB. The current library will be used to find the file. You may also enter a specific library name.

The "Type of information" (TYPE) prompt will accept many different values. This is an important part of the DSPFD command. Using this parameter will enable the DSPFD command to provide a subset of all available information. The default for this parameter is *ALL, meaning all file description information will be provided. Allowable values for the "Type of information" parameter are

*ALL	All the information for the type of file is displayed.
*BASATR	Information common to all files is displayed. This may not be all the information available for the type of file specified; it is instead the base attributes for all files.
*ATR	Information that is meaningful for the type of file selected is displayed.
*ACCPTH	This value will show access path information for physical and logical database files. The composite key will be shown if the access path is keyed and uses multiple key fields.
*MBRLIST	A list of members and their descriptive text is shown for all members in the file. The list is displayed in alphabetic order by member name.
*SELECT	Select and omit criteria are shown if the file type is a logical file.
*SEQ	The collating sequence is displayed for physical and logical files.
*RCDFMT	Record format names and format level information is displayed.
*MBR	Member information for physical and logical files is displayed.
*SPOOL	Spooling information for diskette and printer device files is displayed.
*JOIN	For join logical files, the from file, to file, and join fields are displayed.

Another parameter, "Output," controls the disposition of the output. The *ALL value for the "Type of information" parameter can only be used if the information is to be printed or displayed. The *BASATR value can only be used when the output is directed to an output file. Multiple combinations of "Type of information" values can be used if the information is to displayed or printed, but only one value can be specified if the information is to be directed to an output file.

The "Output" parameter directs the output to either the terminal, a printer (as a spooled file), or to an output file. The "Output" parameter defaults to *, meaning the terminal. Specifying *PRINT for this parameter will direct the information to a printer. The *OUTFILE value will direct the information to an output database file. This is a common usage of the DSPFD command. A program could be written to direct the output to a database file and then access the database file and perform operations based on the information in the file.

Another parameter for the DSPFD command is the "File attributes" (FILEATR) parameter. This parameter can narrow the selection of files selected with this command to just those files that have the attribute specified. The types of attributes that can be selected are

*ALL	All file types are selected. You cannot use *ALL if the output is being directed to a database file (*OUTFILE for the "Output" parameter).
*DSPF	Display device files are selected.
*PRTF	Printer device files are selected.
*DKTF	Diskette device files are selected.
*TAPF	Tape device files are selected.
*CMNF	Communication device files are selected.
*BSCF	Bisynchronous communication files are selected.
*MXDF	Mixed files are selected.
*PF	Physical files are selected.
*LF	Logical files are selected.
*ICFF	Intersystem communication files are selected.
*SAVF	Save files are selected.
*DDMF	Distributed data management files are selected.

As mentioned earlier, a file description contains a wealth of information about the file. Some of the information is only valuable to the operating system, while other information can be very important to the user or programmer. The following will examine some of the more important pieces of information available from the DSPFD command. An example of the output generated by the DSPFD command is (see Figure 3–2).

The "Creation date" field shows the date that the file was created. The "Maximum members" field shows the maximum number of members that can be in this file, while the "Number of members" field shows the current number of members in the file. The "Member size" field has three parts; the first is the initial number of records made available when the file was created, the second is the number of records that will be added to the file when more records are needed, and the third is the maximum number of increments that will be made to the file when more records are required. The defaults for these values (from the Create Physical File command) are 10,000, 1,000, and 3, respectively.

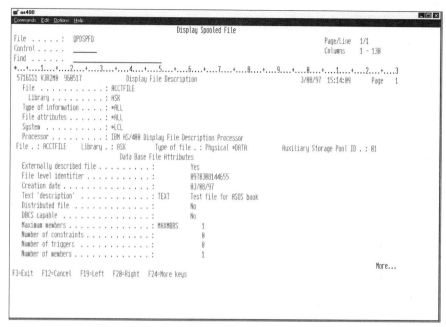

Figure 3–2: DSPFD output display

Another field is the "Maximum record wait time." This is the amount of time OS/400 will wait when trying to retrieve a record from the file before it will signal an error. The "Record format level check" (LVLCHK) parameter is either a *YES or *NO value. If the value is *YES then level checking is in effect for the file. This refers to the OS/400 practice of ensuring that files and programs are "in sync," as mentioned earlier in this chapter.

"Access Path Description" information is also kept in the file description. This will show the type of access path for the file and also key information if the access path is keyed.

"Member" information is also displayed. The name of the member, the number of records in the member, the creation date of the member, and other information will be displayed for each member in the file. Details concerning number of records, increments, and maximum number of records are shown. Facts regarding the last date and time the file was changed, saved, restored or used are also made available.

Remember that this type of information can be placed in an output file. You can create your own file management system by accessing the file descriptions for files in a library. The next section will discuss library operations.

3.6.10 Working with Files

OS/400 provides a command that will allow you to work with multiple files. The Work with Files (WRKF) command presents a list of files upon which you can perform operations. The following shows the WRKF command:

```
WRKF FILE(PRODLIB/*ALL) FILEATR(PF).
```

The WRKF command requires an entry for "File" (FILE) and "Library" if appropriate. The file name may be generic, which will allow you to work with all files in a specific library or in many libraries. You may also enter the special value *ALL, which will allow you to work with all files.

Another parameter that can be entered to further select files to be displayed in the list is the "File attributes" (FILEATR) parameter. This parameter defaults to *ALL, meaning all files shall be displayed regardless of the attribute type of the file.

The file attributes that may be selected are

*ALL	All files regardless of attribute type.
BSCF38	A bisyncronous communication file in System/38 format.
CMNF38	Communication files in System/38 format.
DDMF	Distributed data management files.
DFU	Data File Utility files.
DFUEXC	Data File Utility files in System/38 format.
DFUNOTEXC	Data File Utility files in System/38 format that are not executable.
DKTF	Diskette files.
DSPF	Display files.
DSPF38	Display files in System/38 format.
ICFF	Intersystem communication files.
LF	Logical files.
LF38	Logical files in System/38 format.
MXDF38	A mixed file in System/38 format.
PF	Physical files.
PF38	Physical files in System/38 format.
PRTF	Printer files.
PRTF38	Printer files in System/38 format.
SAVF	Save files.
TAPF	Tape files.

The WRKF command display is shown here (see Figure 3–3).

```
as400                                                              _□×
Commands  Edit  Options  Help
                          Work with Files

 Type options, press Enter.
   1=Create   3=Copy   4=Delete    5=Display physical file member
   8=Display file description      9=Save    10=Restore   13=Change description

 Opt   File          Library     Attribute   Text
 __    _____
 __    ACCTFILE      ASK         PF          Test file for ASOS book
 __    DIALSRC       ASK         PF          TCP/IP Point-to-Point Connection Scri
 __    QCBLSRC       ASK         PF          COBOL Source File
 __    QCLSRC        ASK         PF
 __    QCMDSRC       ASK         PF          Commands Source File
 __    QDDSSRC       ASK         PF
 __    QRPGSRC       ASK         PF
 __    QTXTSRC       ASK         PF
 __    SLIPSRC       ASK         PF          SL/IP Response Source

                                                                   Bottom
 Parameters for options 1, 3, 4, 5, 8, 9, 10 and 13 or command
 ===> _____
 F3=Exit      F4=Prompt   F5=Refresh   F9=Retrieve   F11=Display names only
 F12=Cancel   F16=Repeat position to   F17=Position to
```

Figure 3–3: WRKF display

Note that the files selected are shown in a list. Information shown in the list is the file name, the name of the library containing the file, the attribute of the file, and the text description.

Above the list of files are the options from which you may choose to work with the files. All the file commands discussed (with the exception of Rename Object) may be accessed through the Work with Files display.

Option 3 will allow you to copy a member from one file to another. Option 3 invokes the Copy File (CPYF) command.

Option 4 will delete a file. This option invokes the Delete File (DLTF) command.

Option 5 will display the contents of a member in a file and invoke the Display Physical File Member (DSPPFM) command.

Option 8 will display the file description of the file selected. This option invokes the Display File Description (DSPFD) command.

Option 9 will save the file to diskette or tape. This option invokes the Save Object (SAVOBJ) command.

Option 10 will restore a file to disk that had been saved to tape or diskette. This option invokes the Restore Object (RSTOBJ) command.

Option 11 will change the text description of a file. This optional description can be up to 50 characters long, and is usually created when the file is created. Option 11 invokes the Change Object Description (CHGOBJD) command.

Function keys that are available with the WRKF command include the standard <F3> to Exit, <F4> to prompt an option, <F5> to Refresh the screen, and <F12> to Cancel. In addition, the <F6> key will allow you to create a new file. Pressing <F6> will invoke the Create Physical File (CRTPF) command. The CRTPF command was explained earlier in this chapter. The <F11> key will display only names on the screen. This option is handy when there are many files to display; other information is not shown, so more file names can be displayed.

The <F16> and <F17> keys work together. The <F17> key will "pop up" a window and allow entry of a file name (or partial file name). The system will then position the list at the first file name that matches or is greater than the entry specified. The <F16> key will repeat the positioning. Repeating the position is useful when you have rolled up or down from the previous position. Another available function key is the <F9> key. This will recall the last command entered on the command line.

3.7 LIBRARY OPERATIONS

All objects on an AS/400 must be in a library. There are different types of libraries, but any library is basically an object that contains other objects.

The different types of libraries are determined by their attributes. A library may be of type *PROD, meaning a production library, or *TEST, meaning a test or nonproduction library. The main difference between the two types of libraries is that a library of type *PROD cannot be updated by default when in programming debug mode. It can still be deleted or cleared however.

3.7.1 Creating a Library

The first library operation that will be explained is creating a library with the Create Library (CRTLIB) command. The following is an example of the prompted CRTLIB command:

```
CRTLIB LIB(ACCTTEST) TYPE(*TEST) TEXT('Accounting Test').
```

The CRTLIB command needs a "Library name" (LIB) and "Library Type" (TYPE). The TYPE entry may be either *PROD or *TEST. An optional "Text description" (TEXT) can be included. Additional parameters are the "Authority" to be used for security, and the "Auxiliary storage pool id." The Auxiliary storage pool or ASP refers to the area on disk where the library will reside. You may choose to use this parameter for performance reasons.

Note that there is no entry for the size of the library. OS/400 will dynamically allocate space for the library as more objects are added. You do not need to be concerned with library sizing; the operating system handles that issue. The standard function keys are used with this command.

3.7.2 Renaming a Library

Libraries, of course, are another object; an object of type *LIB. As mentioned earlier, all objects must reside in a library. Since that is in fact the case, where do library objects reside? Objects of type library reside in library QSYS, which is part of OS/400.

Therefore, if you wish to rename a library, you will use the same command as you would use to rename any object—the Rename Object (RNMOBJ) command. The only difference between renaming a library object as opposed to any other object is specifying the library in which the library resides, library QSYS. Specify the "Object" (OBJ) name, the library in which the object resides (QSYS), *LIB for the "Object type" (OBJTYPE), and the "New object" (NEWOBJ) name.

The following is an example of the RNMOBJ command used to rename a library:

```
RNMOBJ OBJ(*LIBL/ACCTTEST) OBJTYPE(*LIB) NEWOBJ(ACCTPROD).
```

3.7.3 Deleting a Library

Removing or deleting a library from the system requires the use of the Delete Library (DLTLIB) command. The next example shows the DLTLIB command:

```
DLTLIB LIB(ACCTTEST).
```

The only parameter required for the DLTLIB command is the "Library" (LIB) name. Provide the library name, press <ENTER>, and the library will be deleted.

Realize, however, that a library is an object that contains other objects. When a library is deleted, all the objects within that library must be deleted. This can be a very time-consuming task. Each object in turn will be deleted, and then the library itself will be deleted. Another command that is similar in effect to deleting a library is clearing a library.

3.7.4 Clearing a Library

The command to clear a library is Clear Library (CLRLIB). Clearing a library will remove the contents of a library without actually deleting the library itself. The CLRLIB command is shown below.

```
CLRLIB LIB(ACCTTEST).
```

Specify the "Library" (LIB) name and press <ENTER>. The contents of the library will be cleared, but the library itself will remain on the system. This is still a time-consuming task, but usually quicker than deleting the library.

3.7.5 Copying a Library

The contents of a library may be copied into another library. Of course, this can be done with appropriate copy commands such as Copy File (CPYF), but if you need to create an exact copy of a library, the Copy Library (CPYLIB) command is very useful.

You may wish to create an exact copy of a library to aid in system development to provide a copy of the production data. To accomplish this, use the CPYLIB command

```
CPYLIB FROMLIB(STDLIB) TOLIB(MFGUSER1) CRTLIB(*YES).
```

The CPYLIB command requires an "Existing library" (FROMLIB) name and a "New library" (TOLIB) name. Another parameter for the CPYLIB command is the "Create library" (CRTLIB) prompt. This prompt (which can have a value of *YES or *NO) will determine if a new library should be created. Note that this prompt defaults to a value of *YES. Enter the parameters needed and press the <ENTER> key. The contents of the existing library will be copied to the new library.

3.7.6 Displaying the Contents of a Library

The Display Library (DSPLIB) command will display the objects that are contained within a library. The DSPLIB command is

```
DSPLIB LIB(MFGUSER1) OUTPUT(*PRINT).
```

The only parameters needed for the DSPLIB command are the "Library" (LIB) name (which defaults to *LIBL, meaning the library list) and "Output" (OUTPUT) (which defaults to *, meaning display to the terminal). The output from the DSPLIB command may also be printed by specifying the special value *PRINT for the "Output" prompt. Provide the appropriate parameters and press the <ENTER> key to display the contents of the library.

The display provided by the DSPLIB command contains a variety of information. The library name and type are displayed, as well as the number of objects contained in the library and the ASP (Auxiliary Storage Pool) of the library.

The objects in the library are displayed in a list. Information shown for each object includes the object name, the type, attribute, and size of the object, the text description of the object, and the "freed" status of the object.

"Freed" status refers to an action that can take place when the object is saved. A parameter on a save operation determines if the storage area allocated for that object should be freed. If storage is freed, then the storage area the object used would be made available to other objects on disk. If storage is not freed, the storage area is not made available, and the object continues to have the same amount of storage allocated.

The <F17> key will position the display at the top of the list and the <F18> key will position the display at the bottom of the list. Two options are available for each object in the list: 5 to display full attributes, and 8 to display service attributes.

The 5 and 8 options invoke another command, the Display Object Description (DSPOBJD) command. The DSPOBJD command displays the system information that is contained within an object. A full attribute display shows all the attributes associated with an object, while the service attribute display shows information concerning saves, restores, and system information.

Some of the types of information displayed from the DSPOBJD command are

- Object attribute.
- Owner of the object.
- Creation information.
- Change and usage information.
- Storage information, including size and ASP.
- Save and restore information, including the date of the last save and restore.
- Source file, library, and member if the object is a program or command. Other information for a program object is the level of the compiler, the object control level, and whether the user has modified the object.

3.7.7 Working with Libraries

OS/400 provides a convenient way to perform operations on several libraries. The Work with Libraries (WRKLIB) command will produce a list of libraries upon which you may perform different actions.

The WRKLIB command only requires the library name with which you wish to work. The following shows the WRKLIB command:

```
WRKLIB LIB(ACCT*).
```

You may specify a specific library for the "Library" (LIB) name prompt. You may also specify a generic name (beginning with certain characters prefixed by an asterisk), *LIBL, meaning the libraries in your library list, or *ALL, meaning all libraries on the system. Indicate the library name and press the <ENTER> key. The following display will be shown (see Figure 3–4):

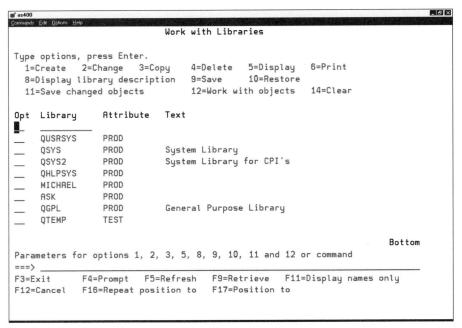

Figure 3–4: WRKLIB display

Note that the libraries selected are shown in a list. Information shown in the list is the library name, the attribute of the library (*PROD or *TEST), and the text description.

Above the list of libraries are the options from which you may choose to perform operations on the libraries. A description of the options, and the commands they execute, are explained below.

Option 2 will allow you to change the library. Items you may change are the type of the library (*PROD or *TEST) and the text description of the library. This option executes the Change Library (CHGLIB) command.

Option 3 will copy the contents of a library to a different library. Option 3 invokes the Copy Library (CPYLIB) command.

Option 4 will delete a library. This option runs the Delete Library (DLTLIB) command.

Option 5 will display the contents of a library. Option 5 invokes the Display Library (DSPLIB) command.

Option 6 will display the contents of a library to a printer. Option 6 invokes the Display Library (DSPLIB) command with the "Output" parameter set to *PRINT.

Option 9 will save the library to diskette or tape. This option invokes the Save Library (SAVLIB) command.

Option 10 will restore a library to disk that had been saved to tape or diskette. This option invokes the Restore Library (RSTLIB) command.

Option 11 will save a changed object in the library to tape or diskette. The objects that meet the criteria to be saved will have been changed since the last time the entire library has been changed. Option 11 invokes the Save Changed Objects (SAVCHGOBJ) command.

Option 12 invokes the Work with Objects (WRKOBJ) command. This command will allow you to perform operations on the objects contained within the selected library. Operations available through the WRKOBJ command are

- Displaying and editing the authority to an object.
- Copying the object.
- Deleting the object.
- Renaming the object.
- Displaying and changing the description of the object.

Option 13 will change the object's description. This option executes the Change Object Description (CHGOBJD) command. You may change the "Text description" of the object and also reset the "Days last used" value.

Option 14 will remove all objects from the library. This option invokes the Clear Library (CLRLIB) command.

Function keys that are available with the WRKLIB command include the standard <F3> to Exit, <F4> to prompt an option, <F5> to Refresh the screen, and <F12> to Cancel. In addition, the <F6> key will allow you to create a new library. Pressing <F6> will invoke the Create Library (CRTLIB) command. The CRTLIB command was explained earlier in this chapter. The <F11> key will display only names on the screen. This option is handy when there are many files to display; other information is not shown, so more file names can be displayed.

The <F16> and <F17> keys work together. The <F17> key will "pop up" a window and allow entry of a library name (or partial library name). The system will then position the list at the first library name that matches or is greater than the entry specified. The <F16> key will repeat the positioning. Repeating the position is useful when you have rolled up or down from the previous position. Another available function key is the <F9> key. This will recall the last command entered on the command line.

4

The AS/400 User Environment

This chapter will explain the OS/400 user environment. OS/400 provides a complete user environment for the interface between you and the operating system, OS/400. This chapter will describe the user profile, security, determining the characteristics of your session, and other user related activities. In addition, library lists will be described, and library list commands explained.

4.1 USERS

Each user on an AS/400 has a specific user name. This user name identifies the user to the operating system for security and access privileges. Each user also has a password. This password provides (or prohibits) access to the system. The necessity of the password is determined by the level of OS/400 security in place. This will be discussed later in this chapter.

In addition, the user profile associated with the user name contains a wealth of information for OS/400. Information such as the environment in which the user will execute, the amount of disk space allowed, and ownership of objects created by the user are all determined by the user profile. The following section will examine the user profile and the information contained within the profile.

4.1.1 User Profiles

As mentioned, the user profile contains a great deal of information concerning the user. The following list will explain some of the more important portions of the user profile.

User Profile—The name assigned to this user profile. The user ID.

User Class—The type of user associated with this user profile. The possible values are

*SECOFR—Security officer. The security officer is given all object authority, security administrator authority, save system authority, job control authority, service authority, and spool control authority.

*SECADM—Security administrator. At security level 10 or 20, the security administrator is given all object authority, security administrator authority, save system authority, and job control authority, At security level 30 or 40, the user is given security administrator authority, save system authority, and job control authority.

*PGMR—Programmer. At security level 10 or 20, the programmer is given all object authority, save system authority, and job control authority. At level 30 or 40, the programmer is given save system authority and job control authority.

*SYSOPR—System operator. At security level 10 or 20, the system operator is given all object authority, save system authority, and job control authority. At level 30 or 40, the system operator is given save system authority and job control authority.

*USER—User. At security level 10 or 20, the user is given all object authority and save system authority. At security level 30 or 40, the user is given no special authorities.

Special Authority—The special authorities granted to a user. Special authorities are required to perform certain functions on the system. Special authorities cannot be removed for the QSECOFR or the QSYS user profiles. The special authorities are

*SAVSYS—Save system authority to save, restore, and free storage for all objects on the system.

*JOBCTL—Job control authority to change, display, hold, release, cancel, and clear all jobs that are running on the system or that are on a job or output queue. The user also has the authority to start the system, start writers, and stop active subsystems.

*SECADM—Security administrator authority to create or change user profiles, if the user is authorized to the create user profile or change user profile commands. This does not allow special authorities to be granted that this user profile does not have. To give *SECADM special authority to another user, a user must have both *ALLOBJ and *SECADM special authorities.

*ALLOBJ—All object authority for accessing any system resource.

*SERVICE—Service authority to perform system service functions, such as save and restore.

*SPLCTL—Spool control authority to manipulate other user's spooled files.

*USRCLS—Special authorities are granted to the user based on the value entered in the user class prompt.

*NONE—No special authorities are granted.

Group Profile—Specifies the group profile name. The current user of this command must have *OBJECT and *CHANGE authority to the profile specified on the group profile prompt. Possible values are

*NONE—No group profile name is used with this user profile.

A specific group name that is used with this user profile to determine a job's eligibility for getting access to existing objects and special authority.

Owner—The user profile that is the owner of newly created objects. Possible values are

*USRPRF—The user profile that is used with the job is made the owner of the object.

*GRPPRF—The group profile is made the owner of newly created objects and is given all authority to the object.

Group Authority—The specific authority granted to the group profile for newly created objects. If *GRPPRF is specified for the OWNER parameter, this parameter cannot be specified. Possible values are

*NONE—No group authority is granted.

*CHANGE—The user can change the object and perform basic functions on the object. Change authority allows the user to perform all operations on the object except those limited to the owner or controlled by object existence authority and object management authority. Change authority provides object operational authority and all data authority.

*ALL—The user can control the object's existence, specify the security for the object, change the object, change the owner for the object, and perform basic functions on the object. All authority allows the user to perform all operations on the object except those limited to the owner or controlled by authorization list management rights. If the object is an authorization list, the user cannot add, change, or remove users, or transfer ownership of the authorization list.

*USE—The user can perform basic operations on the object, such as run a program or read a file. The user is prevented from changing the object. Use authority provides object operational authority and read authority.

*EXCLUDE—Prevents the user from accessing the object.

Initial Menu—The name of the menu that is shown when the user signs on the system. Possible values are

MAIN—The AS/400 main menu.

*SIGNOFF—The system signs off the user when the initial program ends.

A specific menu name and the library of the menu that is called when the user signs on.

Initial Program—Specifies, for an interactive session, the name of the program that is called whenever a new routing step is started that has QCL or QCMD as the request processing program. Possible values are

*NONE—No program is called when the user signs on the system.

A program name and library of the program that is called.

Limit Capabilities—Specifies if the capabilities of the user should be limited for controlling the values of their initial program, initial menu, current library, and the Attention key handling program. Possible values are

*NO—The capabilities of the user are not limited. The program, menu, and current library values can be changed by the user when signing onto the system. The user may use the Change Profile (CHGPRF) or Change User Profile (CHGUSRPRF) command to change the values of the initial program, initial menu, current library, or Attention key handling program in their user profile.

*PARTIAL—The capabilities of the user are partially limited. The program and current library may not be changed when the user is signing on to the system. The menu may be changed at sign on, and commands may be run from a menu command line. The user may change the initial menu value with the CHGPRF or CHGUSRPRF commands.

*YES—The capabilities of the user are limited. The program, menu, and current library values cannot be changed when signing on to the system. Commands may not be run from a menu command line.

Message Queue—The name of the message queue that is used by this user. The message queue is created if it does not already exist. The user profile being created is the owner of the message queue. Possible values are

*USRPRF—A message queue with the same name as that specified in the user profile prompt is used as the message queue for this user. This message queue is located in QUSRSYS.

A specific name and library of the message queue that is used for this user may be given.

Output Queue—Specifies the name of the output queue that is used by this user. The output queue must already exist. Possible values are

*DEV—An output queue with the same name as specified on the "Printer device" prompt is used as the output queue for this user.

A name and library of a specific output queue.

Printer Device—The printer that is used to print the output for this user. The file is placed in an output queue with the same name as the printer when *DEV is specified on the output queue prompt. Possible values are

*SYSVAL—The default system printer specified in the system value QPRTDEV is used.

A specific name of a printer.

Special Environment—The special environment in which the user operates after signing on. Possible values are

*SYSVAL—The system value QSPCENV is used to determine the system environment after the user signs on the system.

*NONE—The user operates in the AS/400 system environment after signing on.

*S36—The user operates in the System/36 environment.

Assistance Level—This is the level with which certain command displays will be shown. Possible value are

*SYSVAL—The system value QASTLVL determines the assistance level.

*BASIC—Basic command usage is shown. More advanced capabilities are available by changing the assistance level (with <F21>) while executing the command.

*INTERMED—This assistance level provides the same displays as earlier versions of OS/400. All capabilities are available from the display.

*ADVANCED—This level provides command displays without showing function key legends and more list elements on the screen.

Attention Program—This is the program that will be executed when the user presses the attention key (<ATTN>). The current program will stop executing, and the attention program will execute. When the attention program terminates, the original program will resume execution. The possible values for this parameter are

*SYSVAL—The system value QATNPGM contains the name of the attention program.

*NONE—No attention key program is used. No action will result if the <ATTN> is pressed by the user.

*ASSIST—The Operational Assistant program will be executed.

Program name—The name of a specific program (and library if required) may be specified. This program will execute when the <ATTN> key is pressed.

User Options—The User Options determine certain characteristics of the interaction with the system. The parameter values that cause the characteristics are specified for this parameter; their presence causes the characteristic to be used. The possible values are

*CLKWD—This value will cause the CL keywords to be displayed when prompting a command.

*EXPERT—This value will cause more detailed information to be shown on a display.

*ROLLKEY—This value will reverse the system default action of the roll keys.

*NOSTSMSG—This value will eliminate status messages being sent to the user.

*STSMSG—This value will allow status messages to be sent to the user.

*HLPFULL—This value will provide a full page rather than a window display when accessing the help function.

*PRTMSG—This value will cause a status message to be sent to the user when one of the user's spooled files is printed.

The user profile entries "User class" and "Special authority" determine the level of access granted to a user for public authority. This will be explained in more detail later in this chapter. The "Special environment" entry determines in what environment the user will operate: native OS/400 or System/36.

The "Initial program" entry is used to name a program that will be executed when you sign on to the system. This program usually will establish the library list, set any special interactive session requirements, and run a program or display a menu that you will use on the system. This, in effect, can restrict a user to only the programs and menus that are applicable to their job requirements.

The "Initial menu" entry is used in place of the main OS/400 menu. This menu is displayed upon sign on, and you can be restricted to only execute options from that menu. If the menu does not provide a command line, you will not be able to execute any OS/400 commands, regardless of your access level.

The "Message queue," "Output queue," and "Printer" entries contain the name of the environment objects that are associated with the user. The "Group profile" parameter determines if this user profile is associated with a group. If set to the special value *NONE, the user profile is not associated with a group. If set to the name of another profile, that profile is the name of the group profile. Group profiles are discussed in the next section.

4.1.2 Group Profiles

Group profiles provide a mechanism to group users and their public authority to objects. A group profile is established as is any profile with the CRTUSRPRF command. The difference is in the user profiles whose "Group profile" parameter is set to the group profile name. These user profiles receive their public authorization from the authorization level that is part of the group profile. In other words, the authority level is determined for a number of users, not just a single user.

Some considerations of group profiles are that a group profile cannot be a member of another group, a user can be a member of only one group, a group can have authority over many objects, and a member of a group can share all authorities and special authorities granted to that group.

This mechanism can make the administration of security easier. When a user is transferred from one department to another, the system administrator does not need to change all the authorities given to that user. The system administrator would instead change the "Group profile" in the transferred user's profile. This would immediately change the user's authority and public access to objects and reflect the new group's authorities. This also provides for easier changes for many members in a group if authorization to objects change.

A parameter in the user profile that works with the group profile concept is the "Owner" parameter. If this parameter is set to the special value *USRPRF, then the user that creates the object is the owner of the object. If the "Owner" parameter contains the special value *GRPPRF, then the group profile associated with that user is the owner of the object. The "Group authority" parameter determines the type of authority the group will have to newly created objects if the user profile is the owner of the objects. The different values for this entry are *NONE, *ALL, *CHANGE, *USE, and *EXCLUDE.

Object ownership is an important component of OS/400 security. Every object is assigned an owner when created. The owner of an object always has all authority to the object unless specifically revoked, and can also grant authority to the object to other users. Another factor in object ownership is that the user profile that owns the object cannot be deleted from the system until all objects it owns are either deleted or their ownership is transferred to a different user profile.

OS/400 user profile related commands include Display User Profile (DSPUSRPRF), Create User Profile (CRTUSRPRF), Change User Profile (CHGUSRPRF), Delete User Profile (DLTUSRPRF), and Work with User Profiles (WRKUSRPRF). These commands are usually available only to the system administrator or to a user with *SECOFR (Security Officer) or *SECADM (Security Administrator) special authority.

4.2 USER SECURITY

Security on an AS/400 is a very complex interrelationship between users and objects. Two types of security are present on an AS/400: private security and public security. Private security refers to authorization that is specifically granted to a user or group. Public security includes authorization levels that are granted to users who are not specifically granted authority to an object. In other words, private security is specific to a user profile while public security is for all other users.

Private security is authority given specifically to a user for an object or resource. Public security is used when a user has no specific authority for an object, when a user is not on an authorization list for an object, when a user's group profile does not have specific authority for the object, or when a user's group profile is not on the authorization list for an object.

4.2.1 AS/400 Security Levels

The system security level determines the type of control that OS/400 will place upon users and objects. Most AS/400 installations use security level 30 or 40. This is known as resource security and is discussed later in this chapter.

AS/400 security levels are controlled by system value QSECURITY. System value QSECURITY can have values of 10, 20, 30, or 40. These values correspond to the four levels of security available on an AS/400. QSECURITY can only be changed by a user with *ALLOBJ (all object) and *SECADM (security administrator) authority. When the security level is set, and the system goes through an IPL, that security level is in effect for all users of the system.

Security level 10 is also known as unsecured. This may be the original security setup when the system is shipped from IBM. No password is required with level 10 security. A user profile will be created at sign-on if none exists. The user does not have to be known to the system, and the system security officer or administrator does not need to set up a user profile.

Once signed on, a user has access to all data and processes.

Security level 20 is known as password security. The user profile must exist and the password must match. The system security officer must have created the user profile and the password. Once signed on, a user has access to all data and processes. The capabilities of a user can be limited.

Security level 30 is known as resource security. All the level 20 restrictions are in effect. In addition, the user only has access to data and processes specifically granted to that user. The user must have been granted *CHANGE authority to device descriptions to be able to use a device such as a terminal or printer.

Level 40 security is resource security with limited system object manipulation. In addition to the level 30 restrictions, the user cannot directly access certain system objects.

4.2.2 Resource Security

Resource security is level 30 or level 40 security. This type of security means that access to objects (or resources) must be specifically granted to users. This type of authority to objects is accomplished when creating an object with the "Authority" parameter. This authority is the public authority granted to all users that are not granted specific authority to the object.

Specific authority to an object may be granted to a user through object authority commands such as Grant Object Authority (GRTOBJAUT), Edit Object Authority (EDTOBJAUT), or Revoke Object Authority (RVKOBJAUT). The authority for an object may be displayed with the Display Object Authority (DSPOBJAUT) command. These commands may be accessible only to the system security officer.

4.2.3 Types of Authority

The authority that may be granted to a user or the public consists of user-defined object authorities and user-defined data authorities. These object and data authority classifications are combined into system-defined authorities which are usually used for object authority manipulation.

The four user-defined object authorities are

*OBJOPR—Object Operational, which allows the user to view the description of the object and use the object as determined by the user's data authorities.

*OBJMGT—Object Management, which allows the user to specify the security for the object, move or rename the object, and add members to database files.

*OBJEXIST—Object Existence, which allows the user to control the object's existence and ownership. This authority is needed to allow deletion, save and restore, or transfer of ownership, but is not needed for save and restore if the user has *SAVSYS special authority.

*AUTLMGT—Authorization List Management, which allows the user to add and remove users and their authorization on the authorization list that secures that object.

The four user-defined data authorities are

*READ—Read, which means the user can display the contents of an object or run a program.

*ADD—Add, which allows the user to add entries to an object (jobs in a job queue, records in a file).

*UPD—Update, which allows the user to change entries in an object.

*DLT—Delete, which allows the user to remove entries from an object.

The user-defined object authorities or user-defined data authorities may be used to grant authority to a specific user or to the public. However, since these authorities are usually needed in combination, the following system-defined authorities are usually used.

*ALL—All object authorities and all data authorities.

*CHANGE—Object operational authority and all data authorities.

*USE—Object operational authority and *READ data authority.

*EXCLUDE—Prevents the user from accessing the object.

4.2.4 Authorization Lists

Another technique used for grouping users and authorizations to objects is known as authorization lists, which contain a list of users and the authorization each user has to all the objects the list secures. This eliminates having to give each user authority to many objects, and each user can have different authority to the objects.

A command used with authorizations lists is the Work with Authorization Lists (WRKAUTL) command. This command provides an access to the list to change the users and their user names.

Another command that can be used to provide users with similar authority is the Grant User Authority (GRTUSRAUT) command. This command copies authorities from one user profile to another. This command takes a significant amount of time to execute and increases the time needed for system saves.

4.3 PASSWORD PROTECTION

A computer's security system is only as strong as the weakest link. That weak link can often be a password. It is very difficult to gain access to an AS/400 that is properly set up with level 30 or level 40 security. However, if a person knows (or is able to guess) a password of a user with high authority, that person could gain access to the system and perhaps damage or misappropriate important business data.

The first line of defense against unauthorized access is the password. Your password should be changed on a regular basis and should not be easy for someone to guess. More hints for password selection follow this section.

4.3.1 Changing Your Password

The command to change your password is the Change Password (CHGPWD) command. This command has no parameters so you must enter the command and press the <ENTER> key to be presented with the following display:

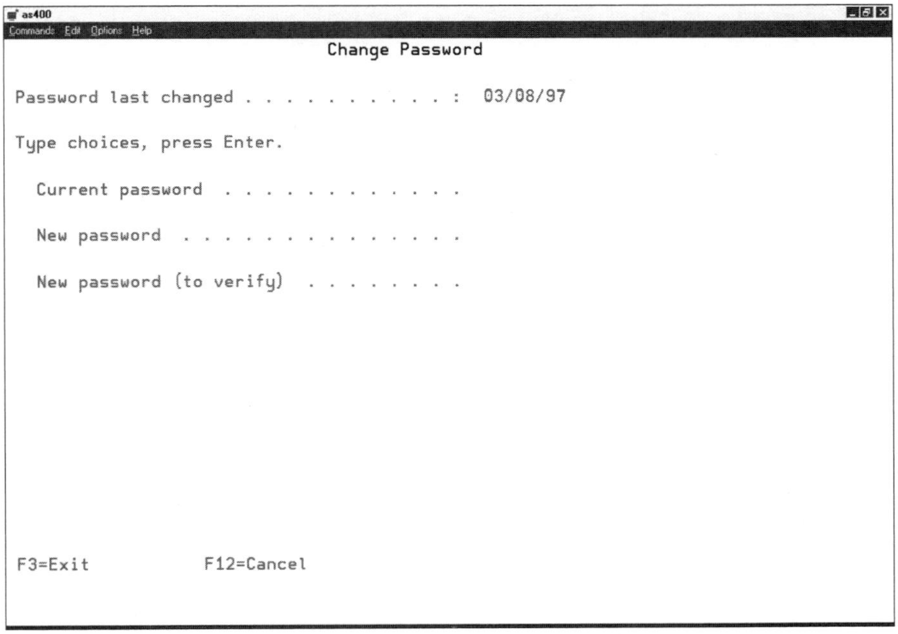

```
 as400                                                              _ B X
Commands  Edit  Options  Help
                            Change Password

 Password last changed . . . . . . . . . . :   03/08/97

 Type choices, press Enter.

   Current password . . . . . . . . . . .

   New password . . . . . . . . . . . . .

   New password (to verify) . . . . . . .









 F3=Exit          F12=Cancel

```

Figure 4–1: CHGPWD display

The display shows the last date your password was changed and accepts input for the current password and the new password. Enter your current password and your new password. You will also need to enter your new password again for verification. Make sure you type your new password and the verification exactly the same or your password will not be changed. None of the input fields will display as they are all nondisplay fields.

Enter your old password, new password, and the new password verification. Press the <ENTER> key and your password will be changed.

4.3.2 Selecting Your Password

Selecting a password that is both easy to remember and, more importantly, hard for others to guess, is an important part of system security. A few recommendations may help you to select a good password. The system security officer usually sets up some system values that will enforce some password selection criteria.

Some ideas for password selection are

- Never use a person's name, especially that of a family member.
- Do not use significant dates such as birthdays or anniversaries.
- Avoid passwords that are related to your job or business such as ACCT, COMPUTER, SALES, and so on.
- It is usually a good practice to use passwords that cannot be found in a dictionary. Some password validation programs reject passwords that can be found in a dictionary.
- Never reuse a password. Always select a new password.
- Use a combination of digits and letters.

A password may be up to 10 digits in length and must begin with an alphabetic character. The remaining characters may be alphabetic, numeric, or some special characters. Some system values that may provide rules for password selection are

QPWDLMTAJC—limits adjacent digits in a password. If this value is true, digits cannot be repeated.

QPWDLMTCHR—limits the characters that may be in a password. Characters can be selected that are not valid in a password.

QPWDLMTREP—limits repeating characters in a password. If true, this value prohibits characters from being repeated.

QPWDMAXLEN—the maximum password length. The maximum allowable length is ten characters, which is also the default.

QPWDMINLEN—the minimum password length. The minimum is one character, the default.

QPWDPOSDIF—limits password character positions from being reused from the old password to the new password. If this value is true, like characters in the same positions in the old and new passwords cannot be used.

QPWDRQDDGT—requires a digit in the password. If true, this value will enforce needing a numeric digit in the password.

QPWDRQDDIF—is the duplicate password control value. This value, if set to true, will prohibit an old password from being reused as the new password.

QPWDVLDPGM—a password validation program. If specified, this value would contain the name of a program that will validate a new password when a password is changed.

4.4 WHO IS ON THE SYSTEM?

An AS/400 is a multiuser system and may have many users on the system at one time. A method to determine who is on the system is to use the Work with Active Jobs (WRKACTJOB) command. This command shows all jobs that are currently active on the system. Since an interactive session is a job, and the job name for an interactive session contains the user name, using this command will show users that are currently logged onto the system.

```
                         Work with Active Jobs                 APPLSPEC
                                                    03/08/97  15:26:37
 CPU %:      .0     Elapsed time:   00:00:00     Active jobs:   73

 Type options, press Enter.
   2=Change   3=Hold   4=End   5=Work with   6=Release    7=Display message
   8=Work with spooled files   13=Disconnect ...

 Opt   Subsystem/Job   User      Type  CPU %  Function        Status
 █     QBATCH          QSYS      SBS    .0                     DEQW
 _     QCMN            QSYS      SBS    .0                     DEQW
 _     QCTL            QSYS      SBS    .0                     DEQW
 _       MONLINEMSG    QPGMR     BCH    .0   PGM-MONLINEMSG    MSGW
 _       QSYSSCD       QPGMR     BCH    .0   PGM-QEZSCNEP      EVTW
 _     QINTER          QSYS      SBS    .0                     DEQW
 _       QPADEV0002    MICHAEL   INT    .0   CMD-WRKACTJOB     RUN
 _     QSERVER         QSYS      SBS    .0                     DEQW
 _       QSERVER       QPGMR     ASJ    .0                     EVTW
                                                                  More...
 Parameters or command
 ===> _____
 F3=Exit     F5=Refresh   F10=Restart statistics   F11=Display elapsed data
 F12=Cancel  F23=More options  F24=More keys
```

Figure 4–2: WRKACTJOB display

Note the "User" column. This shows the names of the users currently signed on to the system. The "Job" column shows the device (terminal) that they are using.

Another technique to determine who is on the system is the Work with Configuration Status (WRKCFGSTS) command. Use this with the *DEV qualifier, as in WRKCFGSTS *DEV. This shows all the devices on the system with the corresponding job that are using the device. The following display shows the WRKCFGSTS *DEV display:

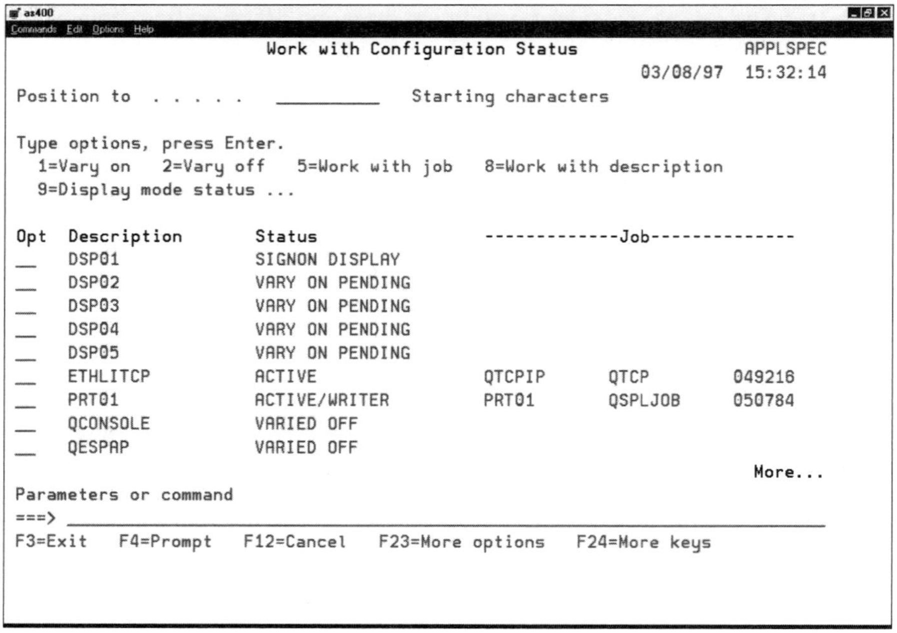

```
 as400                                                                    _ @ x
Commands  Edit  Options  Help
                     Work with Configuration Status              APPLSPEC
                                                      03/08/97   15:32:14
   Position to  . . . . .   _____    Starting characters

   Type options, press Enter.
     1=Vary on    2=Vary off    5=Work with job    8=Work with description
     9=Display mode status ...

   Opt   Description      Status        -------------Job-------------
   __    DSP01            SIGNON DISPLAY
   __    DSP02            VARY ON PENDING
   __    DSP03            VARY ON PENDING
   __    DSP04            VARY ON PENDING
   __    DSP05            VARY ON PENDING
   __    ETHLITCP         ACTIVE          QTCPIP      QTCP       049216
   __    PRT01            ACTIVE/WRITER   PRT01       QSPLJOB    050784
   __    QCONSOLE         VARIED OFF
   __    QESPAP           VARIED OFF
                                                                 More...
   Parameters or command
   ===> _____
   F3=Exit   F4=Prompt   F12=Cancel   F23=More options   F24=More keys
```

Figure 4–3: WRKCFGSTS *DEV display

4.5 WHERE IS MY OUTPUT?

With the plethora of output queues, printers, and options for printing, it may be easy to lose track of where your printer output "disappeared to." Three different OS/400 commands may be used to help you find your output.

If you know with which output queue your job (batch job or interactive session) is associated, use the Work with Output Queue (WRKOUTQ) command and specify the output queue. This will show all the spooled files in the output queue.

Another command that is very helpful in finding output is the Work with Spooled Files (WRKSPLF) command. This command will show all the spooled files that were generated by your job, regardless of the output queue in which the spooled files reside.

Another technique is to display information about your current interactive session. This technique is discussed in the next section.

4.6 DISPLAYING INFORMATION ABOUT YOUR SESSION

The Display Job (DSPJOB) command shows information about a job that is in the system, active or inactive. Information that can be displayed about a job or interactive session includes (1) Job status attributes; (2) Job definition attributes; (3) Job run attributes, if active; (4) Spooled files; (5) Job log, if active or on job queue; (6) Program stack, if active; (7) Locks, if active; (8) Library list, if active; (9) Open files, if active; (10) File overrides, if active; and (11) Commitment control status, if active.

Note that one of the items of information that can be displayed is your spooled files. The DSPJOB command will show any spooled files that were created by your session. The DSPJOB command can be entered on any command line. The default for the DSPJOB command is the current job—your interactive session.

But what if you want to see your spooled files (or any other job related information) while executing a program or command? OS/400 provides a technique that allows you to interrupt an executing program or command to display your job information. The System Request function will interrupt a program or command and show the following display. Press the <SYSRQ> key and a dashed line will appear at the bottom of your terminal. You may enter the option you need (if known) or press the <ENTER> key to see a menu of options.

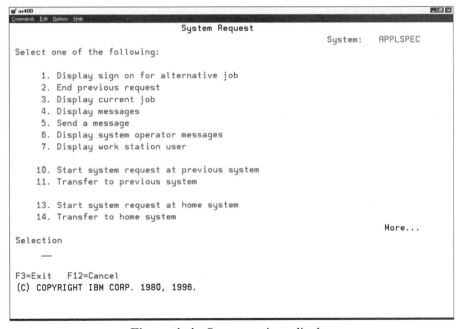

Figure 4–4: Sysreq options display

Option 3 will execute the DSPJOB command. Another common option is 1, which allows you to sign on to an alternative job and have two sessions from the same terminal. This capability may be limited at your installation. Option 2 is dangerous and should only be used with care. This option stops the currently executing program or command.

Option 4 calls the Display Messages (DSPMSG) command, while option 5 executes the Send Message (SNDMSG) command. Option 6 runs the DSPMSG command for message queue QSYSOPR, the system operator's message queue. Option 90 will sign you off from the system. Use caution with option 90; it will stop the currently executing program or command (as does option 2) as well as sign you off from the system.

After you have completed your tasks and are returned to the System Request options menu, press the <ENTER> key to return to the display from where you had pressed the <SYSRQ> key. Please see Chapter 15 ("Advanced Topics") for more information about the System Request menu.

4.7 LIBRARY LISTS

OS/400 will search for a specified object by name. The object could be a file, a program or command, a message queue, or any other type of object. When OS/400 cannot find a referenced object, it will signal an error and abort the search. Library lists provide a method for OS/400 to search through designated libraries to find objects that you request or require for use. Libraries to be searched are grouped together in "lists" to create "search paths."

There are two methods for specifying an object name. The first method is to use a fully qualified object name. This technique will specify the library name and the object name in the format: *libnam/objnam*, where *libnam* is the library name and *objnam* is the name of the object. Since both the library name and the object name are specified, OS/400 will immediately be able to find the object.

The other technique is to use the library list. The library list is a list of libraries that OS/400 will search to find the designated object. OS/400 will search the library list from top to bottom to find the referenced object. An important consideration is that OS/400 will use the first object with the designated name that it encounters in the library list. This may or may not be the actual object you wish to access.

Since you can fully qualify an object name and be assured that OS/400 will find the correct object, why would you use a library list? The power of the library list lies in the very fact that you do not need to specify the name of the library. This saves you (and any programs you use) from knowing the library in which the object is located. In addition, you may move the object to a different library. As long as the new library is in your library list, OS/400 will be able to locate the object.

Another use of the library list is in testing new software. You could place your test data files and test programs in a library that is higher in the library list than your production data and programs. Using this technique will enable you to test and develop new software without impacting production objects.

Library lists may be established in a number of different ways. A library list can be associated with your interactive session through the use of an initial program that is specified in your user profile. Certain system values also may be used to establish your library list. System value QSYSLIBL contains the system portion of a library list, while system value QUSRLIBL contains the user portion of the library list. OS/400 also furnishes commands to manipulate your library list.

A complete library list consists of four sections: the user portion of the library list, and the system portion of the library list. In addition, special library classifications are the current library (*CUR) and the product library (*PRD).

This section will discuss library lists, their different components, and how to manipulate and use library lists.

4.7.1 Displaying Your Library List

The OS/400 command Display Library List (DSPLIBL) will display the contents of your library list. The only parameter available with the DSPLIBL command is "Output." You may direct the output of the DSPLIBL command to the screen (the default of *) or to *PRINT, which will direct the output to a printer. Enter the DSPLIBL command and press <ENTER> to view your library list.

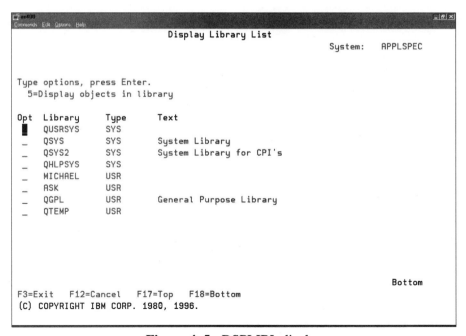

Figure 4–5: DSPLIBL display

As you can see from the DSPLIBL display, the libraries are displayed in order. This is the order that OS/400 will use to search for an object with an unqualified name. The first libraries displayed (and searched) are libraries with a type of *SYS. These libraries are in the system portion of your library list. Libraries such as QSYS, QUSRSYS, and QHLPSYS are often found in the system portion of a library list. The following type is the product library with a type of *PRD. This will be discussed later in this chapter. The next library in order is the current library with a type of *CUR. This type of library will also be discussed later in this chapter. The remaining portion contains libraries in the user portion of your library list. Libraries such as QTEMP (a temporary library) and QGPL (the general purpose library) are usually found in the user portion of the library list.

The DSPLIBL command offers one option: option 5 to display objects in a library. This option executes the Display Library (DSPLIB) command and allows you to view descriptions of the objects in a library. The DSPLIB command shows the same information as can be shown in the Display Object Description (DSPOBJD) command.

4.7.2 Changing Your Library List

Since a library list exists to serve as a search path for unqualified object names, you may need to change your library list. You may need to change the list to "point" to different libraries when testing or when accessing a different application. This type of library list changing may also be done from within an application. You may only change the user portion of your library list. The system portion of the library list must be changed by a system administrator.

Three commands are available to change your library list: the Add Library List Entry (ADDLIBLE) command, the Remove Library List Entry (RMVLIBLE) command, and the Edit Library List (EDTLIBL) command. The EDTLIBL command encompasses the functionality of both the ADDLIBLE and RMVLIBLE commands.

The ADDLIBLE command is

```
ADDLIBLE LIB(PRODLIB) POSITION(*LAST).
```

Specify the "Library" (LIB) to be added to your library list. The other parameter, "Library list position" (POSITION), consists of two parts: the "List position" parameter and the "Reference library" parameter. The "List position" parameter defaults to a special value of *FIRST, meaning that the library to be added should occupy the first position in the user portion of the library list.

Other special values for the "List position" parameter are *LAST meaning the last position in your library list, and *BEFORE, *AFTER, and *REPLACE. These last three special values work with the "Reference library" parameter. The *BEFORE special value indicates that the library to be added should occupy the position before the library specified in the "Reference library" parameter. The *AFTER special value means the library to be added should be placed in the position after the reference library, while the *REPLACE means that the added library should occupy the position of the "Reference library," which will remove the library specified in the "Reference library" parameter.

Enter the appropriate parameters and press <ENTER> and the new library will be added to the user portion of the library list.

The Remove Library List Entry (RMVLIBLE) command requires one parameter: the name of the library that will be removed from the user portion of the library list. Specify the name of the library to be removed and press <ENTER>. The library specified will be removed from the library list.

The Edit Library List (EDTLIBL) command provides the functions of the ADDLIBLE and RMVLIBLE commands in a full screen display. The EDTLIBL command requires no parameters, so enter the EDTLIBL command and press <ENTER>. The following shows the EDTLIBL display:

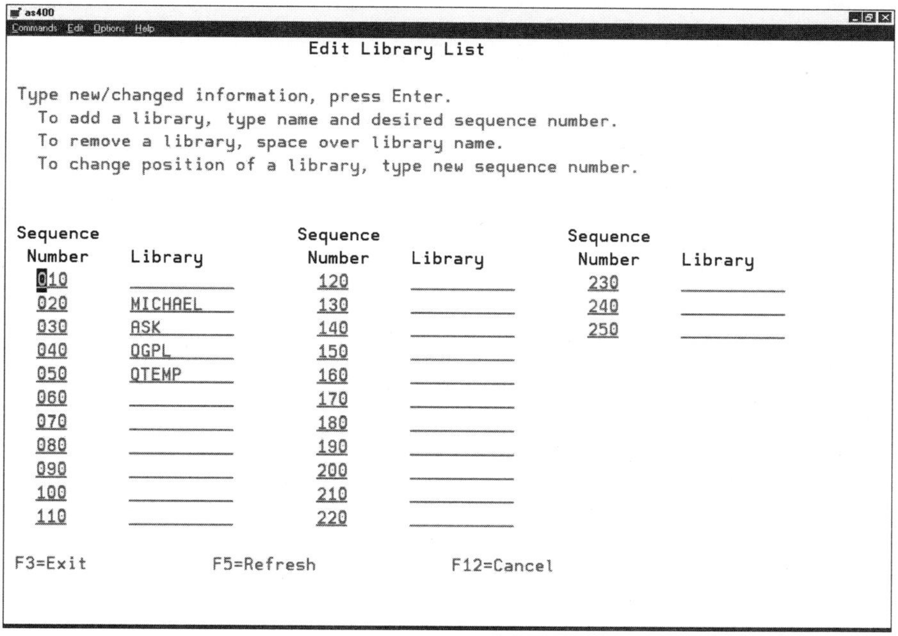

Figure 4–6: EDTLIBL display

Notice that all the libraries in the user portion of your library list are displayed in sequence and that next to each library name is a sequence number. Three functions may be performed from this display: adding a library to the library list, removing a library from the library list, and changing the position of libraries in the library list.

Enter the library to be added to the library list and its sequence number. The library will be added in the correct position according to the sequence number. To remove a library from the library list, space over the library name. This will remove the library from the list.

Changing the position of a library in the library list merely requires a change in its sequence number. Change the sequence number to be in the correct sequence for the new position.

After all changes have been made, press the <ENTER> key to update the library list.

4.7.3 The Current Library

The current library (type *CUR) is a special library in the library list. The search position is after the system portion of the library list and before the user portion. The current library is often a personal library. This allows objects to be located in a library before the rest of the libraries (in the user portion) are searched.

The Change Current Library (CHGCURLIB) command requires one parameter: the "Current library." This parameter will usually be a specific library name and may also contain the special value *CRTDFT. This special value means that no library should be in the current library portion of the library list. If this special value is used and a program or command attempts to create or access an object in the current library, library QGPL will be used instead.

Specify the new current library and press <ENTER> to make the change.

4.7.4 The Product Library

The product library (type *PRD) is another special library in the library list. The search position is after the system portion of the library list and before the current library and the user portion. The product library is a library that contains an application. This allows objects to be located in a special library so the rest of the libraries are not searched. This can simplify management of library lists as the library containing the application will be searched for the correct objects.

5

Queues and Writers

This chapter will explain the creation and use of output queues, printer writers, and message queues in the OS/400 system environment. This environment provides the interaction between the user and OS/400 objects. Output that you generate, such as reports and listings, is directed to an output queue. Printer writers provide the interface between the output queue and the printer device. Messages, whether system messages or conversational messages from another user, are placed in your message queue.

5.1 OUTPUT QUEUES

Output queues exist to receive output generated from a batch program or from your interactive session. An output queue is basically a "holding" area that serves to store your printed output. Printed output items that are placed in an output queue are known as spooled files. The files are spooled so that they will not be immediately printed. This concept of spooling is a common function with midrange, mainframe, and networked computers. This allows output to be generated without needing a printer to be available at that time. In addition, the program producing the output would not need to wait for the slower printer device.

Another item is necessary to actually print output. This item is a job known as a printer writer. A printer writer is associated with an output queue and provides the interface between the output queue's spooled files and the actual printer device. Printer writers will be discussed following output queues.

Output queues are objects of type *OUTQ. These objects can reside in any library, but they will quite often be in library QGPL. This is a handy library to contain output queues since QGPL is usually in all job and user library lists (explained later) and the program or session can find the queue by searching the library list.

5.1.1 Creating an Output Queue

Creating an output queue requires the use of the Create Output Queue (CRTOUTQ) command. An example of this command is

```
CRTOUTQ OUTQ(MFGOUTQ) TEXT(Manufacturing output queue).
```

The CRTOUTQ command requires an entry for the "Output queue" (OUTQ) and the "Library" if needed. The "Output Queue" entry must follow the format of OS/400 object names. Note that the default for the "Library" prompt is *CURLIB, meaning the current library.

Another prompt, "Order of files on queue" (SEQ), has two possible values. The first value (and the default) is *FIFO, which stands for "First In, First Out." This means that the order of files are determined by the time that they were placed in the queue from earliest to latest. The other possible value, *JOBNBR, will place the files on the queue based on the date and time that the job that produced the output entered the system.

An optional "Text description" (TEXT) can be up to fifty characters of descriptive text. This is helpful when working with several output queues (as explained later) as the description of the output queue can describe the function of the queue or the location of the optionally attached printer.

The CRTOUTQ command usually works quite well with just the parameters that are first shown on the display. The additional parameters are usually not required, but are available for special needs. An additional parameter for the CRTOUTQ command is the "Display any file" (DSPDTA) prompt. The default value of *NO will check the security of the user attempting to display, change, or send the spooled file entry. If the user does not have authority to the spooled file entry, OS/400 will stop the attempt. The other possible value, *YES, will allow any user to view any spooled file regardless of authorization level. In either case, the user must have authority to read the output queue.

The "Job separators" (JOBSEP) prompt refers to the practice of placing a separator page between printed spooled files that were produced by different jobs. This can help users to find their printout when several spooled files are printed. The separator pages contain information such as the job name and number, the name of the user that created the output, and date and time the job created the output. The permissible values are a number in the range of 0 though 9, and the special value *MSG. A "Job separators" value of 0 means that no job separators will be printed. A value on the range of 1 through 9 indicates the number of job separator pages that will be printed. The *MSG value will send a message to the message queue identified in the "Start Printer Writer" command that was used to connect the output queue to a printer writer.

The "Operator controlled" (OPRCTL) parameter has two possible values, *YES and *NO. A value of *YES indicates that a user with job control authority can control the queue and the spooled files on the queue. An entry of *NO means that a user must have additional authority to control the queue.

"Authority to check" (AUTCHK) indicates the type of authority needed to control all the files on the output queue. The default value of *OWNER indicates that only the owner of the output queue can control all the files on the queue. A value of *DTAAUT means that any user with read, add, and delete authority to the output queue can control all the files there.

5.1.2 Changing an Output Queue

The command to change characteristics of an output queue, the Change Output Queue (CHGOUTQ) command, is shown below.

```
CHGOUTQ OUTQ(MFGOUTQ) SEQ(*JOBNBR).
```

Note that the parameters are almost identical to the Create Output Queue command. The CHGOUTQ command is used to change the characteristics that could have been established when the output queue was created.

5.1.3 Clearing an Output Queue

Use the Clear Output Queue (CLROUTQ) command to remove all the spooled file entries from an output queue. This process can be time-consuming and resource-consuming depending on the number of entries in the output queue. An example of the CLROUTQ command is

```
CLROUTQ OUTQ(MFGOUTQ).
```

Enter the "Queue name" (OUTQ) and the "Library" values as appropriate and press the <ENTER> key. All spooled files will be removed from the specified output queue.

5.1.4 Deleting an Output Queue

The command to remove an output queue from the system is the Delete Output Queue (DLTOUTQ) command. This command will permanently remove the output queue from the system and will delete all spooled file entries contained in the output queue. An example of the DLTOUTQ command is

```
DLTOUTQ OUTQ(MFGOUTQ).
```

Enter the "Output queue" (OUTQ) to be deleted and the "Library" name if needed. Note that the "Library" name defaults to *LIBL, meaning the library list will be searched for the output queue. Press the <ENTER> key and the output queue will be removed.

5.1.5 Holding an Output Queue

As mentioned earlier, an output queue may be attached to a printer through a printer writer. If an output queue is connected to a writer, spooled file entries will print. If you wish to temporarily stop the printing of spooled files, you may "hold" the output queue with the

Hold Output Queue (HLDOUTQ) command. This will temporarily stop printing because the output queue will not make spooled files available to the printer writer. An example of the HLDOUTQ command is

```
HLDOUTQ OUTQ(MFGOUTQ).
```

Enter the "Output queue" (OUTQ) name, and the name of the "Library" if required. Press the <ENTER> key and the output queue will be held, temporarily stopping printing. A message will be sent to the message queue specified with the "Start Printer Writer" command when the output queue is held. A spooled file that is in the middle of printing will continue to print to completion.

5.1.6 Releasing an Output Queue

Allowing a held output queue to continue printing requires the Release Output Queue (RLSOUTQ) command. The command, shown below, requires the "Output queue" (OUTQ) name and the name of the "Library" if required.

```
RLSOUTQ OUTQ(MFGOUTQ).
```

Enter the values needed and press the <ENTER> key. The held output queue will be released and will continue to print with the next spooled file in the output queue.

5.1.7 Working with Output Queues

As with most types of OS/400 objects, there is a command to perform operations on output queues presented in a list. This command is the Work with Output Queue (WRKOUTQ) command. An example WRKOUTQ command is

```
WRKOUTQ OUTQ(MKT*).
```

Enter the "Output queue" (OUTQ) name and the "Library" name if required. The "Output queue" prompt defaults to *ALL, meaning all output queues. You may narrow this selection by specifying only one library, or be specifying *LIBL for the "Library" name prompt. Specifying *ALL for the "Output queue" prompt and *LIBL for the "Library" name prompt will show all the output queues in your library list.

Another parameter, "Output" (OUTPUT), allows direction of the output from the WRKOUTQ command to the display (*) or to a printer (*PRINT). Enter the values as needed and press the <ENTER> key. The following display will then be shown (see Figure 5–1):

```
as400
Commands  Edit  Options  Help
                        Work with All Output Queues

Type options, press Enter.
   2=Change    3=Hold      4=Delete    5=Work with   6=Release   8=Description
   9=Work with Writers    14=Clear


Opt     Queue         Library       Files     Writer         Status
  __    MRD           ASGPL           0                       RLS
  __    QDKT          ASGPL           0                       RLS
  __    QPFROUTQ      ASGPL           0                       RLS
  __    QPRINT        ASGPL           0                       RLS
  __    QPRINTS       ASGPL           0                       RLS
  __    QPRINT2       ASGPL           0                       RLS
  __    TEMP          ASGPL           0                       RLS
  __    TEST          ASGPL           0                       RLS
  __    GARYG         GARYG           0                       RLS
  __    JOGA          JOGA            2                       RLS
  __    QCSOUTQ       QCSLIB          0                       RLS
  __    GBSS          QDCPLDND        0                       RLS
                                                                   More...
Command
===> _____
F3=Exit    F4=Prompt    F5=Refresh    F12=Cancel    F24=More keys
```

Figure 5–1: WRKOUTQ *ALL display

If multiple output queues were selected, a list of the output queues available through your selection criteria will be shown. Information displayed through the WRKOUTQ command includes the queue name, the library that contains the queue, the number of spooled file entries in the queue, the writer (if any) attached to the queue, and the status of the queue ("RLS" is released and "HLD" is held).

The available options are shown above the list of output queues. All of the commands that have been discussed are available from the WRKOUTQ display.

Option 2 will allow you to change characteristics of the output queue. Option 2 invokes the Change Output Queue (CHGOUTQ) command.

Option 3 will temporarily stop an output queue from delivering spooled files to a printer writer. Option 3 calls the Hold Output Queue (HLDOUTQ) command.

Option 5 will allow you to work with the spooled files in an output queue. This option calls the Work with Output Queue (WRKOUTQ) command for the output queue specified. This display is shown later in this chapter.

Option 6 will release the temporarily held output queue. Option 6 invokes the Release Output Queue (RLSOUTQ) command.

Option 8 allows you to change the description of the output queue. This option invokes the Change Output Queue (CHGOUTQ) command.

The standard "work with" function keys are available with the WRKOUTQ *ALL command, including <F3> to Exit, <F4> to Prompt an option, <F5> to Refresh the screen, <F9> to Recall a command, and <F12> to Cancel.

When a single output queue is specified with the WRKOUTQ command, or option 5 is selected from the WRKOUTQ *ALL display, the WRKOUTQ screen will be displayed. This screen provides access to the spooled files contained within an output queue.

5.1.8 Spooled Files

Several commands are available to manipulate spooled files. Though these commands exist, often users will use the WRKOUTQ command or the "Work with Spooled Files" (WRKSPLF) command. The difference between these two "work with" commands is in their orientation. The WRKOUTQ command will allow you to manipulate spooled files in a certain output queue, while the WRKSPLF command will allow you to work with spooled files selected by user or job regardless of the output queue in which the spooled files reside. The WRKOUTQ command's orientation is by output queue regardless of job or user, while the orientation of the WRKSPLF command is by job or user, regardless of output queue. Both commands provide access to the same underlying commands. The commands to manipulate and control spooled file entries will be discussed in the following section.

When a spooled file is created, it is placed into an output queue. As explained, an output queue may be attached to a printer writer that directs the output queue to a printer device. This means, of course, that an output queue may not be attached to a printer, in which case the spooled file will remain on the output queue until either deleted or moved to another queue with an attached printer.

You may decide to keep spooled files in an output queue to view them from the terminal. This, of course, saves paper, but it is also a technique used by programmers and users to determine if the output should be printed. Reviewing the output could identify an error that would preclude printing, or perhaps not all output that is generated needs to be printed. Occasionally, the results of the output can be viewed on-line and never need to be printed. Whatever the reason for not printing, OS/400 provides a command to display a spooled file.

5.1.9 Displaying Spooled Files

The Display Spooled File (DSPSPLF) command will allow you to view the output from a terminal. This command is shown here.

```
DSPSPLF FILE(CHKRPT) SPLNBR(*LAST).
```

The required parameters are the name of the "Spooled file" (FILE) and the name of the job that produced the spooled file. The "Job name" (JOB) defaults to *, meaning the current job. Using this default would display a spooled file with the name you specify that was generated from the current interactive session. This is a useful default, as you will often generate output during a session and then wish to view the output.

The other parameter, "Spooled file number" (SPLNBR), refers to the number of the spooled file with the name and job information specified. This number allows OS/400 to differentiate between similarly named spooled files. This parameter defaults to a value of *ONLY, which provides the spooled file that is unique to the name and job. The value *LAST is helpful in that it will display the last spooled file with the specified name and job. You may also enter the specific spooled file number in a range of 1 through 9999.

The DSPSPLF command will show the spooled file on the display. The following shows a sample spooled file display (see Figure 5–2):

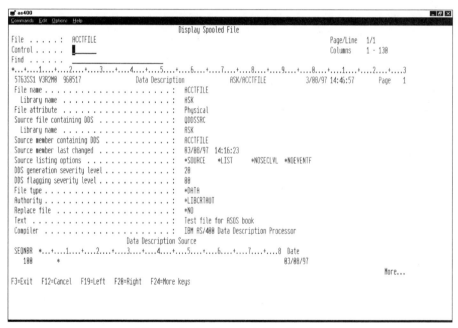

Figure 5–2: Spooled file display

The heading of the display will show the spooled file name, the current page, line numbers, and column numbers currently being displayed. The "Control" and "Find" fields allow you to maneuver around the file to display different portions of the spooled file and to search for information within the spooled file.

The "Control" field allows you to enter certain commands that will move the viewing window. This allows you to view different parts of the spooled file. The allowable "Control" field values are the same as for the Display Physical File Member command discussed in Chapter 2 ("The AS/400 Command Language").

The "Find" field allows you to search the spooled file for a specific character string. Entering a value in the "Find" field and pressing the <F16> key will cause OS/400 to find the value specified. Press the <F16> key again to repeat the search for the same value. If you wish to further qualify the search, you may press the <F14> key. This will display a screen where you may specify options such as columns to search. This can narrow down and expedite the search.

Another function key that is used with the DSPSPLF command is the <F11> key. Pressing <F11> will display the spooled file information in folded format. This causes the command to show only one record of the spooled file, but the entire record will be visible.

If the number of columns in the spooled file is greater than the number of columns your terminal can display, you can use the <F19> and <F20> keys to move the viewing window to the left and right. If your terminal will display the entire width of the spooled file (as with a 132 column terminal) the entire width of the spooled file will be shown. While the windowing commands entered in the "Control" field will also provide this function, it is simpler to move back and forth with the <F19> and <F20> keys.

5.1.10 Selecting Spooled Files

There are two methods that can be used to select spooled files for some spooled file commands. A spooled file name may be used, or the special value *SELECT in the place of the spooled file name. This special value allows a different type of selection criteria.

If a "Spooled file" name is selected, you must specify the job information for the job that created the spooled file. The "Job name" defaults to *, meaning the current interactive session. If the spooled file was created by another job, specify the "Job name," "User" name, the "Number" of the job, and the "Spooled file number." This will allow OS/400 to select the correct spooled file.

The special value *SELECT for the "Spooled file" prompt will show additional parameters. These parameters allow you to select a spooled file based on four different criteria: "User name," "Print device," "Form type," and "User data." These values can be mixed and matched to provide the correct selection criteria. Note that each parameter may use the special value *ALL. This is used to provide a default response for one or more of the selection criteria.

5.1.11 Holding a Spooled File

A spooled file may be held so it will not print. The command to hold the spooled file, the Hold Spool File (HLDSPLF), command is show below.

```
HLDSPLF FILE(CHKRPT) OPTION(*PAGEEND).
```

The HLDSPLF command requires the name of the "Spooled file" (FILE) to hold. Note that the special value *SELECT may be used. Specify the spooled file name and the job information or the special value *SELECT and the other selection criteria.

Another parameter available with the HLDSPLF command is the "When to hold file" (OPTION) parameter. This parameter has two possible values, *IMMED (the default), which means to hold the spooled file immediately, and *PAGEEND, which indicates that the spooled file should be held after the current page has been printed.

Enter the appropriate information and press the <ENTER> key. The spooled file(s) selected will be held from printing.

5.1.12 Releasing a Spooled File

A spooled file that is held may be released to allow it to print. The command to release the spooled file is the Release Spool File (RLSSPLF) command. An example of this command is

```
RLSSPLF FILE(CHKRPT).
```

The RLSSPLF command requires the "Spooled file" (FILE) name to delete. Note that the special value *SELECT may be used. Specify the spooled file name and the job information or the special value *SELECT and the other selection criteria.

Enter the appropriate information and press the <ENTER> key. The held spooled file(s) will be released and made available to be printed.

5.1.13 Deleting Spooled Files

After you have viewed the spooled file, you may wish to remove it from the system. This is a good housekeeping practice as a spooled file takes up disk space on the AS/400, and is also another job of which OS/400 must be aware. Use the Delete Spooled File (DLTSPLF) command to remove a spooled file from the system. An example of this command is

```
DLTSPLF FILE(CHKRPT).
```

The DLTSPLF command requires the "Spooled file" (FILE) name to delete. Note that the special value *SELECT may be used. Enter the spooled file name and the job information or the special value *SELECT and the other selection criteria.

Enter the appropriate information and press the <ENTER> key. The spooled file(s) selected will be permanently removed from the system.

5.1.14 Changing the Attributes of Spooled Files

The attributes of spooled files can be changed. You may do this to change information such as number of copies, the output queue where the spooled file will be contained, or the form type of the spooled file. The command to change the attributes, Change Spooled File Attributes (CHGSPLFA), is shown below.

```
CHGSPLFA FILE(CHKRPT) OUTQ(QPRINT).
```

The criteria for the spooled file selection is the same as for other spooled file manipulation commands. You need to either specify a "Spooled file" (FILE) name or the special value *SELECT. Enter the appropriate selection criteria to identify the spooled file. There are several items that can be changed with this command.

The "Output queue" (OUTQ) parameter may be changed to move the spooled file to a different queue. This is often done to change the location of a spooled file to a queue that has a printer writer attached. Enter the name of the output queue to which you wish to transfer the spooled file.

Another parameter that is often changed is the "Copies" (COPIES) parameter. This parameter can have a value between 1 and 255.

The "Form type" (FORMTYPE) parameter may be changed to reflect a different type of form that this spooled file should use when printing. The spooled file will trigger a message when it begins to print, indicating that the form type is different from the previous spooled file.

Many other attributes of spooled files are available to be changed with the command. Change the parameters as needed and press the <ENTER> key.

5.1.15 Sending Spooled Files to Another System

The Send Network Spool File (SNDNETSPLF) command allows you to send a file to a user on another AS/400. The SNDNETSPLF command format is

```
SNDNETSPLF FILE(CHKRPT) TOUSRID((CFO HQ)).
```

The "Spooled file" (FILE) name needs to be entered, as well as the "User identifier" (TOUSRID) information. The identifier information consists of a "User ID" and an "Address." This will direct OS/400 to send the spooled file to the user at another location. The selection criteria for the spooled file is similar to other spooled file commands.

5.1.16 Working with a Single Output Queue

The information that is displayed when working with a single output queue is similar to the display when working with several output queues. The difference is in the placement of the information on the display.

The queue name and library are displayed. The status indicated in the upper right corner refers to the status of the output queue. The possible status values are

HLD—The queue is currently being held as a result of a HLDOUTQ command.

HLD/WTR—The queue is held and is attached to a printer writer.

RLS/WTR—The queue is released and is attached to a writer.

RLS—The queue is released and is not attached to a writer.

The following is an example of the WRKOUTQ display when a single queue is specified or selected (see Figure 5–3):

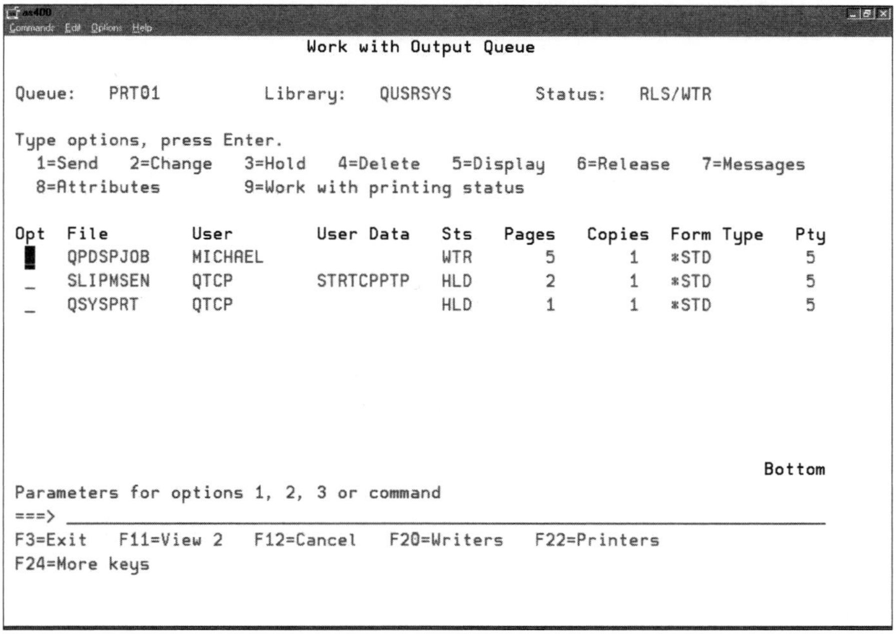

```
 as400                                                                    _|B|x|
 Commands  Edit  Options  Help
                            Work with Output Queue

    Queue:     PRT01         Library:    QUSRSYS        Status:    RLS/WTR

    Type options, press Enter.
      1=Send    2=Change    3=Hold    4=Delete    5=Display    6=Release    7=Messages
      8=Attributes          9=Work with printing status

    Opt   File        User        User Data    Sts    Pages    Copies   Form Type   Pty
     ▮    QPDSPJOB    MICHAEL                   WTR      5        1       *STD        5
     _    SLIPMSEN    QTCP        STRTCPPTP    HLD      2        1       *STD        5
     _    QSYSPRT     QTCP                      HLD      1        1       *STD        5



                                                                    Bottom
    Parameters for options 1, 2, 3 or command
    ===> _____
    F3=Exit    F11=View 2    F12=Cancel    F20=Writers    F22=Printers
    F24=More keys
```

Figure 5–3: WRKOUTQ display view 1

This display shows the spooled files within an output queue and is referred to as the "view 1" display. This display is also shown when the WRKOUTQ command is first executed. More information relating to the individual spooled files can be shown by pressing the <F11> key. This will show "view 2," which provides different information. The following is an example of the "view 2" display (see Figure 5–4):

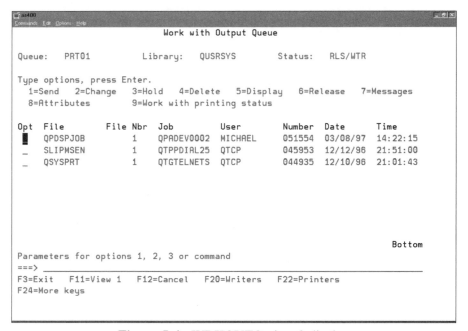

Figure 5-4: WRKOUTQ view 2 display

Information shown on the "view 1" display includes the name of the spooled file and the name of the user that created the spooled file. The user data associated with the spooled file is shown. User data is ten characters of information that can be specified with the spooled file. Other information shown is the status of the spooled file. The following are the possible values for the status of a spooled file:

RDY—The file is ready and available to be written.

OPN—The spooled file is open. A process is currently writing records to the spooled file.

CLO—All records have been written to the spooled file, but the process writing the records has not yet been completed.

HLD—The spooled file is in a held state.

SAV—The file has been written and has a status of save. The spooled file will remain in the output queue after it is printed.

WTR—The spooled file is currently at the printer being written.

PND—The spooled file is in a pending state waiting to be written.

PRT—The spooled file has been completely written but the update of the status of the printing is not yet complete.

MSGW—The spooled file is at the writer but a message is waiting. This can often be a forms change message.

*CHG—The spooled file was changed using option 2.

*HLD—The spooled file was held using option 3.

*RLS—The spooled file was released using option 6.

Other available information includes the number of pages in the spooled file, the number of copies to be printed, the form type associated with the spooled file, and the priority on the output queue.

Information shown on the "view 2" display is the spooled file number, the name of the job, user, and job number of the job that created the spooled file, and the date and time the spooled file was created.

The options shown above the list of spooled files call different spooled file commands. These commands have been discussed in the preceding section.

Option 1 will send the spooled file to a user on another system. This option calls the Send Network Spool File (SNDNETSPLF) command.

Option 2 will change the spooled file attributes. This option calls the Change Spool File Attributes (CHGSPLFA) command. This option is similar to option 8. The difference is that with this option you can specify the keyword and value on the command line for the parameter to be changed.

Option 3 will hold the spool file to stop it from being printed. This option calls the Hold Spool File (HLDSPLF) command.

Option 4 will remove the spooled file from the system. This option calls the Delete Spool File (DLTSPLF) command.

Option 5 allows you to view the contents of the spooled file. This option calls the Display Spooled File (DSPSPLF) command.

Option 6 will release a spooled file that is currently held. This option calls the Release Spooled File (RLSSPLF) command.

Option 7 will display any messages that may be available. These messages will be in the output queue specified with the Start Printer Writer command. This option calls the Display Message (DSPMSG) command.

Option 8 will allow you to work with the attributes of the spooled file. This option calls the Work with Spooled File Attributes (WRKSPLFA) command. You will be able to change the same options as with the CHGSPLFA command.

Option 9 allows you to work with the status of a printer. The spooled file must be at a printer for this command to be valid. This option calls the Work with Printer Status (WRKPRTSTS) command.

5.2 PRINTER WRITERS

Printer writers provide the interface between spooled files on an output queue and the actual printer device. A printer writer (or writer) is a job that usually runs in subsystem QSPL. This job monitors a specified output queue. When spooled file entries are made available in the output queue, through being placed in the queue or being released in the queue, the writer will direct the spooled file to the printer device. There is no association between an output queue, a writer, and the actual device until the writer is started.

Messages are sent from the printer writer job to the output queue specified in the Start Printer Writer (STRPRTWTR) command. A variety of messages may be sent from a printer writer. These messages may be error messages that indicate a problem with the printer, such as a paper jam or an out of paper condition. Another common message is a forms type change. This is sent as a result of a spooled file that is to be printed that has a different forms type than the previous spooled file printed. Different forms types may be standard paper (*STD), invoices, statements, or any type of form that has special length or width requirements.

A printer writer, such as an output queue or a spooled file, may be held to temporarily stop printing or released to continue printing. Printer writers need to be started, as they are a job like any job that runs on an AS/400. Writers will often be started automatically when the system is powered on. A writer can be stopped when the need no longer exists for that printer writer. This stops the association between the output queue, the writer, and the physical device.

5.2.1 Starting a Printer Writer

The command to start a writer and create the association with the queue and the device is the Start Printer Writer (STRPRTWTR) command. This command is

```
STRPRTWTR DEV(SALESWTR) MSGQ(*REQUESTER).
```

The STRPRTWTR command requires the name of the "Printer" (DEV). This is the system name of the actual device and contains either the printer name or special values *ALL or *SYSVAL. *ALL starts all printers; *SYSVAL looks in the list of system values to determine the printer name(s) to start.

The "Output queue" (OUTQ) prompt defaults to a value of *DEV. You may either enter the name of the output queue (and the library if necessary) or accept the default. The default value of *DEV will associate the writer with an output queue that has the same name as the printer. This is a common practice.

Another prompt to be examined is the "Queue for writer messages" (MSGQ) prompt. This is the message queue to which writer messages will be sent. The default value is *DEVD, which means that the message queue specified on the printer device description will be used. Another special value is *REQUESTER. When this value is used, writer messages will go to the message queue of the user who started the writer. You may also specify an output queue and the library if desired for this prompt.

Another parameter for the STRPRTWTR command is the "Form type options" (FORMTYPE) prompt. This determines which form types will be processed by this writer. This parameter has two parts: the "Form type" and the "Message option." The "Form type" defaults to the special value *ALL, which means that spooled files with any form type will be processed by the writer. Another special value is *FORMS. This indicates that the writer will print all the spooled files with the same form type, then the next group of spooled files with a different form type, and so on. This is helpful in reducing the number of forms changes needed. *STD means that spooled files with the standard form type (*STD) will be printed. You may also enter a specific form type for this prompt. The writer will only process spooled files with the specified form type.

The "Message option" prompt of the FORMTYPE parameter defaults to a value of *NOMSG. This means that a message will only be sent to the message queue when the forms type needs to be changed. The other value, *MSG, indicates that a message will be sent to the message queue every time a new spooled file is sent to the printer. This could become quite annoying when many spooled files are printed.

The "File separators" (FILESEP) parameter defaults to *FILE, which indicates that the presence and number of file separator pages will be determined by the spooled file being printed. You may also specify a value between 0 and 9 for the number of separator pages to be printed between each spooled file entry.

Additional parameters for the STRPRTWTR command are the name of the "Writer" (WTR) (which defaults to the device name), which "Spooled file" (FILE) to print (which defaults to *NONE, meaning no specific spooled files, or *ALL, meaning all spooled files), "Align page" (ALIGN) (which defaults to allowing the writer to determine if the printer needs to be aligned) and the "Starting page" (PAGE) number. While the starting page number is more easily handled with the Hold Writer and Release Writer commands for an active writer, you may use this parameter when starting a writer to start at a specific page number.

Enter the appropriate information and press the <ENTER> key. A system message will be displayed that indicates that the writer has been started.

5.2.2 Stopping a Printer Writer

You may desire to end a printer writer. This will disable the association between the output queue, the writer, and the printer. The command to end a printer writer is the End Writer (ENDWTR) command. This command is

```
ENDWTR WTR(SALESWTR) OPTION(*IMMED).
```

Specify the "Writer" (WTR) to end. Remember the default for the writer name (established when the writer is started) is the same as the name of the printer. You may enter a specific writer, special value *SYSVAL (which will use the system values to determine the correct writer), or special value *ALL (which will end all active writers on the system).

Another parameter that can be specified is the "When to end writer" (OPTION) prompt. Three special values are available for this prompt: *CNTRLD, *IMMMED, and *PAGEEND. *CNTRLD uses a system value to determine the length of time to wait before ending the writer. This value is usually thirty seconds. *IMMED will end the writer immediately. *PAGEEND will end the writer at the end of the current page, even if the printer is in the middle of a spooled file.

Enter the information needed and press the <ENTER> key. The writer(s) will end in the time frame specified.

5.2.3 Holding a Writer

A writer may be held to temporarily stop printing. You may need to hold the writer to correct the printer alignment or to restart printing of a spooled file at a specific page. A message is sent to the message queue established with the Start Printer Writer command when the writer is held. The command to hold a printer writer is Hold Writer (HLDWTR). An example of this command is

```
HLDWTR WTR(SALEWTR).
```

The name of the "Writer" (WTR) must be specified as well as a value for the "When to hold writer" (OPTION) parameter. The special values *CNTRLD, *IMMMED, and *PAGEEND have the same meaning as for the End Writer command as discussed above.

Enter the appropriate values and press <ENTER>. The writer will be held and a message will be sent to the writer's message queue.

5.2.4 Releasing a Writer

A writer that is held may be released through the use of the Release Writer (RLSWTR) command. This will allow a temporarily held writer to begin printing again. This command is

```
RLSWTR WTR(SALESWTR) OPTION(*BEGIN).
```

The name of the "Writer" (WTR) must be specified as well as the "Resume writing" (OPTION) parameter. The "Resume writing" parameter determines the position in the spooled file where the writer will resume writing. This prompt has several possible values. These values are

*CURRENT—Can only be used when the writer is not actively writing a file and will resume printing at the current location in the spooled file.

*BEGIN—The writer will resume printing at the beginning of the spooled file.

*BYPASS—The writer will resume printing with the next spooled file in the queue and will hold the current spooled file.

+number—The number of pages in the spooled file that the writer will move forward before it resumes printing.

–number—The number of pages in the spooled file that the writer will move backward before it resumes printing.

Options *BYPASS, +number, and -number are only valid if the printer writer was held while it was writing the spooled file.

The "Starting page" (PAGE) prompt allows you to resume printing the held spooled file at a specific page number within the spooled file.

Enter the information as needed and press the <ENTER> key. You may receive a message that the printer needs to be aligned. This may happen if the writer was writing a spooled file and you selected an option which will change the alignment.

5.2.5 Changing a Printer Writer

Attributes of the printer writer may be changed. This may be used to change the output queue with which the writer is associated, to change form types, or to change the number of file separators. The command to change a printer writer, Change Writer, (CHGWTR), is

```
CHGWTR WTR(SALEWTR) FILESEP(1).
```

This command requires the "Writer" (WTR) name to be entered. This may be a specific writer name or the special value *SYSVAL, which indicates the CHGWTR command should use the system values to determine the correct writer.

The available writer values to change are the same as the values in the Start Printer Writer command. These values are "Output queue" (OUTQ), "Form type options" (FORMTYPE), and number of "File separators" (FILESEP).

The "When to change writer" (OPTION) prompt has two possible values that can be used: *NORDYF, which is the default, and *FILEEND. These options control when the change will occur to the writer. *NORDYF indicates that the change will occur when no files exist in the queue that match the current form type being processed by the writer. *FILEEND means that the change will happen after the current spooled file has finished printing.

Specify the appropriate values and press the <ENTER> key. The change to the writer will take place as you have specified.

5.2.6 Working with Printer Writers

Of course, OS/400 provides a command to work with all printer writers. This command, Work with Writers (WRKWTR), is

```
WRKWTR WTR(*ALL).
```

You may specify a specific "Writer" (WTR) with which to work, or use the special values *PRT or *ALL. *PRT, which is the default, will show a list of all printers on the system and any writers attached to those printers. Special value *ALL will show all currently active writers on the system.

The "Output" (OUTPUT) parameter allows you to direct the output of the WRKWTR command (a list of printers or writers) to either the terminal (*) or to a spooled file (*PRINT).

Another prompt, "Display format" (DSPFMT), determines in what format the output should be displayed. Special value *INLENV (the default) means that the user profile value *SPCENV will be checked to determine the environment. *S36FMT will display the output in System/36 format, while *NORMAL will display the output in native OS/400 format.

Enter the parameters as appropriate and press <ENTER>. The following screen (as shown with using default value *PRT for the "Writer" prompt) will be displayed (see Figure 5–5):

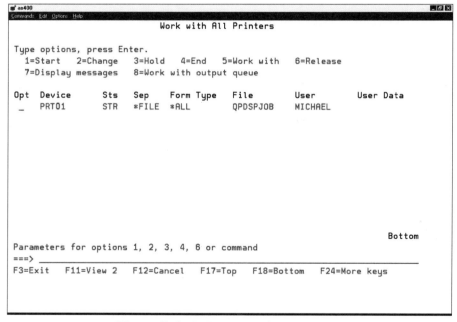

Figure 5–5: WRKWTR display view 1

The WRKWTR display has two parts. The next screen is an example of "view 2" of the WRKWTR display. This display is accessible by pressing <F11> on the "view 1" display.

The information that is shown on the two "views" of the WRKWTR command include

- The printer device name.
- The status of the writer.
- The number of separator pages.

- The current form type being processed.
- The spooled file name.
- The user that created the spooled file.
- The 10 character user data information.
- The name of the printer writer.
- The name of the output queue being processed.
- The name of the library the contains the output queue.

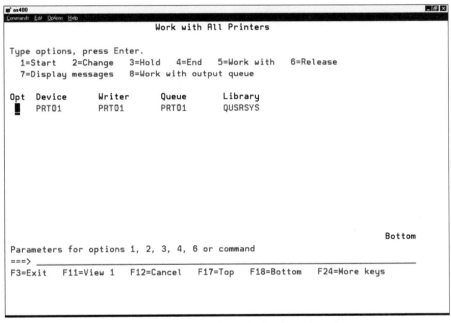

Figure 5–6: WRKWTR display view 2

The WRKWTR command uses the standard "work with" command function keys such as <F3> to Exit, <F4> to Prompt an option, <F5> to Refresh the screen, <F9> to Recall a command, and <F12> to Cancel.

The WRKWTR command allows you to perform operations on multiple writers. The following section will detail the options that are available with the WRKWTR command. All options run commands that have been previously discussed in this chapter.

Option 1 will start a printer writer. This option calls the Start Printer Writer (STRPRTWTR) command.

Option 2 will allow you to change the characteristics of the writer. This option calls the Change Writer (CHGWTR) command.

Option 3 will hold the writer. This option calls the Hold Writer (HLDWTR) command.

Option 4 will end a writer. This option calls the End Writer (ENDWTR) command.

Option 5 will allow you to work with the writer. The display for this command is shown later.

Option 6 will allow you to release a held writer. This option calls the Release Writer (RLSWTR) command.

Option 7 will display any messages associated with the writer. This option runs the Display Message (DSPMSG) command using the message queue established on the Start Printer Writer command.

Option 8 will allow you to work with the contents of the output queue associated with the writer. This option calls the Work with Output Queue (WRKOUTQ) command.

When Option 5 is selected, the following display is shown (see Figure 5–7):

```
as400                                                                    _ | & | x
Commands  Edit  Options  Help
                        Work with Printer Writer

Writer . . . . . . . :   PRT01         User . . . . . . . . :   QSPLJOB
Number . . . . . . . :   050784

Started by user  . . . . . . . . . . . :   DONNA
Status:
   Writing  . . . . . . . . . . . . . :   N
   Waiting on message . . . . . . . . :   N
   Held . . . . . . . . . . . . . . . :   N
   End pending  . . . . . . . . . . . :   N
   Hold pending . . . . . . . . . . . :   N
   Between files  . . . . . . . . . . :   N
   Between copies . . . . . . . . . . :   N
   Waiting for data . . . . . . . . . :   N
   Waiting for device . . . . . . . . :   N
   On job queue . . . . . . . . . . . :   N

                                                              More...
Press Enter to continue.


F3=Exit      F5=Refresh    F6=Messages   F10=Release   F11=Hold   F12=Cancel
F14=Queue    F24=More keys
```

Figure 5-7: WRKOUTQ option 5 display

This command uses the standard function keys such as <F3> to Exit, <F5> to Refresh the screen, and <F12> to Cancel. Other available function keys perform writer commands such as:

<F6>—will display the writer messages (DSPMSG).

<F10>—will release a held writer (RLSWTR).

<F11>—will hold the writer (HLDWTR).

<F14>—will allow you to work with the output queue (WRKOUTQ).

<F13>—will change the writer (CHGWTR).

<F17>—will allow you to display the writer job (DSPJOB).

<F18>—will end the writer (ENDWTR).

Information that is presented from Option 5 includes

The name of the writer.

The name of the system user.

The job number of the writer.

The name of the user who started the writer.

Several possible status conditions may be shown such as:

Currently writing.

Waiting for a message reply.

Writer is held.

Writer has an end pending because of an ENDWTR command.

Writer has a hold pending.

Writer is between files.

Writer is between copies.

Writer is waiting for data.

Writer is on the job queue.

The name of the spooled file being written.

The file number of the spooled file.

The name of the job that created the spooled file.

The name of the user who created the spooled file.

The job number of the job that created the spooled file.

The current page number being written.

The total number of pages in the spooled file.

The number of copies that remain to be produced.

The total number of copies.

The name of the printer device.

The type of printer device.

The number of separator pages.

When the align forms message will be sent.

The output queue that contains the spooled file.

The library that contains the output queue.

The status of the output queue.

The form type in effect.

If a message will be sent to notify you upon completion.

If the writer will end automatically after printing.

The message queue where printer messages will be sent.

The library of the message queue.

The next output queue if the writer has been changed.

The library that contains the next output queue.

The next form type if the writer has been changed.

The next number of separators if the writer has been changed.

When changes will take effect if the writer has been changed.

5.3 MESSAGE QUEUES

Messages and message handling are integral parts of OS/400. Processes running on an AS/400 communicate with each other through the use of messages, and several commands are available to be used in a programming situation. These commands will not be discussed here, instead we will concentrate on the commands that allow you to interact with messages.

Messages are sent (whether from a process or another user) to a message queue. A message queue is an OS/400 object of type *MGSQ. As with any OS/400 object, an object of type *MSGQ must reside in a library.

A message queue is simply a "holding area" for messages. You can display, delete, or reply to messages depending on the type of message that was sent. Two types of message queues exist on an AS/400 with which users will interact: user message queues and workstation message queues.

A user message queue is a queue that is associated with a specific user. Regardless of the terminal used to sign on to the system, the user message queue will be accessible to that user. Contrast this with a workstation message queue. This type of queue is associated with the terminal, not the user. A message sent to a workstation message queue is available to any user that signs on to the system using that workstation.

5.3.1 Creating a Message Queue

User message queue creation is normally performed by a system manager as part of establishing a new user id. Workstation message queue creation is done automatically when a new workstation is added to the system. The command to create a message queue is the Create Message Queue (CRTMSGQ), is shown here.

```
CRTMSGQ MSGQ(MKTUSER) TEXT('Marketing User').
```

Enter the name of the "Message queue" (MSGQ) to be created and optionally the "Library" name. Message queues are often created in library QGPL to ensure that other users on the system will have that message queue in their library list.

It is considered a good practice to establish either a user or a workstation message queue to have the same name as the user or workstation. This is not a requirement and having the same name provides no association to OS/400. The actual association is done when the user profile is created (or changed) or when the workstation device description is created (or changed). Using the same name merely provides a way to remember the message queue name.

An optional "Text description" (TEXT) can be added. This can be helpful when working with several message queues.

Specify the appropriate values and press the <ENTER> key to create the message queue.

5.3.2 Deleting a Message Queue

When a message queue is no longer required, it may be removed from the system. The command to remove a message queue from the system is the Delete Message Queue (DLTMSGQ) command. An example of the DLTMSGQ command is

```
DLTMSGQ MSGQ(MKTUSER).
```

Enter the name of the "Message queue" (MSGQ) and the "Library" if needed. Note that the "Library" prompt defaults to a value of *LIBL meaning the library list will be searched for the message queue to be deleted. Press <ENTER> to remove the message queue from the system.

5.3.3 Changing a Message Queue

The characteristics of a message queue may need to be changed to fulfill different requirements. Use the following Change Message Queue (CGHMSGQ) command to change these characteristics:

```
CHGMSGQ MSGQ(MKTUSER) DLVRY(*BREAK).
```

The "Message queue" (MSGQ) name and optionally the "Library" name should be specified. The characteristics of the message queue default to a value of *SAME, meaning that the characteristic should not change.

Characteristics that can be changed include the type of "Delivery," the "Severity code filter," the "Text description," and other additional parameters.

The "Delivery" (DLVRY) parameter determines how the reception of messages should be announced to the user. A value of *HOLD means that the message will be placed in the message queue and the "Message Waiting" (MW) indicator should be illuminated at the terminal. A value of *BREAK indicates that in addition to placing the message in the queue, the terminal screen will clear and the message will "break" into the display on the terminal. This is used at a message queue level primarily for system operations. This will allow messages to be immediately displayed and available to an operator so that they may take corrective action. This technique of "breaking" into a session can also be accomplished with the Send Break Message (SNDBRKMSG) command.

The "Severity code filter" (SEV) refers to the severity code that is part of each message. More severe errors have higher severity codes. If you do not wish to see informational errors, set the level higher (perhaps to 40).

Enter the appropriate values and press <ENTER> to change the message queue.

5.3.4 Clearing a Message Queue

A single message may be deleted when viewed by pressing the appropriate function key. To remove all the messages from a message queue, use the Clear Message Queue (CLRMSGQ) command. This command is shown here.

```
CLRMSGQ MSGQ(MKTUSER) CLEAR(*KEEPUNANS).
```

Enter the "Message queue" (MSGQ) name and the name of the "Library" if needed. The "Clear" (CLEAR) parameter refers to which messages should be cleared and defaults to a value of *ALL. This default value will remove all the messages from the queue. The other choice, *KEEPUNANS, will retain all messages that have not yet been answered.

Specify the values needed and press the <ENTER> key to clear the message queue.

5.3.5 Working with Message Queues

As you might expect, OS/400 provides a command to work with multiple message queues. This command is the Work with Message Queues (WRKMSGQ) command. An example of this command is shown below

```
WRKMSGQ MSGQ(PLANT*).
```

Specify the name of the "Message queue" (MSGQ) and the "Library" name if needed. Note that you may specify the special value *ALL for the message queue, as well as a generic (ending with *) name. This will allow you to subset the list of message queues. Press <ENTER> to work with the message queues selected. The following display will be shown (see Figure 5–8):

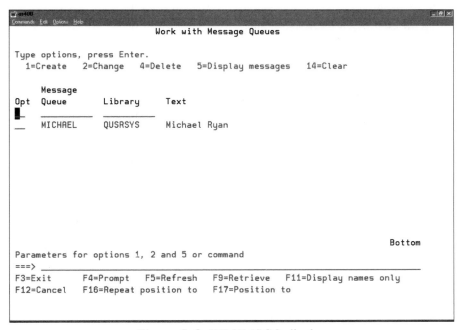

Figure 5–8: WRKMSGQ display

The WRKMSGQ command uses the standard "work with" command function keys such as <F3> to Exit, <F4> to prompt an option, <F5> to Refresh the screen, <F9> to recall a command, and <F12> to Cancel.

The WRKMSGQ command allows you to perform operations on multiple message queues. The following details the options that are available with the WRKMSGQ command. All options run commands that have been previously discussed in this chapter.

Option 2 will change a message queue. This option calls the Change Message Queue (CHGMSGQ) command.

Option 4 will remove a message queue from the system. This option calls the Delete Message Queue (DLTMSGQ) command.

Option 5 will display the messages in the queue. This option calls the Display Message (DSPMSG) command and is explained in the next section.

Option 13 will allow you to change the text description associated with the message queue object. This option calls the Change Object Description (CHGOBJD) command.

Option 14 will clear the messages from the message queue. This option calls the Clear Message Queue (CLRMSGQ) command.

5.3.6 Message Operations

Several commands allow you to work with messages. You may display messages and send various types of messages. In addition, several advanced commands are available to manipulate and control messages from within a program. This section will deal with messages from a user's perspective.

5.3.7 Displaying Messages

Messages are sent to a user message queue or a workstation message queue. To view these messages, use the Display Message (DSPMSG) command. This command is shown here

```
DSPMSG MSGQ(*SYSOPR).
```

The required parameter "Message queue" (MSGQ) defaults to the value *WRKUSR. This indicates that messages will be shown from the workstation message queue ("WRK") first. After messages are shown from the workstation queue, messages will be shown from the user message queue. If no messages exist in the workstation message queue, only the user message queue will be displayed. Since it is common AS/400 practice to utilize the user message queue more than the workstation message queue, you will usually see only your user message queue displayed.

Other special values for the "Message queue" prompt are *SYSOPR, which will display messages in the system operator message queue (QSYSOPR), and *WRKSTN, which will only show the messages in the workstation message queue. You may also enter a specific message queue. The "Library" parameter may be specified to identify the library containing the message queue; special values *LIBL (meaning search the library list), and *CURLIB (meaning use the current library), may also be used for the "Library" prompt.

The "Output" (OUTPUT) parameter allows you to direct the output to a terminal (the default *) or to a printer by specifying *PRINT. Enter the values as appropriate and press <ENTER> to display the messages. The defaults are usually what is required to display messages directed to you, so prompting this command is ordinarily not needed.

The following display will be shown. This display shows the messages in the specified message queue.

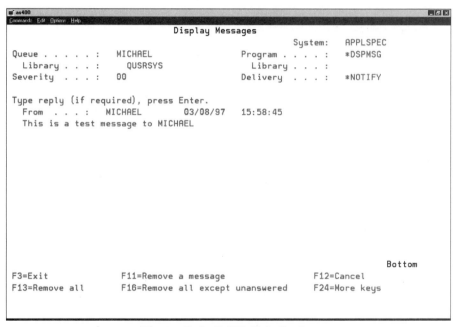

Figure 5–9: DSPMSG display

Note that the messages are in descending order based on the time they were delivered to the message queue. Each message contains the date and time the message was sent. To see more information about a message, place your cursor on the message and press the <HELP> or <F1> key. This will show you the second level message text and other information such as the type of message and its severity code.

Certain messages known as "inquiry messages" require a reply. These messages are identified by the underlined input field directly beneath the message. Some of these messages, especially system error messages, also provide the reply options that the message will accept. Chapter 2 ("The AS/400 Command Language") provides a description of system error messages and their allowable replies.

An "ad hoc" inquiry message may be sent to you from another user. These messages may have no preset reply value. You would enter your response to the message and press <ENTER>, which sends the reply back to the user that issued the message. Inquiry messages will be discussed in more detail later in this section.

Several function keys are available on the DSPMSG display. Some standard keys, such as <F3> to Exit and <F12> to Cancel, are available. The <F10> key is useful when you wish to update the message display with any new messages that have arrived since you first began displaying the message queue. The <F11> key allows you to remove a message from the message queue. Place your cursor on the messages to be removed and press <F11> to delete a message. The <F13> key will remove all messages from the message queue, and the <F16> key will remove all messages from the queue except for inquiry messages that have not yet been answered.

After viewing the messages (and deleting any messages that are no longer needed) press the <F3>, <F12>, or <ENTER> key to exit from the DSPMSG display.

5.3.8 Sending a Message

An impromptu message may be sent from a user to another user or to a workstation message queue. This is accomplished by using the Send Message (SNDMSG) command. This command is shown here.

```
SNDMSG MSG('Bagels in the conference room!') TOUSR(*ALLACT).
```

The first prompt is the "Message text" (MSG) prompt. This provides the area in which you will enter your message.

The next parameter is the "To user profile" (TOUSR) prompt. You may enter a specific user profile name or a special value. The special values that are allowable for this prompt are: *SYSOPR, meaning send the message to the system operator's message queue (QSYSOPR), or *ALLACT, which indicates that the message could be sent to all active user profiles. This is a technique that can be used to broadcast certain system wide information. Another special value that can be used is *REQUESTER, which means send the message to the user message queue for interactive sessions, and to the system operator's message queue for batch jobs.

These are the only parameters needed for the majority of impromptu messages. You would only need to enter the "Message text" and the "To user profile" information and press the <ENTER> key. The message will be sent to the user profile specified.

Additional parameters are available for the SNDMSG command. Another parameter that may be used is the "To message queue" (TOMSGQ) parameter. This parameter is mutually exclusive with the use of the "To user profile" parameter. The "To message queue" parameter allows you to specify any message queue, including a workstation message queue. You may also specify the "Library" if required.

The "Message type" (MSGTYPE) additional parameter may have two values: *INFO, which is the default, and *INQ. The *INFO value will send an informational message; no reply is needed. A message type of *INQ indicates an inquiry message where a reply is needed. Specifying a message as an inquiry message will, when the message is displayed, provide an input area for the recipient of the message to send their reply.

The last additional parameter, "Message queue to get reply" (RPYMSGQ), specifies the message queue to which the reply from an inquiry message will be sent. The default for this parameter is *WRKSTN, meaning the workstation message queue from the workstation where the message was sent. You may also indicate a specific message queue. The "Library" prompt allows you to fully qualify the message queue name.

5.3.9 Sending a Break Message

You may wish to send a message that will be seen immediately, as in the case of a system emergency. You may do this by sending a break message. A break message will "break" into the user's display and show the message. This is done through the use of the Send Break Message (SNDBRKMSG) command. This command is shown here.

```
SNDBRKMSG MSG('SIGN OFF IMMEDIATELY') TOMSGQ(*ALLWS).
```

As you can see, the parameters for this command are very similar to the parameters for the SNDMSG command. One difference is that you cannot send a break message to a user profile, only to a workstation message queue. Another possible value for the "To work station message queue" (TOMSGQ) is special value *ALLWS, which means send the break message to all workstation message queues. This is used when you must immediately reach all users on a system.

The "Message queue to get reply" (RPYMSGQ) defaults to *QSYSOPR, the system operator's message queue. You may also specify another message queue and the "Library" if needed.

Enter the appropriate values and press <ENTER>. The message will be sent to the workstation message queues specified and will break into the display.

6

Basic Editing with the Source Entry Utility (SEU)

The Source Entry Utility (SEU) is the primary text editor for the AS/400. While there are other text editors that may be used from third-party vendors, SEU is almost always a part of the OS/400 licensed programs.

Basic SEU is an old text editor. A form of SEU (although different from the full screen SEU on an AS/400) has been in use for IBM midrange computers since the early S/3X days. SEU is available in both the native AS/400 mode and the System/36 Execution Environment. This chapter will explain the native AS/400 mode of SEU.

Different methods allow access to SEU. One method is to use the Start Source Entry Utility (STRSEU) command. Another is to start with the Start Programmer Menu (STRPGMMNU) command. This command also provides access to other functions. Both of these methods will be discussed in this chapter. A third alternative for starting SEU is through the Programming Development Manager or PDM. PDM is described in Chapter 12 ("Programming Development Manager (PDM)").

SEU is used to edit members in a source file. A source file is a physical file that has an attribute of *SRC. No other files may be edited with SEU. If information that is contained in a nonsource file needs to be changed, use the Data File Utility (DFU) or a data file-oriented editor. Another technique that will work for some files is to copy the data file (using CPYF) into a source file, edit the data, and then copy the information back to the data file. This technique will only work with files containing text information, not numeric information.

A source physical file usually contains many members, while a data physical file often has only one member. The members in a source physical file must have names that follow the standard OS/400 naming convention (one to ten character names) with the first being alphabetic.

6.1 STARTING SEU

The Start Source Entry Utility (STRSEU) command is used to directly access SEU. One of the important aspects of this command is that it "remembers" the last source file, library, and member that you last edited. You are also able to select the source file and member by specifying the special value *SELECT for either of these prompts.

The following is an example of the STRSEU command:

```
STRSEU SRCFILE(DEVELOP/QRPGSRC) SRCMBR(MAP014).
```

Note that this command provides for a "Source file" (SRCFILE) name and an optional "Library" name, a "Member" (SRCMBR) name, a "Type" (TYPE) name, and an "Initial option" (OPTION). The following is an example of the display that would be presented to you if you had specified a source file and library name, and specified *SELECT for the member name (see Figure 6–1):

```
  as400                                                      _ 8 X
Commands  Edit  Options  Help
                     Work with Members Using SEU

Source file . . . . . .   QRPGSRC          Library . . . . .   ASK
Position to . . . . . . . . . . . . . . . . . . . . . . . . .   _____
New member  . . . . . . . . . . . . . . . . . . . . . . . . .   _____
   Type for new member . . . . . . . . . . . . . . . . . . . .  RPG
   Text  . . . . . . . .   _____

Type options, press Enter.
   2=Edit       4=Delete     5=Browse        6=Print

Opt Member         Type        Text
 _  DS0100R        RPG         Sales order entry
 _  DS0200R        RPG         Sales order Maintenance
 _  DS0210R        RPG
 _  DS0220R        RPG         Sales order Maintenance - remove from rem count



                                                             Bottom
 F3=Exit         F5=Refresh       F12=Cancel       F14=Display date
 F15=Sort by date                 F17=Subset
                          (C) COPYRIGHT IBM CORP. 1981, 1996.
```

Figure 6–1: STRSEU with member list

The "Type" prompt can be one of several values. The type of the member may be only informative or, depending on the type, may also provide syntax checking. SEU can check the statements entered for proper syntax according to the member type.

Depending on the member type selected, SEU will also default to a specifically named source file, such as QRPGSRC for a member type of RPG. While SEU supports certain member types, you are free to choose any type you wish. Of course, SEU can only provide syntax checking for the member types it supports.

The types available to be used with SEU are:

BAS—BASIC language source. Syntax checked.

BASP—BASIC procedure. Syntax checked.

C—C language source. No syntax checking.

CBL—COBOL language source. Syntax checked.

CL—Command language source. Syntax checked.

CLP—Command language procedure. Syntax checked.

CMD—Command. Syntax checked.

DFU—Data File Utility program. Syntax checked.

DSPF—Display file DDS statements. Syntax checked.

FTN—FORTRAN source. Syntax checked.

ICFF—Intersystem Communication file DDS statements. Syntax checked.

LF—Logical file DDS statements. Syntax checked.

MNUDDS—DDS for menu. Syntax checked.

MNUCMD—Commands for menu. No syntax checking.

MNU—Menu. No syntax checking.

PAS—Pascal source. No syntax checking.

PF—Physical file DDS statements. Syntax checked.

PLI—PL/1 source. Syntax checked.

PRTF—Printer file DDS statements. Syntax checked.

QRY—Query/400 source. Syntax checked.

REXX—REXX procedure source. No syntax checking.

RPG—RPG source. Syntax checked.

RPT—Report source. Syntax checked.

SPDCT—Spelling dictionary. No syntax checking.

SQLC—SQL statements for C source. No syntax checking.

SQLCBL—SQL statements for COBOL source. Syntax checked.

SQLFTN—SQL statements for FORTRAN source. Syntax checked.

SQLPLI—SQL statements for PL/1 source. Syntax checked.

SQLRPG—SQL statements for RPG source. Syntax checked.

TBL—SQL table definition. No syntax checking.

TXT—Text. No syntax checking.

In addition, SEU provides syntax checking and allows different source types for the System/38 and System/36 environments.

The source file name and the library name are displayed. In addition, there are prompts for positioning the list and for new member options. The "Position to" prompt allows you to specify the member name (or partial member name) with which you wish the list to begin. You may also specify the special value *TOP to take you to the top of the list and special value *BOT to go to the bottom of the list. The "New member" prompt, which includes the "Type for new member" prompt and the "Text" prompt, allows you to choose a new member to edit.

Below these prompts is the list of members contained within the source file you specify. The member name, type, and associated descriptive text are displayed. Alternate displays are also available; these will be explained later in this section. In front of each member name is an option area. This option area is used to enter the option for the member. As with all OS/400 lists, multiple options may be specified or different members.

Option 2 allows you to edit the member. Option 4 will remove the member from the source file and provide confirmation prior to the deletion. Option 5 will allow you to browse the member, where you can see the contents of the member but are not able to make any changes. Option 6 will print the member and place the spooled file in the output queue specified for your interactive session.

Several function keys are available on this display. Standard function keys such as <F3> to Exit, <F5> to Refresh the display, and <F12> to Cancel the display are available, as well as functions that are unique to SEU.

These unique function keys are <F14> to display the member types, <F15> to sort by date or by name, and <F17> to provide a subset of the list of members. This subset option will display the Subset Member List display. The member list may be subsetted based on a partial name match, member type, date of creation or of last change, or member description.

To edit an existing member in the file, place a 2 in the "Option" area of the display. To edit a new member, place the "New member" name, the "Type for new member," and the optional "Text" description in the appropriate areas of the display. Press <ENTER> to edit the existing or new member. When you invoke SEU to create a new member, you are presented with the following screen. If you were editing an existing member, the member would be displayed, available for modifications. The following pages are an example of using SEU. Various functions will be explained and step-by-step screen examples will be shown (see Figure 6–2):

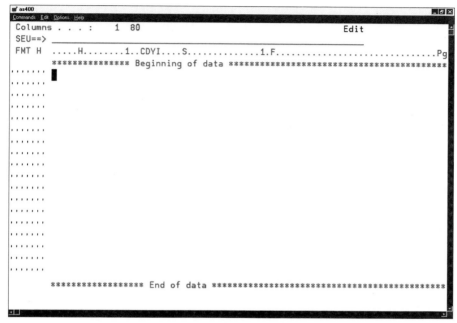

Figure 6–2: SEU initial screen for new member

The top of the screen shows several pieces of information. The left side shows the range of columns currently being displayed. Below the column range is a prompt line beginning with the characters SEU==>. This prompt does not allow you to enter system commands (<F21> does—more about that later), but does allow you to enter SEU commands such as FIND and column or row positioning. The library, file, and member names are shown on the right side of the top of the screen.

The "********** Beginning of data ************" line is at the top of the file. All statements will be entered in the input area below this line. The left side of the input area (which currently contains a series of " ' "characters (for example, """""""), is the SEU sequence number area. You usually do not need to be concerned about SEU sequence numbers as SEU will automatically increment the sequence numbers of newly added lines. They are a consideration, however, when trying to copy a source file member to a data file member or vice versa.

When copying a source file member to a data file member with the Copy File (CPYF) command, use the FMTOPT(*CVTSRC) option. This will remove sequence numbers when copying from a source member to a data member, and add sequence numbers when copying from a data member to a source member.

Sequence numbers are incremented by ten with each line added. New lines that are added between existing lines will be sequenced by .10 or .01, depending on the range in which they need to fit.

SEU is a full-screen editor, which means you are able to move your cursor around the screen to make changes. SEU on other IBM midrange systems (except the System/38) were line editors, meaning you could only edit one line at a time. Since the primary programming language used on the AS/400 (RPG/400) is a columnar-oriented language, SEU provides the capability of prompting for the many different RPG source types. The prompt key, <F4>, can be used to prompt for a format in which to enter information. Another technique to use the prompting function is to enter an SEU prompting command in the sequence number area and prompt for a specific format. The method of selecting prompt types is shown later in this chapter.

The following are examples of the full screen mode and nonfull screen mode displays (see Figures 6–3 and 6–4):

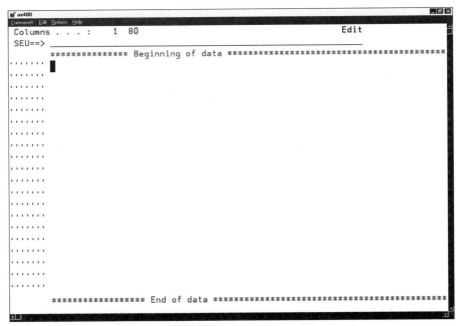

Figure 6–3: Full screen mode display

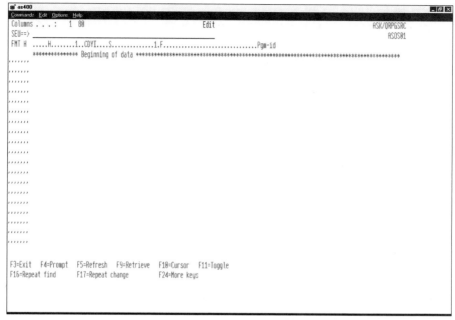

Figure 6–4: Nonfull screen mode display

6.2 EDITING OPERATIONS

Since SEU on the AS/400 is a full screen editor, movement around different portions of the member is accomplished through the use of the cursor keys and the roll keys. Basic editing operations will be explained in the following sections.

6.2.1 Cursor and Page Movement

Use the up and down cursor control keys to move to a previous or subsequent line from the current cursor position. Use the left and right cursor control keys to move a character at a time to the left or right. You can scroll to different portions of the member by using the

<ROLL UP> and <ROLL DOWN> keys. Remember that the roll keys work by "rolling" the member, not the screen. In other words, by pressing the <ROLL UP> key you will move the information "behind" the screen, not the screen position. The <ROLL UP> key will move downward in the source member (increasing sequence numbers), while the <ROLL DOWN> key will move upward in the member (decreasing sequence numbers). Note that this action can be changed by the system manager through a change in a system value.

6.2.2 Function Keys

Many functions keys are used in SEU. The available function keys and their meanings are as follows:

<F1>—Help. The help display is quite extensive in SEU. Context level help may be used, as well as a complete index to different help topics.

<F3>—Exit. The exit key will take you to the Exit display where you can specify options such as resequencing and printing. This screen, and an explanation of the options, is given later in this chapter.

<F4>—Prompt. Use the prompt key to prompt the line that the cursor is on. Note that in the event of a specific prompt (such as in RPG/400), the appropriate prompt will appear with the information already entered on the line in the proper positions.

<F5>—Refresh. This key is used to refresh the display. Any options (such as copy or move functions) that were entered will not be done if the screen is refreshed.

<F9>—Retrieve. The retrieve key will recall the last command that was typed on the SEU command line. This will not recall the last system command entered unless the system command line window (using <F21>) is currently displayed.

<F10>—Cursor. The cursor key will move the cursor between the input area and the SEU command line.

<F11>—Previous record. The <F11> key will provide a prompt for the previous record (line).

<F13>—Change session defaults. This key will display the SEU Session Defaults screen and allow you to make changes in the settings for this SEU session. Options such as uppercase only or lowercase allowed and number of lines to roll are specified using this screen. Changing the SEU environment is explained in the *Customizing the SEU Environment* section later in this chapter.

<F14>—Find and Change options. This function key will display a screen that allows you to specify information, such as the number of columns to search, or to search by the date a line was modified. This topic will be further discussed in the *Using the Find and Change Functions* section later in this chapter.

<F15>—Browse and Copy options. The <F15> key will display a screen that provides options to browse another source member (and enabling copying from that member) or to view a spooled file. These functions will be explained in the *Utility Operations* section later in this chapter.

<F16>—Repeat Find. The repeat find key will allow you to repeat the searching operation specified through the use of the SEU FIND command or specified from the Find/Change options display.

<F17>—Repeat change. The repeat change function will repeat the last change operation specified.

<F18>—DBCS conversion. This function key will convert between double-byte character set characters and standard characters.

<F19>—Left. The left function key will display the screen of characters that are to the left of the current cursor position.

<F20>—Right. The right function key will display the screen of characters that are to the right of the current cursor position.

<F21>—System command. This function key will display a window in which system commands may be entered. The window will be displayed until the <F3> key is pressed to exit the window function. Any system command may be entered, including calling a program.

<F23>—Select prompt. This function key provides a display where a prompt may be selected for use. This is very useful for columnar-oriented languages such as RPG/400. After the appropriate prompt has been selected, SEU will return to the input screen and provide the prompt requested. This screen is shown later in this chapter.

<F24>—More keys. Since all the function keys cannot be shown on the screen at one time, the <F24> key will show the different function keys and a short description of the function.

6.2.3 Inserting Lines

New lines are inserted into a new or existing member by overtyping the letter I in the sequence number area. The letter I, in either upper or lowercase, will insert a blank line following the line in which the I was entered. The sequence number where the I was overtyped will not be affected.

Multiple lines may be inserted by specifying a number after the I character. The following example shows five lines being inserted into an RPG/400 source member. Note that if nothing is entered on the inserted lines, they will not be added to the source member. In other words, you cannot add multiple blank lines to a member; you need to specify at least one blank space on each line (see Figure 6–5):

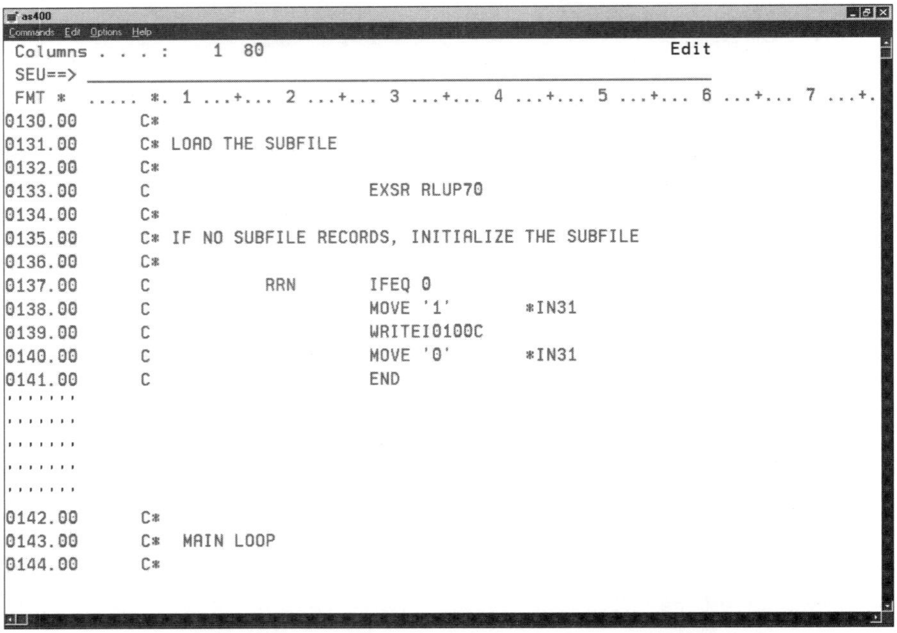

```
as400                                                                    _ 6 ×
Commands  Edit  Options  Help
  Columns . . . :    1  80                                    Edit
  SEU==> _____
  FMT *  ..... *. 1 ...+... 2 ...+... 3 ...+... 4 ...+... 5 ...+... 6 ...+... 7 ...+.
0130.00      C*
0131.00      C* LOAD THE SUBFILE
0132.00      C*
0133.00      C                  EXSR RLUP70
0134.00      C*
0135.00      C* IF NO SUBFILE RECORDS, INITIALIZE THE SUBFILE
0136.00      C*
0137.00      C         RRN      IFEQ 0
0138.00      C                  MOVE '1'       *IN31
0139.00      C                  WRITEIO100C
0140.00      C                  MOVE '0'       *IN31
0141.00      C                  END
''''''''
''''''''
''''''''
''''''''
''''''''

0142.00      C*
0143.00      C*   MAIN LOOP
0144.00      C*
```

Figure 6–5: SEU example showing a 5 line insert

The IP code, for input with the prompt, may also be used. In addition, an insert command may be entered in the format IPx, where the x is the prompt code. Prompting is explained in a subsequent section in this chapter.

6.2.4 Copying and Moving Lines

Statements within an SEU member may be copied or moved to another location in the member. An SEU copy will make a duplicate of the line in another location in the source member, while a move will change the position of the line within the member. A copy will produce a new line, while a move will delete the original line and copy the line to a different location.

A copy or move is performed by placing appropriate characters in the sequence position area of the lines to be copied or moved. The character for a copy is a C, and the character for a move is M. Associated with the copy or move characters are the target characters. The target characters may be either A to copy or move the line after the line with the A in the sequence number area, or a B to move or copy the line before the target line.

Enter a C for copy or an M for move on the source line, and an A for after or a B for before on the target line. After the appropriate characters have been entered into the sequence number area, press the <ENTER> key. This will perform the copy or move. Remember that you can use <F5> to refresh the screen before the <ENTER> key is pressed. This will refresh the screen and cancel the pending copy or move.

A block copy or move may be performed by specifying CC or MM at the beginning of the block of lines, and CC or MM at the end of the block of lines.

The following is an example of a copy operation. Note that the lines to be copied have the CC characters in the sequence number area, and the target line has an A in the sequence number area. This will copy the block of lines delimited by the CC characters to after the line with the A (see Figure 6–6):

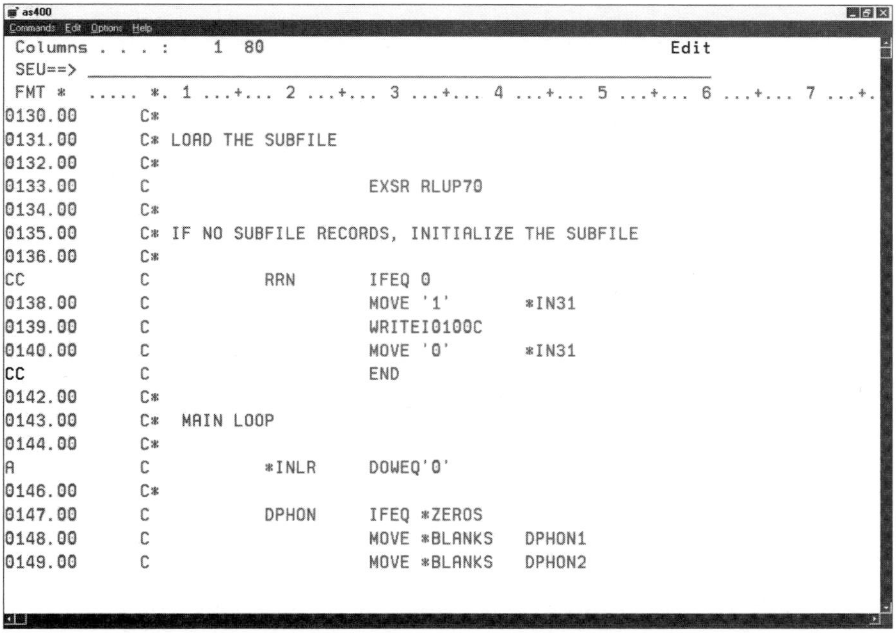

Figure 6–6: Before and after block copy operation

6.2.5 Deleting lines

Lines may be deleted from a source member by entering a D or DD (for a block delete) in the sequence number area of the line(s) to be deleted. This will permanently remove the lines from the source member.

Enter a D to delete a single line or a DD at the beginning of a block and a DD at the end of a block to delete a group of lines.

The following is an example of deleting several lines from a source member (see Figure 6–7):

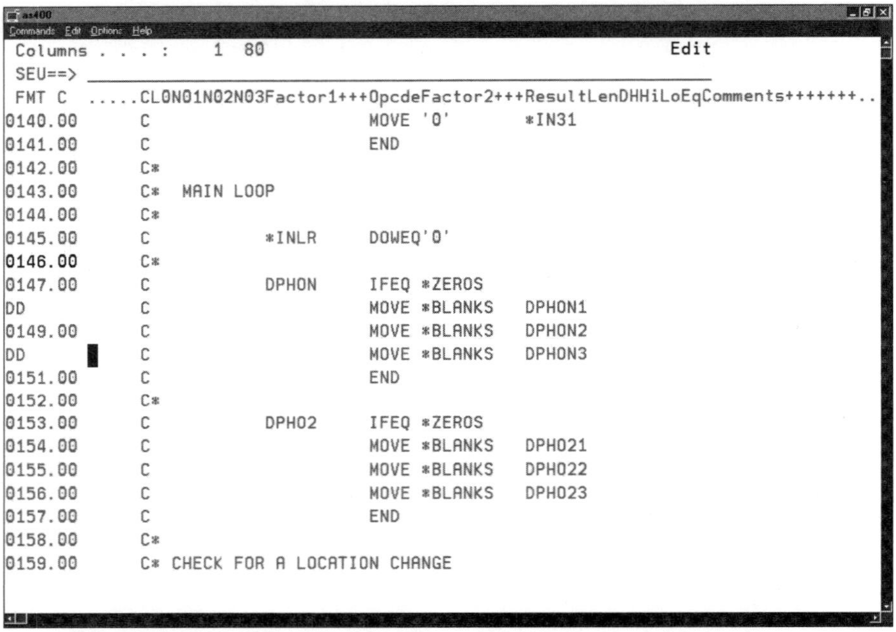

```
as400                                                                    _ 8 X
Commands  Edit  Options  Help
 Columns . . . :    1  80                                        Edit
 SEU==> _____
 FMT C  .....CLON01N02N03Factor1+++OpcdeFactor2+++ResultLenDHHiLoEqComments+++++++..
0140.00    C                        MOVE 'O'       *IN31
0141.00    C                        END
0142.00    C*
0143.00    C*  MAIN LOOP
0144.00    C*
0145.00    C          *INLR         DOWEQ'O'
0146.00    C*
0147.00    C          DPHON         IFEQ *ZEROS
DD         C                        MOVE *BLANKS   DPHON1
0149.00    C                        MOVE *BLANKS   DPHON2
DD         ▮ C                      MOVE *BLANKS   DPHON3
0151.00    C                        END
0152.00    C*
0153.00    C          DPHO2         IFEQ *ZEROS
0154.00    C                        MOVE *BLANKS   DPHO21
0155.00    C                        MOVE *BLANKS   DPHO22
0156.00    C                        MOVE *BLANKS   DPHO23
0157.00    C                        END
0158.00    C*
0159.00    C* CHECK FOR A LOCATION CHANGE
```

Figure 6–7: Before and after of deleting three lines from a member

6.2.6 Other Line Commands

Other line commands may be entered in the sequence number area, including setting tabs, excluding lines, shifting lines, and other commands. The following is a list of SEU line commands:

A, Ax

After (target)

> Use this command to copy or move lines after this line; it establishes the target line. The Ax command will repeat the command, creating duplicates of the copied line(s).

B, Bx

Before (target)

Use this command to copy or move lines before this line. Establishes the target line. The Bx command will repeat the command, creating duplicates of the copied line(s).

C, Cx, CC, CR, CRx, CCR

Copy line

Use this command to copy the line or block of lines to a specified target. The Cx command will cause duplicates of the copied line. The CC command marks the beginning and end of a block of lines to copy. The CR command will retain the command upon completion.

COLS

Display columns

This command will display a column line.

D, Dx, DD

Delete lines

Use this command to delete a line. The Dx command will delete x number of lines. The DD command marks the beginning and end of a block of lines to delete.

F, Fff, F?

Display format line

This command will display a format line. The Fff command will display ff format. The F? will prompt for a format.

I, Ix, IF, IFx, IFff, IFffx, IF?, IF?x, IP, IPff, IP?, IS, ISx

Insert line

This command will insert a line. The Ix command will insert x number of lines. IF will insert a line and display the current format. The IFff command will insert a blank line and display the ff format. IP will insert a line and prompt using the previous line's format. The IS command will insert a line and initialize the line as the skeleton line.

L, Lx, LL, LLx, LT, LLT, LLTx

Shift data left

> This command will shift data in the line to the left. If data is in the column to be shifted, the shift will terminate. The Lx command will shift data x characters to the left. The LL command will shift a block of data. The LT command will shift data to the left and truncate any data in the first x columns.

M, Mx, MM

Move line

> This command will move the line or block of lines to a specified target. The Mx command will cause duplicates of the moved line. The MM command marks the beginning and end of a block of lines to move.

O, Ox, OO

Overlay (target)

> The overlay line command specifies a target for a move or copy operation. The target line will be overlaid by the source line. The Ox command will overlay x number of times. The OO command indicates the beginning and end of a block of lines to overlay.

P, Pff, P?

Display prompt

> This command will show the line in a format. The Pff command will display the line in the ff format. The P? command will display the format prompt screen.

R, Rx, RR, RRx, RT, RRT

Shift data right

> The command will shift data in the line to the right. If data is in the column to be shifted, the shift will terminate. The Rx command will shift data x characters to the right. The RR command will shift a block of data. The RT command will shift data to the right and truncate any data in the last x columns.

RP, RPx, RPP, RPPx

Repeat line

> The RP command will repeat the source line. The RPx command will repeat the line x times. The RPP command marks the beginning and ending of a block of lines to repeat.

S

Skeleton line

> This command creates a skeleton line of the line specified.

SF, SFx

Show first record

> This command will show the first line of an excluded group. The SFx command will show the first x lines from an excluded group.

SL, SLx

Show last record

> This command will show the last line of an excluded group. The SLx command will show the last x lines from an excluded group.

TABS

Set/display tabs

> The TABS command will allow you to set and display tab settings. Specify TABS on the SEU command line or the Change Session Defaults screen.

W, Wx

Window to line

> The window command will window to column 1. The Wx command will window to column x.

X, Xx, XX

Exclude line

> The exclude command will exclude a record. This will cause the record
> not to be displayed, but will not remove the record from the member. The
> Xx command will exclude x lines. The XX command marks the beginning
> and end of an excluded block of lines.

+, +x

Roll display forward

> This command will roll the display one line forward. The +x command
> will move the display x lines forward.

−, −x

Roll display backward

> This command will roll the display one line backward. The -x command
> will move the display x lines backward.

x

Go to line

> Specifying a number in the sequence number area will move the display
> so that the specified line number is at the top of the screen.

6.2.7 Formats and Prompts

Certain languages require source statements to be entered in certain positions. RPG/400, the
most popular programming language on an AS/400, has definite requirements for column
positions of variables and operation codes. SEU provides a method for specifying and
prompting for the format to be used when entering new source lines or modifying existing
source lines.

Prompting the format for a statement will provide a split screen display where the
upper part of the screen shows the statement being prompted and the lower portion of the
screen is the prompt.

Different techniques may be used to specify a format for a member. One technique is to
use the prompt key, <F4>. Pressing <F4> while the cursor is on a statement will split the screen
and place the information from the source statement into the correct fields in the prompt.

SEU knows what prompt should be used by a combination of the member type and the statement type. RPG/400 has many different statement types that may be used. SEU will examine position 6 in the statement line for an RPG/400 source member. Position 6 contains the specification type which determines which prompt should be displayed.

This technique will not work for a new statement being entered. In this case, you could place the characters "IPx" in the sequence number area with the "x" being replaced by the format desired. After working with SEU for some time one becomes familiar with the common format codes. SEU also provides an option to determine the proper format code. You can display a screen with the available format codes for the specific member type by pressing the <F23> function key. The following is an example of pressing the <F23> function key (see Figure 6–8):

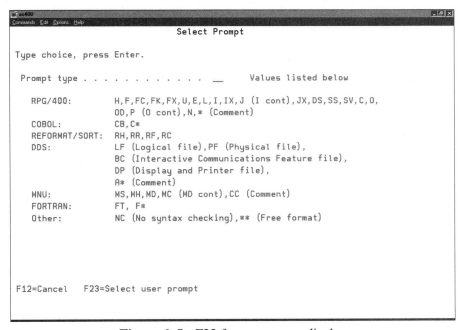

Figure 6–8: F23 format prompt display

Prompts may be entered for RPG/400 statements, COBOL statements, SORT specifications, Data Description Specifications (DDS), Menu (MNU) statements, FORTRAN statements, a free format, and a no syntax checking format. Multiple formats are available for the different statement types.

RPG/400 has many different format types due to the different types of specifications in the language. The standard H, F, E, I, C, and O formats exist, as well as continuation formats. Continuation format characters follow the primary format character and allow appropriate information to be entered for continuation or special statements. For instance, the I format will allow you to enter the information for the record portion of an Input specification, while the J format allows entry of field information.

After the appropriate format code has been entered, press the <ENTER> key to return to the editing screen. The correct format will be prompted on the display.

SEU can identify errors when entering source statements based on the format type. Since SEU knows the format type, syntax checking will show an error if incorrect information is entered. This will not find all of the compilation errors that may occur, but grammatically incorrect statements will be identified. SEU shows the incorrect portion of the statement in reverse video, making the error obvious. The following is an example of a syntactically incorrect statement (see Figure 6–9):

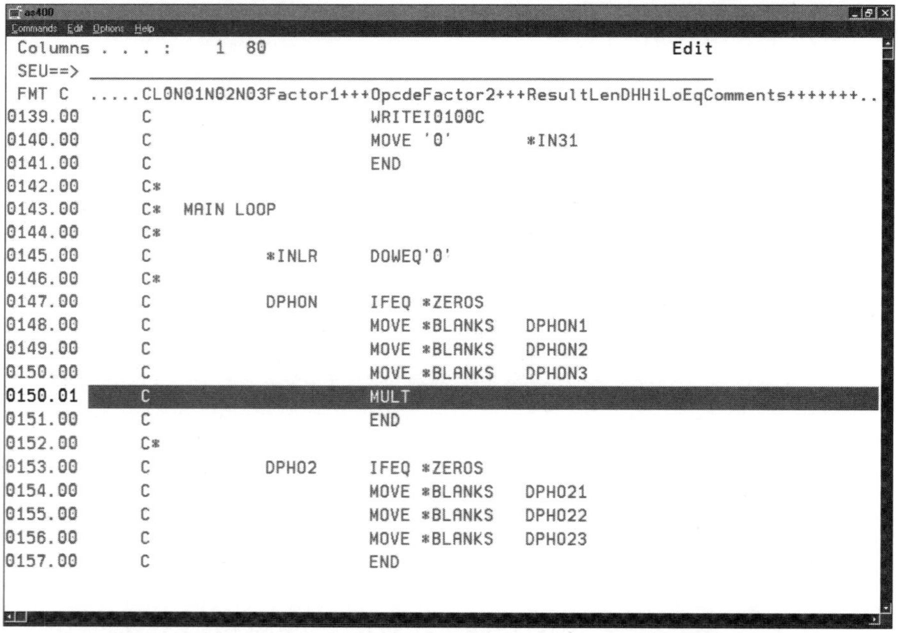

Figure 6–9: Missing factor 2 with RPG MULT operation

The RPG/400 operation code MULT (multiplication) allows an optional entry in Factor One (column 18) and requires entries for the Operation Code (column 28), Factor Two (column 33), and the Result Field (column 43). In this example, Factor Two is missing. The field in error (columns 33 through 42) is shown in reverse video and an error message is shown at the bottom of the screen. SEU also places the cursor at the point where it detected the error.

You could then prompt the line (with <F4>) to enter the correct information. You do not need to prompt the line; you could simply use the cursor keys to move to the error area and correct the error. In fact, many people that are familiar with SEU and the type of member that they are editing use the full screen mode than the prompt mode.

Remember that SEU will only perform syntax checking for certain types of members. These members were listed earlier in this chapter. If SEU does not support syntax checking for the member type, or if the format type is NC for no checking, or if you type ** for free format, SEU will not perform syntax checking. In addition, you can specify when SEU will perform syntax checking. This is explained in a following section, *Customizing the SEU Environment*.

6.2.8 SEU Command Line

The SEU command line (SEU==>) allows you to enter SEU commands. These commands may also be entered by using function keys, but the SEU command line allows a shortcut if you know the command you need to execute. The <F10> key will toggle between the statement input area and the SEU command line. The <F9> key will recall the last SEU command line command entered. Commands that may be used, and their abbreviations, if available, are:

FIND (F)—This command will allow you to specify a string of characters to search. You may also access the FIND command by using the <F14> key and accessing the Find/Change options screen. You cannot specify a date search when using the SEU command line, but most other search options are available. To find a string from SEU command line input, enter the find command in the following form:

FIND string direction search columns.

The only required parameter is the string for which you are searching. The optional direction may be one of the following: N or NEXT for the next occurrence, P or PREV for the previous occurrence, F or FIRST for the first occurrence, L or LAST for the last occurrence, or A or ALL for all occurrences. The search parameter may be either X to search excluded lines, or NX to search the lines that are not excluded. The columns parameter allow you to specify the beginning and ending columns in which to search. If the ending column number is omitted, the search will be from the specified starting position to the end of each record (the remaining columns).

Since the only required parameter is the search string, a find command such as FIND CUST would search for the next occurrence of the string CUST in the nonexcluded lines within the entire record. Using an asterisk (*) for the search string will cause SEU to search for the previously entered string. This is handy when changing direction, as in FIND * PREV, which will find the string previously entered, but will search backwards for the previous occurrence.

CHANGE (C)—The CHANGE command will allow you to change strings of characters in the source member. You may also access the CHANGE command from the Find/Change Options screen which is accessible by using the <F14> function key. As with the FIND command, most search options are available.

The format for using the CHANGE command from the SEU command line is

CHANGE fromstring tostring direction search columns.

The "fromstring" is the string that you are searching for in order to change, and the "tostring" is the string that will replace the fromstring. The direction, search, and columns parameters are the same as described above for the FIND command.

SAVE—This command will save the contents of the source member to disk, but will not exit SEU. You may also save, but not exit, SEU via the End of SEU Options screen, which is accessible with the <F3> key. The SAVE command is good for saves of work in progress. You will be prompted for confirmation if any syntax errors exist in the member.

CANCEL (CAN)—This command cancels any editing that has been done to this member and returns you to the selection list. You may also cancel any changes via the End of SEU Options screen, which is accessible with the <F3> key. You will be prompted for confirmation if you have changed the member or if there are any pending line operations when the CANCEL command is issued.

FILE—This command saves the member you are editing and exits SEU after the member is saved. You may also save and exit SEU via the End of SEU Options screen, which is accessible with the <F3> key. You will be prompted for confirmation if any syntax errors exist in the member when the FILE command is issued.

TOP (T)—The TOP command will move the display to the top or start of the source member.

BOTTOM (B)—This command will move the display to the bottom of the source member.

SET (S)—The SET command allows you to establish certain SEU environment options. These options may also be set with the Change Session Defaults function key, <F13>. You may set the following environment options:

MATCH—This option forces a match in case when searching or replacing.

CAPS—The CAPS option allows only uppercase entry.

TABS—This option allows you to use the tab settings that were established with the TABS line command.

ROLL—The ROLL option will accept an entry that determines the number of lines to roll when the <ROLL UP> or <ROLL DOWN> keys are pressed. Available entries are H(alf), F(ull), C(ursor), D(ata), or a number from 1 to 999.

EXPERT—This option will place SEU into expert mode, which means that a full screen entry area will be shown on the display and no format indication or function key legends will appear. SET EXPERT YES establishes full screen mode; SET EXPERT NO is the standard display showing function keys and complete prompts.

SHIFT—This option determines if data may be shifted with a CHANGE operation. SET SHIFT YES allows data to be shifted, while SET SHIFT NO restricts data from being shifted during a change operation. Please see the "Allow data shift" discussion in the next section for futher details.

6.2.9 Using the Find and Change Functions

The find and change functions are accessed by pressing the <F14> key. The Find/Change options display allows you to specify the strings for which to search and, optionally, a replacement string. The following is an example of the Find/Change options screen (see Figure 6–10):

```
 as400                                                              _ 8 X
Commands  Edit  Options  Help
                          Find/Change Options

  Type choices, press Enter.

    Find  . . . . . . . . . . . .    _____
    Change  . . . . . . . . . . .    _____
    From column number  . . . . . .   1_         1-80
    To column number  . . . . . . .   80_        1-80 or blank
    Occurrences to process  . . . .   1          1=Next, 2=All
                                                 3=Previous
    Records to search . . . . . . .   1          1=All, 2=Excluded
                                                 3=Non-excluded
    Kind of match . . . . . . . . .   2          1=Same case
                                                 2=Ignore case
    Allow data shift  . . . . . . .   N          Y=Yes, N=No

    Search for date . . . . . . . .   97/03/08   YY/MM/DD or YYMMDD
      Compare . . . . . . . . . . .   _          1=Less than
                                                 2=Equal to
                                                 3=Greater than

  F3=Exit   F5=Refresh      F12=Cancel   F13=Change session defaults
  F15=Browse/Copy options   F16=Find     F17=Change
```

Figure 6–10: Find/change options display

You can also achieve the find and change functions through the SEU command line FIND and CHANGE commands; however, this display provides an easier method of entering the parameters needed for a find or change.

Specify the value to search for in the first parameter, "Find." The second parameter, "Change," is only used if you wish to find a character string and then change it to another character string. Note that the display will be positioned at the point where the character string is found.

The next two parameters, "From column number" and "To column number," delimit the beginning and ending column numbers in which the search will take place. If these parameters are specified, only the character strings that are found within the column limits will be identified.

The "Occurrences to process" parameter can have three values. The value for this parameter determines the direction and number of occurrences for the search. A value of 1 (the default) will search for the next occurrence of the "Find" value. A value of 2 will search for all occurrences, which is usually used for Change operations. A value of 3 will search backwards for the previous occurrence of the "Find" value.

The "Records to search" parameter determines which records to search. A 1 in this parameter is the default and indicates that all records (either forward to the end of the member or backward to the beginning of the member) will be searched. A value of 2 means that only records that have been excluded will be searched, while a value of 3 indicates that only the nonexcluded records will be searched.

The "Kind of match" parameter determines the case checking of the search. If a 1 is entered for this parameter, then only strings that are exactly the same case as the "Find" value will be located. A value of 2 allows the search to disregard case checking.

The "Allow data shift" parameter refers to changing information in the member. A value of Y indicates when the search finds the specified string; if the string that is to replace the found string is a different size than the found string, the data in the record will be shifted to accommodate the new string. This may pose a problem will a columnar language, such as RPG/400. A value of N will prohibit the data shifting.

The last parameter, "Search for date," allows a search for the date information that is a part of every record of the member. Enter the date information in the form of year, month, and day (YY/MM/DD or YYMMDD). The other portion of this parameter, "Compare," allows you to specify a 1 to search for the records that are less than the specified date, a 2 to find the records that are equal to the specified date, or a 3 to search for records that are greater than the date specified. Note that you cannot search for a "Find" string and a date with the same search.

After the appropriate search and change parameters have been specified, press the <ENTER> key. This will initiate the search. After the first occurrence has been found, press the <F16> key to search again. The <F16> key and the <F17> key (for changes) may be entered at any time during an edit session. This allows you to enter the search or change information once and use the information for searches at other times during the edit session.

6.3 UTILITY OPERATIONS

SEU provides utility operations that allow you to browse a member, copy all or a portion of another member, view spooled files, or view the entries in an output queue. The viewing of spooled files is especially valuable to a programmer, who can split the screen, view compiled output, and search for error in the compile listing.

These options are accessible from the SEU editing screen by pressing <F15>. The following screen is shown for the Browse/Copy options display (see Figure 6–11):

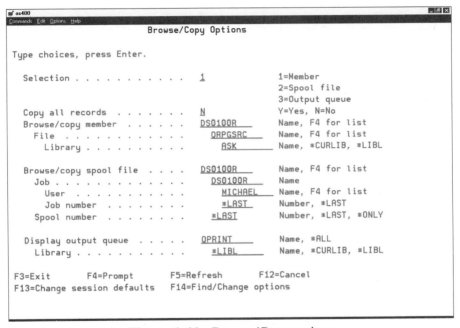

Figure 6–11: Browse/Copy options

The "Selection" screen will accept a value of 1 to browse or copy another member, a value of 2 to view a spooled file, and a value of 3 to examine the entries in an output queue.

6.3.1 Browsing or Copying Members

A "Selection" of 1 requires the "Browse/copy member" information to be completed. The first parameter, "Copy all records," refers to copying a member. The default of N will allow you to specify a beginning and ending block of records to copy from the member. An entry of Y will copy all the records in the member. In either case, a target for the copy must be specified.

After entering the appropriate value for the "Copy all records" parameter, specify the "Browse/copy member," the "File" in which the member is located, and "Library" in which the file is located. Note that if the library is specified, the file may be selected from a list by pressing <F4> in the "File" prompt area. If the library and file are specified, the member may be selected from a list by pressing <F4> in the member prompt area.

After the appropriate member has been selected, press <ENTER> to begin the browse/copy operation. The screen will be split horizontally, with the original member being displayed on the top half of the screen, and the member being browsed on the bottom half of the screen. The split display is shown below (see Figure 6–12):

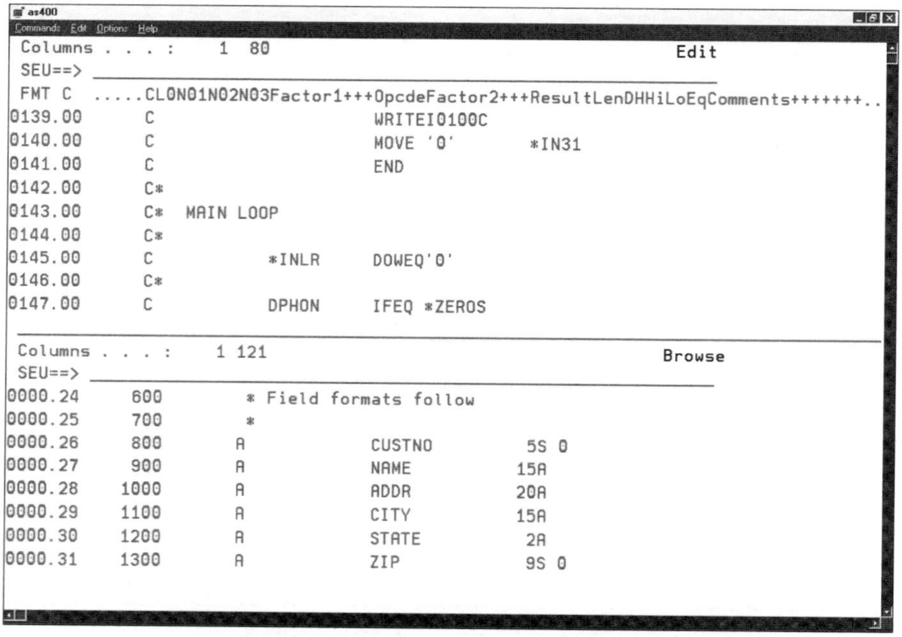

Figure 6–12: Browse/copy split screen display

After browsing the member, press <F12> to cancel the browse operation and restore the screen to display the original member.

Copying records from another member utilizes the same technique as browsing, with the addition of specifying the records to copy and the location for the copied records in the original member. Specifying the location of the records to be copied is done in the same manner as copying records within a member. Enter an A in the sequence number area to copy the records after the specified line, or B to copy the records before the line.

If Y was the response to the "Copy all records" prompt, and a target location has been specified in the original member, then all records from the "Browse/copy member" will be copied to the original member without SEU displaying the split screen. If all records are to be copied and a target is not specified, or if N was the response to the "Copy all records" prompt, the split screen display will be shown. Select the target for the records to be copied.

If N was the response to the "Copy all records" prompt, you must select the records to be copied. Select the records by entering the CC line command in the beginning and ending records to be copied (or a single C if only one record is to be copied). Enter the source record(s) indication and the target location, then press <ENTER> to copy the record(s) to the original member.

The following illustrates a split screen display with the block of source records and the target location specified (see Figure 6–13):

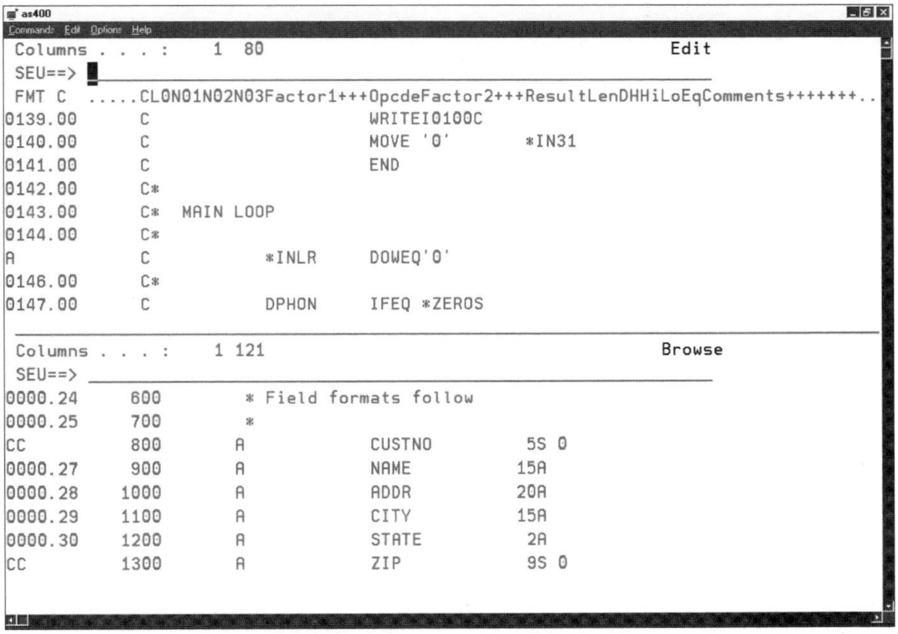

```
as400                                                                    _ 8 X
Commands  Edit  Options  Help
  Columns . . . :    1   80                                         Edit
  SEU==>
  FMT C  .....CLON01N02N03Factor1+++OpcdeFactor2+++ResultLenDHHiLoEqComments+++++++..
 0139.00       C                        WRITEIO100C
 0140.00       C                        MOVE '0'        *IN31
 0141.00       C                        END
 0142.00       C*
 0143.00       C*  MAIN LOOP
 0144.00       C*
 A             C            *INLR       DOWEQ'0'
 0146.00       C*
 0147.00       C            DPHON       IFEQ *ZEROS

  Columns . . . :    1  121                                         Browse
  SEU==>
 0000.24        600           * Field formats follow
 0000.25        700           *
 CC             800         A             CUSTNO          5S 0
 0000.27        900         A             NAME            15A
 0000.28       1000         A             ADDR            20A
 0000.29       1100         A             CITY            15A
 0000.30       1200         A             STATE           2A
 CC            1300         A             ZIP             9S 0

```

Figure 6–13: Split screen with source and target shown

6.3.2 Browsing or Copying a Spooled File

Entering option 2 for the Browse/Copy Options "Selection" will allow you to view a spooled file. An entry must be made for the "Browse/copy spool file" parameter. Other parameters that are required are the "Job" name, the "User" name, the "Job number," and the "Spool number."

SEU will default the parameters for viewing a spooled file to the appropriate entries needed to identify a batch compilation of the member being edited. This allows the results of the last compilation of the member to be displayed without requiring the entry of the job-related information.

The spooled file will be shown in the bottom half of the split screen, with the member being displayed in the upper half of the screen. You may move your cursor into the lower half of the screen and use the <ROLL UP> and <ROLL DOWN> keys to examine different portions of the spooled file.

You may search for errors in the compiled listing when the spooled file is being displayed on the split screen. Note that this is the only time a spooled file may be searched for errors; in other words, displaying a spooled file outside of this SEU facility will not provide error message searching.

Search for errors by specifying *ERR as the search string on the SEU command line with the FIND command. This special FIND option will search for error messages within a spooled file. The advantage of this technique is that you can view the error messages in the lower half of the screen and make changes to the member in the upper half of the screen. This saves the programmer from having to print out the compile listing and make changes while viewing the listing.

Another advantage of using SEU to review the compiler listing is that more information is available here than from the printed listing. When an error is located using FIND *ERR, the compiler error message is highlighted at the bottom of the screen. You may place your cursor on this highlighted message and receive the second level help associated with the message.

Copying lines from the spooled file into a source member is accomplished in the same way as copying from one member to another. Specify the lines to copy with block CC line commands, and the target for the copy with the A or B line command. This can be a handy method of providing documentation for an on-line system—produce print screens of the displays used, then copy the spooled files into a source member for further editing.

The following is an example of a split screen display of a source member with its corresponding compilation listing (see Figure 6–14).

6.3.3 Viewing an Output Queue

Entering option 3 for the Browse/Copy Options "Selection" will allow you to view the contents of an output queue. This selection executes the Work with Output Queue (WRK-OUTQ) command. This is the same display as shown in Figure 5-1 in Chapter 5 ("The AS/400 System Environment").

6.4 CUSTOMIZING THE SEU ENVIRONMENT

You may change the defaults for your SEU session by specifying commands on the SEU command line or by pressing <F13>. The changes made to the session environment are only in effect for the current SEU session. The following is an example of the Change Session Defaults screen accessed by using the <F13> key (see Figure 6–15).

```
as400                                                          _ □ ×
Commands Edit Options Help
 Columns . . . :    1  80                              Edit
 SEU==>  _____
 FMT A*  .....A*. 1 ...+... 2 ...+... 3 ...+... 4 ...+... 5 ...+... 6 ..+... 7 ...+.
         *************** Beginning of data *******************************************
0001.00       *
0002.00       * Record format REC01
0003.00       *
0004.00    A          R REC01
0005.00       *
0006.00       * Field formats follow
0007.00       *
0008.00    A             CUSTNO      5S 0
 _____
 Columns . . . :    1 121                              Browse
 SEU==> █_____
0000.40
0000.41  SEQNBR  *...+....1....+....2....+....3....+....4....+....5....+....6....+..
0000.42   400              R REC01
0000.43   800                CUSTNO      5S 0B    COLHDG('CUSTNO')
0000.44   900                NAME       15A  B    COLHDG('NAME')
0000.45  1000                ADDR       20A  B    COLHDG('ADDR')
0000.46  1100                CITY       15A  B    COLHDG('CITY')
0000.47  1200                STATE       2A  B    COLHDG('STATE')
```

Figure 6–14: Member and compile listing

```
as400                                                          _ □ ×
Commands Edit Options Help
 EDTOPTS                    Change Session Defaults

 Type choices, press Enter.

   Amount to roll . . . . . . . . . .   H        H=Half, F=Full
                                                 C=Cursor, D=Data
                                                 1-999
   Uppercase input only . . . . . . .   Y        Y=Yes, N=No
   Tabs on  . . . . . . . . . . . . .   N        Y=Yes, N=No
   Increment of insert record . . . .   0.01     0.01-999.99
   Full screen mode . . . . . . . . .   N        Y=Yes, N=No
   Screen size  . . . . . . . . . . .   1        1=27x132, 2=24x80
   Source type  . . . . . . . . . . .   PF
   Syntax checking:
     When added/modified  . . . . . .   Y        Y=Yes, N=No
     From sequence number . . . . . .   _____  0000.00-9999.99
     To sequence number . . . . . . .   _____  0000.00-9999.99


   Set records to date  . . . . . . .    /  /    YY/MM/DD or YYMMDD
                                                            More...
 F3=Exit     F5=Refresh    F12=Cancel
 F14=Find/Change options   F15=Browse/Copy options
```

Figure 6–15: SEU change session defaults screen <F13>

The first option that may be modified is the "Amount to roll." This option may have a value of H to roll a half page, a value of F to perform a full page roll, a value of C to perform the roll so that the line the cursor is on will be at the top or bottom line of the display when the roll key is pressed, or a value of D for a roll of a full page minus one line. This option is analogous to the SET ROLL command entered on the SEU command line.

The next option, "Uppercase only," determines if upper and lowercase or only uppercase information may be entered into the input area. While most AS/400 programming languages require uppercase for variable names and operation codes, you may wish to enter literal strings or comments in lowercase. A value of Y for this option will change all information entered to uppercase, while a value of N will allow both upper- and lowercase entry.

The "Tabs on" options determines if the tab key may be used. This may be helpful when trying to place information into columns. RPG/400 uses specific column positions for the entry of variable names and operation codes, so tabs are usually not used. A value of Y for this option will enable tabs, and a value of N (the default) will disable tabs.

The "Increment of insert" option determines the sequence numbering for new lines that are added to the source member. You may specify a range from 0.01 to 999.99, with .01 being the default.

The "Full screen" option may have a value of Y or N. A Y value indicates that SEU should use all of the screen for the statement input area. This eliminates the function key legend and the format indication. The function keys used by SEU are still active even though the function key legend may not be visible. While you can see more of the input area, you would have to go to this screen and set the "Full screen" option to N to identify the function key usage. This function can be accessed through the SEU command line SET EXPERT command.

The "Screen size" option identifies to SEU the size of the screen that your display will support. Some terminals are a full 27 row by 132 column display. If your terminal supports this size display, enter 1 for this option. If your terminal supports the more standard 24 rows by 80 columns, enter a 2 for this option.

The "Source type" option contains the source type that SEU is using for syntax checking and prompting. You may change the source type as needed; you may do this if the defaults you selected when you started SEU are not correct. You will probably receive an informational message from SEU if this option is changed. The message will show that the error count may be wrong due to the source type change. You should disregard this message if you have changed this option to the correct source type.

The next option, "Syntax checking," refers to when and where you want the source statements to be checked for correct syntax. The first portion of this option, "When added/modified," determines if the statements should be checked for when they are added or modified ('Y'). If they are not checked at this time, they will be checked when you attempt to change the member. The next two portions of this option, the "From sequence number" and "To sequence number," determine the sequence numbers where you want syntax checking to occur. You may specify a value of zero to 9999.99, or leave these entries blank. Blank entries indicate to SEU that all source statements should be checked for proper syntax.

The "Set records to date" option will set all the statements in the source member to have the same changed date. This could be used to "fix" the member's statements at a given point so that any new statements that were added or modified would be apparent. Specify a date in YY/MM/DD order, meaning year, month, and day. The statements have their changed date in YY/MM/DD order so that they can be searched by date.

Press the <ENTER> key after you have changed any of the session defaults needed. These defaults will be in effect for the current SEU session.

6.5 SYSTEM COMMAND LINE

The system command line is accessible by pressing <F21>. A window will overlay the display in which you may enter any valid OS/400 command. The <F4> key may be used to prompt the command, the <F9> key is used to retrieve the previous command, and the <F12> key is used to cancel the window. The following is an example of the system command line (see Figure 6–16):

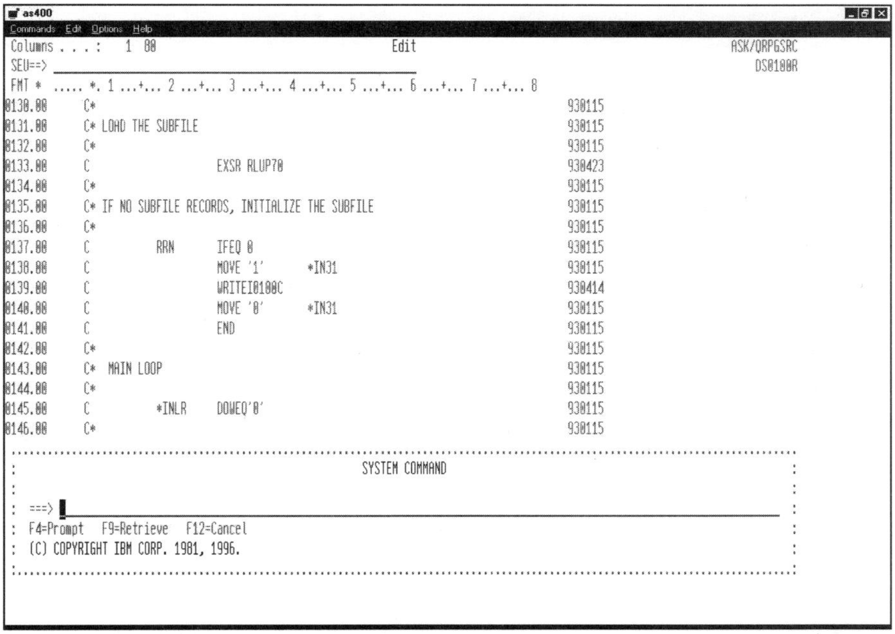

Figure 6–16: F21 system command line overlaying an RPG/400 edit

6.6 GETTING HELP IN SEU

The help facility is SEU is very robust and covers the topics well. Some of the topics covered are the use of function keys, the line commands (in detail), the SEU command line commands, and the different option screens available in SEU.

Help is available by pressing the <HELP> key or by pressing <F1>. Moving to the top of the help display will allow you to view all the SEU help available. You may press <F2> to view the expanded help, and <F14> to print the help text.

The following is an example of a help screen from within SEU (see Figure 6–17):

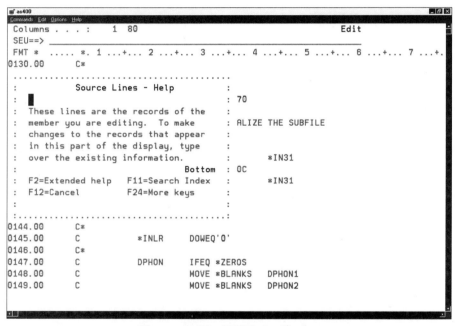

Figure 6–17: SEU help display

6.7 EXITING AND SAVING YOUR WORK

The SEU Exit display is reached by pressing the <F3> key. This display will allow you to save the member, create a new member, resequence the member, and other utility operations. The save and cancel options that are available on this screen are also available with SEU command line commands. The following illustrates the SEU exit screen (see Figure 6–18):

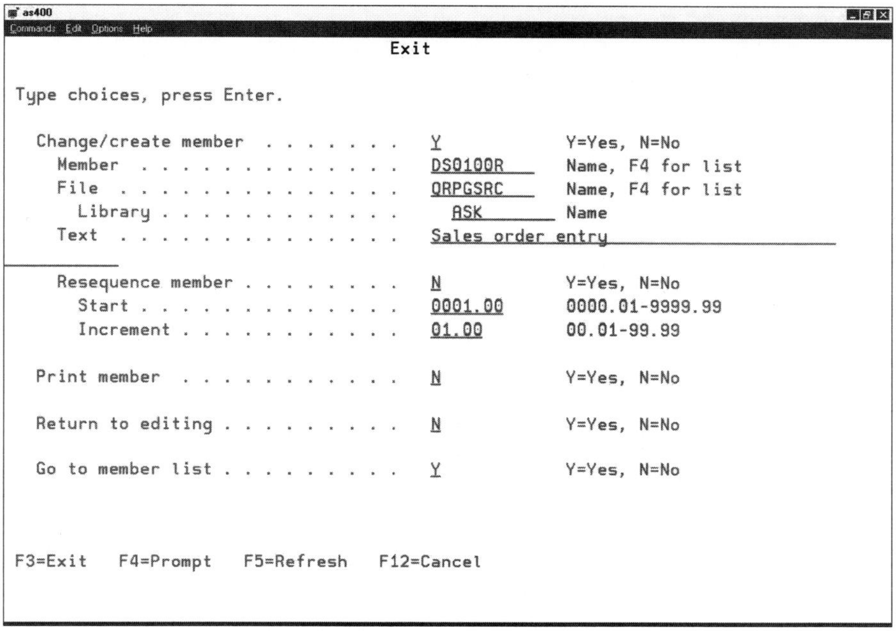

```
 as400                                                            _ [] X
 Commands  Edit  Options  Help
                                Exit

 Type choices, press Enter.

     Change/create member  . . . . . . .    Y            Y=Yes, N=No
        Member  . . . . . . . . . . . .    DS0100R      Name, F4 for list
        File  . . . . . . . . . . . . .    QRPGSRC      Name, F4 for list
          Library . . . . . . . . . . .    ASK          Name
        Text  . . . . . . . . . . . . .    Sales order entry

     Resequence member . . . . . . . .    N            Y=Yes, N=No
        Start . . . . . . . . . . . .    0001.00      0000.01-9999.99
        Increment . . . . . . . . . .    01.00        00.01-99.99

     Print member  . . . . . . . . . .    N            Y=Yes, N=No

     Return to editing . . . . . . . .    N            Y=Yes, N=No

     Go to member list . . . . . . . .    Y            Y=Yes, N=No



 F3=Exit    F4=Prompt    F5=Refresh    F12=Cancel

```

Figure 6–18: SEU exit screen

The first parameter, "Change/create member," requires a response of Y or N. This parameter will default to Y if you have made any changes to the member. If you do not wish to save the changes made to the member, change this parameter to N.

The next parameter specifies the name of the "Member," "File," and "Library" in which to save the member. If you wish to change the name of the member, to overlay another member with this member, or to change the library or file name, change the information associated with this prompt. Note that you may use the <F4> key to prompt for the file or member name.

The "Text" parameter is the optional fifty character text description that is to be associated with this member. It is a good practice to specify the "Text" description so you may more easily identify the member in a list of members.

The "Resequence member" parameter allows you to specify Y to have SEU resequence the line numbers or N for SEU to bypass the resequencing. The next parameters, "Start" and "Increment," will allow you to specify the starting line number for resequencing and the sequencing increment. These parameters default to 0001.00 and 01.00, respectively. Resequencing the member will not change the order of the statements in the source member.

When the "Print member" prompt defaults to N the SEU will not print the member when exiting SEU. A response of Y will cause SEU to print the member. The spooled file will be produced in your default output queue.

The next prompt, "Return to editing," will normally default to N, meaning that SEU should return to the command line or menu from which SEU was invoked. An entry of Y will be placed in this parameter if any syntax errors exist in the member. You may also place a Y in this prompt if you wish to save the member and then return to editing; however, it may be simpler to use the SEU command line SAVE command.

The "Go to member list" prompt also defaults to N, meaning that SEU will not produce a list of the members in the file. You may wish to change the value of this parameter to Y if you are editing several members in a file.

Enter the appropriate information (usually the defaults are appropriate) and press the <ENTER> key to process the request.

6.8 THE PROGRAMMER'S MENU

Another method of invoking SEU is through the use of the Programmer Menu. This menu provides access to several program development functions. This menu will be briefly described in this section.

The Programmer Menu is invoked with the Start Programmer Menu (STRPGMMNU) commands shown here (see Figure 6–19).

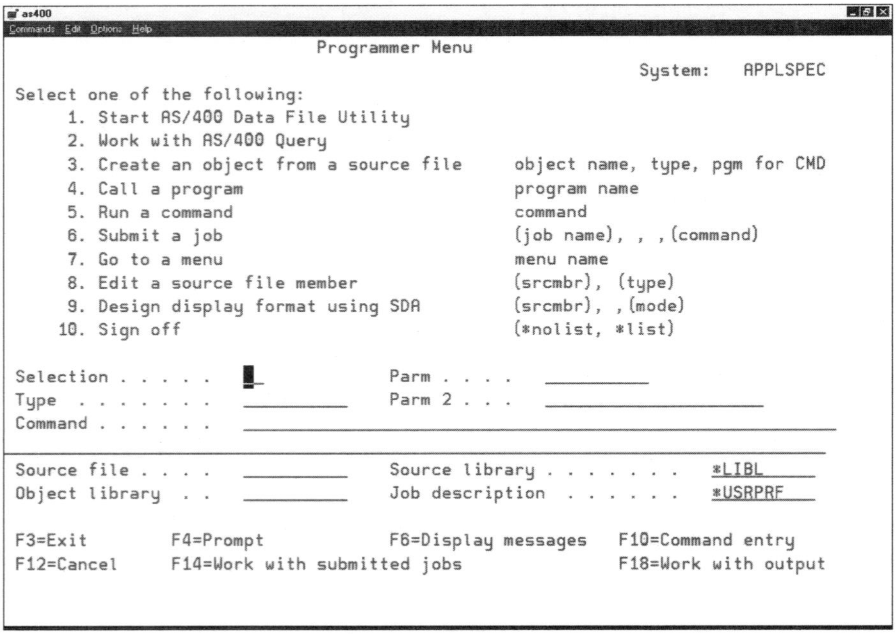

Figure 6–19: STRPGMMNU display

The Programmer Menu provides the following options:

Option 1 will execute the Start Data File Utility (STRDFU) command to allow you to create, list, or update a data file.

Option 2 will run the Start Query (STRQRY) command to allow you to query a data file.

Option 3 will create an object from a source member. The appropriate create command (CRT...) is chosen by OS/400 based on the "Type" parameter.

Option 4 will call the program specified in the "Parm" field.

Option 5 will run the command specified in the "Command" prompt.

Option 6 will submit the job specified in the "Parm" field. The submitted job will use the job description specified on the "Job description" parameter.

Option 7 will display the menu specified in the "Parm" field.

Option 8 will invoke SEU. Optional parameters are the names of the member specified in the "Parm" field and the "Type" of the member. Required parameters are the name of the "Source file" and the "Source library."

Option 9 will execute the Start Screen Design Aid (STRSDA) command to allow you to create, change, and test display files.

Option 90 will run the SIGNOFF command.

Function keys that are available from the Programmer Menu are the standard <F3> to exit, <F4> to prompt a command, and <F12> to cancel. Other function keys are <F6> to display messages (DSPMSG command), <F10> for the command entry screen (CALL QCMD command), <F14> to Work with Submitted Jobs (WRKSBMJOB command), and <F18> to Work with Output (WRKSPLF command).

7

Command Language Programs

7.1 WHAT IS A CL PROGRAM?

A CL (Command Language) program is a compiled object that contains standard OS/400 commands which accomplish a task on the system. CL programs often contain additional commands that are not available interactively. These additional commands provide program control, file (and other object) access, and error handling. CL program source statements are created with the Source Entry Utility (SEU) or with any source editor available for an AS/400. The source file that is used for CL program members may be any name, but the OS/400 default name is QCLSRC. The member should type CLP for Control Language Program.

Almost every task that is performed by a CL program could be performed if you entered the commands, one at a time, into the system. An advantage of CL programs is that they automate repetitive processes. Rather than having an operator or user enter many commands interactively, a CL program can execute the individual commands in a group. You can save time since the commands are all executed consecutively as a group.

Another advantage of CL programs is that the commands will be executed the same way each time you run the program. The number of errors can thus be reduced.

An example of using a CL program is the initial program. An initial program is usually a CL program, though it may be written in any supported language. This program, which is accessed as a result of the "Initial program" (INLPGM) parameter in a user profile, is executed each time a user signs on to the system. While the initial program may provide almost any system function, initial programs are often used to establish a library list and the current library, associate system objects with the interactive session (such as output queues, message queues, and session attributes), or run an application. A sample initial program is provided later in this chapter.

Programming in CL is similar to programming in any language. CL programs contain program flow commands, mathematical and logical operators, parameter passing, string handling operators, and the ability to call other programs. CL programs do not need to be complex to be effective. Many CL programs are only a few lines in size, but provide consistent, accurate processing.

CL programs may also be very complex and involved. While a programming language such as RPG or C may be better suited to complex programming requirements, a CL program has benefits in that it provides an excellent access to system resources. Another programming language may not provide this capability. An example of a CL program that is used to start system printers is provided later in this chapter.

A common use for CL programs is to call many other programs. This type of CL program provides a "controlling" function for other programs. Programs may be executed in a certain order, often with the output of one program used as the input to another. A CL program such as this may be used for job streams, nightly routines, or system development. An example of a CL program that executes other programs is shown later in this chapter.

7.2 GUIDELINES FOR WRITING CL PROGRAMS

A CL program may be as structured or as unstructured as any other type of program. While a CL program does not have the control structures that may be found in other programming languages (such as the DO WHILE/UNTIL, CASE, or FOR structures), a CL program may be written in a structured manner.

Producing small sections of code that perform a single function promotes structure. The technique of creating small CL programs that accomplish a single action also lends itself to structured programming.

An important guideline for writing CL programs is to use comments. The CL program may contain as many comments as needed to identify the intent and the action of the CL program. A comment in a CL program is accomplished by using /* to begin a comment, and */ to end the comment. The following is an example of comments in a CL program:

```
/* This line is a comment */.
```

Any characters may be placed between the comment character groups.

Another significant aid in writing CL programs is documentation. While a program listing may be good (although they tend to get out of date quickly), having a description of the CL programs, the inputs and outputs, and a change history is very helpful. This allows the user or operator to determine which programs should be executed, and also what type of recovery is appropriate if the system or application fails.

Debugging CL programs (and their associated commands) requires a thorough knowledge of the CL program, the commands the CL programs are executing, and a good working knowledge of OS/400. Since a CL program interacts closely with the resources of the system, you should have a basic understanding of the AS/400.

One technique to debug CL programs is to use the Display Job Log (DSPJOBLOG) command. You will be able to see the CL statements as they execute. Use the Display Job (DSPJOB) command to identify files that are open and any messages that the program is passing to the user, or messages that OS/400 is passing to the CL program. The Log CL Program (LOGCLPGM) parameter for a job may need to be adjusted so the appropriate amount of information is being written to the job log.

The OS/400 debugging command Start Debug (STRDBG) may also be used, along with the associated command to set breakpoints (Add Breakpoint (ADDBKP)) and to see the contents of variables [Display Program Variable (DSPPGMVAR)]. Remember to enclose the CL variable name in quotation marks when using the DSPPGMVAR command.

7.3 CL PROGRAM COMPONENTS

A CL program must begin and end with the PGM and ENDPGM statements. The PGM statement marks the beginning of the program and provides the mechanism for passing parameters into the program. The CALL command (described below) passes the optional parameters into the CL program and the PGM statement receives the parameters. An example of the PGM statement is

```
PGM PARM(&PRT).
```

This statement indicates the beginning of the program and accepts the &PRT parameter. The ENDPGM statement marks the end of the program. This statement is simply ENDPGM, with no other information (except an optional label) allowed on the line.

All variables used in a CL program must be declared with the DCL statement. A CL variable name begins with an ampersand (&). The DCL statement has required parameters for the name and type of the variable, and optional parameters for the length and an initial value. Use the prompt <F4> key to prompt the DCL statement. You will find that the prompt key is invaluable when creating a CL program since you can use the prompt key on all commands and statements.

Prompting the DCL statement provides the following display (see Figure 7–1).

The "CL variable name" (VAR) entry determines the name of the variable. The name must begin with an ampersand and may be a total of ten characters long.

The "Type" (TYPE) parameter determines the data type of the CL variable and may be one of three special values. *CHAR indicates the variable is a character variable. Character variables may contain numeric, alphabetic, or special characters. String operators (explained later) may be used to manipulate the data contained within the variable. A variable of type *DEC means that the variable is a decimal variable and will contain numeric information. Numeric operations may be used on this data type. *LGL means a logical variable; it may contain a value of 1 (for true) or 0 (for false). Logical variables are used as "flags" for decisions within the program.

The "Length of variable" (LEN) parameter has two entries: "Length" and "Decimal positions." The "Length" entry contains the length of the variable being declared; the "Decimal positions" (only valid for variables of type *DEC) entry contains the number of decimal positions. The "Length of variable" may be left blank as OS/400 will provide defaults for the variable length. The default for a character variable is 255, fifteen digits with nine decimal positions for a decimal variable, and one for a logical variable.

```
as400                                                                  _ 8 X
Commands  Edit  Options  Help
                        Declare CL Variable (DCL)

Type choices, press Enter.

Label . . . . . . . . . . . . .      _____
CL variable name . . . . . . .       _____    Variable name
Type . . . . . . . . . . . . .       _____           *DEC, *CHAR, *LGL
Length of variable:
   Length . . . . . . . . . . .       _____          Number
   Decimal positions  . . . . . .     _____          Number
Initial value  . . . . . . . . .     _____
                                     _____
                                     _____
                                     _____
                                     _____
                                     _____
                                     _____  . . .


                                                              More...
F3=Exit   F4=Prompt   F5=Refresh   F12=Cancel   F13=How to use this display
F24=More keys
```

Figure 7–1: DCL statement prompt

The remaining parameter, "Initial value," (VALUE) will allow you to establish a beginning value for a variable. This is an optional parameter. If left blank, OS/400 will initialize character variables to blank, decimal variables to zero, and logical variables to false (0).

The following are examples of declaring variables:

```
/*    A character variable */.
      DCL   VAR(&CHARVAR) LEN(25)

/*    A decimal variable with 2 decimal positions and an   */
/*    initial value of 4.95.   */
      DCL   VAR(&DECVAR) LEN(8 2) VALUE(4.95)

/*    A logical variable        */.
      DCL   VAR(&LGLVAR)
```

The contents of a CL variable are changed with the use of the Change Variable (CHG-VAR) command. This command may be used to perform string manipulation or numeric operations on variables. The syntax for the CHGVAR is

```
CHGVAR VAR(&varname) VALUE(newvalue).
```

where &varname is the CL program variable to be changed, and newvalue is the new value to be placed in the CL variable. The newvalue may be a constant, a variable, or an expression. Examples of using the CHGVAR command are

```
/*   Replacing the contents of one variable with        */
/*   another.                                            */
CHGVAR VAR(&OUTFILE) VALUE(&INFILE)


/*   Replacing the contents of a variable with a        */
/*   constant.                                           */
CHGVAR VAR(&BASE) VALUE(12)


/*   Replacing the contents of a variable with an       */
/*   expression.                                         */
CHGVAR VAR(&LOOP) VALUE(&LOOP + 1)
```

Numeric CL variables may be used in mathematical operations. CL uses the four basic numeric operators: addition, subtraction, multiplication, and division. These operators will be most likely used in a CHGVAR statement to assign a new value to a CL variable. The standard algebraic symbols for the operations used are: + for addition, − for subtraction, * for multiplication, and / for division.

The mathematical operations may be as complicated as you wish, but you may find that a language with better mathematical capabilities (RPG, COBOL) may be more suitable for complex math. The expressions are processed from left to right, with operations in parentheses performed first. Multiplication and division have a higher order of precedence than addition and subtraction. Some examples of using mathematical operations in CL are

```
/*   A simple accumulator.                                  */
CHGVAR VAR(&LIBSIZE) VALUE(&LIBSIZE + &NEWSIZE)


/*   Decrementing a counter.                                */
CHGVAR VAR(&COUNT) VALUE(&COUNT - 1)


/*   A more complex statement.                        */
CHGVAR VAR(&TEMP) VALUE((&BAL + &INAMT - &OUTAMT) / &RATIO)
```

Just as CL programming provides a mathematical capability, CL programming also provides the ability to manipulate string variables and constants. The *CAT, *BCAT, and *TCAT operators all concatenate strings together.

The *CAT operator will link two entire strings, with the resulting string containing the complete contents of both strings. The *BCAT operator concatenates two entire strings, placing a space in between. The *TCAT operator concatenates two strings and trims the trailing blanks from the first string with no spaces between the strings. The following examples will clarify the different string operators:

```
/*    An example of concatenation.                           */
DCL VAR(&FIRST) LEN(4) VALUE('Mary')
DCL VAR(&LAST) LEN(3) VALUE('Doe')
DCL VAR(&FULL) LEN(8)

CHGVAR VAR(&FULL) VALUE(&FIRST *CAT &LAST)
/*    After this line of code has executed, &FULL           */
/*    will have the value "MARYDOE."                         */

CHGVAR VAR(&FULL) VALUE(&FIRST *BCAT &LAST)
/*    After this line of code has executed, &FULL           */
/*    will have the value "MARY DOE."                        */

CHGVAR VAR(&FULL) VALUE(&LAST *CAT "," *CAT &FIRST)
/*    After this line of code has executed, &FULL           */
/*    will have the value "DOE, MARY."                       */

/*    Concatenation with trailing blanks.              *
DCL VAR(&FIRSTNAME) LEN(10) VALUE('Mary       ')
DCL VAR(&LASTNAME) LEN(3) VALUE('Doe')
DCL VAR(&FULLNAME) LEN(14)

CHGVAR VAR(&FULLNAME) VALUE(&FIRSTNAME *CAT &LASTNAME)
/*    After this line of code has executed, &FULLNAME        */
/*    will have the value "MARYDOE."                    */

CHGVAR VAR(&FULLNAME) VALUE(&FIRSTNAME *BCAT &LASTNAME)
/*    After this line of code has executed, &FULLNAME        */
/*    will have the value "MARYDOE."                    */

CHGVAR VAR(&FULLNAME) VALUE(&FIRSTNAME *TCAT &LASTNAME)
/*    After this line of code has executed, &FULLNAME        */
/*    will have the value "MARYDOE".                    */
```

The strength of CL programming lies in the ability to execute OS/400 commands. Almost all commands may be used in a CL program. Certain commands may not be used (such as some "work with" commands), but the majority of commands may be included in a CL program. In addition, several commands may only be used in a CL program. Commands such as CHGVAR and RCVF (Receive File) are only valid within a CL program, as are declaratives such as DCL (Declare) and DCLF (Declare File).

Some commands that are used often in CL programs are the "Start" (STR...) commands, commands to end a process (END...), create commands (CRT...), commands to copy objects (CPY...), and display commands (DSP...). Display commands deserve special attention as they provide a flexibility for CL programs that allow them to interact with objects on the system.

Many (but not all) display commands have an output (OUTPUT) parameter and an output file (OUTFILE) parameter. The OUTPUT parameter can contain a value of *NONE, which will prevent the output being displayed on the screen. The OUTFILE parameter directs the output (that is usually displayed) into a physical file on the system. A CL program could then access the data stored in this physical file. OS/400 uses predefined record and file formats for the output file data. These predefined formats may be examined to determine the record and field names. These records and fields would be used in a program.

An example of this technique could be a CL program that executes a Display File Description (DSPFD) into an output file. This output file could then be opened and read to obtain file characteristics such as the names of the members. The members could then be processed by sending them over a network to another AS/400.

Another use of this technique would be to use the Display Object Description (DSPOBJD) into an output file for certain object types. The resulting file could then be used to gather information about the objects on the system. While not all display commands provide the capability to direct their output to an output file, the commands that do have this capability provide a way to interact with the system.

7.4 PROGRAM FLOW CONTROL

The flow of a CL program is controlled through the use of the IF (and ENDIF) conditional statements and the GOTO (and label) statements. As mentioned earlier, CL programming does not provide the control structures as do other languages.

A conditional statement in CL uses logical operators. The logical operators available in CL programming are the standard operators available in most languages. The logical operators may be represented in algebraic format or in a Fortranlike format. The logical operators and the conditions they represent are

>	or	*GT	Greater Than
<	or	*LT	Less Than
=	or	*EQ	Equal To
>=	or	*GE	Greater Than or Equal To
<=	or	*LE	Less Than or Equal To
<>	or	*NE	Not Equal To

These operators are used in IF statements to provide decision making within the CL programming. The format for the simple IF statement is

```
IF (cond) THEN(stmt).
```

where cond is a condition between a variable or a constant and another variable or constant, and stmt is the statement (or group of statements) that will be executed if the condition evaluates to true.

The IF statement may execute a group of statements by using the DO and ENDIF constructs. The format is then

```
IF (cond) THEN(DO)
     stmt
     stmt
      .
      .
ENDIF .
```

The ELSE clause may be used to provide an alternate course of action if the condition evaluates to false. The ELSE clause may also be used with the DO construct to provide execution of a group of statements. The format for using the ELSE clause is:

```
IF (cond) THEN(stmt)
ELSE stmt
ENDIF

or

ELSE(DO)
     stmt
     stmt
      .
      .
ENDIF .
```

Examples of IF statements are

```
/*   Compare a variable to a constant. If the      */
/*   statement is true, change the value of variable    */
/*   &RATE to 100.                                  */
IF (&NAME *EQ 'Bill') THEN CHGVAR VAR(&RATE) VALUE(100)
/*   Execute several statements if the condition is*/
/*   true.                                          */
IF (&RATE = 100) THEN(DO)
     CALL '*LIBL/ADDPAY'
     DLTF QTEMP/TEMPFILE
     CHGVAR VAR(&DONE) VALUE('1')
ENDIF
```

```
/*    Execute a statement if the condition is    true,*/
/*    execute a different statement if false.             */
IF (&TITLE = 'President') THEN CHGVAR VAR(&BOSS) VALUE('1')
ELSE CHGVAR VAR(&BOSS) VALUE('0')
```

Using the above IF statement as an example can show how a variable defined as type logical (*LGL) may be used. If variable &BOSS was declared as a logical, the following IF statement would be valid:

```
IF (&BOSS) THEN some CL statement....
```

A logical variable may have a value of 1 for true and 0 for false. The IF statement needs then to test only the variable.

Statements in a CL program may be bypassed or executed repetitively by transferring control to a label. Any CL statement may have a label. The label consists of one to ten characters followed by a colon (label:). The CL statement would then follow the label.

A label exists primarily as a target for the GOTO statement. The GOTO statement is often used in conjunction with an IF statement to provide an alternate flow of control through the CL program. The format of the GOTO command is

```
GOTO CMDLBL(label).
```

Note that the colon is not included when referencing the label in the GOTO command. An example of the GOTO command used with the IF statement is

```
IF (&RATE *LT 5.00) THEN(GOTO CMDLBL(PASS))
other
      CL
        statements

PASS: continue with program.
```

Labels are used with the GOTO command to produce looping. This allows the CL program to repetitively execute commands until a condition has been reached. An example of looping in a CL program is

```
        CHGVAR VAR(&COUNT) VALUE(1)
TOP:    SNDMSG MSG('Sign off now!') TOUSR(*ALLACT)
        CHGVAR VAR(&COUNT) VALUE(&COUNT + 1)
        IF (&COUNT *LT 10) THEN GOTO(CMDLBL(TOP))
        other CL commands....
```

This (perhaps annoying) segment of CL code will send the message "Sign off now" to all active users ten times.

7.5 HANDLING ERRORS

Error handling within CL programs is accomplished through the use of the Monitor Message (MONMSG) command. This command will monitor for a message produced by OS/400 (or a user message) and take the specified action. The action specified may be no action; in this case, the MONMSG command exists to ignore the message.

   If an error message is sent to a CL program and the program does not monitor for the message, the CL program will be interrupted. The user executing the program (or the system operator for a batch job) will then need to respond to the message. The MONMSG command may eliminate the need for this user intervention.

   The format for the MONMSG command is

```
MONMSG MSGID(msgid) CMPDTA(compdata) EXEC(action)
```

where msgid is the message id of the message for which the program is monitoring, compdata is the compare data (which is optional), and action is the optional action to be taken when the message is encountered in the CL program.

   The "MSGID" parameter is the id of the monitored message. The appropriate message id may be found in the IBM CL Reference Guide. The "CMPDTA" parameter may be used if the message contains specific data for which you are comparing. The "EXEC" parameter may contain a CL command to be executed when the message is sent to the CL program. An example of using the MONMSG command is

```
MONMSG MSG(CPF0000).
```

   This MONMSG command will monitor for all error messages that may occur in a CL program. This message is the first message in the CPF series and serves to monitor for all messages that begin with CPF. You may monitor for other messages with this technique, such as RPG, CBL. In the example shown, the "EXEC" parameter is not specified, so no action will be taken if an error message occurs.

   An example of an action taken as a result of the message is

```
MONMSG MSG(CPF1234) EXEC(GOTO CMDLBL(EXIT)).
```

   Control will transfer to label "EXIT" if message "CPF1234" is encountered.

   The MONMSG command may be placed in two different places in a CL program. If the MONMSG command is placed at the top of the program (after any DCL statements and before the first executable statement), the action specified by that MONMSG command will be done if that message is encountered anywhere in the program. This is an example of global monitoring. If the MONMSG command is placed immediately following an executable statement, the MONMSG is only in effect for that statement. The same message could be encountered later in the program, but the previously encountered MONMSG will not be in effect.

7.6 CREATING CL PROGRAMS

CL programs are created with the Create CL Program (CRTCLPGM) command. CL programs may also be created from the "Create Object" option from the programmer menu (STRPGMMNU). The CRTCLPGM command uses several defaults that allow you to specify fewer parameters. Ensuring that the target library for the compiled object is your specified current library (*CURLIB) will enable you to specify only the program name. An example of the CRTCLPGM command is shown below

```
CRTCLPGM PGM(NIGHTCL) SRCFILE(TESTLIB/QCLSRC) .
```

The "Program" (PGM) and the associated "Library" parameter specifies the name and location of the compiled object to be created.

The "Source file" (SRCFILE) and the associated "Library" parameter specifies the name and location of the file that contains the member of CL program statements. Note that the "Source file" defaults to the IBM default of QCLSRC, and the "Library" parameter defaults to *LIBL.

The "Source member" (SRCMBR) is the name of the member that contains the CL source statements. This parameter defaults to *PGM, meaning the name of the source member is the same as the name of the program object to be created.

The "Text description" (TEXT) may contain up to fifty characters of descriptive text that identifies the program object. This parameter defaults to *SRCMBRTXT, which means that the text description for the program object should be the same as the description for the member that contains the source statements.

The "Source listing options" (OPTION) parameter allows you to specify options for the compile listing. The default is to list the source statements and all diagnostics.

The "Generation options" (GENOPT) parameter determines if the object should be produced if no errors are found in the compilation. The default is to produce the object. You may wish not to generate the object if you are compiling only to determine compilation errors.

The "User profile" (USRPRF) parameter determines if the authorities of the user of the program object (*USER, the default) should be used when executing the program, or if the authorities of the owner of the object (*OWNER) should be used. The default for this parameter is *USER. Note that the use of *OWNER may permit a security breach since the owner of the program could have different authorities than the user of the program.

The "Log commands" (LOG) parameter determines if the commands executed in the CL program should be logged into the job log when the program is executed. The default, *JOB, indicates that the attributes of the interactive or batch should be used to determine whether command logging should be done. The special value *YES or *NO will cause the commands to be logged or not logged, regardless of the job's attributes.

The "Allow RTVCLSRC" (ALWRTVSRC) determines if the source of the compiled program object may be retrieved by using the Retrieve CL Source command. This may be helpful if the source for the program is lost.

The "Replace program" (REPLACE) parameter defaults to *YES, which means that an existing program object of the same name will be replaced when the compilation is successful. *NO means that the existing program will not be replaced.

The "Target release" (TGTRLS) allows you to compile the program object to the current release of OS/400 (*CURRENT, is the default), the previous release (*PRV), or an earlier release.

The "Authority" (AUT) parameter defaults to *LIBCRTAUT, which means the authority associated with the library will be the authority for the object. Other authority values are available.

Specify the appropriate values and press <ENTER> to create the CL program. The compilation may be done interactively or in batch. A batch submission may be done with the Submit Job (SBMJOB) command or through the programmer menu. The compile listing will be placed in the output queue associated with your interactive session or the batch job.

7.7 EXECUTING CL PROGRAMS

CL programs are invoked with the OS/400 command CALL. The CALL command requires the name of the program (and optionally the library) to execute and an optional list of parameters that are to be passed to the program. An example of calling a CL program is

```
CALL STRPRINT PARM(PRT01).
```

Note that since a CL program executes OS/400 commands, the program would use the CALL statement to execute another program. This is how a CL program may be a controlling program for a job stream. The program that is to be called may be a CL program, an RPG program, or any program object that can be produced on the AS/400.

Parameters are passed to a CL program when the program is called through the PARM parameter of the CALL command. The general format is

```
CALL program-name PARM(parm1 parm2 etc).
```

The parameters specified in the PARM parameter are separated by a space. The CL program parameters are specified in the PARM statement in the order in which they are declared on the PGM statement in the CL program. The parameters passed should match in number and in type to the parameters that the CL program expects.

Character value parameters do not need to be surrounded with quotation marks unless the character value contains embedded spaces. A numeric parameter must be passed in packed decimal format. A number specified in packed decimal format is designated in hexadecimal format. An example of this format follows. The parameter being passed into the CL program is the number 123

```
CALL CLPROG PARM(x'123f').
```

This parameter properly passes the numeric value 123 into CL program CLPROG. If the number was passed into the CL program as the numeric value 123 [CALL CLPROG

PARM(123)], the command processor would interpret the number as x'F1F2F3 (display format) and the CL program would abort with a data decimal error when the parameter was accessed in the program.

A CL program may be executed either interactively or in batch. Executing interactively uses the CALL command, while executing in batch uses the Submit Job (SBMJOB) command. An example of using the SBMJOB command to call a CL program is

```
SBMJOB JOB(MYJOB) RQSDTA('CALL STRPRINT PARM(PRT01)').
```

The SBMJOB command uses a "Request Data" (RQSDTA) parameter to indicate the information that is passed to the batch job processor. The "Request Data" is the CALL command with the parameters of the CL program name and the parameters for the CL program.

Note the difference between a CL program (which is CALLed) and a command. The name of a command is entered on the command line; you do not need to indicate to OS/400 to "run" anything. Commands are discussed in more detail later in this chapter.

7.8 SAMPLE CL PROGRAMS

An example of an initial program is shown below. An initial program is specified in your user profile and is executed when you sign on to the system. While an initial program may contain any commands, they often are used to establish an environment. The following CL program will add entries to the library list, change the current library, establish an output queue, and execute another program. All error messages are monitored globally.

```
/*    Initial program for user ACCTUSER.              */
        PGM

/*    Monitor for all errors.                         */
        MONMSG MSGID(CPF0000)

/*    Add accounting files to the library list.    */
        ADDLIBLE LIB(ACCT_PROG)
        ADDLIBLE LIB(ACCT_FILE)

/*    Change the current library.                    */
        CHGCURLIB CURLIB(ACCT)

/*    Establish the output queue.                    */
        CHGJOB OUTQ(ACCTOUTQ)

/*    Call the accounting program.                   */
        CALL 'ACCTPGM'

    ENDPGM.
```

The next CL program example will start a printer. The printer to be started is passed in as a parameter to the program. The printer will be started and then changed to provide a file separator page. Messages are monitored for specific commands.

```
/*     Start the print writer to device specified.              */
           PGM             PARM(&PRT)

           DCL             VAR(&PRT) TYPE(*CHAR) LEN(10)
/*     Start the printer and monitor for writer already         */
/*     started.                                     */
           STRPRTWTR       DEV(&PRT) MSGQ(*REQUESTER)
           MONMSG          MSGID(CPF3310)

AGAIN:

/*     Change the writer to add a separator page.               */
           CHGWTR          WTR(&PRT) FILESEP(1) OPTION(*FILEEND)

/*     Monitor for the 'Writer not available for change'        */
/*     message. This message would result if the printer was    */
/*     still in the process of being started. If the message    */
/*     is issued, delay ten seconds and try again.              */
           MONMSG          MSGID(CPF3459) EXEC(DO)
               DLYJOB          DLY(10)
               GOTO            CMDLBL(AGAIN)
           ENDDO

       ENDPGM.
```

The next CL program is an example of a "controlling" CL program. This program executes several programs. If a program to be executed is not found, the program will issue a message and abort. The "program not found" message is monitored globally, with a program message sent and the program aborted if the message is encountered.

```
/*     Execute the nightly batch jobs.                      */
           PGM

/*     Abort if program not found error message encountered.   */
           MONMSG MSGID(CPD0170) EXEC(GOTO CMDLBL(ABORT))

/*     Execute the programs.                                   */
           CALL PGM(MERGE)
           CALL PGM(REBUILD)
           CALL PGM(REPORTS)

/*     If no errors have occurred, exit normally.              */
           GOTO CMDLBL(OK)

ABORT:     SNDBRKMSG MSG('Error in nightly jobs!') TOMSGQ(QSYSOPR)
OK:        ENDPGM.
```

7.9 WHAT IS A COMMAND?

Actions performed on an AS/400 by users are as a result of executing commands. You use commands for every action performed on an AS/400. A command name is a single word which is entered from a command line, executed from within a CL program, or executed from a menu.

A command is associated with a program in that the program is run when the command is executed. This association is established when the command is created. Just as a program can have parameters passed into it, a command may pass parameters into the associated program. Note that while any type of program may be associated with a command, CL programs are usually used.

A command may be only a simple method of executing a CL program by providing a single word to enter. A command may also be very complex and provide validity checks on the data entered as command keywords. A command merely provides an interface to a CL program. The interface is standard; however, all commands have the same appearance, use the same function keys, and operate in the same manner. This provides for consistency in the user interface. In addition, both IBM and user-written commands may be executed from a CL program.

Commands are often used to execute utility programs. Using commands to execute utility programs can reduce the amount of keying by the user by enabling execution with the entry of a single word. Use of a command can also ensure that the same programs and commands are used for each execution. A user may enter a command to execute several programs rather than calling each program individually. Commands may also provide a mnemonic aid for the user of the utility program. The user would not need to remember all the program names, just a simple mnemonic command name.

Utility programs are often used for saving libraries, moving members and files, starting jobs or devices, and other common system tasks. An example command that calls a utility program to start a printer is illustrated later in this chapter.

Commands are constructed in a similar manner as CL programs but have a very specific syntax. The source statements for commands are created with the Source Entry Utility (SEU) or any editor available on an AS/400. The source file that is used for command members may be any name, but the OS/400 default name is QCMDSRC. The member should be of type CMD for command.

Commands have several statements which may be used when constructing the command. Some of the command statements are used for validity and consistency checking between keyword values, while others are used for almost all commands. The CMD and PARM statements are used in most commands and are explained here.

CMD—This is a required statement and has a function which is similar to the PGM statement in a CL program. The CMD statement identifies the member as a command and provides the ability to use the PROMPT keyword. The PROMPT keyword is optional. The function of the PROMPT keyword is to display a prompt heading on the top line of the screen. An example of the CMD statement is

```
CMD PROMPT('Start Printer').
```

This prompt will be displayed on the top line of the screen if the command is prompted (<F4>).

PARM—This is an optional statement, but is common in commands. This statement accepts input to the command in the form of keywords. The information entered into the keyword is passed to the associated CL program when the user presses <ENTER>. The keyword definition is similar to the definition of DCL statements in CL programs. Some of the more common PARM entries for keywords are shown below. Prompting the PARM statement provides the following display (see Figure 7–2):

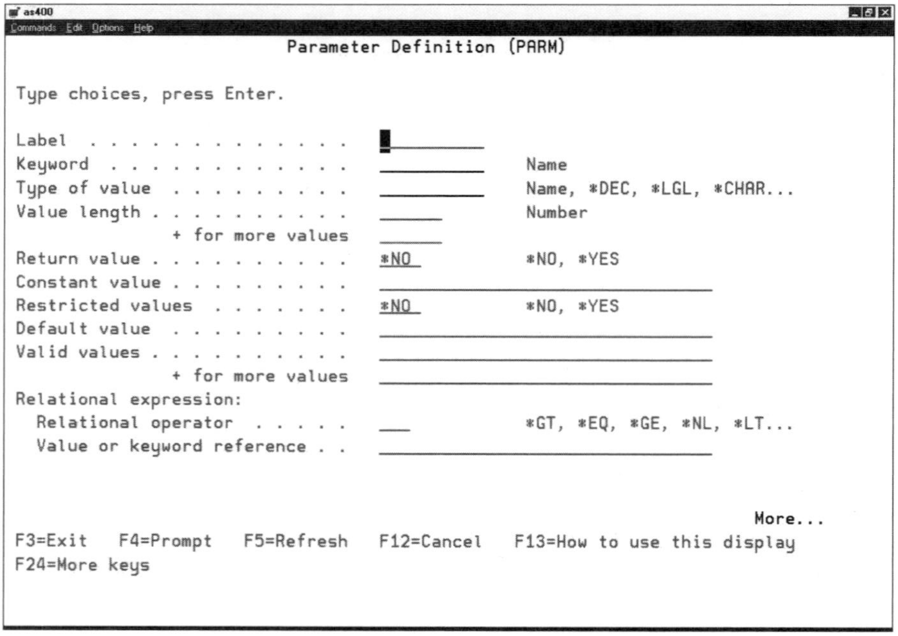

```
 as400                                                        _ 5 X
Commands  Edit  Options  Help
                      Parameter Definition (PARM)

 Type choices, press Enter.

 Label  . . . . . . . . . . . .   ▌_____
 Keyword  . . . . . . . . . . .   _____      Name
 Type of value  . . . . . . . .   _____      Name, *DEC, *LGL, *CHAR...
 Value length . . . . . . . . .   _____        Number
            + for more values    _____
 Return value . . . . . . . . .   *NO           *NO, *YES
 Constant value . . . . . . . .   _____
 Restricted values  . . . . . .   *NO           *NO, *YES
 Default value  . . . . . . . .   _____
 Valid values . . . . . . . . .   _____
            + for more values    _____
 Relational expression:
   Relational operator  . . . .   ___           *GT, *EQ, *GE, *NL, *LT...
   Value or keyword reference . .  _____


                                                          More...
 F3=Exit   F4=Prompt   F5=Refresh   F12=Cancel   F13=How to use this display
 F24=More keys
```

Figure 7–2: Prompt of PARM keyword

The first parameter, "Keyword" (KWD), determines the name of the keyword in which the user will input information. This keyword name follows the standard conventions for names in OS/400.

The next parameter, "Type of value" (TYPE), establishes the type of the keyword. Some of the allowable values are *CHAR, meaning character information, *DEC, meaning a decimal number, and *NAME, meaning a value that must conform to OS/400 conventions for names.

The "Value length" (LEN) parameter determines the length of a keyword.

The "Minimum number of values" (MIN) parameter determines the minimum number of entries that are allowed for this keyword. A value of 1 means that at least one value is required, a value of 0 means that no values are required for this keyword. OS/400 will produce an error message if an incorrect number of entries are provided.

The "Prompt" (PROMPT) parameter allows the command to show a short description of the keyword. This is the text that normally appears next to the entry area of a keyword when a command is prompted. Note that pressing <F11> when prompting a command will change the display from showing the keyword prompt text to showing the name of the keyword.

An example of the PARM statement is

```
PARM KWD(FILE) TYPE(*CHAR) LEN(10) MIN(1) PROMPT('File:').
```

This PARM statement will show the legend File: next to the entry area for the keyword. The keyword FILE is of type character, is ten characters long, and requires at least one value.

Other command statements such as QUAL and DEP provide relationship and consistency checking with keywords.

A command is created with the Create Command (CRTCMD). An example of this prompted command is as follows:

```
CRTCMD CMD(NIGHT) PGM(TESTLIB/NIGHTCL).
```

The first parameter, "Command" (CMD), will be the name of the command to be created. The "Library" parameter defaults to *CURLIB, meaning the current library. You may specify a "Library" name if needed.

The next parameter, "Program to process command" (PGM), determines the CL program that will be run when the command is executed. The "Library" parameter indicates the library in which the command processing program is located. This program does not need to exist when the command is created; however, it must be present when the command is executed.

The "Source file parameter" (SRCFILE) is the name of the file (and "Library") where the source statements for the command are located. The file name defaults to the IBM suggested file name of QCMDSRC.

The "Source member" (SRCMBR) parameter determines the name of the member that contains the command source statements. This parameter defaults to *CMD, meaning the name of the member containing the source statements is the same as the command to be created.

Specify the appropriate parameters and press the <ENTER> key to create the command. The command will be able to be used from a command line, a menu, or from within a CL program when the command is created.

The following example commands would execute the example CL programs described earlier in this chapter. The first example command will be associated with the CL program to start the printer; the second command would be associated with the program to run the nightly jobs.

```
CMD PROMPT('Start Printer').
PARM KWD(PRINTER) TYPE(*CHAR) LEN(10) MIN(1)
```

Note that this command uses the PARM statement to set up the parameter passing between the command and the CL program that processes the command input. The command parameter PRINTER would be passed to the CL program and fill CL variable &PRT.

This command could be created with the following CRTCMD command:

```
CRTCMD CMD(TEST/STRPRT) CPP(TEST/STRPRTCL).
```

The following display shows the prompted STRPRT command (see Figure 7–3).
The next command will execute the nightly jobs

```
CMD PROMPT('Execute Night Jobs').
```

This is the only statement needed in the command. No parameters are being passed to the CL program that processes this command.

This could be created with the following CRTCMD command:

```
CRTCMD CMD(TEST/NIGHT) CPP(TEST/NIGHTCL).
```

Prompting this command would display the following (see Figure 7–4).

Note the message at the bottom of the screen. This message indicates that no parameters are used with this command and to press the <ENTER> key to execute the command.

```
as400                                                              _ |&|X|
Commands  Edit  Options  Help
                        Start Printer (STRPRT)

Type choices, press Enter.

Enter Printer to Start:  . . . .  _____      Character value

















                                                         Bottom
F3=Exit    F4=Prompt    F5=Refresh    F12=Cancel    F13=How to use this display
F24=More keys
```

Figure 7–3: Strprt command prompted

```
as400                                                              _ |&|X|
Commands  Edit  Options  Help
                        Execute Night Jobs (NIGHT)


















F3=Exit    F5=Refresh    F12=Cancel    F13=How to use this display    F24=More keys

No parameters to show; press Enter to run, F3 to exit.
```

Figure 7–4: Night command prompted

8
Operations

8.1 SAVES AND RESTORES

Information is a company resource. Many companies could not operate without the information contained on their computer. The loss of data, even for a short period of time, could cost a company their place in the market. Most businesses realize the importance of regularly scheduled backups to save their information. The ability to reconstruct data and transactions after a failure is critical. Fortunately, OS/400 provides a dependable interface to the save and restore process.

The architecture of an AS/400 provides an impetus to regular saves of the data. Since OS/400 employs a single-level architecture, any loss of a disk unit causes all data on the system to be lost. OS/400 will normally attempt to balance the disk usage across all available disk units. Objects are spread across the available disk. This provides faster access time since multiple disks may be accessed concurrently, but it makes the data more vulnerable to loss. The disk drives used on an AS/400 are very reliable, but hardware has been known to malfunction. In addition, "people" errors may also cause the need for data to be restored.

One type of system activity that would cause the need for data to be restored is the failure of an OS/400 object. An object failure, while rare, can require that the object be restored from a saved version. Another problem that can occur is an object being lost or damaged. This condition is also rare but does happen. System failures such as power loss, failure of a disk unit, or operating system errors can lower the integrity of data. Disasters such as fire, flood, or hurricanes can cause all data to be lost.

Errors that cause loss of data may also be caused by authorized or unauthorized users of the system. Programming errors, operator errors, disgruntled employees, or "hackers" may cause data to be removed or corrupted. These errors would not necessarily be intentional; OS/400 is a complex operating system and the object orientation may allow several objects to be affected with one operation.

Regardless of the reason for data loss or object corruption, the data and operating system on an AS/400 should be saved on a regular basis. Most businesses will save the data on a daily basis, with a full system save on a weekly basis. The frequency of saving data will be dependent on the activity of the system.

OS/400 provides many different options for saving the system, saving user libraries and objects, and for restoring information previously saved to tape, diskette, or a save file. The following sections will detail the save and restore process for the entire system, certain libraries, and selected objects. The process used to restore the data will be explained, as will tape and diskette operations. This chapter also contains an explanation of configuring local devices and concludes with an explanation of problem determination and resolution.

8.1.1 Saving the System

Saving the system consists of saving the licensed internal code, local and remote communication configuration objects, OS/400 required libraries, and security objects such as user profiles and authorization lists. Note that this does not save the rest of the data contained on disk. Objects in user libraries (all nonOS/400 required libraries) must be saved separately. Therefore, saving the entire system consists of saving the system and saving all the user libraries.

The command to save the system, Save System (SAVSYS), is shown here.

```
SAVSYS DEV(TAP01).
```

The first parameter, "Tape device" (DEV), requires you to specify the name of the tape device to which you will save the system. For example, TAP01 is commonly used to designate the first tape drive. Also note that the system may only be saved to tape. Other objects such as libraries and files may be saved to tape, diskette, or a save file.

Another parameter, "Volume identifier" (VOL), defaults to the special value *MOUNTED. This indicates that the save process should use the volume identifier of the tape that is currently mounted. You may also specify a volume identifier that could be unique for this save operation. Volume identifiers are discussed in more detail in the *Tape and Device Operation* section.

The "File expiration date" (EXPDATE) parameter defaults to special value *PERM, which means that the information on the tape will not expire. Information on a tape may only be removed when the expiration date has passed. Making the expiration date permanent means that this tape cannot be overwritten without operator intervention. You may also specify a date when this tape will expire.

The "End of tape option" (ENDOPT) parameter defaults to *REWIND, which means that the tape will be rewound when the save is completed. Special value *LEAVE means that the tape will be left at the ending position when the save is complete. A value of *UNLOAD indicates that the tape will be rewound and unloaded. This saves the step of unloading the tape when the save is done.

Another parameter that may be used with the save process is "Clear" (CLEAR), which defaults to *NONE. This means that the tape will not be automatically cleared when the save process is initiated.

8.1.2 Saving User Libraries

Saving user libraries consists of saving nonoperating system libraries. The command to save user libraries is the Save Library (SAVLIB) command. You may save individual libraries (up to fifty at one time) or save all nonsystem libraries. The SAVLIB command is shown here.

```
SAVLIB LIB(*NONSYS) DEV(TAP01).
```

The first parameter, "Library" (LIB), indicates the library or libraries to save. You may enter a library name or multiple library names. You may also use special values to indicate the libraries to save. These special values include

*NONSYS—saves all nonsystem libraries. These libraries include all user-created libraries and IBM libraries QGPL and the licensed program libraries. The system must be in a restricted state (only the controlling subsystem may be active). The libraries will be saved in alphabetical order. This is the value used when saving the entire system.

*ALLUSR—saves all user-created libraries and all IBM libraries that contain user-created information. Note that licensed program libraries and QGPL will not be saved unless they contain user-created information.

*IBM—saves all libraries with objects that were created by IBM. IBM libraries QDOC, QRECOVERY, QRPLOBJ, QSPL, QSRV, QSYS, and QTEMP will not be saved.

The next parameter, "Device" (DEV), indicates the device to be used for saving the libraries. You may specify a device that exists on the system (such as TAP01 for a tape drive or DKT01 for a diskette drive) or special value *SAVF, which indicates that the information will be saved in a save file. This save file could be transmitted to another system or saved with the Save Save File Data (SAVSAVFDTA) command which saves the contents of a save file. If you do specify *SAVF, you will need to enter a name for the "Save file" (SAVF) parameter. You may specify multiple tape or diskette devices for this parameter. The advantage in doing this is OS/400 can move to the next specified tape or diskette drive when the volume on the current drive is full. This can save time when saving multiple libraries.

The parameter, "Volume identifier" (VOL), defaults to special value *MOUNTED. This indicates that the current volume in the drive should be used. You may also specify a volume name. If specified, the same volume name must be used when restoring the information.

The parameter, "Sequence number" (SEQNBR), allows you to specify the sequence number of the volume on which you will save the information. This parameter defaults to special value *END, which means that the information being saved is saved after the last sequence numbered object on the volume (if any). You may also enter a specific sequence number if desired.

The parameter, "Label" (LABEL), allows you to specify a name for the information to be saved. The special value *LIB is the default. This default value means that the label associated with the information is the same as the library being saved. You may also specify a unique label identifier.

The "File expiration date" (EXPDATE) parameter allows you to specify a date before which the information cannot be automatically removed from the volume. The special value *PERM is the default and indicates that the information may not be overwritten or deleted from the volume.

The "End of tape option" (ENDOPT) parameter defaults to special value *REWIND, which means (if using tape) that the tape will be rewound after saving the information. Other special values that may be used are *LEAVE and *UNLOAD. *LEAVE will leave the tape at the point where the saved information ends. *UNLOAD will rewind the tape and unload the tape drive allowing the tape to be removed.

8.1.3 Saving Document Library Objects

A complete save of the system requires that document library objects be saved. These objects are associated with the Officevision/400 product, and include documents, folders, and mail items. The Save Document Library Object (SAVDLO) command is used to save these objects. An example of the SAVDLO command follows

```
SAVDLO DLO(*ALL) FLR(*ANY) DEV(DKT01).
```

The first parameter, "Document library object" (DLO), indicates which objects should be saved. You may indicate specific objects to save, or use one of several special values. The available special values include

> *ALL—all document library objects are to be saved. Note that this is the required entry if folders are to be saved. This would be the value specified for a complete system save.

> *MAIL—all mail objects that are not filed will be saved.

> *SEARCH—allows you to specify search criteria to be used. If an object meets the specified criteria, the object will be saved. Search criteria include: contents of folders, items marked for storage, items whose expiration date has not yet passed, any items created after a specified date, objects with a specific owner or document class, or objects changed after a certain date or time.

The "Folder" (FLR) parameter allows you to specify the folders that are to be saved. The default for this parameter is *ANY, meaning that all folders should be saved.

The "Device" (DEV) parameter allows you to specify the device (or devices) upon which the system will save the document library objects. You may also specify *SAVF, which will save the information to a save file, in which case you will need to enter a name for the "Save file" (SAVF) parameter.

Other parameters include the "Volume identifier" (VOL), "Sequence number" (SEQNBR), "Label" (LABEL), and "End of tape option" (ENDOPT).

8.1.4 Saving Objects

Individual objects may also be saved. This action is not performed as part of an entire system save, but can be used when a certain object needs to be saved. Objects to be saved may be specified by name (in a number of libraries), by type (in a number of libraries), or by a group of objects (in a single library).

The function of this command is to save objects. While the same information may be saved as when using the SAVLIB command, the SAVOBJ command will save the individual objects rather than the entire library. The command to save objects is the Save Object (SAVOBJ) command. An example of this command is shown here.

```
SAVOBJ OBJ(TEST*) LIB(TESTLIB) DEV(*SAVF) SAVF(TESTSAVE).
```

The first parameter, "Objects" (OBJ), indicates the objects to be saved. You may specify a single object name, a list of object names (up to fifty), a generic object name, or the special value *ALL. Special value *ALL means that all objects in the specified libraries will be saved.

Specifying a generic value allows you to save objects that fit the generic name criteria. All the objects that are to be saved by specifying a generic name must be in a single library. A generic name is a name specified with an asterisk (*) or series of asterisks. Placing an asterisk at the end of the name will match any object whose name begins with the characters. Placing an asterisk at the beginning of the name will select any object whose name ends with the specified characters. Asterisks may be placed at the beginning and end of the name in which case an object will be selected if it contains the specified characters. An asterisk may also be specified between characters to select any object where the beginning and ending characters match the indicated characters.

The "Library" (LIB) parameter indicates the library or libraries that contain the objects to be saved. Up to fifty library names may be specified. Only one library name may be entered if a generic "Object" name is used.

The "Device" (DEV) parameter indicates the device to be used for saving the objects. Specifying special value *SAVF will save the information to a save file, and you will need to enter a name for the "Save file" (SAVF) parameter.

The "Object types" (OBJTYPE) parameter allows you to specify the types of objects to be saved. The default for this parameter is *ALL, meaning that objects of any type will be saved. You may also enter a specific object type or a list of object types.

Other parameters include the "Volume identifier" (VOL), "Sequence number" (SEQNBR), "Label" (LABEL), and "End of tape option" (ENDOPT).

8.1.5 Additional Save Commands

Other save commands and options are available to save certain objects from the system. These commands are

Save Changed Objects (SAVCHGOBJ)—This command will save objects that have been changed since the last SAVLIB of the library containing the object.

Saving database files (SAVOBJ)—This command and specifying the "File member" (FILEMBR) parameter will save database files.

Save Licensed Programs (SAVLICPGM)—This command will save the licensed programs on your system. This may be used to distribute licensed programs to other AS/400 systems through an agreement with IBM.

Save Security Data (SAVSECDTA)—This command will save security-related information such as user profiles and authorization lists.

Save Save File Data (SAVSAVFDTA)—This command will save the contents of a save file. Certain save commands allow you to save the information into a save file. This command will save the save file to tape or diskette. This is used to save information from the system at a later time or to send saved information to another system.

Save Storage (SAVSTG)—This command will save the internal microcode contained on the system. This command is used for disaster recovery purposes.

You have the option to "free" storage when saving objects. "Freeing" storage means that the contents of the object will be removed from the system after the object has been successfully saved. This will reduce the disk space requirements if the objects do not need to be online after being saved. An empty object will remain on disk, providing the description of the object for other system processes, including restores of the information.

8.1.6 Restore Process

Information that is saved from the system may need to be restored at some point. System problems may cause a loss of data, an older version of an object may need to be restored to regain functionality, or historical data may be retrieved for comparison purposes.

Whatever the reason for regaining data that was previously saved, OS/400 provides restore commands that can operate on a library, object, or system information. Generally, the restore command to be used is based on the save command that was originally used to save the information.

When restoring an object, the following factors should be considered:

Objects saved by separate commands should usually be restored with separate commands.

The original library must exist when restoring an object, or the object must be restored to a different library. OS/400 will not create a library to contain the restored object.

Multiple occurrences of the same object saved on the same volume will have different sequence numbers. You may need to provide the sequence number to restore the specific object desired.

An object may be restored to a system regardless of whether the object is on the system at that time. If the object is on the system and storage has not been freed, the information contained in the object will be overwritten.

The command to restore a library is the Restore Library (RSTLIB) command. This command would be used to restore a library that was saved with the SAVLIB command. An example of this command is shown here.

```
RSTLIB SAVLIB(TESTLIB) DEV(TAP01).
```

The RSTLIB command is similar to the SAVLIB command. The first parameter, "Saved library" (SAVLIB), indicates the name of the library to be restored. A specific library name may be specified, or the special values *NONSYS, *ALLUSR, or *IBM may be specified. These special values have the same meaning as for the SAVLIB command.

The second parameter, "Device" (DEV), allows you to specify the device (tape or diskette) from which the library will be restored. Special value *SAVF may be used to indicate that the saved library resides in a save file. You will need to include a value for the "Save file" parameter if this special value is used.

Other parameters include the "Volume identifier" (VOL), "Sequence number" (SEQNBR), "Label" (LABEL), and "End of tape option" (ENDOPT).

8.1.7 Restoring Objects

Objects may be restored by using the Restore Object (RSTOBJ) command. Again, this command is similar to its counterpart, the SAVOBJ command. This command is shown here.

```
RSTOBJ OBJ(*ALL) SAVLIB(TESTLIB) DEV(DKT01) OBJTYPE(*FILE).
```

The first parameter, "Objects" (OBJ), allows you to specify the object or objects to be restored. Up to fifty objects may be specified in a list, or you may specify a generic object name. The special value *ALL may also be used to restore all the objects in the specified library.

The "Saved library" (SAVLIB) parameter allows you to specify the name of the library that contains the saved objects.

The "Device" (DEV) parameter will indicate the name of the device from which the objects will be restored. You may also specify *SAVF to restore information from a save file, in which case you will need to make an entry for the "Save file" parameter.

The "Object types" (OBJTYPE) parameter allows you to specify the types of objects to restore. This parameter defaults to *ALL which means all object types will be restored.

The "Option" (OPTION) parameter may be used to determine which objects in a library should be replaced. The available special values for the "Option" parameter are as follows:

*ALL—old objects are replaced and new objects added. This is the default.

*OLD—only old (existing) objects are replaced in a library.

*NEW—only new (not existing) objects are added to a library. Old objects are not replaced.

*FREE—only objects whose storage has been freed are replaced.

Another parameter, "Restore to library" (RSTLIB), may be used to specify a new library name to use when restoring the library.

8.1.8 Additional Restore Commands

Other restore commands are available to restore certain objects to the system. These commands are

Restore Authority (RSTAUT)—This command will restore user authorities that were saved with the SAVSECDTA command.

Restore Configuration Object (RSTCFGOBJ)—This command will restore the device configuration of the system. The information to be restored will have been saved with the SAVSYS command.

Restore Document Library Object (RSTDLO)—This command will restore objects such as unfiled mail, folders, and documents. These objects would have been saved with the SAVDLO command. This command may be very system-intensive depending on the options selected.

Restore Licensed Program (RSTLICPGM)—This command will restore licensed programs that were saved using the SAVLICPGM command.

Restore User Profile (RSTUSRPRF)—This command will restore the user profiles that were saved with the SAVSECDTA command.

8.1.9 Save and Restore Media

Different save and restore commands may use different media. The following list shows the media type that may be used when saving information. Information may be saved on tape, diskette, or in a save file. While different types of commands may be used when saving and restoring information, the restore command used is usually similar to the save command originally used.

- SAVDLO—Tape, diskette, or save file.
- SAVCHGOBJ—Tape, diskette, or save file.
- SAVLIB—Tape, diskette, or save file.
- SAVLICPGM—Tape only.
- SAVOBJ—Tape, diskette, or save file.
- SAVSAVFDTA—Tape or diskette.
- SAVSECDTA—Tape or save file.
- SAVSYS—Tape only.

8.2 TAPE AND DISKETTE OPERATION

Tapes and diskettes are used on an AS/400 to save and restore information and to provide a platform for copied information. IBM (and third-party vendors) provides many different options for tape and diskette devices on an AS/400. Round reel tape (at both 1600 and 6250 BPI), $1/4$-inch cartridge tape, 8 mm tape, and diskette (both 8-inch and $5^{1}/4$-inch) provide for many different tape and diskette options.

Regardless of the type of tape or diskette, certain concepts apply. An important point is that a diskette or a tape must be initialized before use. The initialization of a tape or diskette provides certain identifying information. Operations will usually fail if attempted on tapes or diskettes that have not been initialized. Using uninitialized media with a save operation will cause a message to be sent to the operator. The operator may choose that the media be initialized, but this takes more time for the save operation.

A volume is a name given to a tape or diskette or a series of tapes or diskettes used for the same operation. You may specify a volume name for a tape or diskette. When using multiple tapes or diskettes, such as with a save operation, the series of tapes or diskettes may all have the same volume name. Most tape and diskette operations allow you to use the special value *MOUNTED for the volume name. This allows you to use whatever volume is mounted regardless of the name. The volume name does provide a safeguard, if a command specifically requires a certain volume, the command will not execute until the appropriate volume is mounted.

An owner-id may also be specified for a tape or diskette volume. This identifying information ensures the correct tape or diskette volume is used in processing.

A label name is the name of the file (or object) as it is stored on the tape or diskette. Accessing a specific object on a diskette or tape usually requires providing the label name. The Display Tape (DSPTAP) and Display Diskette (DSPDKT) commands allow you to view the labels on the volume.

Another important concept in tape and diskette operations is a device file. A device file provides an interface between the device and the system. Device files are used when reading or writing records on a tape or diskette. The device file identifies the tape or diskette unit to be used, and other characteristics such as the volume identifier, the label name, the type of file, the block and record length, the exchange type (for diskettes), and the code (EBCDIC or ASCII) to be used.

The standard naming convention for tape and diskette devices is TAPxx for tape devices and DKTxx for diskette devices, where the xx is the number of the device. You may have multiple devices on your system (the number of devices is model-dependent), which can make for faster operations. Operations may be faster since OS/400 can switch to a different device when it is done with the volume faster than an operator can unload and load a new volume. Note that other naming conventions are possible depending on the value of system value QDEVNAMING.

8.2.1 Initializing a Diskette

The first step when using a diskette is to initialize the diskette. Initializing (also known as formatting) is a process that writes identifying information on the diskette and also establishes the format that the diskette will use. Other actions performed by initializing a diskette are checking for active files, formatting the diskette to a specified sector size and density, and testing the diskette for media errors. The command to initialize a diskette is the Initialize Diskette (INZDKT) command. An example of this command is shown here.

```
INZDKT DEV(DKT01) FMT(*SAVRST).
```

The first parameter, "Diskette device" (DEV), identifies the name of the device that will contain the diskette to initialize.

The "New volume identifier" (NEWVOL) parameter defaults to special value *NONE, indicating that this diskette has no specific volume identifier. You may also enter a volume identifier of up to fourteen characters to identify this specific diskette.

The "New owner identifier" (NEWOWNID) parameter defaults to special value *BLANK which provides a blank owner-id. You may also enter an owner identifier of up to fourteen characters to identify this specific diskette.

The "Diskette format" (FMT) parameter determines the format in which this diskette will be initialized. The default is *DATA, which means the diskette will be formatted in single-density format. Other values are 1 for single-density formatting of a single-sided diskette, 2 for single-density formatting of a double-sided diskette, 2D or *DATA2 for double-density formatting of a double-sided diskette, or *SAVRST for the formatting required for save and restore processing.

The "Sector size" (SCTSIZ) parameter determines the sector size of the newly formatted diskette. The default is *STD, which indicates the standard sector size for the type of format that will be used. You may also specify sector sizes of 128, 256, 512, or 1024 bytes per sector.

The "Check for active files" (CHECK) parameter defaults to *YES, which means that if any active files are found (files with an expiration date which has not yet passed), a message will be sent to the operator. The operator may then abort the operation or continue, deleting the active files. A value of *NO for this parameter will cause the diskette initialization to continue without checking for active files.

The "Code" (CODE) parameter indicates whether the information written to the diskette will be in EBCDIC or ASCII code. The default for this parameter is *EBCDIC coding. Information may only be subsequently written to the diskette in the code in which it was formatted.

8.2.2 Copying to a Diskette

Information may be copied to a diskette using the Copy To Diskette (CPYTODKT) command. This command is similar to the Copy File (CPYF) command, which may be used if special requirements exist. The CPYTODKT command is shown here.

```
CPYTODKT FROMFILE(MKTTEST/CONTACTS) TOFILE(MKTLIB/DKTFILE).
```

The first parameter, "From file" (FROMFILE) and the associated "Library," identify the database file from which the records will be copied.

The "Diskette file" (TOFILE) and associated "Library" parameter identify the diskette device file that will be used to provide the characteristics of the destination file.

The "From member" (FROMMBR) parameter defaults to *FIRST, meaning that the first member in the database file will be copied. You may also enter a specific member name, a generic member name, or the special value *ALL to copy all members in the database file.

The "Diskette label" (TOLABEL) parameter determines the name of the file as it will reside on the diskette. The default for this parameter is *FROMMBR, meaning the label will be the name of the database file member that was copied. You may also specify a different label name.

The "Diskette device" (TODEV) parameter identifies the device which will be used in the copy operation. The default is *DKTF, which indicates that the name of the device to be used is specified in the diskette device file in the "Diskette file" parameter. You may also specify a diskette device to use for the copy operation.

The "Volume identifier" (TOVOL) parameter identifies the volume name to be used for this copy operation. The default is *DKTF which indicates that the volume name to be used is specified in the diskette device file in the "Diskette file" parameter. You may also specify a volume identifier to use for the copy operation. The special value *NONE indicates that no volume identifier will be used for this diskette.

The "Copy to exchange type" (TOEXCHTYPE) parameter determines the exchange type of the diskette. This would be used when transferring information to a different type of system. The default is *DKTF, which indicates that the exchange type to be used is specified in the diskette device file in the "Diskette file" parameter. You may also specify exchange types of *STD (which will provide BASIC or H type exchange format depending on the format of the diskette), *BASIC for basic exchange type, *H for H type exchange format, or *I for I format exchange type.

The "File expiration date" (TOEXPDATE) parameter establishes the expiration date of the copied file. The file cannot be overwritten until the expiration date has passed. The default is *DKTF, which indicates that the expiration date to be used is specified in the diskette device file in the "Diskette file" parameter. You may also specify a date (in YY/MM/DD format), or special value *PERM, which indicates that the file is not to be overwritten (permanent).

The "Number of records to copy" (NBRRCDS) parameter specifies the number of records to copy from the database file to the diskette file. The default is special value *END, which means that records will be copied until the end of file on the database file. You may also specify a number of records that will be copied starting from the beginning of the file.

8.2.3 Copying from a Diskette

Information may be copied from a diskette using the Copy From Diskette (CPYFRMDKT) command. This command, similar to the Copy To Diskette (CPYTODKT) command, is shown here.

```
CPYFRMDKT FROMFILE(MKTLIB/DKTFILE) TOFILE(MKTPROD/PROSPECTS).
```

The parameters in the CPYFRMDKT command have the same name and same meaning as the parameters in the CPYTODKT command except that the meanings are reversed. The "Diskette file" (FROMFILE) parameter indicates the name of the diskette device file that is used to copy records from the diskette, while the "To file" (TOFILE) parameter contains the name of the database file that will receive the copied records. The "To file" parameter may also contain the special value *PRINT, which will cause the records on diskette to be printed.

The "Member" (TOMBR) parameter defaults to *FROMLABEL, which causes the name of the member in the database file that contains the copied records to be the name of the file label on diskette.

The "Replace or add records" (MBROPT) parameter determines if the target member will be cleared and new records added, or if the copied records will be appended to the database file member. The default for this parameter is *NONE, which would be used if the "To file" parameter was *PRINT. The special value *ADD will append records to the database file member, while special value *REPLACE will clear the member and then copy the records from the diskette.

8.2.4 Other Diskette Commands

Other diskette related commands are available for diskette operations. These commands are

CHKDKT—This command will search a diskette in a specified device for a unique volume identifier and/or file label.

CLRDKT—This command will delete all files, active and inactive, from a diskette by erasing the file identifiers from the diskette label area.

CRTDKTF—This command will create a diskette device file.

DSPDKT—This command will show the volume label and data file identifier information that is on the diskette. You may specify options of *LABELS to show the labels of the files on diskette, or *SAVRST to show the contents of the saved information on diskette.

OVRDKTF—This command is used to override or replace certain parameters of a diskette device file.

RNMDKT—This command will change the volume name of a diskette.

8.2.5 Initializing a Tape

A tape needs to be initialized before being used. Initializing a tape is different from a diskette as sector size and a specific format do not apply for tapes. A tape is initialized to set the volume label and the recording density. The command to initialize a tape, Initialize Tape (INZTAP), is shown here.

```
INZTAP DEV(TAP01) CLEAR(*YES).
```

The first parameter, "Tape device" (DEV), identifies the device which will contain the tape to be initialized.

The "New volume identifier" (NEWVOL) parameter defaults to special value *NONE, indicating that this tape has no specific volume identifier. You may also enter a volume identifier of up to fourteen characters to identify this specific tape.

The "New owner identifier" (NEWOWNID) parameter defaults to special value *BLANK, which provides a blank owner-id. You may also enter an owner identifier of up to fourteen characters to identify this specific tape.

The "Volume identifier" (VOL) parameter serves to identify the tape that is currently in the tape drive. The default is special value *MOUNTED, which means that the volume identifier of the mounted tape will not be checked. You may specify a volume name to ensure that the correct tape is being initialized.

The "Check for active files" (CHECK) parameter defaults to *YES, which means that if any active files are found (files with an expiration date which has not yet passed), a message will be sent to the operator and the operation aborted. A value of *NO for this parameter will cause the tape initialization to continue without checking for active files. A value of *FIRST means that the initialization process will only check the first file on the tape. If that file's expiration date has passed (or there are no files on the tape), the tape will be initialized without checking any other files. If the first file has not yet expired, a message will be sent to the operator and the process aborted.

The "Tape density" (DENSITY) parameter determines the density to which the tape will be initialized. The default value of *DEVTYPE indicates that the standard tape device density will be used. You may also specify values of 1600, 3200, 6250, 10000, 16000, 38000, or 43200 bits per inch. The tape device must be able to initialize a tape to the density specified.

The "Code" (CODE) parameter indicates whether the information written to the tape will be in EBCDIC or ASCII code. The default for this parameter is *EBCDIC coding. Information may only be subsequently written to the tape in the code in which it was formatted.

The "End of tape option" (ENDOPT) parameter determines the status of the tape after the initialization process has completed. The default value of *REWIND means that the tape should be rewound to the beginning of the tape marker. This would position the tape for further operations. Specifying special value *UNLOAD indicates that the tape should be rewound and unloaded after the initialization is complete.

The "Clear" (CLEAR) parameter determines if the tape should have both the labels and the data removed from the tape. The default value of *NO means that only the labels are removed. The files are not available after the initialization process is completed. A value of *YES means that the labels and the actual data will be removed from the tape. You may need to choose this option to ensure that all data is physically removed from the tape. This option will cause the initialization process to take much longer.

8.2.6 Copying to a Tape

Information may be copied to a tape using the Copy To Tape (CPYTOTAP) command. This command is similar to the Copy File (CPYF) command, which may be used if special requirements exist. The CPYTOTAP command is shown here.

```
CPYTOTAP FROMFILE(SALES/SALESRPT) TOFILE(MKTLIB/SALESTAP).
```

The first parameter, "From file" (FROMFILE) and the associated "Library" parameter, identifies the database file from which the records will be copied.

The "Tape file" (TOFILE) and associated "Library" parameter identifies the tape device file that will be used to provide the characteristics of the destination file.

The "From member" (FROMMBR) parameter defaults to *FIRST, meaning that the first member in the database file will be copied. You may also enter a specific member name, a generic member name, or the special value *ALL to copy all members in the database file.

The "File sequence number" (TOSEQNBR) parameter determines the sequence number of the file that receives the copied records. This differentiates files with the same name that contain different information. This parameter defaults to *TAPF, which indicates that the sequence number to be used is specified in the tape device file in the "Tape file" parameter. You may specify a sequence number in the range of 1 through 9999 or special value *END, which causes the file to be copied to the end of the tape.

The "Tape label" (TOLABEL) parameter determines the name of the file as it will reside on the tape. The default for this parameter is *FROMMBR, meaning the label will be the name of the database file member that was copied. You may also specify a different label name.

The "Device" (TODEV) parameter identifies the device which will be used in the copy operation. The default is *TAPF, which indicates that the name of the device to be used is specified in the tape device file found in the "Tape file" parameter. You may also specify a tape device to use for the copy operation.

The "Copy to reels" (TOREELS) parameter determines the type of labeling in use on the tape. The default is *TAPF, which indicates that the labeling method used is specified in the tape device file found in the "Tape file" parameter. You may also specify one of the following special values: *SL, which indicates the receiving value has standard labels, *NL, which indicates the volume has no labels, or *LTM, which indicates the volume has no labels but does have a leading tape mark before the first data record.

The "Record length" (TORCDLEN) parameter determines the record length of the file on tape. The default is *FROMFILE, which means the record length of the file on tape containing the copied records will have the same record length as the database file from which the records will be copied. Special value *TAPF indicates that the record length to be used is specified in the tape device file found in the "Tape file" parameter. Special value *CALC means that record length of the existing tape file will be used. You may also specify a record length in a range of 1 through 32,767.

The "End of tape option" (TOENDOPT) parameter determines the status of the tape after the initialization process has completed. The default for this parameter is *TAPF, which indicates the end of tape option to be used is specified in the tape device file found in the "Tape file" parameter. Special value *REWIND means that the tape should be rewound to the beginning of tape marker. This would position the tape for further operations. Specifying special value *UNLOAD indicates that the tape should be rewound and unloaded after the initialization is complete.

8.2.7 Copying from a Tape

Information may be copied from a tape using the Copy From Tape (CPYFRMTAP) command. This command is similar to the Copy To Tape (CPYTOTAP) command. The CPYFRMTAP command is shown here.

```
CPYFRMTAP FROMFILE(MKTLIB/SALESTAP) TOFILE(*PRINT).
```

The parameters in the CPYFRMTAP command have the same name and same meaning as the parameters in the CPYTOTAP command except that the orientation is reversed. The "Tape file" (FROMFILE) parameter indicates the name of the tape device file that is used to copy records from the tape, while the "To file" (TOFILE) parameter contains the name of the database file that will receive the copied records. The "To file" parameter may also contain the special value *PRINT, which will cause the records on tape to be printed.

The "Member" (TOMBR) parameter defaults to *FROMLABEL, which will cause the name of the member in the database file that will contain the copied records to be the name of the file label on tape. You may also specify a member name or special value *FIRST to copy the records from the tape to the first member in the database file.

The "Copy from reels" (FROMREELS) parameter is equivalent to the "Copy to reels" parameter on the CPYTOTAP command. The default for the first parameter, "Label processing type," is *TAPF, which indicates the label option to be used is specified in the tape device file found in the "Tape file" parameter. You may also specify one of the following special values: *SL, which indicates the value has standard labels, *NL, which indicates the volume has no labels, *NS, which means the volume has nonstandard labels, *BLP, which means to bypass label processing, or *LTM, which indicates the volume has no labels but does have a leading tape mark before the first data record. The second parameter, "Number of reels," indicates the number of reels of tape that contain the file to copy. The default is *TAPF; and you may also specify a number in a range from 1 through 255 to indicate the number of reels.

The "Record length" (FROMRCDLEN) determines the length of the records on tape. The default of *TAPF indicates the record length to be used is specified in the tape device file found in the "Tape file" parameter. Special value *CALC means that the system will determine the record length. You may also specify the record length directly.

The "Replace or add records" (MBROPT) parameter determines if the target member will be cleared and new records added, or if the copied records will be appended to the database file member. The default for this parameter is *NONE, which would be used if the "To file" parameter was *PRINT. The special value *ADD will append records to the database file member, while special value *REPLACE will clear the member and then copy the records from the tape.

8.2.8 Other Tape Commands

Other tape related commands are available for tape operations. These commands are

CHKTAP—This command will search a diskette in a specified device for a unique volume identifier and/or file label.

CRTTAPF—This command creates a tape device file.

DSPTAP—This command will show the volume label and data file identifier information that is on the tape. You may specify options of *LABELS to show the labels of the files on tape, or *SAVRST to show the contents of the saved information on tape.

OVRTAPF—This command will override certain parameters associated with a tape device file.

VFYTAP—This command will verify if a specified tape unit is operating. It is usually used in CL programs.

8.3 CONFIGURING LOCAL DEVICES

Local devices are easily configured for operation with OS/400. System value QAUTOCFG controls automatic configuration of devices on an AS/400. If this system value is set to Y, devices will be configured automatically when they are attached to the system and powered on. A value of N requires that a device description be created for each newly added device.

With automatic configuration the system will recognize that a new device has been added and will create the appropriate device description for the new device. Note that every time a device is added (or moved to a new port) and powered on, the system will create a new device description. This may cause unnecessary device descriptions to be created on the system.

A common practice is to turn on automatic configuration when adding a device and turn off automatic configuration when the devices have been added. This will reduce the number of device descriptions to only those needed.

OS/400 provides a number of different attachment types for workstation and printer devices. Traditional twinaxial (twinax) attachment is available, as well as an ASCII workstation attachment for ASCII workstations. In addition, token-ring and Ethernet LAN attachments for PCs may be used. The number and type of workstation controller attachments that are available is dependent on the type and size of your AS/400.

The following section will show the commands and procedures for creating a twinaxial workstation and a twinaxial printer without the use of automatic configuration. The creation of ASCII devices are similar to creating the twinaxial counterparts. LAN-attached PCs require configuration of both the AS/400 and the PC.

8.3.1 Configuring a Local Workstation Device

The Create Device Description Display (CRTDEVDSP) command creates a local workstation device description. An example of this command is shown here.

```
CRTDEVDSP DEVD(MKTDSP) DEVCLS(5251) MODEL(11).
```

The first parameter, "Device description" (DEVD), will be the name of the device to be created. This is one of the reasons why you may want to manually create a device description. The device naming conventions with automatic configuration may not meet your needs.

The "Device class" (DEVCLS) parameter allows you to specify the class of workstation description to create. The allowable values are *LCL for a locally attached device, *VWS for a virtual display device (used for Display Station Pass-through), or *RMT for a remotely attached device (used with a remote workstation controller).

The "Device type" (TYPE) parameter will indicate to the system the type of device description that will be created. This parameter will determine the system's interaction with the device in terms of color, display size, and other attributes. While a device will usually operate if the type is wrong, the attributes (especially color) will not be correct. This parameter requires a four-digit number that is recognized by the system. If you are creating a device description for a nonIBM device, check the documentation for the workstation to determine which IBM device the workstation will emulate. An IBM device will have the device type printed on the device. Some device types are not recognized by the system and must be configured as a different device type. The allowable values for this parameter are 3179, 3180, 3196, 3197, 3477, 5251, 5291, 5292, or 7561. The 5251 value will work as a base default for almost all devices.

The "Device model" (MODEL) parameter further defines the type of device. This parameter is dependent on the device type, and is printed on the device or included in the nonIBM device's documentation. Different models require a different value for this parameter; consult the *AS/400 Device Configuration Guide* for details.

The "Port number" (PORT) parameter is the port number on the workstation controller to which this device will be attached. Different controller models have a different number of ports. Check with your system manager for this value.

The "Switch setting" (SWTSET) parameter indicates the address of this specific workstation. The number will be in a range of 0 through 6. Check with your system manager for this value.

The "Online at IPL" (ONLINE) parameter determines if this workstation should be brought online after the system completes an IPL (Initial Program Load). The default for this parameter is *YES since workstations are usually activated at IPL. A value of *NO will require this workstation to be manually varied before it can be used.

The "Attached controller" (CTL) parameter refers to the workstation controller to which this workstation will be attached. The workstation controller should have already been created, perhaps by automatic configuration. Check with your system manager for this value.

The following parameters, "Keyboard language type" (KBDTYPE) and "Character identifier" (CHRID), default to a value of *SYSVAL, which indicates that the system values for these parameters will be used as the value. This is usually what is wanted because the different workstations will generally use the same keyboard language and character set. There are multiple values available for these parameters; consult the *AS/400 Device Configuration Guide* for a complete list.

The "Allow blinking cursor" (ALWBLN) parameter determines if the cursor is allowed to blink. A value of *YES will allow the cursor to blink, while a value of *NO will produce a solid cursor.

The "Text description" (TEXT) parameter allows you to specify a fifty-character description of this device. This description will be shown when commands such as Display Object Description (DSPOBJD) are used.

8.3.2 Configuring a Local Printer

The Create Device Description Printer (CRTDEVPRT) command creates a local printer device description. An example of this command is shown here.

```
CRTDEVPRT DEVD(MKTPRINTER) DEVCLD(4214) MODEL(1).
```

The first parameter, "Device description" (DEVD), will be the name of the printer device description to be created. This is one of the reasons why you may want to manually create a device description. The device naming conventions with automatic configuration may not meet your needs.

The "Device class" (DEVCLS) parameter allows you to specify the class of printer description to create. The allowable values are *LCL for a locally attached printer, *VWS for a virtual printer device (used for Display Station Pass-through), or *RMT for a remotely attached printer (used with a remote workstation controller).

The "Device type" (TYPE) parameter will indicate to the system the type of printer device description that will be created. This parameter will determine the system's interaction with the device in terms of form capabilities, fonts, points sizes, and other attributes. A printer may not work correctly if the type is wrong. This parameter requires a four-digit number that is recognized by the system. If you are creating a printer device description for a nonIBM printer, check the documentation to determine which IBM device the printer will emulate. An IBM printer will have the device type printed on the printer. Some device types are not recognized by the system and must be configured as a different device type. The allowable values for this parameter are *IPDS, 3812, 4214, 4234, 4245, 5219, 5224, 5225, 5256, and 6252.

The "Device model" (MODEL) parameter further defines the type of printer. This parameter is dependent on the device type and is printed on the device or included in the nonIBM device's documentation. Different models require a different value for this parameter; consult the *AS/400 Device Configuration Guide* for details.

The "Advanced function printing" (AFP) parameter indicates if the printer supports advanced function printing. A value of *YES indicates that the printer supports advanced function printing, while a value of *NO indicates the printer does not.

The "AFP attachment" (AFPATTACH) determines how an advanced function printer is attached to the system. The default is *WSC, which indicates the printer is attached via a workstation controller. The other allowable value is *APPC, which indicates the printer is a remote printer and uses APPC/APPN communications as an attachment.

The "Port number" (PORT) parameter is the port number on the workstation controller to which this printer will be attached. Different controller models have a different number of ports. Check with your system manager for this value.

The "Switch setting" (SWTSET) parameter indicates the address of this specific printer. The number will be in a range of 0 through 6. Check with your system manager for this value.

The "Online at IPL" (ONLINE) parameter determines if this printer should be brought online after the system completes an IPL (Initial Program Load). The default for this parameter is *YES since printers are usually activated at IPL. A value of *NO will require this printer to be manually varied on before it can be used.

The "Attached controller" (CTL) parameter refers to the workstation controller to which this printer will be attached. The workstation controller should have already been created, perhaps by automatic configuration. Check with your system manager for this value.

Parameters "Font identifier" (FONT) and "Form feed" (FORMFEED) refer only to the 3812, 5219, or *IPDS printers. The "Maximum pending requests" (MAXPNDRQS), "Print request timer" (PRTRQSTMR), and "Form definition and library" (FORMDF) refer to advanced function printing capable printers. Consult the *AS/400 Device Configuration Guide* for details about these parameters if you have these types of printers.

The "Printer error message" (PRTERRMSG) parameter determines if the printer will send an informational or inquiry message to the operator for recoverable errors. The special value *INQ will send an inquiry message to the operator which will require a response. Special value *INFO indicates the printer will send an information message.

The "Message queue and library" (MSGQ) parameter determines the message queue to which printer messages will be sent. The default is message queue QSYSOPR, which is the system operator's message queue. You may also specify a message queue to which the messages will be sent.

The "Text description" (TEXT) parameter allows you to specify a fifty-character description of this device. This description will be shown when commands such as Display Object Description (DSPOBJD) are used.

8.4 OPERATIONAL ASSISTANT

Operational Assistant is an interface that allows users to perform sophisticated system tasks without requiring an in-depth knowledge of the commands needed to perform those tasks. Operational Assistant (OA) provides a seamless interface for system tasks such as managing user jobs and output, managing the system, performing backups, and performing system cleanup tasks. The actions performed via OA are the same as would be performed by executing system commands. OA is being upgraded by IBM with each new release of OS/400, providing more functionality for system operations.

OA is a menu-driven interface that can show the displays of the underlying commands; it can also show displays that are more general and less complex. The less complex displays are the screens that are shown when the assistance level for the command is set to *BASIC. A command assistance level may be set to one of the following values:

*BASIC—provides basic, less complex displays.

*INTERMED—provides intermediate displays (the displays used before the implementation of assistance level modification).

*ADVANCED—provides advanced displays with more information and little or no function key legends or instructions.

*SYSVAL—indicates the value established in system value QASTLVL that should be used.

The OA display can be shown for the following command displays. Note that these commands may be displayed with the assistance level set to one of the above values.

- Display Message (DSPMSG).
- Work with Configuration Status (WRKCFGSTS).
- Work with Messages (WRKMSG).
- Work with Spooled Files (WRKSPLF).
- Work with User Jobs (WRKUSRJOB).
- Work with User Profiles (WRKUSRPRF).
- Work with Writers (WRKWTR).

The main OA menu can be accessed by invoking the ASSIST menu. This menu may be invoked directly with the GO ASSIST command. In addition, setting system value QATNPGM to a value of *ASSIST will provide the OA menu as the attention key-handling program for users. In this case, the ASSIST menu will be displayed when the user presses the <ATTN> key. The ASSIST menu is shown in Figure 8–1.

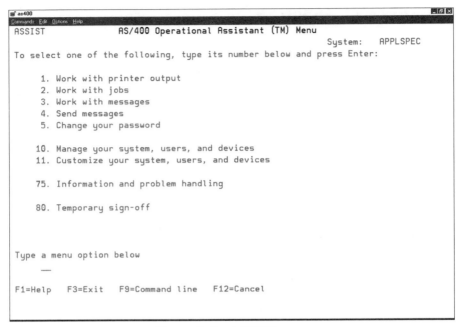

Figure 8–1: ASSIST menu

The standard function keys are used with the ASSIST menu. In addition, using the <F9> will provide you with a command line (if authorized) on which you may enter commands.

Option 1 will allow you to work with printer output by executing the Work with Spooled Files (WRKSPLF) command. The WRKSPLF command is explained in Chapter 5 ("Queues and Writers").

Option 2 will run the Work with User Jobs (WRKUSRJOB) command. The WRKUSR-JOB command allows you to view the status of user batch jobs and performs job-related tasks such as holding a job from executing, releasing a held job, ending a job, responding to messages issued by a job, and displaying a job queue.

Option 3 will invoke the Work with Messages (WRKMSG) command, and option 4 will allow you to send a message to another user with the Send Message (SNDMSG) command. The WRKMSG command and the SNDMSG command are explained is Chapter 5, ("Queues and Writers").

Option 5 will execute the Change Password (CHGPWD) to allow you to change your password. The CHGPWD command is explained in Chapter 4, ("The AS/400 User Environment").

Option 10 displays the MANAGESYS menu to enable you to perform system-related activities such as device operations, backups, working with user profiles, system power operations, and system cleanup operations. Note that you may also access this menu directly (GO MANAGESYS). The MANAGESYS menu is shown in Figure 8–2.

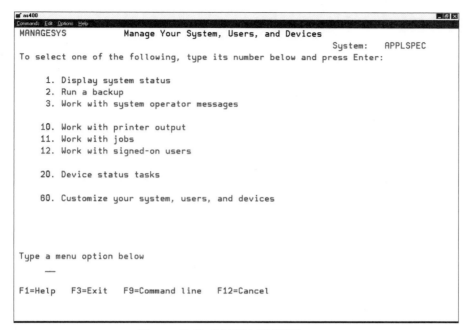

Figure 8–2: MANAGESYS menu

Option 1 executes the WRKSYSSTS command, which displays the status of the system, including CPU utilization and disk usage.

Option 2 on the MANAGESYS menu provides for backup of the system and user libraries. This option displays the BACKUP menu. Note that this menu may be accessed directly (GO BACKUP). Options 1, 2, and 10 execute the Save Library (SAVLIB) command with different values for the Library (LIB) parameter. Option 11 executes the Save System (SAVSYS) command. The SAVLIB and SAVSYS commands are discussed earlier in this chapter. Defaults are provided for the device to which information will be saved, checking for information on the tape or diskette, and other operational parameters.

The BACKUP menu is shown in Figure 8–3.

Option 1, Run daily backup, uses the schedule for a predefined daily backup.

Option 2, Run weekly backup, uses the schedule for a predefined weekly backup.

Option 3, Run monthly backup, uses the schedule for a predefined monthly backup.

Option 10, Back up the IBM-supplied libraries, runs the SAVLIB command with a parameter of LIB(*IBM).

Option 11, Back up the entire system, invokes the SAVSYS command. Figure 8–4 is shown to ensure you are executing the correct menu option.

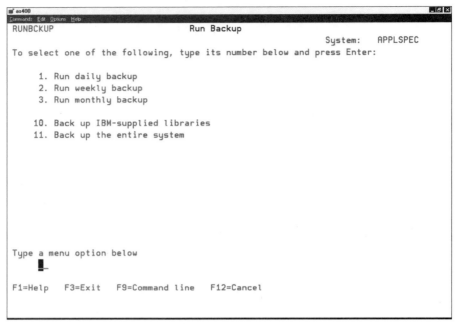

Figure 8–3: BACKUP menu

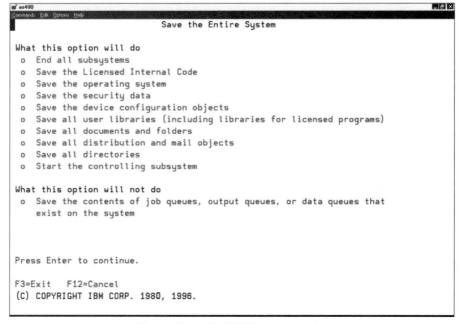

Figure 8–4: SAVSYS information

Option 3 from the MANAGESYS menu, Work with system operator messages, will execute the DSPMSG MSGQ(QSYSOPR) command.

Option 10 from the MANAGESYS menu, Work with printer output, will execute the WRKSPLF command.

Option 11 from the MANAGESYS menu, Work with jobs, will execute the WRKUSRJOB STATUS(*ALL) command.

Option 12 from the MANAGESYS menu, Work with signed-on users, will execute the WRKUSRJOB STATUS(*ACTIVE) command.

Option 20 enables you to examine the status of devices on the system. Choosing option 1 will display the DEVICESTS menu. This menu is shown below (see Figure 8–5):

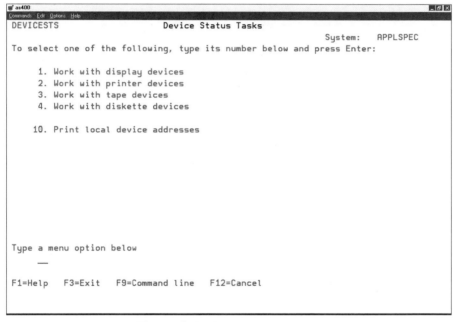

Figure 8–5: DEVICESTS menu

The DEVICESTS menu has five menu options. Options 1 through 4 allow you to work with different types of devices on the system. The same command, Work with Configuration Status (WRKCFGSTS with a parameter of CFGTYPE(*DEV)), is executed (with a different CFGD parameter) for options 1 through 4. The WRKCFGSTS command is discussed later in this chapter.

Option 1, Work with display devices, invokes the WRKCFGSTS CFGTYPE(*DEV) command with a parameter of CFGD(*DSP).

Option 2, Work with printer devices, executes the WRKCFGSTS CFGTYPE(*DEV) command with a parameter of CFGD(*PRT).

Option 3, Work with tape devices, runs the WRKCFGSTS CFGTYPE(*DEV) command with a parameter of CFGD(*TAP).

Option 4, Work with diskette devices, runs the WRKCFGSTS CFGTYPE(*DEV) command with a parameter of CFGD(*DKT).

Option 10 on the DEVICESTS menu, Print local device addresses, will execute the Print Device Address (PRTDEVADDR) command. This command will create a report showing the addresses of the local devices that are attached to the system. This report is excellent documentation for readdressing devices when they are moved. An example of the PRTDEVADDR report is shown below (see Figure 8–6):

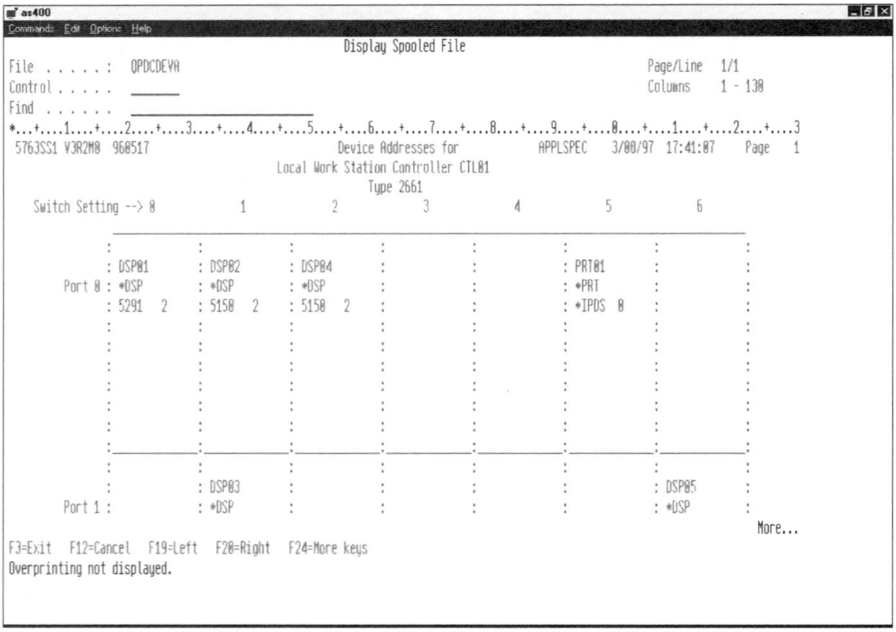

```
as400
Commands  Edit  Options  Help
                              Display Spooled File
File . . . . . :   QPDCDEVA                                        Page/Line   1/1
Control . . . . .  _____                                           Columns     1 - 130
Find . . . . . .   ______________________
*...+....1....+....2....+....3....+....4....+....5....+....6....+....7....+....8....+....9....+....0....+....1....+....2....+....3
 5763SS1 V3R2M0  960517                    Device Addresses for          APPLSPEC    3/00/97  17:41:07    Page    1
                                  Local Work Station Controller CTL01
                                               Type 2661
   Switch Setting --> 0          1          2          3          4          5          6
              ______________________________________________________________________
             :          :          :          :          :          :          :          :
             : DSP01    : DSP02    : DSP04    :          :          : PRT01    :          :
      Port 0 : *DSP     : *DSP     : *DSP     :          :          : *PRT     :          :
             : 5291   2 : 5150   2 : 5150   2 :          :          : *IPDS  0 :          :
             :          :          :          :          :          :          :          :
             :          :          :          :          :          :          :          :
             :          :          :          :          :          :          :          :
             :          :          :          :          :          :          :          :
             :          :          :          :          :          :          :          :
             :__________:__________:__________:__________:__________:__________:__________:
             :          :          :          :          :          :          :          :
             :          : DSP03    :          :          :          :          : DSP05    :
      Port 1 :          : *DSP     :          :          :          :          : *DSP     :
                                                                                            More...
F3=Exit   F12=Cancel   F19=Left   F20=Right   F24=More keys
Overprinting not displayed.
```

Figure 8–6: PRTDEVADDR report

Option 60 from the MANAGESYS menu, Customize your system, users, and devices, allows you to customize options on your system. This is explained below as option 11 on the ASSIST menu.

Option 11 from the ASSIST menu, Customize your system, users, and devices, allows you to customize options on your system. The SETUP menu is displayed and is shown in Figure 8–7.

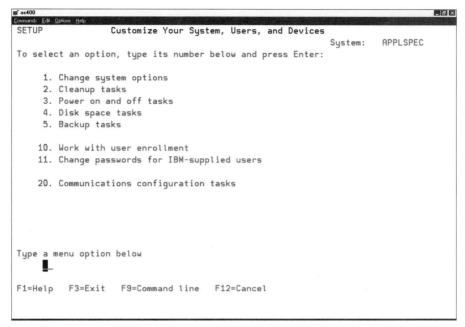

Figure 8–7: SETUP menu

Option 1 from the SETUP menu, Change system options, is an abbreviated version of the WRKSYSVAL command. This option allows you to change some of the most common system values in an easy interface.

Option 2 on the SETUP menu, Cleanup tasks, displays the CLEANUP menu to enable scheduling and execution of cleanup tasks. Job and history logs, journal receivers, messages, spooled files, and OfficeVision/400 calendar items are created each day on an AS/400 system. Many of these items will need to be saved for some amount of time, but older items may be removed from the system. Removing these items will save disk space and will also improve the efficiency of the system, as OS/400 will have fewer objects to maintain and monitor.

The functions available through Operational Assistant make the task of cleanup much easier. Cleanup operations may be scheduled with selectable time periods based on the length of time the item has been on the system. The CLEANUP menu is shown in Figure 8–8, and may also be directly accessed (GO CLEANUP).

Option 1, Change cleanup options, allows you to start or end scheduled cleanups, and to change the time periods associated with different system items. Selecting option 1 will display the screen in Figure 8–9.

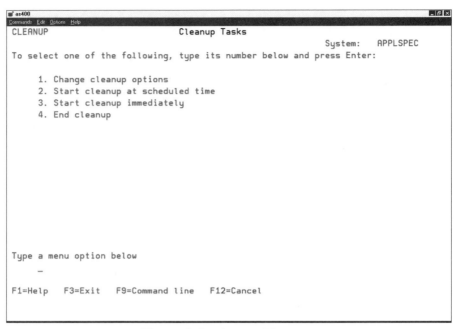

Figure 8–8: CLEANUP menu

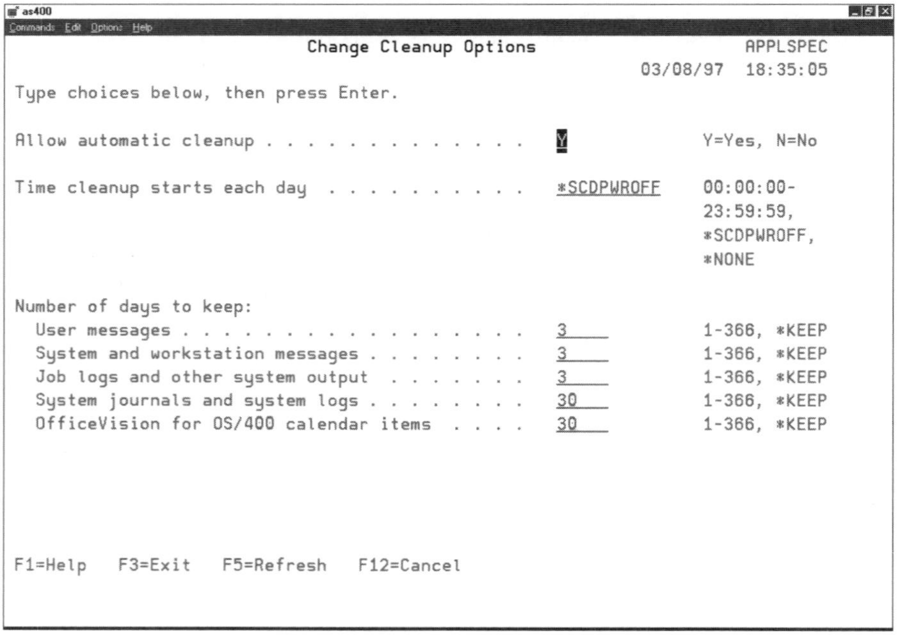

Figure 8–9: Change cleanup options

The first prompt, "Allow automatic cleanup," determines if cleanup tasks will be executed.

The "Time cleanup starts each day" prompt allows you to specify when the cleanup tasks should execute. The special value *SCDPWROFF will cause the cleanup tasks to be executed when the system is power cycled.

The following prompts determine, for each of the listed items, the number of days the item should be kept on the system before it is removed. The special value *KEEP indicates the item should be kept on the system and not removed.

Option 2, Start cleanup at scheduled time, schedules the cleanup process.

Option 3, Start cleanup immediately, will cause the cleanup process to begin executing regardless of the scheduled time.

Option 4, End cleanup, will remove the cleanup process from the schedule. Option 2 (or the STRCLNUP command) will need to be executed to again schedule the cleanup tasks.

Option 3 on the SETUP menu, Power on and off tasks, allow you to maintain a schedule of system power on and off events. This process allows you to schedule these events based on the day of the week, holidays, and different maintenance or work schedules. The POWER menu is displayed when option 11 is selected. This menu may be accessed directly (GO POWER) and is shown here (see Figure 8–10).

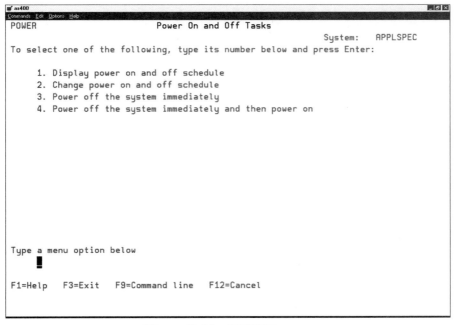

Figure 8–10: POWER menu

Option 1, Display power on and off schedule, displays the following screen. This display indicates when the system will be powered on and powered off. A description field is included to identify the reason for the power cycle (see Figure 8–11).

```
as400                                                                          _ 8 X
Commands  Edit  Options  Help
                        Display Power On/Off Schedule                     APPLSPEC
                                                        03/08/97  18:29:43
      Start list at . . . . . . .  █_____   Date


                           Power    Power
      Date      Day        On       Off        Description
      03/08/97  Sat

      03/09/97  Sun
      03/10/97  Mon
      03/11/97  Tue
      03/12/97  Wed
      03/13/97  Thu
      03/14/97  Fri
      03/15/97  Sat

      03/16/97  Sun
      03/17/97  Mon
      03/18/97  Tue
                                                              More...
      Press Enter to continue.


      F1=Help   F3=Exit   F12=Cancel
```

Figure 8–11: Display power on/off schedule

Option 2, Change power on and off schedule, uses the previous display to allow you to maintain the schedule.

Option 3, Power off the system immediately, executes the Power Down System (PWRDWNSYS) command with a parameter of OPTION(*IMMED). This will immediately end all subsystems and power down the system. The system will not be automatically restarted.

Option 4, Power off the system immediately and then power on, invokes the Power Down System (PWRDWNSYS) command with parameters of OPTION(*IMMED) and RESTART(*YES). This will immediately end all subsystems and power down the system. The system will then be automatically restarted. This produces a power cycle effect.

Option 4 from the SETUP menu, Disk space tasks, produces a menu where you may collect disk space information, print disk space information, work with libraries, work with folders, and work with objects by owner.

Option 5 from the SETUP menu, Backup tasks, produces a menu where you may run a backup, display the status of backups, set up backups, initialize a tape, and initialize a tape set.

Option 10 on the SETUP menu, Work with user enrollment, allows easy access to functions for the maintenance of directory and OfficeVision/400 enrollment entries. These functions are explained in Chapter 10, ("Using OfficeVision/400").

Option 11 on the SETUP menu, Change passwords for IBM-supplied users, provides a simple method to change the passwords for the default IBM-supplied users. These passwords are for the security officer (QSECOFR), the system operator (QSYSOPR), the programmer (QPGMR), the user (QUSER), service (QSRV) and basic service (QSRVBAS).

Option 20 on the SETUP menu, Communications configuration tasks, provides a easy to use interface for communication configuration tasks.

Option 75 from the ASSIST menu, Documentation and problem handling, enables you to examine on-line documentation, use the system supplied help functions, and use the on-line error determination and resolution facilities. These functions are discussed in Chapter 1, ("Getting Started") and later in this chapter.

Option 80 from the ASSIST menu, Temporary sign-off, enables you to sign off the system temporarily. You will be returned to this menu when you sign on to the system again.

8.5 ERROR DETERMINATION

OS/400 provides excellent error reporting and determination features. Several sources of error information are available, and OS/400 also has a feature that allows you to analyze and report problems to IBM. This section will examine the different methods and sources of error information. The following section will identify the steps needed to analyze problems (with OS/400's help) and to report a problem to IBM.

The most common source of error or problem determination is from the users of the system. Users will notice (and hopefully report) problems such as slow response time, lost jobs or reports, abnormal ends to batch or interactive jobs, or inaccurate results on reports or in programs. Other problems that may be reported would be system or program error messages, or indications of problems from system status commands.

The most common indication that an error has occurred is from messages in the system operator's message queue (QSYSOPR). Displaying messages from this queue will show errors that have occurred at a system level. These messages may or may not require a response depending on the severity of the message. Placing the cursor on the message and pressing the <HELP> key (or <F1>) will display the second-level help. This second-level help may provide more information to help correct the problem. The example shown in Figure 8–12 is displaying the system operator's message queue (DSPMSG QSYSOPR).

Another important source of error information is the job log. The job log is a record of the messages received, commands executed, and results from an interactive session or a batch job. A great deal of information can be collected depending on the value of the LOG parameter in the user profile or job description. The job log for an interactive session may be printed when the user signs off the system by specifying SIGNOFF OPTION(*LIST). A batch job's job log may often be kept by the system for later examination.

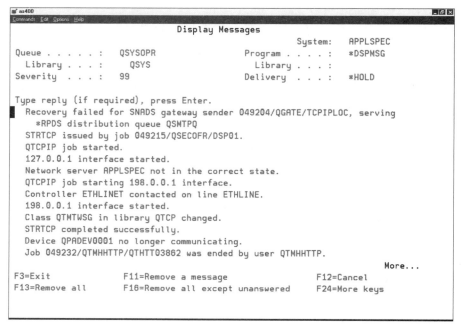

Figure 8–12: DSPMSG QSYSOPR

The display shown in Figure 8–13 is an example of a job log with errors. Note that information such as the time and date of job initiation, commands that were executed, and error messages received are all shown in the log. This information could be provided to the system manager to help in identifying a problem.

The history log is another tool for problem identification. The history log is similar to a job log except the history log is a record of system events. Interactive session and batch job initiation and termination are shown in the history log as are important system events such as system errors.

The command to display the contents of the history log is Display Log-History (DSPLOG LOG(QHST)). The output of this command may be directed to the terminal (the default) or to a printer. You may specify optional starting and ending times and specific error messages to be displayed. The following figure shows a portion of a history log (see Figure 8–14).

Second-level help may be accessed when displaying the history log by placing the cursor on the line containing the message and pressing the <HELP> or <F1> keys.

Another source of information is the error log. This log keeps a record of all the errors occurring on the system. While the QSYSOPR message queue or the history log may have the information you need to identify a problem, the error log may contain the historical information required. The command to print the error log is Print Error Log (PRTERRLOG).

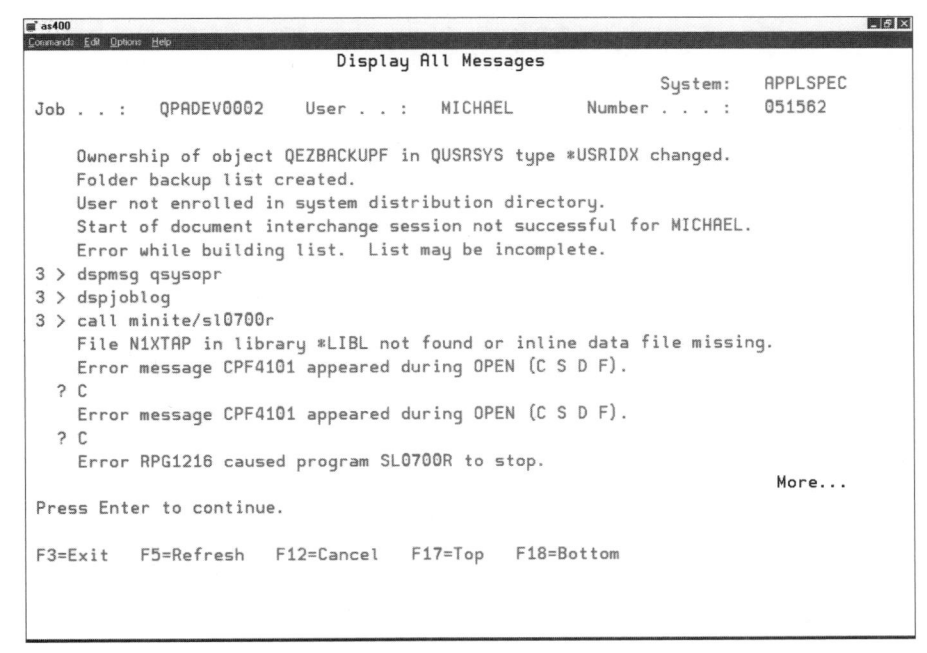

Figure 8–13: Job log

```
as400                                                              _ 8 X
Commands  Edit  Options  Help
                    Display History Log Contents
Job 050794/QTMHHTTP/QTHTT20250 started on 02/26/97 at 13:49:49 in subsystem Q
Job 050787/QTMHHTTP/QTHTT17283 was ended by user QTMHHTTP.
Job 050787/QTMHHTTP/QTHTT17283 ended on 02/26/97 at 13:50:55; 3 seconds used;
Job 050795/QTMHHTTP/QTHTT20865 started on 02/26/97 at 13:51:53 in subsystem Q
Job 050788/QTMHHTTP/QTHTT18092 was ended by user QTMHHTTP.
Job 050788/QTMHHTTP/QTHTT18092 ended on 02/26/97 at 13:53:00; 3 seconds used;
Job 050796/QTMHHTTP/QTHTT21454 started on 02/26/97 at 13:53:59 in subsystem Q
Job 050797/QSECOFR/PRTSYSRPT started on 02/26/97 at 13:56:07 in subsystem QBA
Job 050797/QSECOFR/PRTSYSRPT ended on 02/26/97 at 13:58:21; 79 seconds used;
Device PRT01 no longer communicating.
Hardware failure on device PRT01.
Job 050798/QSECOFR/PRTSYSRPT started on 02/26/97 at 14:05:48 in subsystem QBA
Job 050798/QSECOFR/PRTSYSRPT ended on 02/26/97 at 14:07:52; 78 seconds used;
Attempting recovery from possible power loss on device PRT01.
Job 050799/QSECOFR/PRTSYSRPT started on 02/26/97 at 14:22:38 in subsystem QBA
Job 050799/QSECOFR/PRTSYSRPT ended on 02/26/97 at 14:23:26; 19 seconds used;
Job 050800/QSECOFR/PRTSYSRPT started on 02/26/97 at 14:23:49 in subsystem QBA
                                                                 More...
Press Enter to continue.

F3=Exit   F12=Cancel
```

Figure 8–14: History log

Several displays also help in identifying problems. These system status commands include Work with Active Jobs (WRKACTJOB), Work with System Activity (WRKSYSACT), Work with Jobs (WRKJOB), Display Job Log (DSPJOBLOG), Work with System Status (WRKSYSSTS), Work with Configuration Status (WRKCFGSTS), Work with Submitted Jobs (WRKSBMJOB), and Work with User Jobs (WRKUSRJOB).

These status displays may not provide an error indication, but will show the status of the system in terms of disk and CPU utilization, jobs (both interactive and batch), and communication status. Specifically, the WRKACTJOB and WRKSYSACT commands can show what jobs are using a greater portion of CPU resources, the WRKSYSSTS command will show the amount of disk and number of addresses used, and the WRKCFGSTS command will show the status of data communications devices and jobs.

8.6 ERROR RESOLUTION

Problems may be analyzed with the help of OS/400. While this is not meant to take the place of system problem analysis, the facility works very well for certain system problems. The first step is to analyze the problem.

A method to analyze problems is to display the messages in the system operator's message queue [DSPMSG MSGQ(QSYSOPR)]. Any messages that have an asterisk next to the message are eligible for problem analysis. Place the cursor on the asterisk and press <F14>. This will take you through several (depending on the problem) steps to analyze the problem. You will need to answer questions and perform certain tests or exercises. The answers and results of the exercises are placed in the problem log. The Analyze Problem (ANZPRB) command provides the same functionality for problems that may or may not be in the QSYSOPR message queue.

For example, in the case of a problem with a device, OS/400 will present a series of steps for you to follow to determine the problem. Some of these steps in this example would be to ensure the power is on to the device, to ensure the device is varied on, to check if the brightness and contrast controls are turned up adequately, and so on. After you have completed this level of problem analysis and have still not corrected the problem, OS/400 will add the problem to the problem log. You may then have the problem electronically reported to your service provider. Reporting problems is explained below.

The problem log is a journal that OS/400 maintains to track problems. You may add a problem to the problem log, report the problem to your service provider, print the log, add notes to a problem, and other functions. The problem log exists so that you may keep track of the problems, report the problems, and have a record of when the problem was corrected.

Reporting the problem to your service provider allows you to electronically transmit information regarding the problem. The service provider can analyze the information and then contact you (electronically or by phone) to update the status of the problem. The service provider could also electronically send a "fix" to the problem.

The Work with Problem (WRKPRB) command produces a display of problems that have occurred on the system. Each problem will be assigned a problem ID which is used to track the problem. This problem ID will be used by your service provider when dealing with the problem. These problems could have a status of "OPENED," which means the problem has not yet been analyzed, "READY," or "PREPARED," which means the problem has been analyzed, or "SENT," which indicates the problem has been sent to the service provider.

The WRKPRB command allows you, at a problem I

D level, to report the problem. Option 8, Work with Problem, will produce a display of options that include reporting the problem. Selecting this option will produce a display showing the contact information for this problem. You may change this information, pressing <ENTER> when complete. This will cause OS/400 to produce another display that allows you to identify the severity level of the problem. Severity levels are

1. "Inability to use the program resulting in a critical impact on operations." This indicates the system has encountered an error whose severity is so great that normal business cannot proceed. This severity level requires an immediate response. An example of this problem would be being unable to access Officevision/400 for a company that utilizes all the functionality of Officevision/400 for their daily activities.

2. "The program is usable but severely restricted." This indicates that limited functionality is available, but the problem restricts function. An example of this problem would be if Officevision/400 could be accessed, but no documents could be printed.

3. "The program is usable without some functions which are not critical to the overall operation." This type of problem will limit function. An example of this problem is where Officevision/400 could be accessed and operations such as printing could be accessed, but the spell check option was not functional.

4. "A circumvention to the problem has been found." This severity level indicates that the program is operating at full function, but a problem still exists. An example could be where a library list change would need to be made manually rather than automatically.

After the appropriate severity level has been selected, the problem will be reported to the service provider electronically using the Electronic Customer Support (ECS) modem. Your AS/400 will automatically dial up the service provider and transmit the problem information.

If the service provider is IBM, a standard set of steps will ensue. The incoming call will be routed to a customer service coordinator who will initially examine the problem. If the problem is hardware-related, IBM will send the information to an IBM service representative who will contact you to make arrangements for a service call. The problem description on your system will be changed to a status of "SENT."

If the problem is software-related, the IBM software database will be searched to find a match with the information you entered in the problem description. If the problem is found and a Program Temporary Fix (PTF) is available, the PTF will either be downloaded electronically or sent on a tape depending on the size of the PTF. If the solution to the problem is not available as a PTF, the problem will be sent to the IBM Software Support Center for further analysis. An IBM software service representative will contact you for more information regarding the problem. The problem description on your system will be changed to a status of "SENT" or "ANSWERED."

9

OfficeVision/400

OfficeVision/400 is a licensed program purchased separately from the OS/400 base operating system. OfficeVision/400 is an office automation package that provides electronic mail, calendar, word processing, and other organizational aides for OS/400 users. This chapter will teach you about

- using the OfficeVision/400 calendar.
- sending and receiving messages (one or two lines of text) and notes (short documents).
- basic editing with the OfficeVision/400 word processor.

9.1 THE OFFICEVISION VISION

OfficeVision/400 was originally the AS/400 component in IBM's enterprisewide OfficeVision solution. The intent of OfficeVision was to implement an office automation solution that embraces Personal Computers, midrange systems, and mainframe systems. The various program components of OfficeVision were to communicate with each other using the IBM System's Application Architecture (SAA). Unfortunately, the enterprisewide OfficeVision plan was discontinued before completed.

Fortunately, OfficeVision/400 took on a life of its own, and it is now commonly used as a stand-alone product to service workstation and PC users who are connected to an AS/400. In this environment, OfficeVision/400 is a central service available to all of the OS/400 users on that AS/400. IBM also offers optional gateway services to bridge OfficeVision/400 with nonOfficeVision mainframe products such as PROFS and NOTES. This chapter will address OfficeVision/400 in this context.

9.2 INVOKING OFFICEVISION/400

OfficeVision/400 may be invoked from the OS/400 Main Menu by selecting option 2 (Office tasks). After a brief pause, the Office Tasks menu appears. Select option 1 (OfficeVision/400) to begin interacting with OfficeVision/400.

NOTE: You must be enrolled as an OfficeVision/400 user. Having an OS/400 user id does not automatically grant you access to OfficeVision/400.

Alternatively, you can use the command-line method to start OfficeVision/400 by entering the command STROFC on any available command line.

Using the STROFC command takes you directly to the OfficeVision/400 opening menu. It is equivalent to entering option 2 (Office tasks) from the Main Menu followed by option 1 (OfficeVision/400) from the Office Tasks menu.

Once OfficeVision/400 has been selected, its opening menu will appear. On this left side of this display are option selections; on the right side are the current time, a calendar display for the current month, and an optional message that indicates if new mail is waiting to be read. A two-character field is located on the left side of the screen underneath the options to permit the entry of one of the listed option numbers (see Figure 9–1):

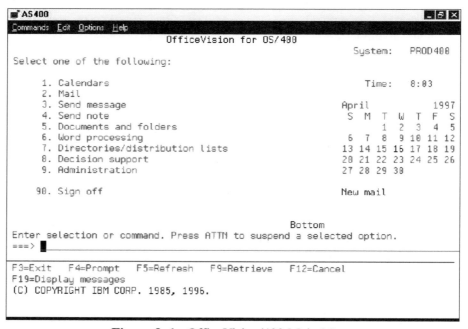

Figure 9–1: OfficeVision/400 Main Menu

The standard implementation of OfficeVision/400 features nine primary options, numbered from 1 to 9, and a sign-off option, number 90. Other custom options may be available at your location. In brief, the standard OfficeVision/400 options are as follows:

1. Calendars—The calendar function can be used as a personal appointment schedule and can display a calendar using a daily, weekly, or six-month perspective. The calendar function also allows you to find common free times on multiple calendars and schedule meetings that include other people.

2. Mail—The mail function allows you to work with mail you have received. You can use this function to read your mail, forward your mail, delete your mail, or perform other activities on your inbound mail.

3. Send message—This function lets you compose and send a brief (one or two line) message to another user.

4. Send note—This function allows you to compose and send a short document using a predetermined OfficeVision/400 format. This function is appropriate for memorandums or other types of concise correspondence.

5. Documents and folders—This multipurpose function permits you to access documents stored in your personal folders or folders that you are allowed to access. This function provides a convenient method for browsing through documents, and sending documents, and for sharing documents between two or more individuals.

6. Word processing—The word processing function is used to access the fully-functional OfficeVision/400 word processor. The word processor may be used to create formal documents such as letters, specifications, or documentation. These documents are then stored in folders for subsequent access.

7. Directories/distribution lists—This function manages lists of people's names whom you may communicate with via electronic mail. Using this function you can create a single name that may be used to send mail to a group of people, or create custom "nicknames" for individuals.

8. Decision support—This menu function may be used to access other, optional utilities, such as business graphics, database query, and interactive data definition functions.

9. Administration—This function allows you to change the environmental and authorization settings for your OfficeVision/400 interactions. The extent of changes you can make is limited, based on your OS/400 security assignments.

90. Sign off—Using the sign-off option terminates your interaction with OfficeVision/400 and signs you off of the AS/400.

Since OS/400 allows for menus to be customized, all of the described options may not be available on your opening menu. Similarly, additional custom options may be available for you to choose from.

9.3 RETURNING TO THE OPENING MENU

After choosing an option from the opening menu, additional menus will be displayed as appropriate for the selected function. If you need to return to the opening menu (for example, to read mail that has just arrived), you can use one of the following techniques:

Suspend the current function using the <ATTN> key:

When you are working with a function selected from the opening menu, you may press the <ATTN> key to temporarily suspend it and return to the opening OfficeVision/400 menu. Suspended functions will be marked by the > character appearing to the left of the option number, and the message "ATTN pressed" will appear above the selection field.

At that point you may select another option, such as 2 to read new mail. To return to a function you have suspended, simply select that option again from the opening menu.

NOTE: The <ATTN> key may be disabled in your user profile and therefore may not be available in OfficeVision/400 (see Figure 9–2):

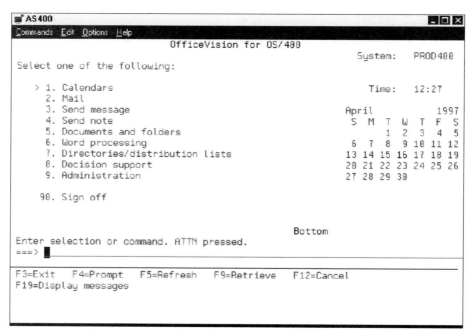

Figure 9–2: OfficeVision with suspended functions

Exit the current function using the <F3> key:

To exit a selected function simply press the <F3> key.

Cancel the current function using the <F12> key:

> Use the <F12> key to return to the previous display. Because some functions have several layers of displays, you may have to press the <F12> key several times to return to the opening menu.

9.4 LEAVING OFFICEVISION/400

To terminate OfficeVision/400 activity, you must first return to the OfficeVision/400 opening menu. At that point you can perform one of the following activities:

> Press <F3> or <F12> to leave OfficeVision/400, but remain signed on to the AS/400.

> Select option 90 to sign off the AS/400. This will automatically terminate your interaction with OfficeVision/400.

If you attempt to terminate your interaction with OfficeVision/400 and you have any suspended functions that remain unresolved, an Exit OfficeVision/400 menu will appear asking if you want to abandon the suspended function(s) (see Figure 9–3):

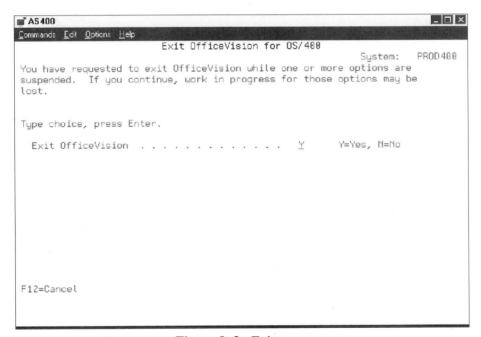

Figure 9–3: Exit menu

If you enter Y in this menu, all suspended functions will be terminated. If you enter N, you will be returned to the opening menu. At that point you can return to each suspended function, finish your activity, and then exit from it.

NOTE: You should not attempt to exit OfficeVision/400 while the word processing function is suspended. OfficeVision/400 may not detect that the word processor function is suspended and terminate without asking for confirmation. If this happens, any work-in-progress document is lost.

9.5 OPTION 1: THE CALENDAR FUNCTION

Select option 1 from the OfficeVision/400 opening menu to access the calendar function. The calendar function supports three viewing perspectives: daily, weekly, and six-month. You can change your current perspective and default perspective through the use of the <F11> and <F13> keys, as described in this chapter (see Figures 9–4 through 9–6):

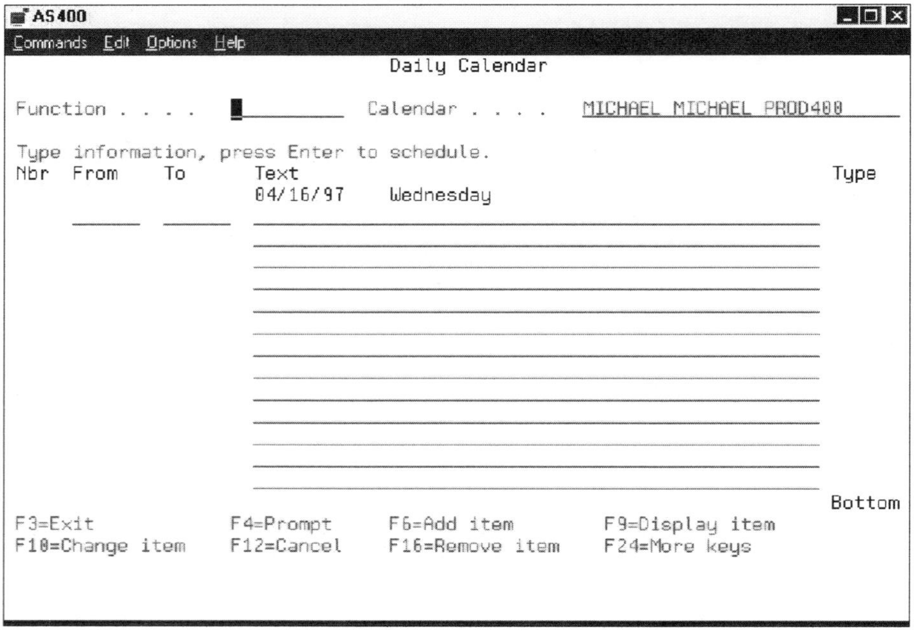

```
 AS400                                                          _ □ ✕
Commands  Edit  Options  Help
                              Daily Calendar

Function . . . .   ▮_____    Calendar . . . .   MICHAEL MICHAEL PROD400

Type information, press Enter to schedule.
Nbr  From    To     Text                                          Type
                    04/16/97    Wednesday
     _____  _____  _____
                     _____
                     _____
                     _____
                     _____
                     _____
                     _____
                     _____
                     _____
                     _____
                     _____
                     _____
                     _____
                                                              Bottom
F3=Exit           F4=Prompt      F6=Add item     F9=Display item
F10=Change item   F12=Cancel     F16=Remove item F24=More keys
```

Figure 9–4: Daily view

NOTE: If you do not have a calendar associated with your user name, you will need to create one using the administrative functions described in the *More Calendar Tasks* section of this chapter.

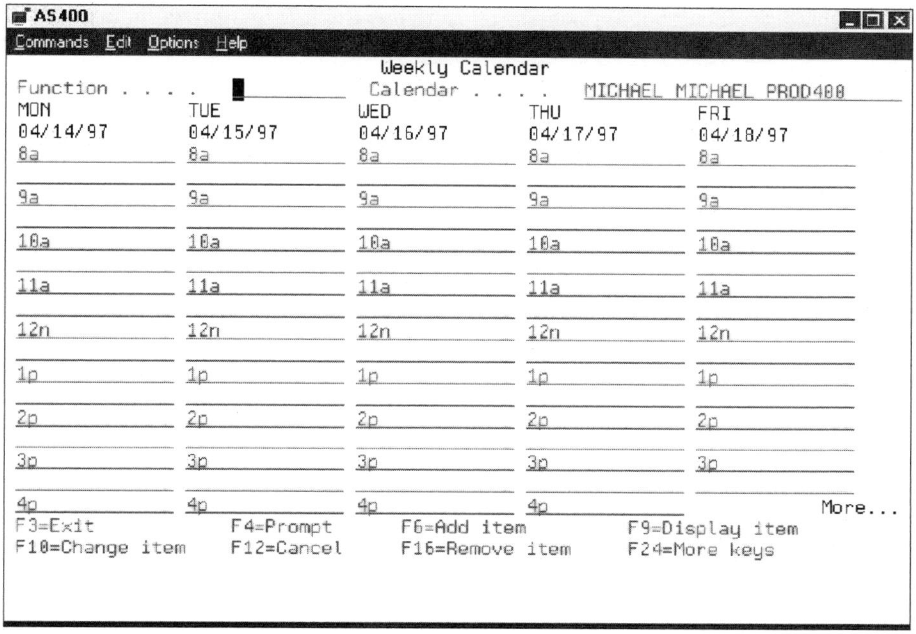

```
■ AS400                                                            _ □ ×
Commands  Edit  Options  Help
                              Weekly Calendar
Function . . . .  ■_____     Calendar . . . .   MICHAEL MICHAEL PROD400
MON               TUE           WED              THU             FRI
04/14/97          04/15/97      04/16/97         04/17/97        04/18/97
8a_____8a_____8a_____8a_____8a_____

9a_____9a_____9a_____9a_____9a_____

10a_____10a_____10a_____10a_____10a_____

11a_____11a_____11a_____11a_____11a_____

12n_____12n_____12n_____12n_____12n_____

1p_____1p_____1p_____1p_____1p_____

2p_____2p_____2p_____2p_____2p_____

3p_____3p_____3p_____3p_____3p_____

4p_____4p_____4p_____4p_____More...
F3=Exit           F4=Prompt       F6=Add item          F9=Display item
F10=Change item   F12=Cancel      F16=Remove item      F24=More keys
```

Figure 9–5: Weekly view

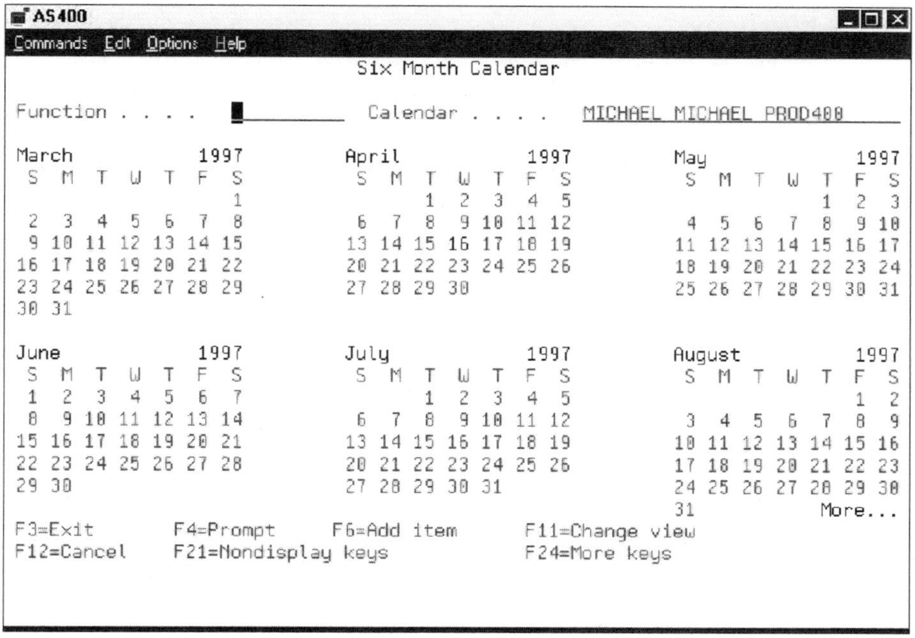

```
■ AS400                                                            _ □ ×
Commands  Edit  Options  Help
                              Six Month Calendar

Function . . . .   ■_____     Calendar . . . .   MICHAEL MICHAEL PROD400

March            1997      April            1997      May              1997
S  M  T  W  T  F  S        S  M  T  W  T  F  S        S  M  T  W  T  F  S
                  1                 1  2  3  4  5                     1  2  3
2  3  4  5  6  7  8        6  7  8  9 10 11 12        4  5  6  7  8  9 10
9 10 11 12 13 14 15       13 14 15 16 17 18 19       11 12 13 14 15 16 17
16 17 18 19 20 21 22      20 21 22 23 24 25 26       18 19 20 21 22 23 24
23 24 25 26 27 28 29      27 28 29 30                25 26 27 28 29 30 31
30 31

June             1997      July             1997      August           1997
S  M  T  W  T  F  S        S  M  T  W  T  F  S        S  M  T  W  T  F  S
1  2  3  4  5  6  7                 1  2  3  4  5                        1  2
8  9 10 11 12 13 14        6  7  8  9 10 11 12        3  4  5  6  7  8  9
15 16 17 18 19 20 21      13 14 15 16 17 18 19       10 11 12 13 14 15 16
22 23 24 25 26 27 28      20 21 22 23 24 25 26       17 18 19 20 21 22 23
29 30                     27 28 29 30 31             24 25 26 27 28 29 30
                                                     31              More...
F3=Exit           F4=Prompt       F6=Add item          F11=Change view
F12=Cancel        F21=Nondisplay keys                  F24=More keys
```

Figure 9–6: Six-month view

After the default calendar appears, you can view the information contained in it or use any of the following keys:

<ROLL UP> and <ROLL DOWN>—If a "More.." message appears below the calendar on the right-hand side, the <ROLL UP> and <ROLL DOWN> keys may be used to move the calendar forward and backward in time.

The <F6> Add item, <F10> Change item, and <F16> Remove item keys may be used to alter the contents of the calendar, as explained in the *Editing a Calendar* section of this chapter.

The <F9> View item and <F11> Change view keys may be used to alter how you look at calendar information. Please consult the *Viewing a Calendar* section of this chapter.

<F13> More tasks—Pressing <F13> brings up a menu of additional calendar tasks. These tasks are described in the *More Calendar Tasks* section.

<F15> Print—Pressing this key brings up a menu allowing you to specify print options for your calendar and send it to an output queue.

<F19> Display message—OfficeVision/400 can be configured to alert you about upcoming activities by sounding a bell and placing a notice in your message queue. The <F19> key is used to display your message queue.

<F21> Nondisplay—Pressing this key reduces the function key display on the bottom of the screen to allow more of the calendar to show. Pressing <F21> again restores the function key display.

<F24> More keys—Pressing <F24> changes the function key display to show additional function keys that are available. Each time you press <F24> the function key display on the bottom of the screen will change.

The main calendar display also contains a field named "Function." You may enter special commands into this field to perform operations that would normally take two or more menu operations. Please see the *Calendar Shortcuts* section of this chapter for more information on this topic.

9.5.1 Editing a Calendar

The primary benefit of a personal calendar is that it allows you to keep track of personal appointments, business meetings, and other important events. With OfficeVision/400 you can employ one or more calendars to keep track of these items.

Items can be added to the calendar you are currently viewing by pressing the <F6> key. In response, OfficeVision/400 brings up a menu on the bottom of the screen requesting you to define the type of item you are adding (see Figure 9–7):

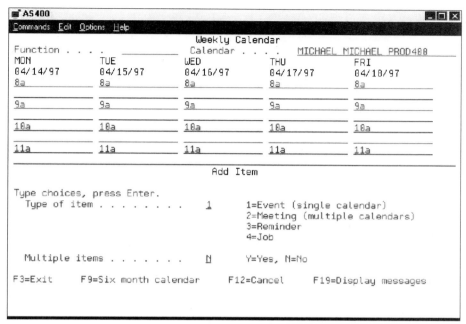

Figure 9–7: Add Item

The OfficeVision/400 calendar supports the following types of items:

1. Event—An event is an item that affects you but does not necessarily involve other individuals from your company. Events include personal appointments, business meetings with individuals from different companies, and so forth. You can instruct OfficeVision/400 to send you a message alerting you to an upcoming event.

    NOTE: If you are using the daily perspective, you can also define an event by entering a time and a brief description directly into the calendar display.

2. Meeting—A meeting is an event that involves multiple persons. When you add a meeting to your calendar, you can find common free times for the desired attendees and provide them with notification of the meeting.

3. Reminder—Unlike an event or a meeting, a reminder has no specific time assigned to it. Reminders may be used to remind you to make a phone call, to perform an errand, or other similar activities. You can instruct OfficeVision/400 to send you a message alerting you about a reminder.

4. and 5.   Job or System/36 procedure—You can also use the calendar func-
            tion to automatically run a job or command for you at a certain date
            and time. To use this feature you must be authorized to submit jobs
            and to access the specific job or command you supply. This is an
            advanced function that should be carefully considered before using.

OfficeVision/400 also allows you to schedule items for one specific date or for multiple dates. This is determined by the "Multiple items" field. If you enter a Y in this field, you
will be defining an item that occurs on two or more dates (for example, a regular status meeting or a series of three appointments). If, however, you enter N you will be defining an event
for a single date.

Once you select the type of item, press the <ENTER> key and additional menus will
appear requesting further definition of the item.

9.5.2 Adding a Calendar Event or Reminder

When you add an single event or a reminder, you are then presented with a simple data
entry menu on the bottom of the screen. In both cases you may change the default date for
the item, supply a description, assign the item a security classification, and optionally
request an alert message. Defining an event also requires establishing the starting and ending times; times are not required for reminders. Times may be specified in a 12-hour format followed by an "a" for "a.m." or a "p" for "p.m." (for example, 8:00a, 4:00p) or in a
24-hour format (13:50, 21:00) (see Figure 9–8).

NOTE: To access the security information for an event, press the <ROLL UP> key
and a second display will appear. You may press <ROLL DOWN> to return to the first display (see Figure 9–9).

If you need more space for a description than is available on the display, press the
<F14> key to obtain additional data entry space.

If you request an alert message by entering a Y in the "Message" field, you will then
be prompted for the date and time you want to receive the alert.

Each reminder and event may be assigned a security level to control which items can
be viewed by other people accessing your calendar. By convention, a "Security" field
assignment of 1 means unclassified, an assignment of 2 means confidential, and an assignment of 3 means personal. The ability for people to see items defined with these access levels is determined when they are given the ability to access your calendar.

Finally, if you are defining an event, you are presented with a "Status" field that
allows you to indicate if the event is tentative (1) or confirmed (2).

When all fields have been defined to your satisfaction, press <ENTER> to post the
item to your calendar.

```
┌─────────────────────────────────────────────────────────────────────────┐
│ ▪ AS 400                                                        _ □ ✕      │
├─────────────────────────────────────────────────────────────────────────┤
│ Commands  Edit  Options  Help                                             │
│                           Weekly Calendar                                 │
│ Function . . . .  _____   Calendar . . . .   MICHAEL MICHAEL PROD400    │
│ MON            TUE            WED            THU            FRI            │
│ 04/14/97       04/15/97       04/16/97       04/17/97       04/18/97       │
│ 8a             8a             8a             8a             8a             │
│                                                                           │
│ 9a             9a             9a             9a             9a             │
│                                                                           │
│ 10a            10a            10a            10a            10a            │
│                                                                           │
│ 11a            11a            11a            11a            11a            │
│                                                                           │
│                             Add Event                                     │
│ Type choices, press Enter.                                                │
│   Calendar . . . . . .   MICHAEL MICHAEL PROD400      F4 for list          │
│   Date/day . . . . . .   04/16/97          MM/DD/YY                        │
│   From/to  . . . . . .    8:00a   9:00a    hh:mmA, hh:mmP                   │
│   Text . . . . . . . .   _____              │
│                          _____              │
│                                                                           │
│   Message  . . . . . .   N              Y=Yes, N=No                        │
│                                                               More...      │
│ F3=Exit     F4=Prompt     F12=Cancel    F24=More keys                      │
│                                                                           │
└─────────────────────────────────────────────────────────────────────────┘
```

Figure 9–8: Add Event

```
┌─────────────────────────────────────────────────────────────────────────┐
│ ▪ AS 400                                                        _ □ ✕      │
├─────────────────────────────────────────────────────────────────────────┤
│ Commands  Edit  Options  Help                                             │
│                           Weekly Calendar                                 │
│ Function . . . .  _____   Calendar . . . .   MICHAEL MICHAEL PROD400    │
│ MON            TUE            WED            THU            FRI            │
│ 04/14/97       04/15/97       04/16/97       04/17/97       04/18/97       │
│ 8a             8a             8a             8a             8a             │
│                                                                           │
│ 9a             9a             9a             9a             9a             │
│                                                                           │
│ 10a            10a            10a            10a            10a            │
│                                                                           │
│ 11a            11a            11a            11a            11a            │
│                                                                           │
│                            Add Reminder                                   │
│ Type choices, press Enter.                                                │
│   Calendar . . . . . .   MICHAEL MICHAEL PROD400      F4 for list          │
│   Date/day . . . . . .   04/16/97          MM/DD/YY                        │
│   Reminder . . . . . .   _____              │
│                                                                           │
│   Message  . . . . . .   N              Y=Yes, N=No                        │
│   Security . . . . . .   1              1=Unclassified, 2=Confidential     │
│                                         3=Personal                        │
│                                                                           │
│ F3=Exit     F4=Prompt     F12=Cancel    F24=More keys                      │
│                                                                           │
└─────────────────────────────────────────────────────────────────────────┘
```

Figure 9–9: Add Reminder

9.5.3 Adding a Calendar Meeting

Adding a meeting is necessarily more complicated than adding an event or a reminder because a meeting involves other peoples and may require the allocation of time in a shared conference room. When you select the add meeting option (2) with "Multiple items" set to N in the Add Item menu, a full screen menu appears (see Figure 9–10):

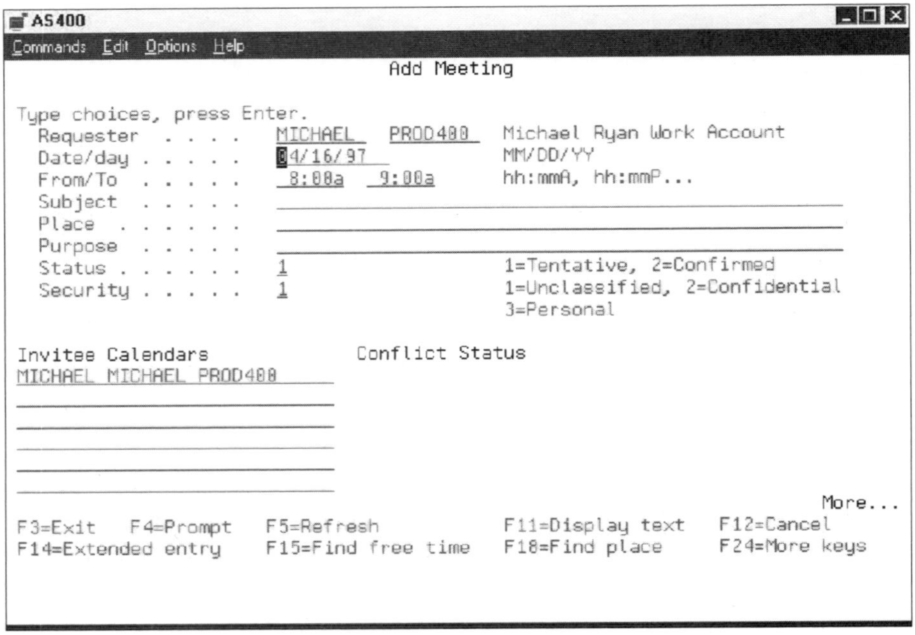
AS400
Commands Edit Options Help
Add Meeting
Type choices, press Enter.
Requester . . . . MICHAEL PROD400 Michael Ryan Work Account
Date/day . . . . . 04/16/97 MM/DD/YY
From/To . . . . . 8:00a 9:00a hh:mmA, hh:mmP...
Subject . . . . .
Place . . . . . .
Purpose . . . . .
Status . . . . . . 1 1=Tentative, 2=Confirmed
Security . . . . . 1 1=Unclassified, 2=Confidential
3=Personal
Invitee Calendars Conflict Status
MICHAEL MICHAEL PROD400
More...
F3=Exit F4=Prompt F5=Refresh F11=Display text F12=Cancel
F14=Extended entry F15=Find free time F18=Find place F24=More keys

Figure 9–10: Add Meeting

On the Add Meeting menu you are defined as the "Requestor" of the meeting and are asked to supply the date and time boundaries of the meeting. Times may be entered in a 12-hour format followed by an "a" for "a.m." or a "p" for "p.m." (for example, 1:30p, 9:00a) or in a 24-hour format (13:50, 21:00).

Following the date and time, you can then define the "Subject," "Place" (location), and "Purpose" of the meeting. Both the "Subject" and "Purpose" fields are free-format data entry areas for text. If you need additional space to define the "Purpose," you can press <F14> for a larger data entry area.

You can enter descriptive text into the "Place" field or you can use OfficeVision/400 to manage the availability of meeting spaces such as conference rooms. If you are using OfficeVision/400 to manage meeting spaces, please refer to the *Scheduling a Meeting Place* section of this chapter.

Like an event, meetings are assigned "Status" and "Security" values. In terms of "Status," a value of 1 means tentative and a value of 2 means confirmed. For the "Security" field, an assignment of 1 means unclassified, an assignment of 2 means confidential, and an assignment of 3 means personal. This assignment will restrict people from seeing the meeting on your calendar, or the calendar of others involved.

In the "Invitee Calendar" fields, enter the names of calendars for the other people you want involved in the meeting. In most cases, the calendar names will directly relate to user names. To obtain a list of calendar names, press the <F4> key while in one of these fields. You can then select from the list of names shown and press <ENTER> to return to the Add Meeting menu. Also note that you can press <ROLL UP> to obtain data entry space for additional names.

Once you have defined the participants in the meeting, you can perform one of two activities.

1. Press <ENTER> to have OfficeVision/400 search the defined calendars to see if all requested participants can attend. If conflicts occur, they will be noted in the "Conflict Status" area of the screen. If the meeting attendance is to your satisfaction, you can press <ENTER> to schedule the meeting. Alternatively, you can find common free time, as described in the next step.

    NOTE: You do not have to resolve conflicts in order to schedule a meeting. OfficeVision/400 permits individuals to have duplicate or overlapping meetings.

2. Press <F15> to find common free time for all participants. After pressing <F15>, the Find Free Time menu appears (see Figure 9–11).

    Use this menu to define the acceptable boundaries that a meeting may fall within. After defining these boundaries, press <ENTER>. OfficeVision/400 will return a list of acceptable meeting times. Select the desired time slot by entering a 1 next to that time and pressing the <ENTER> key. OfficeVision/400 will then complete the meeting definition using that time (see Figure 9–12).

NOTE: If OfficeVision/400 cannot access another person's calendar because of security or because that person uses a different AS/400 system, it will send a meeting notice to that person via electronic mail.

9.5.4 Adding Multiple Items

If you specify Y in the "Multiple items" field in the initial Add Item menu, you will see displays that slightly vary from the screens used to define single occurrence items. The most significant difference is that the multiple item displays include fields that allow you to set specific dates for the recurring item, or to inform OfficeVision/400 of the interval between items and have it automatically generate the dates.

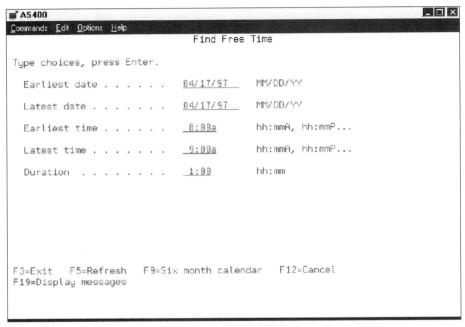

Figure 9–11: Find Free Time

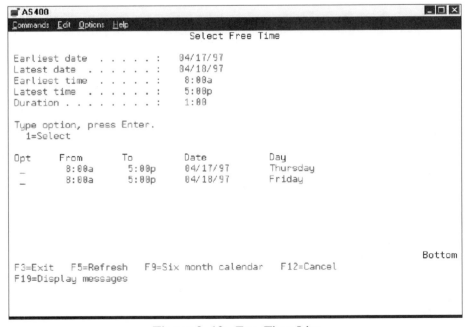

Figure 9–12: Free Time List

9.5.5 Viewing Calendar Information

The amount of item detail displayed on the screen is directly related to the calendar perspective being used.

If you are using a six-month display, no item detail is shown.

If you are using the weekly calendar perspective, brief information about each item will appear.

If you are using the daily perspective, detailed information on each calendar item is presented (see Figures 9–13 through 9–15).

```
 AS400                                                                  _ □ ×
Commands  Edit  Options  Help
                              Six Month Calendar

Function . . . .  ▉_____      Calendar . . . .  MICHAEL MICHAEL PROD400

March            1997        April            1997        May              1997
 S  M  T  W  T  F  S          S  M  T  W  T  F  S          S  M  T  W  T  F  S
                   1                    1  2  3  4  5                      1  2  3
 2  3  4  5  6  7  8          6  7  8  9 10 11 12          4  5  6  7  8  9 10
 9 10 11 12 13 14 15         13 14 15 16 17 18 19         11 12 13 14 15 16 17
16 17 18 19 20 21 22         20 21 22 23 24 25 26         18 19 20 21 22 23 24
23 24 25 26 27 28 29         27 28 29 30                  25 26 27 28 29 30 31
30 31

June             1997        July             1997        August           1997
 S  M  T  W  T  F  S          S  M  T  W  T  F  S          S  M  T  W  T  F  S
 1  2  3  4  5  6  7                   1  2  3  4  5                         1  2
 8  9 10 11 12 13 14          6  7  8  9 10 11 12          3  4  5  6  7  8  9
15 16 17 18 19 20 21         13 14 15 16 17 18 19         10 11 12 13 14 15 16
22 23 24 25 26 27 28         20 21 22 23 24 25 26         17 18 19 20 21 22 23
29 30                        27 28 29 30 31               24 25 26 27 28 29 30
                                                          31          More...
F3=Exit          F4=Prompt      F6=Add item       F11=Change view
F12=Cancel       F21=Nondisplay keys              F24=More keys
```

Figure 9–13: Typical six month calendar

On the daily and weekly perspective, the type of item is shown as "E" for event, "M" for meeting, "R" for reminder,"J" for job, and "P" for procedure. Each item in a given day is also assigned a number showing its relative position in that day. The first item in a day is 1, the second item is 2, and so on.

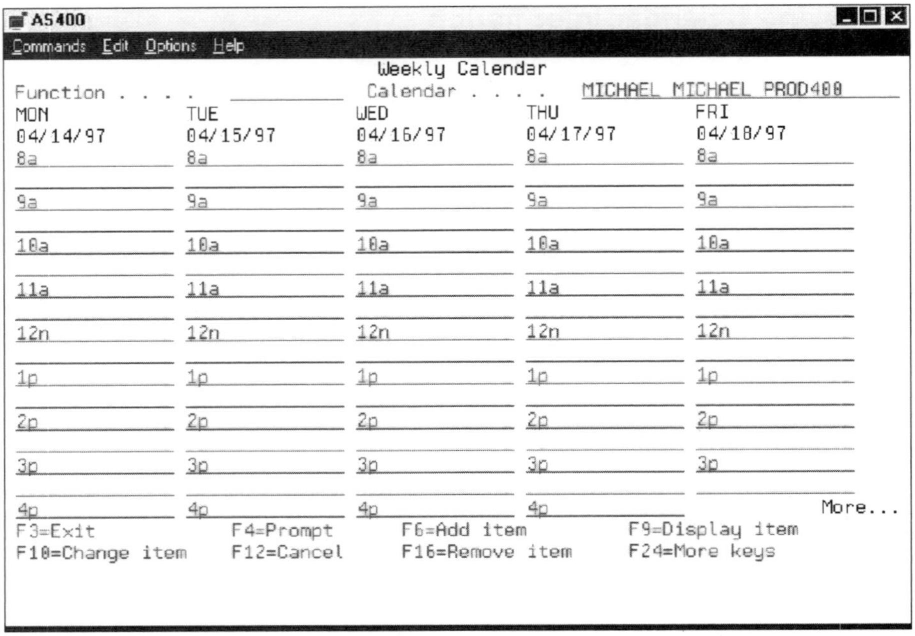

```
■ AS400                                                              _ □ ×
Commands  Edit  Options  Help
                              Weekly Calendar
Function . . . .  _____   Calendar . . . .   MICHAEL MICHAEL PROD400
MON              TUE              WED              THU              FRI
04/14/97         04/15/97         04/16/97         04/17/97         04/18/97
8a_____        8a_____        8a_____        8a_____        8a_____

9a_____        9a_____        9a_____        9a_____        9a_____

10a_____        10a_____        10a_____        10a_____        10a_____

11a_____        11a_____        11a_____        11a_____        11a_____

12n_____        12n_____        12n_____        12n_____        12n_____

1p_____        1p_____        1p_____        1p_____        1p_____

2p_____        2p_____        2p_____        2p_____        2p_____

3p_____        3p_____        3p_____        3p_____        3p_____

4p_____        4p_____        4p_____        4p_____                 More...
F3=Exit                  F4=Prompt        F6=Add item         F9=Display item
F10=Change item          F12=Cancel       F16=Remove item     F24=More keys
```

Figure 9–14: Typical daily calendar

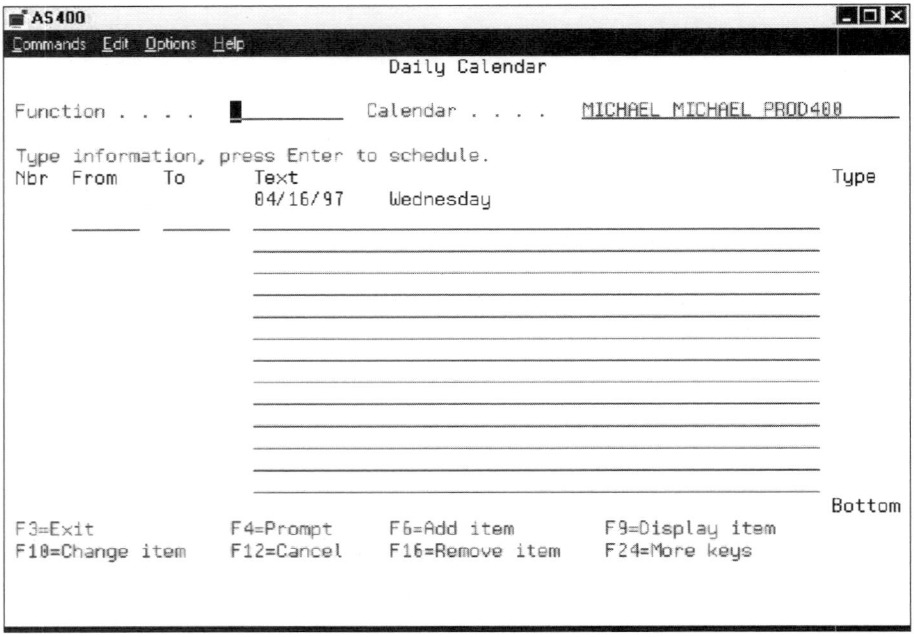

```
■ AS400                                                              _ □ ×
Commands  Edit  Options  Help
                              Daily Calendar

Function . . . .  ■_____     Calendar . . . .   MICHAEL MICHAEL PROD400

Type information, press Enter to schedule.
Nbr  From    To      Text                                            Type
                     04/16/97    Wednesday

     _____   _____   _____

                     _____
                     _____
                     _____
                     _____
                     _____
                     _____
                     _____
                     _____
                     _____
                     _____
                     _____
                                                                    Bottom
F3=Exit                  F4=Prompt        F6=Add item         F9=Display item
F10=Change item          F12=Cancel       F16=Remove item     F24=More keys
```

Figure 9–15: Typical weekly calendar

Because the weekly perspective must fit more information into a limited space, it relies on the placement of special characters to convey further information. The following are examples:

Reminders do not appear in the item list and are noted by the presence of an "R" next to the day.

If items are scheduled before the start of the work day, this will be noted by the presence of a "B" next to the day. You may use the <ROLL DOWN> key to access that period of time.

If calendar items overlap or conflict in a time slot, this will be noted by the presence of two asterisks (**) next to the time.

The following function keys may be used to change the calendar perspective or view additional information about an item:

<F9> Display item—If you are viewing a daily or weekly calendar perspective and want to see all of the information associated with a calendar entry, simply move the cursor to that item and press the <F9> key. Additional information will then appear on the bottom of the screen. You can use <ROLL UP> and <ROLL DOWN> to scroll through the information. Press <F12> to return to the normal calendar display screen.

<F11> Change views—When you press the <F11> key, a menu appears prompting you for the perspective you want to see. By entering the appropriate option in the "Calendar view" field, you can change perspectives. The "Group" and "Composite" selections are advanced options used to manage multiple calendars at once. In addition to the calendar perspective, the Change View menu also allows you to view other calendars you are authorized to access and to specify a specific starting date for the calendar display. After you have made your desired changes, press <ENTER> to return to the primary calendar display (see Figure 9–16).

9.5.6 Calendar Shortcuts

The primary calendar display contains a field named "Function." This field may be used to enter a command to go directly to a specific display or perform a specific function. The commands you may enter into the "Function" field are shortcuts, because they perform an action that may normally require interactions with multiple screens to get to the same point. For example, you can enter VS to change your calendar view to a six-month perspective. The more popular function commands are:

AE—add event.

AM—add meeting.

AR—add reminder.

VD—change to daily perspective.

VS—change to six month perspective.

VW—change to weekly perspective.

A complete list of these function commands may be obtained by positioning the cursor in the "Function" field and pressing the <F4> key.

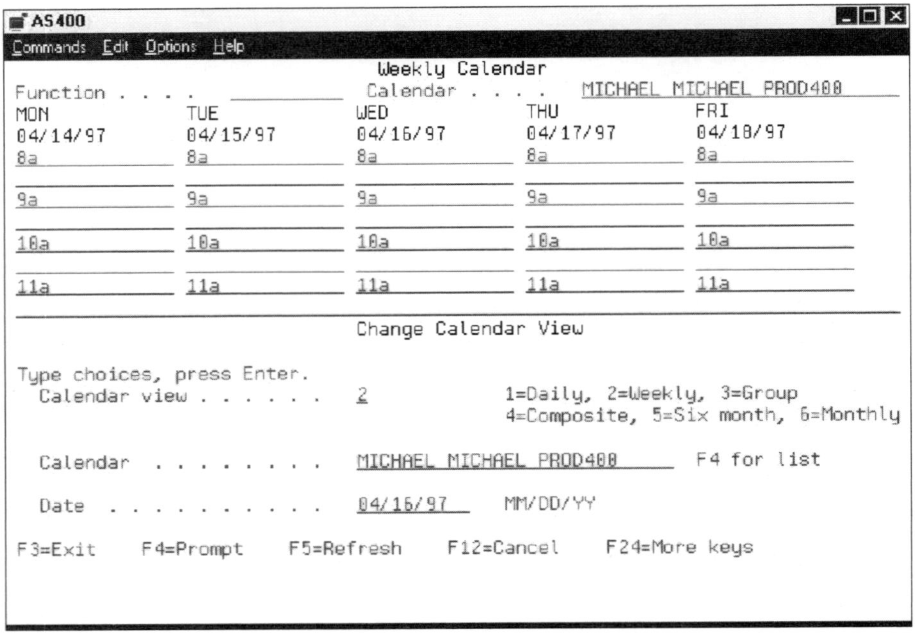

```
 ▄ AS400                                                      ▬ ▢ ✕
 Commands  Edit  Options  Help
                            Weekly Calendar
 Function . . . .  _____   Calendar . . . .   MICHAEL  MICHAEL  PROD400
 MON              TUE            WED             THU             FRI
 04/14/97         04/15/97       04/16/97        04/17/97        04/18/97
 8a _____ 8a _____ 8a _____ 8a _____ 8a _____

 9a _____ 9a _____ 9a _____ 9a _____ 9a _____

 10a _____ 10a _____ 10a _____ 10a _____ 10a _____

 11a _____ 11a _____ 11a _____ 11a _____ 11a _____

                            Change Calendar View

 Type choices, press Enter.
   Calendar view . . . . . .   2            1=Daily, 2=Weekly, 3=Group
                                            4=Composite, 5=Six month, 6=Monthly

   Calendar  . . . . . . . .   MICHAEL MICHAEL PROD400      F4 for list

   Date  . . . . . . . . . .   04/16/97    MM/DD/YY

 F3=Exit     F4=Prompt     F5=Refresh     F12=Cancel     F24=More keys
```

Figure 9–16: Change View

9.5.7 Changing and Removing Items

To change an event or a reminder, use the daily or weekly perspective, move the cursor to the item to be altered and press the <F10> key. The current information on the item will appear on the lower half of the screen. Make the changes you desire and press the <ENTER> key.

To delete an event, a reminder, or a meeting, use the daily or weekly perspective, move the cursor to that item and press the <F16> key. Information on the selected item will then be displayed and you are asked to confirm deletion. Press <ENTER> to delete the item from your calendar or press <F12> to cancel the deletion.

To change a meeting, use the daily or weekly perspective, move the cursor to the meeting to be altered, and press the <F10> key. The current information on the item will appear on the lower half of the screen. The Change Meeting Entry menu appears (see Figure 9–17):

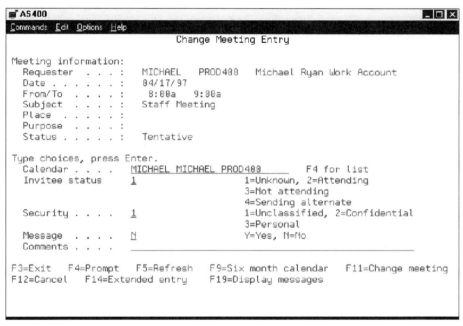

Figure 9–17: Change Meeting

If you are the originator of the meeting, you can press <F11> to change the meeting information. If you are not the originator, you are only permitted to view the information. After making all desired changes, press the <ENTER> key.

9.5.8 Changing and Removing Multiple Items

If you are changing or deleting an item that has multiple occurrences, you will receive a message on the bottom of the display indicating that "multiple occurrences exist." To affect the displayed occurrence only, press <ENTER>. To affect all occurrences of the item, press <F10> (change), or <F16> (delete) as appropriate.

9.5.9 Scheduling a Meeting Place

As previously noted, OfficeVision/400 can help you manage meeting spaces. This is accomplished by establishing a calendar for each meeting area. Once these calendars are established, the Find Place menu can be accessed from either the Add Meeting or Change Meeting menus by pressing the <F13> key (see Figure 9–18):

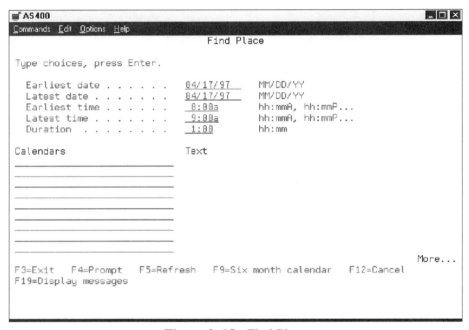

Figure 9–18: Find Place

In the Find Place menu you define the time boundaries that are acceptable for the meeting and enter one or more calendar names corresponding to the meeting spaces that are acceptable. When you press the <ENTER> key, OfficeVision/400 will search those calendars and report on available times (see Figure 9–19).

Once you review the list of available meeting spaces, you can select a place and time for your meeting by entering 1 next to it. When you press <ENTER>, the date, time, and location information will be updated in your meeting item.

9.5.10 More Calendar Tasks

The OfficeVision/400 calendar function includes a secondary menu that allows you to perform a variety of administrative and maintenance tasks. Access to this menu is accomplished by pressing the <F13> key at the primary calendar menu (see Figure 9–20).

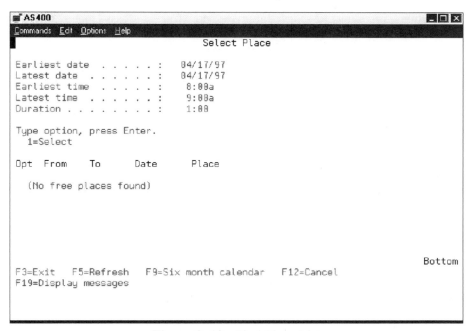

Figure 9–19: Find Place List

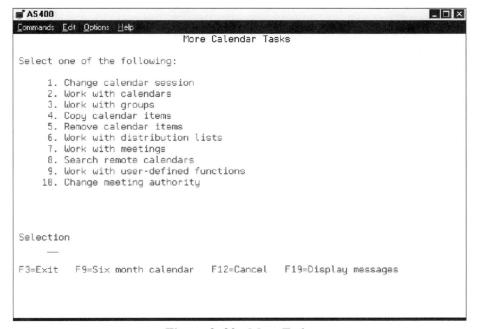

Figure 9–20: More Tasks

The options which may be selected from the More Calendar Tasks menu are as follows:

1. Change calendar session—This option permits you to change various defaults applied to your calendar. This includes the viewing perspective (daily, weekly, or six-month) and the time intervals shown on the weekly calendar.

2. Work with calendars—This option allows you to create a new calendar, delete a calendar, change the basic information about a calendar, or change the authorization access established for a calendar.

3. Work with groups—This option is used to create, delete, or maintain group calendars. A group calendar allows you to access multiple individual calendars through a single group calendar.

4. Copy calendar items—This option allows you to duplicate items within your own calendar or copy them from your calendar to another calendar. This provides a quick way to schedule multiple items that are similar, but not identical.

5. Delete calendar items—This option allows you to delete all items in your calendar that fall within a specified day or range of dates. Unlike the <F16> (delete) key, which deletes a specific item, this option deletes all items that fall within the selected range.

6. Work with distribution lists—Selecting this option takes you to the Work with Distribution List menu. Distribution lists are used primarily by the electronic mail function to allow multiple users to be grouped together under a single name. This collection of users is termed a distribution list. Access to this Work with Distribution lists is available from other points in OfficeVision/400 as well.

7. Work with meetings—This option allows you to change and delete meetings on your calendar. These same functions can be performed by viewing the calendar in weekly or daily perspective and using the <F10> and <F13> key sequence to modify a meeting, or the <F16> key to delete a meeting. The primary difference between the two methodologies is that Work with meetings option presents the meetings in a simple continuous list, as opposed to wherever they fall on the calendar.

8. Search remote calendars—This option permits you to access the calendar of a user on a different AS/400 system. The results of the inquiry will be returned to you in a document sent via the OfficeVision/400 mail system. This is an advanced feature.

9.5.11 Adding a Calendar

If a calendar was not created when you were enrolled as an OfficeVision/400 user, or if you want to have more than one calendar, you can create one through option 2 (Work with calendars) on the More Calendar Tasks menu. Access to the More Calendar Tasks menu may be gained by pressing <F13> at the primary calendar display.

From the Work with Calendars menu, press <F6> to invoke the Create Calendar display (see Figure 9–21):

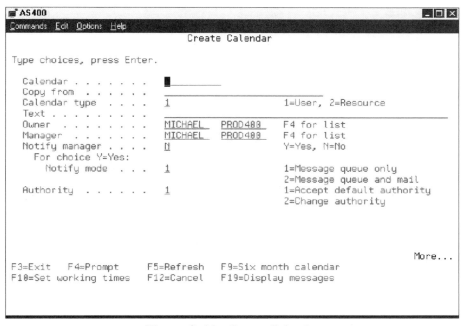

Figure 9–21: Create Calendar

In the Create Calendar display, you can supply a name and a description for a calendar. If you want to create your calendar by making a copy of an existing calendar, you can provide the name of an existing calendar in the "Copy from" field. If you don't know any existing names, you can press <F4> to obtain a list of existing calendars.

Each calendar has an owner and a manager. You are the owner of the calendar. You may also assign yourself as the manager of the calendar. If you establish a different user as the manager of the calendar, you can reroute notification messages to that person and they will be informed of changes in your calendar.

You can also establish the authorization levels for your calendar at creation time. In most cases, you will want to use the default authority.

The final set of entries in the Create Calendar display are used to set the default values supplied when you request OfficeVision/400 to generate an alert message for an event or a reminder. The "Lead time" field is used to compute the time OfficeVision/400 automatically suggests for a notification. The "Automatic prompt" becomes the default value used in the "Message prompt" on the event and reminder displays. And finally, you can control whether you want an alert message sent just to your message queue, or if you want it to be sent to your message queue and appear as inbound electronic mail.

9.6 OPTIONS 2 THROUGH 4: ELECTRONIC MAIL

OfficeVision/400 offers three options for handling electronic mail. Option 2 (Mail) allows you to read and review mail you have sent and received. Option 3 (Send message) allows you to send a brief (two line) electronic message. Option 4 (Send note) allows you to compose a brief document. All of these options are accessible from the OfficeVision/400 opening menu (see Figure 9–22):

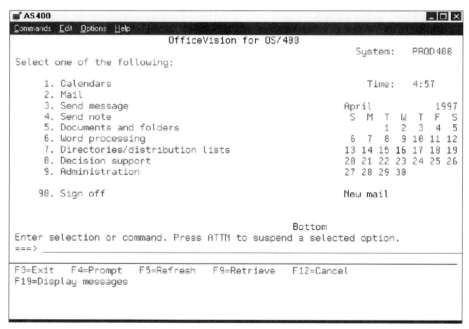

Figure 9–22: Main menu with New Mail

NOTE: You are alerted to the presence of unread mail by the appearance of the message "New mail" on the OfficeVision/400 opening menu.

9.6.1 Option 2: Mail

When you select option 2 (Mail) from the OfficeVision/400 menu, the Work with Mail display appears on your screen. New mail and any mail that you have received and have not deleted will be listed on the display. Each item shows a status, the identity of the sender, a brief description of the item, and the date the mail item was received (see Figure 9–23):

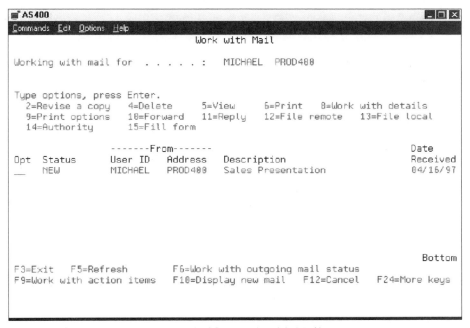

Figure 9–23: Work with Mail

A mail item can be a message, a note, or a document. The handling of a mail item is dependent on its type.

When a message arrives in your mailbox it is given a status of "message." The status for a message remains the same until it is deleted, at which point the entire item disappears.

When a note or a document arrives in your mailbox, it assumes the status of "new." Once you read the item (by selecting the "View" option for the item), its status changes to "opened." If the status of an item is "new*" instead of "new," this indicates that the item has a memo slip attached, which is a note attached to a document to tell the recipient what to do with the document when received. Like a message, notes and documents can be deleted. If you want to retain a copy of a note or document, you can use the "File local" option prior to deleting it.

On the left side of each mail item is a field where you can select an action to take on the item. Multiple actions may be selected and they will be performed one at a time. The available actions are

2. Revise a copy—This action copies the mail item into the OfficeVision/400 word processor so you can alter it and mail it out again. The original mail item is unchanged. When you exit the document and save your changes, you will then be asked where you want it to be sent.

4. Delete—This action removes the item from the list of mail items.

5. View—The view action allows you to see the contents of the mail item. You may use the <ROLL UP> and <ROLL DOWN> keys to page through the item as necessary.

    NOTE: If the mail item has a memo slip attached, you will first see the memo slip. When you press the <ENTER> key you will then see the contents of the item.

6. Print—This action submits the mail item to a printer, with OfficeVision/400 automatically setting the options that control how the item will appear in print. Also see option 9 (Print options).

8. Change details—This action may be selected to change some of the advanced aspects of the mail item. This selection may also be used to indicate that the mail item is an action item by setting the "Action required date" to a future date. An action item may also be indicated when you send mail to others.

9. Print options—This action submits the mail item to a printer, but allows you to set the variables that control how it will appear in print. When you select this action, you will have four display pages of variables to control. Press <ROLL UP> or <ROLL DOWN> to page through the options. Press <ENTER> to submit the item to print.

10. Forward—Selecting "Forward" for a mail item brings up the Forward Mail display where you can select the groups or individuals to whom you want the mail item forwarded. Once you supply these names, press <F10> to forward the item.

11. Reply—This action may be used to compose a note for the individual(s) that sent you the selected mail item. After reviewing the distribution information, you will enter the OfficeVision/400 word processor to compose your reply. Once you have composed your response and exited from the word processor, press <F10> to send it.

12. File remote—This action may be used to save a note or document from the mail list to a folder located on another AS/400. This is an advanced option. Please see the *Document Handling* section of this chapter for more information on folders.

13. File local—This action may be used to save a note or document from the mail list to a folder on your AS/400. Please see the *Document Handling* section of this chapter for more information on folders.

14. Change authority—This action allows you to change the authority assigned to your filed documents. This is an advanced option.

Additional operations may be selected from the Work with Mail display through the use of function keys. The two most used operations are

<F6> Outgoing mail status—Press <F6> to see the status of mail you have sent on the Work with Outgoing Mail Status display. Detailed information on each outbound mail item can also be obtained through this display. You may want to use this function periodically to delete status information on old mail to keep the list manageable (see Figure 9–24):

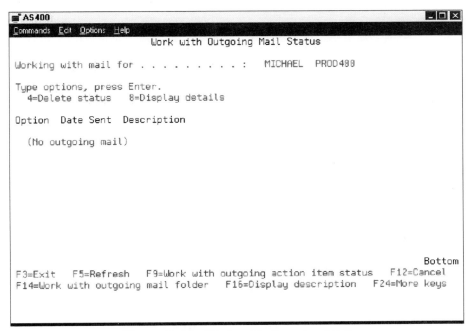

Figure 9–24: Work with Outgoing Mail

<F9> Action items—Pressing <F9> brings up the Work with Action Item display. This display shows mail items that require action by a specific date. An action item may be designated by the sender, or you can indicate an action item for a mail item by selecting option 8 (Change details) on the Work with Mail display (see Figure 9–25):

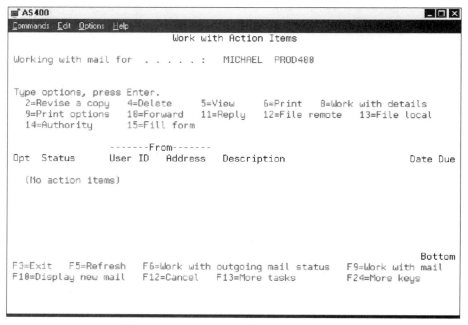

Figure 9–25: Work with Action Items

<F13> More mail tasks—Pressing the <F13> key brings up the More Mail Tasks menu (see Figure 9–26).

This menu can be used to select the following functions:

1. Create local hard-copy reference—The hard-copy reference functions (options 1 and 2) can be used to keep track of documents that were distributed by some other fashion than OfficeVision/400. This includes postal mail and other forms of electronic document exchange (for example, DISOSS). This reference will be stored on your AS/400.

2. Create remote hard-copy reference—The same as option 1, except the reference will be stored on another AS/400.

3. Select mail by status—This function allows you to select mail items based on their status. The selected items will then appear in a Work with Mail display.

4. Print mail reports—This function may be invoked to print all or a selected range of your mail items.

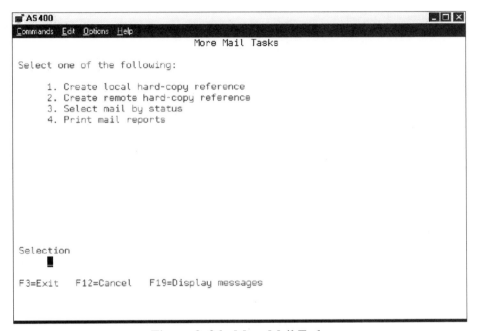

Figure 9–26: More Mail Tasks

9.6.2 Option 3: Send Message

Choosing option 3 from the OfficeVision/400 opening menu brings up the Send a Message menu. This display allows you to enter your message and define who the recipient(s) will be (see Figure 9–27).

At the top of the form you can type the message you want to send. The data entry area is limited to what you see on the screen.

You can send your message to specific individuals, a group of individuals who are defined in an existing distribution list, or both. If you are unsure of what distribution lists are available, you can place the cursor on the first distribution list field and press the <F4> key. The available distribution lists will then be displayed on your screen.

If you want to specify a distribution list, enter its name in the first "Distribution list" field. The second field may be used to specify the name of another AS/400 which contains the distribution list definition. If you leave the second field blank, the AS/400 you are communicating with will be used.

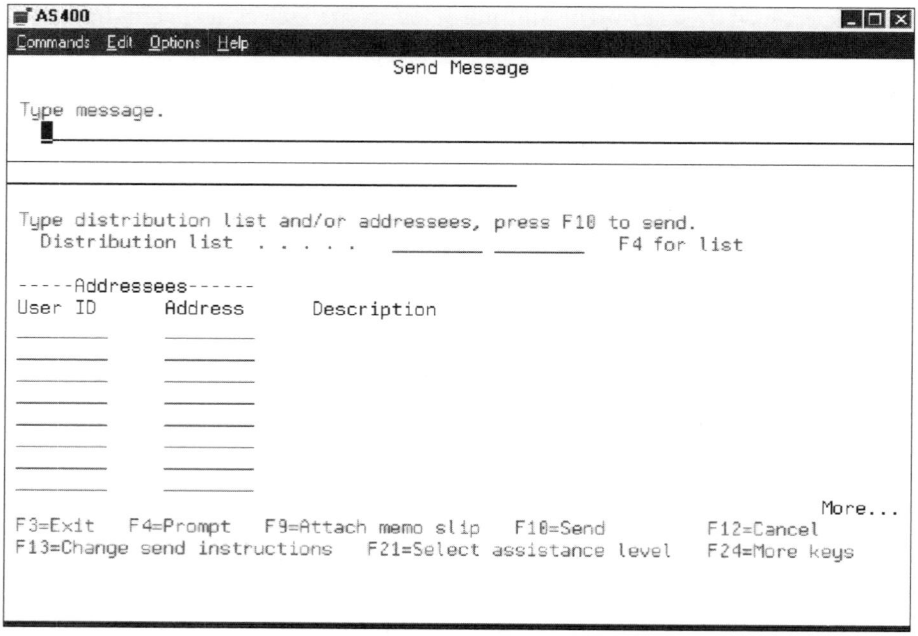

```
AS400                                                        _ □ ×
Commands  Edit  Options  Help
                             Send Message
Type message.
  █_


  _____


Type distribution list and/or addressees, press F10 to send.
  Distribution list  . . . . .      _____  _____    F4 for list

-----Addressees------
User ID       Address      Description
_____      _____
_____      _____
_____      _____
_____      _____
_____      _____
_____      _____
_____      _____
_____                                                      More...
F3=Exit    F4=Prompt   F9=Attach memo slip   F10=Send      F12=Cancel
F13=Change send instructions   F21=Select assistance level   F24=More keys
```

Figure 9–27: Send a Message

In addition to, or instead of, a distribution list, you may specify the "User IDs" (names) of individuals who are to receive the message you have typed. If you do not know what names are available, you can position your cursor in one of the name fields and press the <F4> key to obtain a list of defined names. The "Address" field may be used to specify the name of another AS/400 where the user is located. If the "Address" field is left blank, your local AS/400 is assumed.

After you supply the user and any necessary address information, press the <ENTER> key. OfficeVision/400 will then check the list of recipients and change the display to include the names of all individuals on the distribution list. Any invalid or improper name entries will be also be noted. You may correct any errors and press <ENTER> again to reverify the information (see Figure 9–28).

When all the information meets your satisfaction, press the <F10> key to send the message. Alternatively, you can perform any of the other special activities by pressing the indicated function key before you press <F10>.

<F9> Attach memo slip—If you press <F9> prior to sending the message, the Attach Memo Slip menu appears. You can select any of the indicated actions and then press the <ENTER> key to return to the Send a Message display (see Figure 9–29).

```
┌─────────────────────────────────────────────────────────────────────────┐
│ ■ AS 400                                                        ■ □ ×     │
│ Commands  Edit  Options  Help                                             │
│                          Send Message                                     │
│                                                                           │
│ Type message.                                                             │
│   When are you free for lunch?                                            │
│                                                                           │
│ ─────────────────────────────────────────                                │
│                                                                           │
│ Type distribution list and/or addressees, press F10 to send.             │
│   Distribution list  . . . . .     _____  _____    F4 for list      │
│                                                                           │
│ -----Addressees------                                                     │
│ User ID      Address      Description                                     │
│ MICHAEL      PROD400                                                      │
│ _____      _____                                                      │
│ _____      _____                                                      │
│ _____      _____                                                      │
│ _____      _____                                                      │
│ _____      _____                                                      │
│ _____      _____                                                      │
│                                                               More...     │
│ F3=Exit  F4=Prompt  F9=Attach memo slip  F10=Send      F12=Cancel         │
│ F13=Change send instructions  F21=Select assistance level  F24=More keys  │
│                                                                           │
└─────────────────────────────────────────────────────────────────────────┘
```

Figure 9–28: Send a Message with data

```
┌─────────────────────────────────────────────────────────────────────────┐
│ ■ AS 400                                                        ■ □ ×     │
│ Commands  Edit  Options  Help                                             │
│                          Attach Memo Slip                                 │
│                                                                           │
│ Type choice, press Enter.                                                 │
│                                                                           │
│    Action . . . . . . . . .    1       1=For your information             │
│                                        2=For your comments                │
│                                        3=For your signature               │
│                                        4=For your approval                │
│                                        5=Please handle                    │
│                                        6=Please circulate                 │
│                                        7=Please see me                     │
│                                        8=Please prepare reply             │
│                                                                           │
│                                                                           │
│                                                                           │
│                                                                           │
│                                                                           │
│                                                                           │
│ F3=Exit  F5=Refresh  F12=Cancel  F19=Display messages                     │
│                                                                           │
└─────────────────────────────────────────────────────────────────────────┘
```

Figure 9–29: Attach Memo Slip

<F13> Change defaults—Pressing <F13> before sending the message brings up the Change Default display. You can then change the way that OfficeVision/400 will handle the message in three ways. These are (see Figure 9–30):

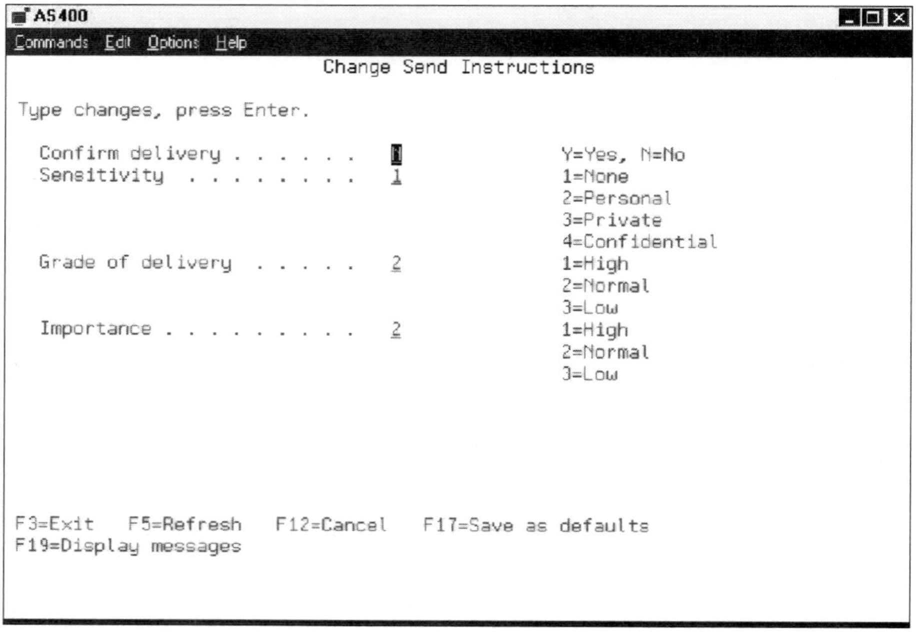

```
▄ AS400                                                              _ □ ×
Commands  Edit  Options  Help
                          Change Send Instructions

Type changes, press Enter.

     Confirm delivery . . . . . .   █          Y=Yes, N=No
     Sensitivity  . . . . . . . .   1          1=None
                                               2=Personal
                                               3=Private
                                               4=Confidential
     Grade of delivery  . . . . .   2          1=High
                                               2=Normal
                                               3=Low
     Importance . . . . . . . . .   2          1=High
                                               2=Normal
                                               3=Low




F3=Exit   F5=Refresh   F12=Cancel   F17=Save as defaults
F19=Display messages

```

Figure 9–30: Change Default

"Confirm delivery"—If this field is set to Y, you will be notified when the message is received by the person(s) to whom it was sent. An N means no special response is generated.

"Personal"—If you set this field to Y, only the person(s) whom you addressed the message to can see the message. An N indicates that other people with the proper access authority can also read it.

"High priority"—If you set this field to Y, the mail item will appear highlighted in each recipient's mailbox. An N means no special highlighting will be used.

NOTE: If you change these fields and want to use them for all future messages, press <F17> (Save defaults).

Once you have completed your entries in the Change Default display, press <ENTER> to return to the Send Message menu. Pressing <F10> will then send that message using the new default values.

9.6.3 Option 4: Send Note

If you want to send a communiqué that is longer than a message, but not as involved as a formal document, you can select option 4 from the OfficeVision/400 opening menu and the Send a Note display appears. The first display will be used to define the recipients of the note; you will then invoke a separate screen to actually create the note (see Figure 9–31):

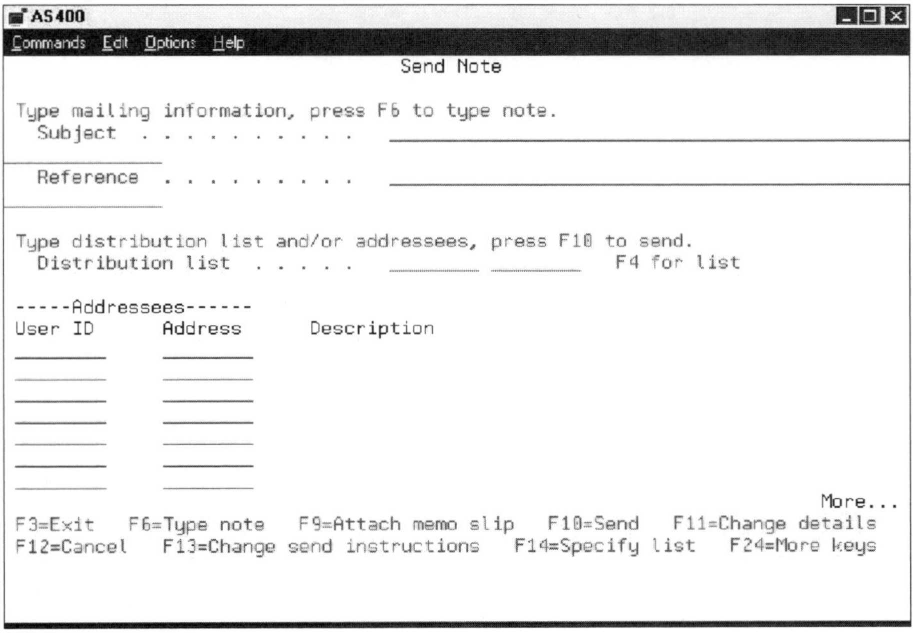

```
[] AS400                                                            _ □ ×
Commands  Edit  Options  Help
                              Send Note

Type mailing information, press F6 to type note.
  Subject  . . . . . . . . . .        _____

  Reference  . . . . . . . .          _____


Type distribution list and/or addressees, press F10 to send.
  Distribution list  . . . . .     _____ _____   F4 for list

  -----Addressees------
  User ID     Address     Description
  _____    _____
  _____    _____
  _____    _____
  _____    _____
  _____    _____
  _____
                                                          More...
F3=Exit   F6=Type note   F9=Attach memo slip   F10=Send   F11=Change details
F12=Cancel   F13=Change send instructions   F14=Specify list   F24=More keys
```

Figure 9–31: Send a Note

At the top of the display you can enter text for a "Subject" and a "Reference" in the designated fields. The rest of the fields are used to define the groups or individuals who will receive the message. These fields have the same meaning as described in the *Send a Message* section of this chapter. A brief review follows:

If a distribution list is specified, the note will be sent to the group of people who are included in the list. If the distribution list resides on another AS/400, the name of that AS/400 must be included.

The names of specific individuals can also be included in the "User ID" fields. If a user resides on another AS/400, the name of that AS/400 must be included as the "Address."

After you define the recipients, you can press <ENTER> and OfficeVision/400 will verify the names you have entered. If you specified a distribution list, the names of the individuals in that distribution list will appear.

When you are satisfied with the distribution information, press <F6> to call up the word processor's Edit display (see Figure 9–32):

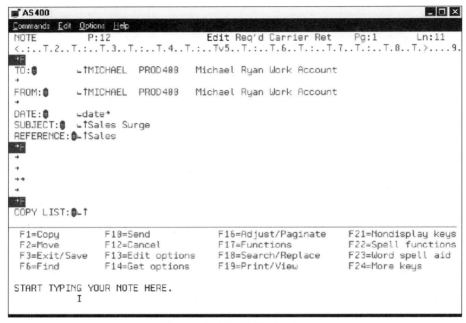

Figure 9–32: Edit display

When the Edit display appears, it will contain the subject text, reference text, and distribution information you supplied in the Send a Note display. Your cursor will automatically be positioned in the start of the area where you can enter the text of your note.

NOTE: For information on using the word processor, please see the *Text Entry* section of this chapter.

Once you have entered your note, press the <F3> key to save the note and return to the Send a Note display. Then press <F10> to send the note to the designated recipients. Alternatively, you can use any of the following function keys prior to pressing <F10>:

<F6> Attach memo slip—Please see the *Send a Message* section of this chapter for a description of this feature.

<F13> Change defaults—Please see the *Send a Message* section of this chapter for a description of this feature.

<F17> Save—If your note is incomplete and cannot be sent, you may press <F17> and OfficeVision/400 will save your work in progress. You can complete the note at a later time by pressing <F16> (Work with saved notes) from the Send a Note menu.

If you used option <F6> or <F13>, you can send the note by pressing <F10> when you return to the Send a Note display.

9.7 OPTIONS 5 AND 6: DOCUMENT HANDLING

Option 5 (Documents and folders) and option 6 (Word processing) on the OfficeVision/400 opening menu are the two functions provided for the creation and maintenance of documents. In this context, a document can be considered any written material, including but certainly not limited to letters, memorandums, proposals, technical specifications, or reports.

One of the key concepts of document handling under OfficeVision/400 is the use of folders. In the simplest sense, a folder is a storage area for documents. Each individual may have one or more folders, so you can organize your documents into logical groups. Furthermore, you can allow other people to access your folders, thus allowing multiple individuals to share access to groups of documents.

Options 5 and 6 both allow you to access documents in folders. Option 5 (Documents and folders) gives you an administrative view of the folders and documents to which you have access. Option 6 (Word processing) allows you to create or edit a document stored in a folder.

9.7.1 Option 5: Documents and Folders

As mentioned, option 5 (Documents and folders) allows you to peruse documents and folders you are authorized to access. Initiation of this function is accomplished by specifying option 5 on the OfficeVision/400 opening menu. In response, the Documents and Folders menu appears (see Figure 9–33).

From the Work with Documents menu, you can select further action by specifying one of the following functions:

1. Work with documents in folders—This option allows you to view and manage documents within a selected folder.

2. Work with folders—This option allows you to view the folders available to you, and optionally access documents within specific folders.

3. Search for documents—This option allows you to search for one or more documents based on a number of qualifications, such as subject, author, or keywords associated with the document. A list of qualifying documents is produced as a result of the search.

4. Work with document lists—This option allows you to access the lists created by option 3 (Search for documents).

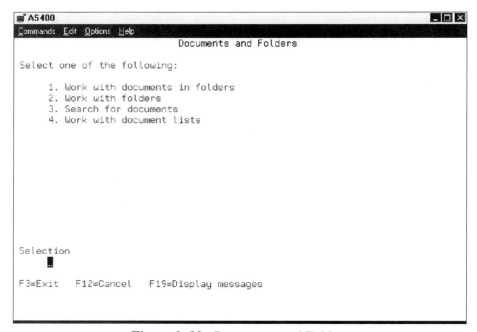

Figure 9–33: Documents and Folders

9.7.2 Documents in Folders

When you select option 1 from the Work with Documents and Folders menu, the Work with Documents in Folders menu appears. This option allows you to manage documents contained in a specific folder (see Figure 9–34).

At the top of the display is a field named "Folder." This is the name of the folder containing the documents that appear on the display. To open a different folder, simply change the name in this field and press <ENTER>.

Below the "Folder" field is a field named "Position to." If you enter the first character or set of characters in a document name and press <ENTER>, the first matching document will appear as the first document on the list of documents.

The remaining portion of the display shows the documents in the folder. Each line in the list contains the document name, description, the last date of revision, and its type. The type will show as "RFTAS400" for documents that can be revised, and as "FFTAS400" for documents that cannot be changed.

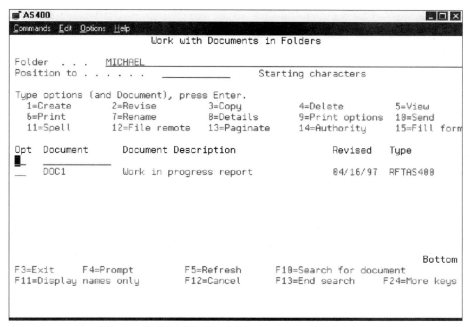

Figure 9–34: Work with Documents in Folders

A field appears to the left of each document name which allows you to select an action to be performed on that document. Supported actions include

1. Create—One of the entries in the list of document names should be blank. Entering a 1 in the "Opt" field and typing in a new document name in the blank field will create a document. After specifying document details, you will be placed in the word processor to work on the document content.

2. Revise—Selecting this option invokes the word processor which allow you to make changes to the selected document.

3. Copy—The copy option allows you to create a new document by copying the contents of an existing document.

4. Delete—This option deletes the referenced document.

5. View—This option allows you to look at the contents of a document.

6. Print—This option may be used to print a document, with the system controlling how the document will be formatted.

7. Rename—This option allows you to change the name of the referenced document.

8. Details—This option allows you to change the administrative details asso-
    ciated with a document (as opposed to the contents of a document). The
    detail information is defined when a document is created.

9. Print opts—You can use this option to print a document and control how
    the document will be formatted for print.

10. Send—This option allows you to send (mail) a document through Office-
    Vision/400.

11. Spell—The spell option checks the spelling in the referenced document.

12. File remote—This option may be used to store the referenced document on
    another AS/400 system.

13. Paginate—This option forces OfficeVision/400 to go through the referenced
    document and reset page breaks according to the format of the document.

14. Authority—This option allows you to control who has access to this doc-
    ument and for what purposes. This is an advanced option.

To select an action, enter the number next to the document name and press
<ENTER>. If you select actions on multiple documents, those actions will be performed
one at a time.

9.7.3 Work with Folders

When you select option 2 from the Work with Documents and Folders menu, the Work with
Folders menu appears. This option allows you to manage folders (see Figure 9–35).

At the top of the display is a field named "Folder." A folder may contain other folders
(which may, in turn, contain other folders). If you want to look at folders contained in a
folder, enter the folder name in this field. If multiple levels of folders are involved, each
folder name must be separated by a forward slash (for example, enck/docs).

Below the "Folder" field is a field named "Position to." If you enter the first character or set of characters in a folder name and press <ENTER>, the first matching folder will
appear as the first folder on the list.

The remaining portion of the screen lists the available folders. Next to each folder
name is a field you can use to select one of the following actions:

1. Create—One of the entries in the list of folder names should be blank.
    Entering a 1 in the "Opt" field and typing in a new folder name in the blank
    field will create a folder by that name.

3. Next level—Folders can, in turn, contain other folders. Use this option to
    access any folders contained in the selected folder.

4. Delete—This option may be used to delete a folder.

5. Work with documents—Selecting this option opens the folder and takes you to the Work with Documents in Folders display.

7. Rename—This option may be used to change the name of a folder.

8. Details—This option allows you to change the description and text profile associated with a folder.

14. Authority—This option allows you to control who has access to this folder and for what purposes. This is an advanced option.

To select an action, enter the number next to the folder name and press <ENTER>. If you select actions on multiple folders, those actions will be performed one at a time.

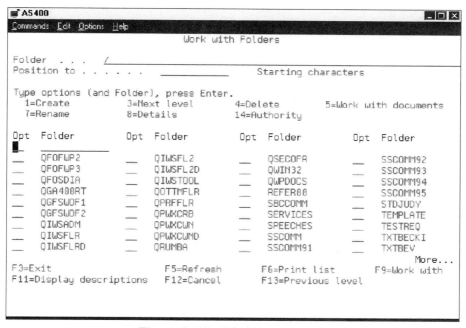

Figure 9–35: Work with Folders

9.7.4 Option 6: Word Processing

If you select option 6 from the OfficeVision/400 opening menu, the Word Processing menu appears. Notice that several of the options overlap the options available through the Work with Documents and Folders menu. The primary reason for this overlap is that the word processing program itself is normally invoked from the Work with Documents in Folders menu. OfficeVision/400 provides multiple paths to that display for your convenience (see Figure 9–36):

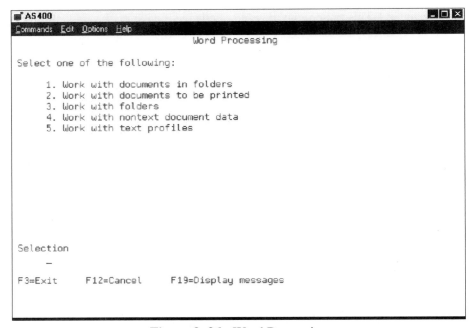

Figure 9–36: Word Processing

You can then select one of the following options from the Word Processing menu:

1. Work with documents in folders—This is the same function previously described in the *Documents in Folder* section of this chapter. From this option you can create new documents or edit existing ones.

2. Work with documents to be printed—This option allows you to see what documents are currently being printed or scheduled to be printed.

3. Work with folders—This is the same function previously discussed in the *Work with Folders* section of this chapter.

4. Work with nontext document data—This option allows you to work with graphics created with the Business Graphics Utility (BGU) or some other graphics program. Note that BGU is an optional program.

5. Work with text profiles—This option allows you to establish or maintain profiles to control the layout and appearance of documents. Profiles are conceptually similar to style sheets.

The "standard" OfficeVision/400 word processor was designed for use with the 5250 family of workstation. OfficeVision/400 does, however, support the following two variations of the standard word processor:

If you are using IBM's PC Support program, and the PC Support Organizer function is active, you will use the "text-assisted" word processor, which is very similar (but not identical) to the standard word processor.

If you are using a foreign terminal type (for example, an IBM 3270 or ASCII display station), you will use the "adapted" word processor. You can tell if you are using the adapted word processor because the <F24> option will be missing from the Edit display.

NOTE: This chapter assumes you are using the "standard" word processor available to native 5250 workstations.

9.7.5 Invoking the Word Processor

As mentioned, the word processor is normally invoked from the Work with Documents in Folders display. From this menu you can either create a new document or revise an existing document.

To create a new document, enter the name in an empty document name field and specify create (1) in the corresponding option field and press <ENTER>. The Create Document Details menu will then appear on your display (see Figure 9–37).

You can then supply information in the Create Document Details menu to clarify the nature and content of your document. In general, you should always enter a "Document description" because this information will appear on the other OfficeVision/400 menus, such as the Work with Documents in Folders menu.

You can also define information in the Create Document Details menu that can later be used as the document search options. For example, you can define the "Subject," "Author," "Keywords," and "Document class" fields and then use any or all of them for search criteria.

After you have entered your qualifying information, press <ENTER> to go to the Edit display of the word processor.

To edit an existing document, specify revise (2) in the corresponding option field on the Work with Documents in Folders menu and press <ENTER>. OfficeVision/400 will then load the document into the word processor and take you directly to the Edit display.

9.7.6 Text Entry

The Edit menu is composed of a status line at the top, a scale line immediately below the status line, a data entry area below the scale line, and a summary of function key purposes in the lower area (see Figure 9–38).

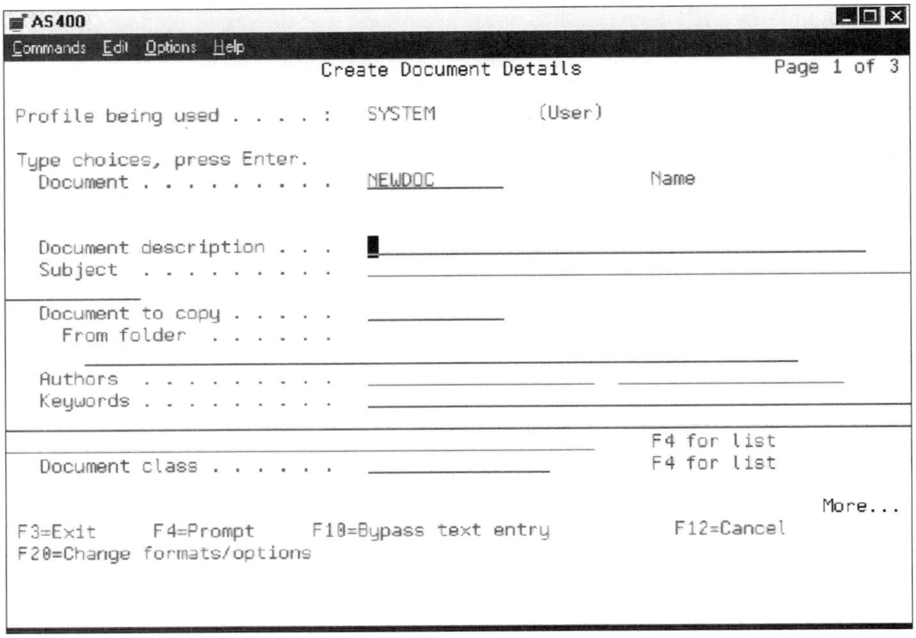

```
 AS400                                                              _ □ ×
 Commands  Edit  Options  Help
                            Create Document Details              Page 1 of 3

 Profile being used . . . . :   SYSTEM        (User)

 Type choices, press Enter.
   Document . . . . . . . . .    NEWDOC             Name

   Document description . . .   █_____
   Subject  . . . . . . . . .   _____

   Document to copy . . . . .    _____
     From folder  . . . . . .
                                _____
   Authors  . . . . . . . . .    _____  _____
   Keywords . . . . . . . . .    _____

 _____  F4 for list
   Document class . . . . . .    _____        F4 for list

                                                                    More...
 F3=Exit     F4=Prompt    F10=Bypass text entry         F12=Cancel
 F20=Change formats/options
```

Figure 9–37: Create Document Details

```
 AS400                                                              _ □ ×
 Commands  Edit  Options  Help
 NEWDOC       P:12               Edit Page End            Pg:1     Ln:7
 <2...T:...T3...T:...T4...T:...T5...Tv...T6...T:...T7...T:...T8...T:...T9>...:..
 ⌐




 F1=Copy          F7=Window         F14=Get options      F20=Format options
 F2=Move          F8=Reset          F15=Tables/Columns   F21=Nondisplay keys
 F3=Exit/Save     F9=Instructions   F16=Adjust/Paginate  F22=Spell functions
 F4=Find char     F11=Hyphenate     F17=Functions        F23=Word spell aid
 F5=Goto          F12=Cancel        F18=Search/Replace
 F6=Find          F13=Edit options  F19=Print/View       F24=More keys
            I
```

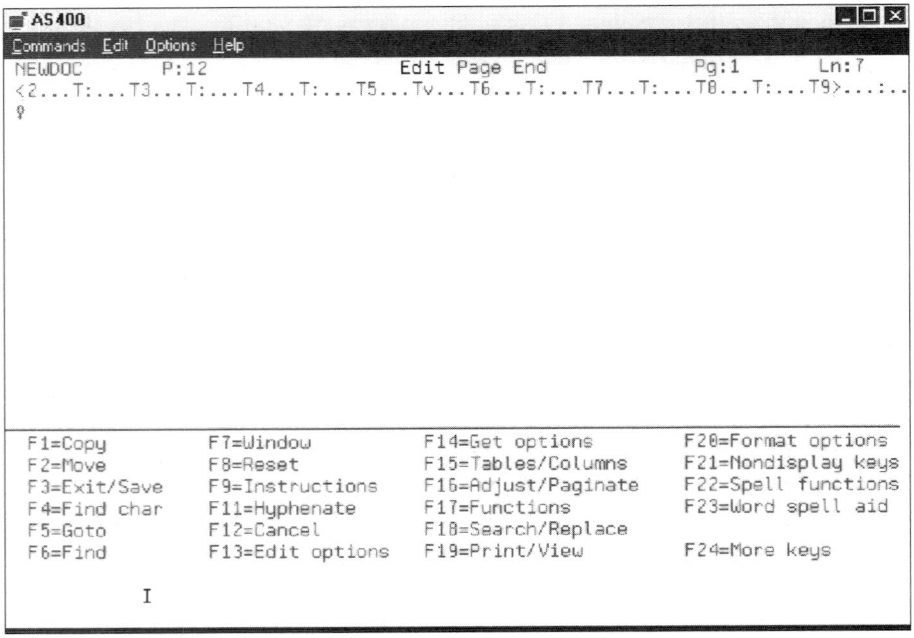

Figure 9–38: Edit menu

The status line (the top line on the display) shows the name of the document, the current pitch (characters per inch), the page number ("Pg") and line number ("Ln") where the cursor is located. If the cursor is on top of a control character, this will also be indicated on the status line. If you are creating a new document, the "page end" control character is automatically entered into the document and the cursor will be positioned on top of it.

The scale line shows the settings for the margins and tabs. The left margin is indicated by the < character, the right margin by the > character, and each tab is noted by a "T." A "v" in the scale line also serves to show the center of the line.

Below the scale line is the area for data entry. The word processor automatically enables insert mode. To enter information into the document, simply begin typing. If you are typing a paragraph, the word processor will automatically perform word wrap when you reach the end of a line. To end a paragraph or a line of text, press the <FIELD EXIT> key. A square block will appear at the end of the line or paragraph and the cursor will move to the next line.

You can move around the document by using the arrow keys to move within the displayed area or the <ROLL UP> and <ROLL DOWN> keys to move forward and backward a screen at a time.

If you need to correct the information in a document, you can move the cursor to the area and follow these basic guidelines.

To delete characters, you can use the <BACKSPACE> key to delete the character to the left of the cursor, or use the <DELETE> key to delete the character underneath the cursor.

To replace characters, make sure insert mode is disabled and simply type over the characters to be changed.

To insert characters, make sure insert mode is enabled, and insert the desired characters or codes.

Other advanced editing tools are available through the use of function keys.

NOTE: The OfficeVision/400 word processor is a powerful and comprehensive product that is as capable and as complicated as any desktop word processor. To learn its full range of capabilities, you should examine the IBM documentation or other books focused on the word processor.

9.7.7 Highlighting

If you want portions of your text to appear and print in bold or underlined type, you can place control characters before and after the text you want highlighted. These control characters occupy extra space when displayed on the screen, but do not occupy any space on the printed output.

Control characters may be inserted as you are typing, or you may plant them after the fact. To insert a control character, hold down the <ALT> key, press the indicated letter key, then release the <ALT> key.

To begin bold type, hold down the <ALT> key, then press B. To end bold type, hold down <ALT>, then press J.

To begin underlined type, hold down the <ALT> key, then press U. To end underlined type, hold down <ALT>, then press J.

Note that the <ALT> J sequence is used to terminate both styles of highlighting. If you combine both bold and underlined type, the <ALT> J sequence terminates both highlights.

To remove highlighting, simply delete the control characters in the same fashion that you delete normal characters. You should make sure you delete both the starting and ending control characters.

9.7.8 Special Functions

The OfficeVision/400 makes liberal use of the function keys available on your terminals. These keys may be used to perform block operations, invoke utility functions, perform search and replace operations, and more. In brief, the keys available to you are as follows:

<F1> Copy—This function may be used to duplicate blocks of information. Move the cursor to the start of the area you want copied and press <F1>. The message "Copy what?" will appear on the bottom of your screen. In response, move the cursor to the end of the area you want copied and press <ENTER>. You will then be asked "To where?" Move the cursor to the desired location and press <ENTER> to insert the copied area.

<F2> Move—This operation follows the same procedure as <F1> (copy), except that the selected area is deleted from its original location after being inserted into the new location.

<F3> Exit/Save—Press <F3> to leave the word processor. You will be given the opportunity to save or abandon your work. Please refer to the *Exiting the Word Processor* section of this chapter.

<F4> Find char—When you press <F4> you will be asked for a single character to look for. When you type the character, the word processor will move the cursor to the next occurrence of that character. To repeat the operation, type the character again. To terminate the operation, press <F8>.

<F5> Goto—Pressing the <F5> key brings up the Select Goto Request display. From this display you can have the word processor take you to a specific line, page, or function. Many of the options on the Select Goto Request display are advanced functions.

<F6> Find—This function allows you to search for the next occurrence of a word or phrase. When you press <F6>, the message "Find what?" appears and you can type the desired word or phrase to be searched. Press <ENTER> to begin the search. You can repeat the search by pressing <F6> then <ENTER>.

<F7> Window—Pressing <F7> allows you to adjust the left column of the display. This is useful when lines of text in a document exceed the width of the display. For example, if you specify a left column of 70, you could see the information contained in columns 70 to 132 of a 132 character report.

<F8> Reset—This key is used to terminate the <F4> function and is also used in some of the advanced operations.

<F10> Instructions—Pressing <F10> provides you with a summary of text instructions. Text instructions are special commands that may be embedded in your document for greater format control. This is an advanced feature.

<F11> Hyphenate—The <F11> key allows you to insert "soft" hyphens in words at the end of the line. These hyphens may be processed or ignored by the word processor as necessary.

<F12> Cancel—The <F12> key discontinues a selected operation and returns you to the Edit display. Pressing <F12> at the Edit display takes you to the Exit Document menu.

<F13> Edit options—Pressing <F13> brings up a menu containing options and defaults for your edit session. You can use this function to customize your editing environment.

<F14> Get options—This function allows you to retrieve another document into your current document, or bring another document up in a split-screen display.

<F15> Tables/Columns—The <F15> key invokes a menu that allows you to define columns for text or the layout for a table.

<F16> Adjust/Paginate—You can use the <F16> option to have OfficeVision/400 set or reset the page breaks for your document. This allows you to maintain an electronic copy of a document that closely matches your printed output.

<F17> Functions—The <F17> key permits you to select additional functions, such as setting up or performing a merge operation.

<F18> Search/Replace—When you press <F18>, a display appears allowing you to define your search/replace criteria. Pressing <ENTER> starts the search/replace operation.

<F19> Print/View—The <F19> key may be used to send your document to the printer, or to obtain an approximate view of how it will appear printed (including headers, footers, and so on).

<F20> Change format—This option allows you to change general layout parameters that affect the document, including margins, line spacing, justification, and page layout.

<F21> Nondisplay keys—The <F21> key can be used to remove the list of function keys from the bottom of the screen (thereby increasing display room for the document), or restore the function key display if disabled.

<F22> Spell functions—Pressing <F22> brings up the Spell Options display. From this display you can launch a spell check on your document.

<F23> Word spell aid—If the spell-checking function locates a misspelled word, you can press <F23> to obtain a list of possible corrections.

<F24> More keys—Pressing <F24> shows additional key sequences available in the word processor. This includes page operations (for example, <ROLL UP>, <ROLL DOWN>) and <ALT> "letter" combinations (for example, <ALT> U, <ALT> B, <ALT> J).

9.7.9 Exiting the Word Processor

When you have completed your additions or changes to the document, press <F3>. The Exit Document menu will then appear (see Figure 9–39).

To save the changes to your document, specify Y in the "Save document" field. If you specify N, all of your changes will be abandoned.

The current name of your document will appear in the "Document name" field. You can change this name and save the document as a new document. Similarly, you can allow the document to be saved to its default folder or specify a new name in the "Folder name" field.

The "Display save options" field allows you bring up an additional menu to change line settings, page settings, error indicators, and other advanced functions. Generally, you should specify N to bypass this option.

Specifying a Y in the "Print document" field submits the document for print. Control of how the document will be formatted is determined by the setting of the "Display print options" field. Specifically, if you want to print the document and control how it will be formatted, you can specify Y in the "Display print options" field. If you want OfficeVision/400 to handle the formatting, you can specify N in the "Display print options" field.

When you have completed the Exit Document menu, press <ENTER>.

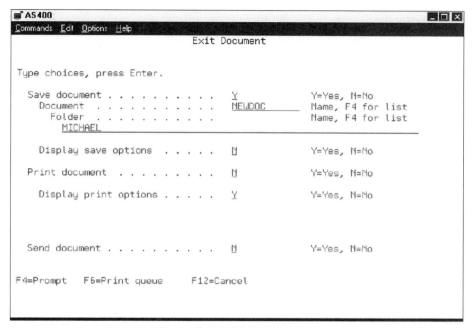

Figure 9–39: Exit Document

9.8 OPTION 7: DIRECTORIES/DISTRIBUTION LISTS

Select option 7 from the OfficeVision/400 opening menu to view and manage distribution information. This information is used by OfficeVision/400 to send mail to individuals you define by name or by distribution group (see Figure 9–40).

NOTE: The extent of information you can view and change using this function is dependent on your authorization levels on the AS/400.

You can select the following actions from the Directories and Distribution Lists menu:

1. Personal directories—This option allows you to create your own personal information area. This could be used, for example, to create a personal telephone directory, an equipment list, or even a home address list. The information maintained in this area does not need to have any relation to any information in OfficeVision/400. This is an advanced function.

2. System directory—This option allows you to see the "User ID" and "Address" for each user defined in OfficeVision/400. This may include both users on your AS/400 and other AS/400 systems.

3. Distribution lists—This option allows you to access distribution lists defined within OfficeVision/400. A distribution list contains multiple user names and allows you to address mail to the name of the distribution list instead of the name of each individual on the list.

4. Nicknames—Nicknames may be used to establish a short name for a user id and address or a distribution list and address. This option allows you to access nickname definitions.

5. Search system directory—This search option allows you find additional information about a user based on his or her name and/or department. The information returned by the search consists of the user id/address, full name, telephone number, and department for the qualifying individual(s).

6. Departments—This option allows you to access information about departments. This includes finding a list of defined departments and showing what users are in a particular department.

Figure 9–40: Directories and Distribution Lists

9.9 OPTION 8: DECISION SUPPORT

Option 8 on the OfficeVision/400 opening menu is used to invoke other optional programs. The number and nature of these optional programs can differ from site to site.

9.10 OPTION 9: ADMINISTRATION

Option 9 on the OfficeVision/400 opening menu may be selected to manage the administrative information associated with your user id. When you select this option, the Administration menu appears (see Figure 9–41):

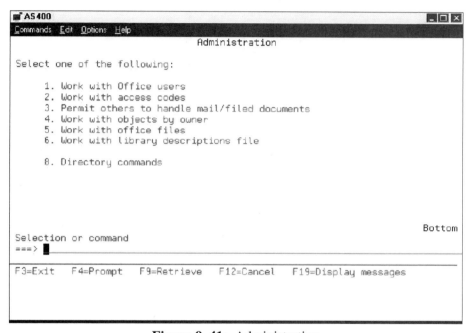

Figure 9–41: Administration

NOTE: If you are the administrator for OfficeVision/400, you will be able to change additional information and you will have additional options on the menu.

The main tasks you can perform from the Administration menu are

1. Change enrollment—The enrollment option allows you to change your environmental settings under OfficeVision/400. This information is broken into the following three categories:

    Directory—This information includes your full name, title, phone number, and other administrative information.

    Environment—This information sets your default folder name, default message notification value, current library assignment, initial directory, and default word processor selection (standard or adapted).

Calendar—This information controls your calendar operations. Settings in this area establish your initial calendar name, the default viewing perspective, and other options as well.

2. Display access codes—Access codes may be assigned to documents and used to control which departments or individuals may have access to them. This option shows the defined access codes.

3. Permit others to handle mail or filed documents—This option allows you to permit individuals to access your mail and documents.

4. Work with objects by owner—This option allows you to work with the information associated with OfficeVision/400 objects, such as calendars, directories, and folders. This is an advanced function.

5. Work with office files—This option allows you to save, restore, copy, or delete your calendar and personal directory files. This is an advanced function.

9.11 COMMAND SHORTCUTS

Many of the menus and screen displays shown in this chapter can be bypassed by keying in commands to take you directly to the function you desire. To use a command, enter the name on the command line and press <F4> to request any prompts it may require. These commands include

CHKDOC—spellcheck a document.

CPYDOC—copy a document.

CRTDOC—create a document.

CRTFLR—create a folder.

DSPDOC—display a document.

DSPFLR—display a folder.

EDTDOC—edit a document.

PAGDOC—paginate a document.

PRTDOC—print a document.

RNMDOC—rename a document.

SNDDOC—send (mail) a document.

STRWP—start the word processors.

WRKDOC—work with documents in folders.

WRKFLR—work with folders.

10

Data File Utility (DFU)

10.1 WHAT IS DFU?

OS/400's Data File Utility (DFU) is a tool to perform operations on data physical files. Operations that may be performed are: changing data within records in files, deleting records from files, and adding records to files.

Both indexed and nonindexed files may be manipulated with DFU. In addition, either a physical or logical file may be selected. Since data files are externally described on an AS/400, DFU will access the definition of the fields and records in the specified file. This provides the capability for DFU to prompt the user or programmer for the fields to be changed in a record. Choosing all fields for the records in a data file is very simple.

DFU creates programs to access the data in a file. You may create a permanent program (and the associated DFU display file) or a temporary program that exists only for your DFU session. The temporary program is useful when a change is needed to a data file (adding, changing, or deleting records) and you do not need to keep a copy of the program.

DFU is a simple utility to maintain records in a data file. DFU has the capability to change the order of fields as displayed on the screen. DFU also optionally produces an audit trail (a printed listing) that shows the before and after images of the records that were added, changed, or deleted. This allows you to verify the accuracy of any changes to the data file.

10.2 STARTING DFU

DFU can be started directly by using the Start Data File Utility (STRDFU) command, the Programmer Menu (STRPGMMNU command), or the PROGRAM menu (GO PROGRAM). Chapter 6, ("Basic Editing with SEU"), contains a description of the Programmer Menu. The STRDFU command uses as defaults the information entered when you last used the command. The STRDFU command is shown here.

```
STRDFU OPTION((2 1)) FILE(ARFILE).
```

The first parameter, "Option" (OPTION), consists of two parts. The first part, "DFU option," allows entries of 1 through 5 and *SELECT. The numbered options correspond to the five DFU Main Menu options, while choosing *SELECT displays the DFU Main Menu. The second part, "Run option," may have a value of 1 to allow updates to the data file, or a value of 2 to display only the information in the data file and not allow the information to be changed.

The next parameter, "DFU program" (DFUPGM), allows you to enter the DFU program to be used or created. The "Library" may also be specified if needed. Special value *PRV is the default and is used to specify the previously used value for this parameter.

The "Database file" (FILE) parameter contains the name of the data physical file that will be manipulated. The "Library" may also be specified. Special value *PRV is the default and is used to specify the previously used value for these parameters.

The "Member" (MBR) parameter contains the name of the member in the data physical file with which records will be added, changed, or deleted. Special value *PRV is the default and is used to specify the previously used value for these parameters.

Enter the appropriate parameters and press <ENTER> to start DFU.

The DFU main menu will be shown if *SELECT was chosen for the "Option" prompt with the STRDFU command. The main menu is shown here (see Figure 10–1):

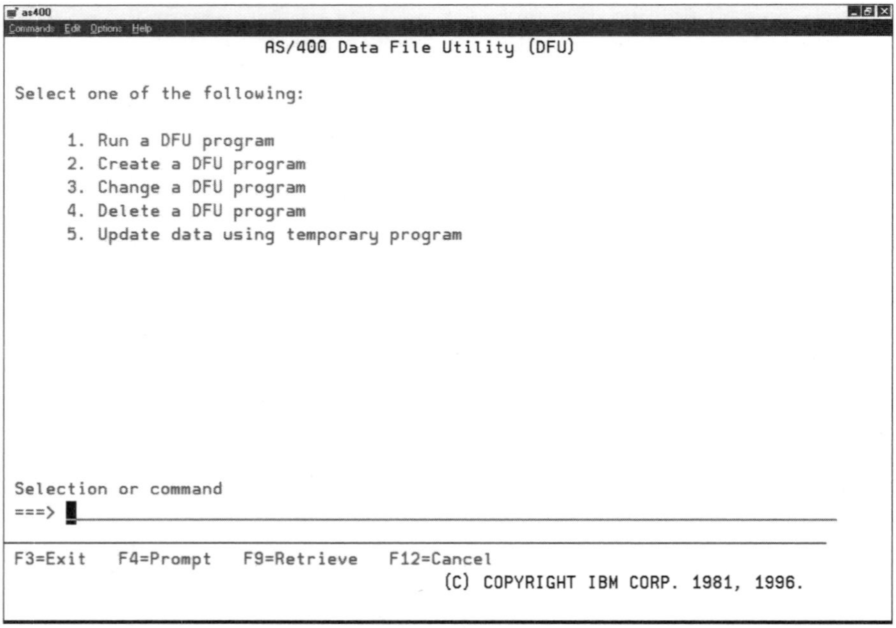

Figure 10–1: DFU main menu

Option 1 will run an existing DFU program. Option 2 will create a new DFU program. Option 3 will allow you to change an existing DFU program. Option 4 will remove an existing DFU program from the system. Option 5 will cause DFU to create a temporary program, which will only exist for the duration of your DFU session.

10.3 CREATING A DFU PROGRAM

Choosing option 2 from the DFU main menu will allow you to create a new DFU program. You could have also specified this with the STRDFU command by entering a value of 2 for the "Option" parameter and entering appropriate information for the "Database file," "Library," and "Member" parameters.

Choosing option 2 from the main menu will display the Create a DFU Program screen. This screen is shown here (see Figure 10–2):

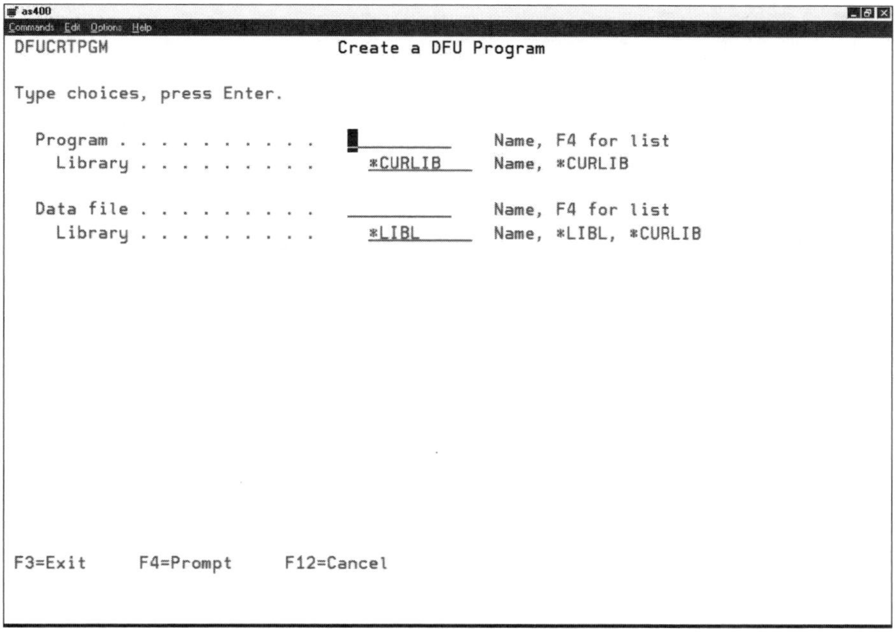

```
as400                                                                _ 8 X
Commands  Edit  Options  Help
 DFUCRTPGM                      Create a DFU Program

 Type choices, press Enter.

     Program . . . . . . . . .    █                Name, F4 for list
       Library . . . . . . . .    *CURLIB          Name, *CURLIB

     Data file . . . . . . . .    _____         Name, F4 for list
       Library . . . . . . . .    *LIBL            Name, *LIBL, *CURLIB










 F3=Exit     F4=Prompt    F12=Cancel
```

Figure 10–2: Create a DFU Program screen

This screen will accept the name of the DFU "Program" to create, and the "Library" in which the DFU program should reside. Enter the appropriate information for "Data file" and "Library" prompts. This will be the data file to be manipulated by the DFU program. Specifying the data file allows DFU to obtain the field and record definitions for the file. Note that you may also prompt (using <F4>) for the name of the program and the data file.

Enter your responses and press the <ENTER> key. A display will be shown that enables you to specify certain general information regarding the DFU program or job. Regardless of whether the file is indexed, certain information is common to both file types (indexed and nonindexed). The examples shown in this chapter assume the file is a nonindexed physical file. The following display is the Define General Information screen (see Figure 10–3):

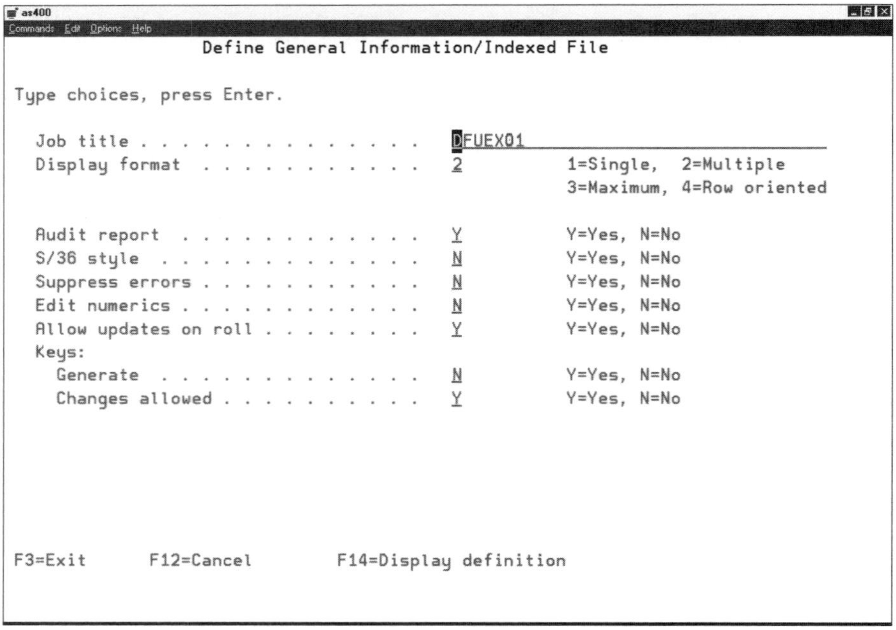

```
 as400                                                                    _ 8 X
Commands  Edit  Options  Help
                     Define General Information/Indexed File

  Type choices, press Enter.

    Job title . . . . . . . . . . . . .   DFUEX01
    Display format  . . . . . . . . . .   2          1=Single,   2=Multiple
                                                     3=Maximum,  4=Row oriented

    Audit report  . . . . . . . . . . .   Y          Y=Yes,  N=No
    S/36 style  . . . . . . . . . . . .   N          Y=Yes,  N=No
    Suppress errors . . . . . . . . . .   N          Y=Yes,  N=No
    Edit numerics . . . . . . . . . . .   N          Y=Yes,  N=No
    Allow updates on roll . . . . . . .   Y          Y=Yes,  N=No
    Keys:
      Generate  . . . . . . . . . . . .   N          Y=Yes,  N=No
      Changes allowed . . . . . . . . .   Y          Y=Yes,  N=No




    F3=Exit      F12=Cancel        F14=Display definition

```

Figure 10–3: Define general information screen

The "Job Title" prompt accepts a string of characters that will be used as a heading and also is printed on the optional audit report.

The "Display format" prompt allows you to define how the fields in the record will be displayed on the screen. DFU will place the fields so that there is space between each field. Entering a value of 1 for the "Display format" parameter will show one column of fields at a time. A value of 2 (the default) will show multiple columns of fields on the screen. DFU will determine the appropriate spacing between the fields, and will cause additional screens to be used if needed. A value of 3 for this parameter will cause DFU to place the maximum number of fields possible on the screen without regard to the columnar format. A value of 4 will place the fields in a row oriented format.

The "Audit report" prompt (Y or N) determines if an audit report should be generated to print the changes made to the data file. The default for this parameter (Y) will cause an audit report to be generated.

The next prompt "S/36 style," determines if the generated DFU program should operate as System/36 DFU or as "native" OS/400 DFU. This parameter defaults to N, meaning not in System/36 style.

The "Suppress errors" prompt refers to the capability of DFU to try to display a record that has an error, such as a data decimal error (invalid data in a numeric field). This parameter defaults to N, meaning that errors will be reported if encountered during the execution of the DFU program.

The "Edit numerics" prompt defaults to N. This means that numeric fields will be entered and displayed as a series of digits without numeric editing such as decimal points and commas. An entry of Y to this prompt will cause additional screens to be displayed; these screens allow you to specify the output editing for numeric fields.

"Allow updates on roll" determines if records should be updated if fields have been changed and the user presses the <ROLL UP> or <ROLL DOWN> keys to access the previous or next record. An entry of Y for this parameter will cause DFU to update the changed record and then roll to the next record.

Note: Other parameters are available depending on the type of file (indexed or non-indexed) selected for processing.

Enter the appropriate parameters and press the <ENTER> key.

The following display shows the Define Audit Control screen. This screen will be displayed if Y was entered for the "Audit report" parameter on the Define General Information Screen (see Figure 10–4):

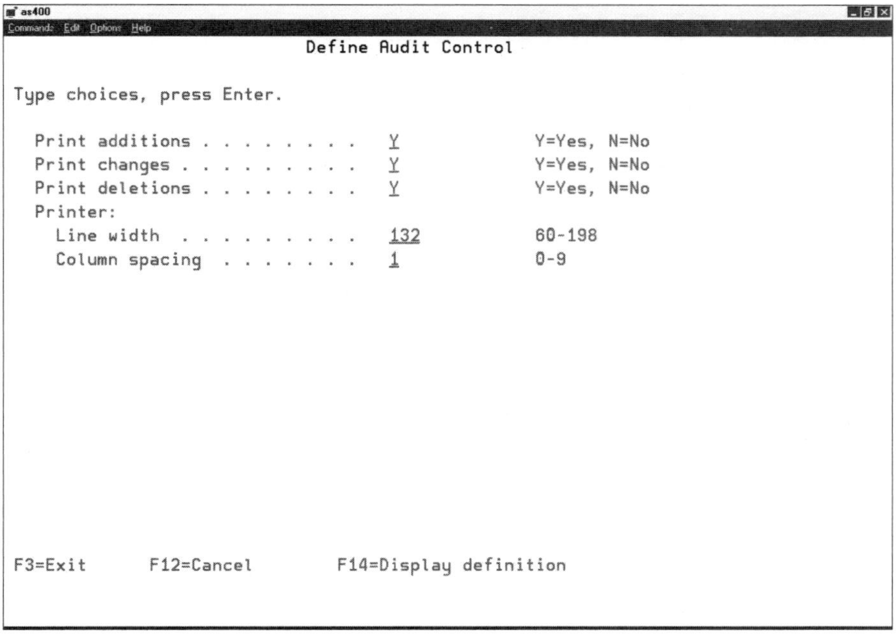
```
                         Define Audit Control

Type choices, press Enter.

  Print additions . . . . . . . .   Y          Y=Yes, N=No
  Print changes . . . . . . . . .   Y          Y=Yes, N=No
  Print deletions . . . . . . . .   Y          Y=Yes, N=No
  Printer:
    Line width  . . . . . . . . .   132        60-198
    Column spacing  . . . . . . .   1          0-9

F3=Exit      F12=Cancel       F14=Display definition
```

Figure 10–4: Define audit control screen

The first three prompts determine if information should be printed for three different operations. These prompts all default to Y. A response of Y for the first prompt, "Print additions," will print the new contents of the newly added record. The next prompt, "Print changes," determines if changed records should be printed. If selected, this prompt will cause the before and after contents of the changed record to be printed. The "Print deletions" prompt controls whether deleted records should be printed.

The "Printer" prompt allows you to define characteristics of the printed audit report. The "Line width" defaults to 132 and may be in the range of 60 to 198. The "Column spacing" parameter determines the amount of space between columns in the printed audit report. The value for this parameter may be between 0 and 9 spaces.

Specify the parameter values and press <ENTER>.

Whether or not the audit report was selected, the next screen that will be displayed is the Work with Record Formats display. This display allows you to select the record format in the data file that you wish to use for the DFU program (see Figure 10–5):

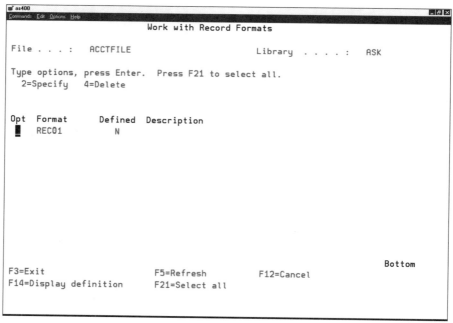

Figure 10–5: Work with record formats display

You may select record formats to be processed with Option 2 and remove record formats from being processed with Option 4. Removing a record format does not remove the record format from the file, just from being used in the generated DFU program.

You may also specify that multiple records be displayed. This provides the capability to access and view multiple records on the screen at one time and may be helpful when entering similar information into more than one record. Place a Y in the "Multiple Records" column for the appropriate record format if you wish to use multiple record processing.

The "Defined" column indicates if the record format has been previously defined for use in this DFU program. This column will be N when creating a new DFU program.

Select the record formats to be used in this DFU program and press <ENTER> to continue. You may also press <F21> to select all record formats in the file, and <F14> to display the file definition.

The next display to be shown is the Select and Sequence Fields display. This display allows you to select the fields to be used in the DFU program and to place the fields in the sequence you wish. Remember that the format of the display is determined on the General Information display. Additional screens containing the fields in a record format will be shown if multiple record formats have been selected.

The following example screen shows how to select and sequence fields (see Figure 10–6):

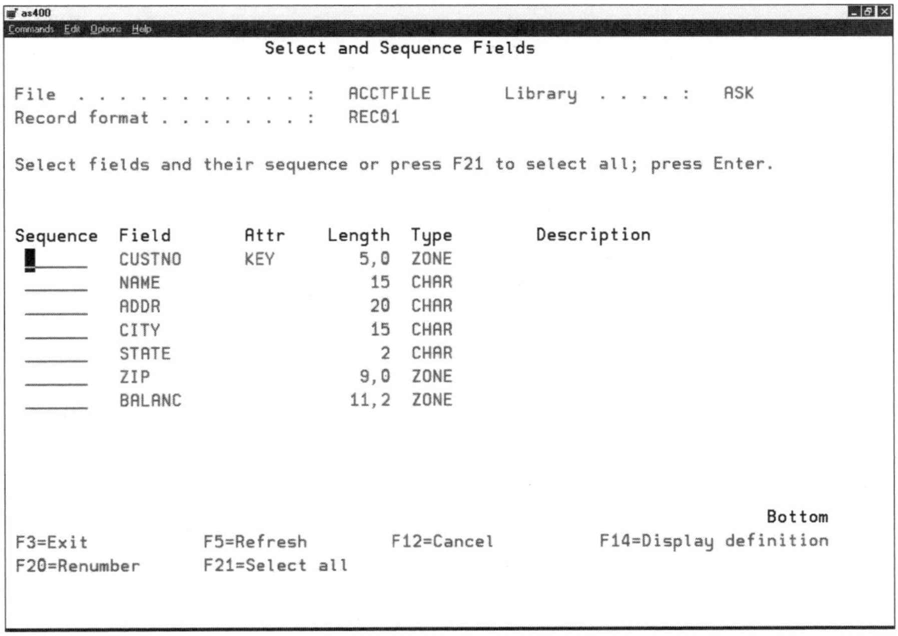

Figure 10–6: Select and sequence fields display

The fields for a record format, along with the description, are shown on this display. The display shows the name of the file, library, and record format containing the fields. Other information displayed on this screen includes the field name, any attributes (such as being part of a key) associated with the field, and the length and type of the field.

Fields are selected by specifying a "Sequence" number. The number specified indicates the position of the field as it will be displayed. You may use <F21> to select all the fields in the format in the order they exist in the file description. Pressing <ENTER> will redisplay the fields in the order you have specified. A message will display on the last line of the screen requesting you to press <ENTER> to confirm your selection or <F17> to confirm and accept the defaults.

Confirming and accepting the defaults will take you to the Exit DFU Program Generation screen. Pressing <ENTER> will display the Work with Fields screen. This display is shown below and allows you to specify extended definitions (see Figure 10–7):

```
as400                                                                   _ 6 X
Commands  Edit  Options  Help
                              Work with Fields

 File  . . . . . . . . . . :      ACCTFILE      Library . . . . :      ASK
 Record format . . . . . . :      REC01

Type options, press Enter.  Press F21 to select all.
   2=Specify extended definition
   4=Delete extended definition


                   Extended
 Opt   Field       Definition   Heading
  _    CUSTNO          N         CUSTNO_____
  _    NAME            N         NAME_____
  _    ADDR            N         ADDR_____
  _    CITY            N         CITY_____
  _    STATE           N         STATE_____
  _    ZIP             N         ZIP_____
  _    BALANC          N         BALANC_____

                                                                   Bottom
 F3=Exit                     F5=Refresh       F12=Cancel
 F14=Display definition      F21=Select all
```

Figure 10–7: Work with fields display

The fields selected will be displayed in the order you specified. The Extended Definition column indicates if an extended definition already exists for the field. You may enter a new "Heading" for a field. This will replace the heading that DFU would otherwise use when displaying the field during DFU program execution.

Pressing <F21> will select all fields for extended definition. You may enter a 2 to provide an extended definition or a 4 to remove an extended definition. The extended definitions illustrate the ease in which fairly complicated operations may be performed with DFU. Some of the extended definition attributes available for a numeric field are

Accumulate—You may specify a field to be accumulated as records are processed. This running total will be shown after program execution and will also print on the audit report.

Extended field heading—DFU will automatically place a heading near the field on the display. You may specify an extended heading on multiple lines. You may also specify that the heading appear above or below the field.

Initial value—An initial value may be specified for a field. This is helpful when the majority of records will have the same value for the field. You may specify a numeric literal or a special value such as the date (*DATE) or time (*TIME).

Validity checks—Specific validity checks may be specified in the extended definition. Validity checks such as mandatory entry, mandatory fill, and modulus checking may be specified. In addition, you can specify that the entered field be compared to a numeric literal or a range of values.

Field exit required—This attribute forces the user to press the <FIELD-EXIT> key to exit the field.

Edit code—You may specify an edit code that will be used to edit the field for display. The default edit code used by DFU is L, providing commas, decimal point, and leading zero suppression. You may also specify an edit word for unique editing requirements.

Extended field definitions for alphanumeric fields include many of the numeric field definition attributes and the following alphanumeric specific definitions:

Alphabetic characters only—This attribute allows only alphabetic characters (no numeric digits or special characters) to be entered into the field.

Validity checks—Validity checks for alphanumeric fields include a name check to ensure that the entered information conforms to OS/400's requirements for a name, and whether blanks are allowed as an entry for a field.

After the extended field definitions have been entered for the selected fields, press <ENTER> to return to the Work with Fields display.

Press <ENTER> or <F3> to proceed to the Exit DFU Program Generation display. This screen is shown in Figure 10–8.

The first prompt, "Save program," will default to Y. This will save the generated DFU program. Entries are also required for other parameters if you wish to save the program.

The "Run program" prompt also defaults to Y. This will run the DFU program. The associated prompt "Type of run" has two allowable values. A response of 1 will run the program and allow data to be updated. A response of 2 will run the program in display mode but not allow any data to be changed.

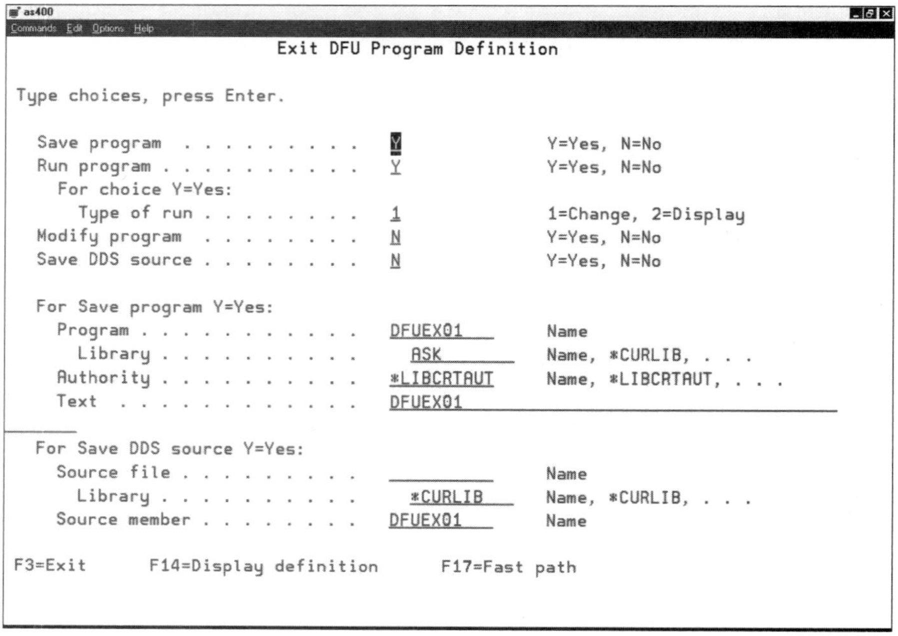

```
as400                                                                    _ [] X
Commands  Edit  Options  Help
                        Exit DFU Program Definition

  Type choices, press Enter.

      Save program  . . . . . . . .  Y          Y=Yes, N=No
      Run program . . . . . . . . .  Y          Y=Yes, N=No
        For choice Y=Yes:
          Type of run . . . . . . .  1          1=Change, 2=Display
      Modify program  . . . . . . .  N          Y=Yes, N=No
      Save DDS source . . . . . . .  N          Y=Yes, N=No

      For Save program Y=Yes:
        Program . . . . . . . . . .  DFUEX01      Name
          Library . . . . . . . . . ASK          Name, *CURLIB, . . .
        Authority . . . . . . . . .  *LIBCRTAUT   Name, *LIBCRTAUT, . . .
        Text  . . . . . . . . . . .  DFUEX01

      For Save DDS source Y=Yes:
        Source file . . . . . . . .               Name
          Library . . . . . . . . . *CURLIB       Name, *CURLIB, . . .
        Source member . . . . . . .  DFUEX01      Name

  F3=Exit     F14=Display definition     F17=Fast path

```

Figure 10–8: Exit DFU program generation screen

The next prompt, "Modify program," will allow you to return to the Define General Information display to change information about the DFU program. A response of Y to this parameter will return you to the definition screen.

The following prompt, "Save DDS source," allows you to save the created DDS source for your DFU program's displays. You may wish to change this parameter to Y to add additional information displayed on the screen, or to reformat the appearance of the screen. The default for this parameter is N. Entries are required for other parameters if you wish to save the DDS source.

If you answered Y to the "Save DFU program" prompt, you must complete the following associated prompts. The "Program" and "Library" prompts will default to the entries made when you selected the Create a DFU program option from the DFU Main Menu. The value in the "Authority" prompt determines the type of public authority that will be granted. This prompt defaults to *LIBCRTAUT, meaning that the program will assume the authority specified in the "Create authority" (CRTAUT) parameter in the library description. You may also choose any of the other public authorities. The "Text" prompt defaults to the name of the DFU program. You may choose up to fifty characters of descriptive text for this program.

A response of Y to the "Save DDS source" prompt requires that entries be made for the following associated prompts. The "Source file," "Library," and "Source member" prompts determine where the DDS source will be saved.

Specify the appropriate parameters and press the <ENTER> key. The DFU program will be executed if you specified Y to the "Run program" prompt.

10.4 RUNNING A DFU PROGRAM

A DFU program may be executed from the Exit DFU Program Definition screen by using the Change Data (CHGDTA) command or through the use of the DFU Main Menu. DFU Main Menu option 1 will execute a DFU program. The following screen will be displayed when option 1 is selected (see Figure 10–9):

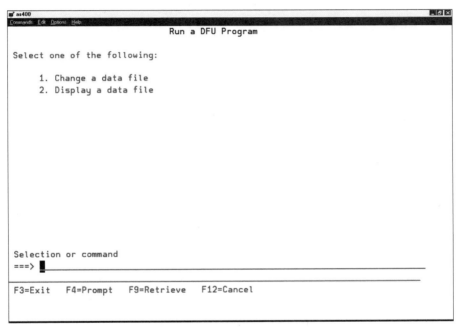

Figure 10–9: Run a DFU program display

Select option 1 to change the data file (including adding new records to the file or deleting existing records) or option 2 to display the data file while not allowing any changes. Press <ENTER> after selecting the option to display the Change a Data File screen (see Figure 10–10).

The "Program" entry is required and specifies the name of the DFU program to be executed. You may also specify the "Library" name if needed.

The "Data file" parameter indicates the name of the data file that will be changed. The "Library" may be specified as well as the name of the "Member" in the data file. The "Member" parameter defaults to the first member in the file. Note that this data file need not be the file with which the DFU program was created. However, if a different data file is selected, it should have the same record format name and field names as the original data file.

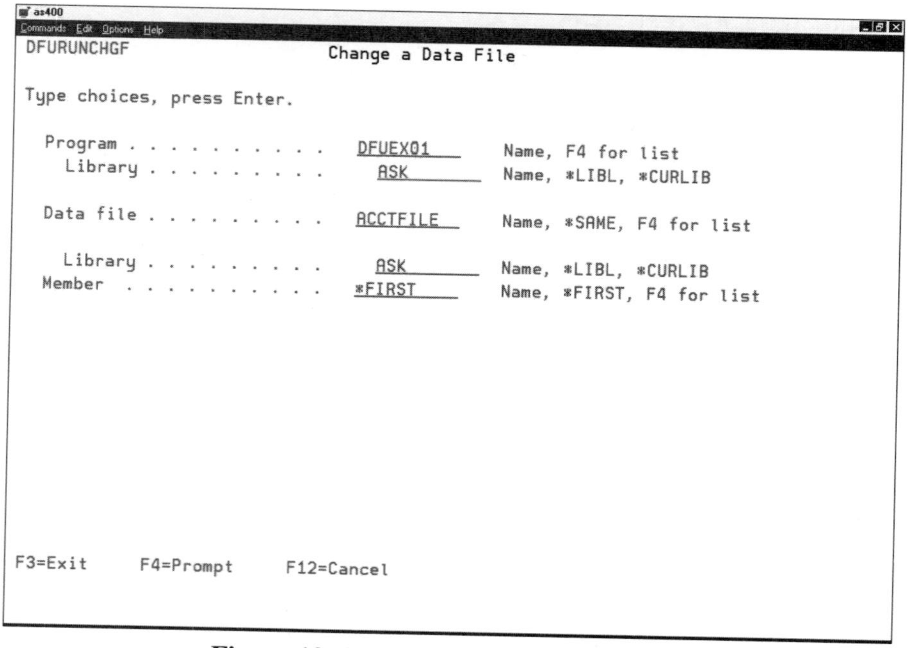

```
 a:400
Commands Edit Options Help                                                    _ 6 x
 DFURUNCHGF                    Change a Data File

 Type choices, press Enter.

    Program . . . . . . . . . .    DFUEX01      Name, F4 for list
       Library . . . . . . . . .    ASK          Name, *LIBL, *CURLIB

    Data file . . . . . . . . .    ACCTFILE     Name, *SAME, F4 for list

       Library . . . . . . . . .    ASK          Name, *LIBL, *CURLIB
    Member  . . . . . . . . . .    *FIRST       Name, *FIRST, F4 for list








 F3=Exit      F4=Prompt     F12=Cancel

```

Figure 10–10: Change a data file display

Press <ENTER> to run the DFU program. The format of the displayed information will depend on the option that was selected when the DFU program was created. The "Display format" parameter specifies the format for the fields to be displayed on the screen. The format may show the fields one at a time, as multiple fields on the screen, as the maximum number of fields possible, or in a row oriented format. The following example screen in Figure 10–11 shows the fields in the default format of multiple fields with DFU providing the default spacing.

10.4.1 Adding New Records

The program will begin in a certain mode depending on the existence of records in the file. If records currently exist, the program will begin in change mode. The program will begin in entry mode if records do not exist in the file. The following example screen (see Figure 10–12) shows the entry mode display.

```
┌─────────────────────────────────────────────────────────────────────┐
│ ▄ as400                                                      _ ⟊ ✕    │
│ Commands  Edit  Options  Help                                        │
│ DFUEX01                              Mode . . . . :   CHANGE          │
│ Format . . . . :   REC01            File . . . . :   ACCTFILE        │
│                                                                       │
│ CUSTNO: ____1__                                                       │
│ NAME:  Ralph Princeton                                                │
│ ADDR:  1 Harvard Lane____                                             │
│ CITY:  Boston_____                                                  │
│ STATE: MA                                                             │
│ ZIP:  ____1234_                                                       │
│ BALANC: ___1472389_                                                   │
│                                                                       │
│                                                                       │
│                                                                       │
│                                                                       │
│                                                                       │
│                                                                       │
│                                                                       │
│ F3=Exit            F5=Refresh          F6=Select format               │
│ F9=Insert          F10=Entry           F11=Change                     │
│                                                                       │
└─────────────────────────────────────────────────────────────────────┘
```

Figure 10–11: Change a data file display

```
┌─────────────────────────────────────────────────────────────────────┐
│ ▄ as400                                                      _ ⟊ ✕    │
│ Commands  Edit  Options  Help                                        │
│ DFUEX01                              Mode . . . . :   ENTRY           │
│ Format . . . . :   REC01            File . . . . :   ACCTFILE        │
│                                                                       │
│ CUSTNO: _____                                                        │
│ NAME:  _____                                                  │
│ ADDR:  _____                                               │
│ CITY:  _____                                                  │
│ STATE: __                                                             │
│ ZIP:  _____                                                       │
│ BALANC: _____                                                    │
│                                                                       │
│                                                                       │
│                                                                       │
│                                                                       │
│                                                                       │
│                                                                       │
│                                                                       │
│ F3=Exit            F5=Refresh          F6=Select format               │
│ F9=Insert          F10=Entry           F11=Change                     │
│                                                                       │
└─────────────────────────────────────────────────────────────────────┘
```

Figure 10–12: Entry mode display

Note that numeric fields contain zeros and alphanumeric fields contain blanks. Remember that the DFU program may set defaults for fields; in this case, the fields would have initial values. The DFU program creation option "Multiple Records" will display and make available multiple records at one time. Other attribute information, such as bold or underline, would be seen when the information is displayed.

Function keys available are <F5> to refresh the screen, <F6> to display a record format selection list and allow you to select a format, <F9> to insert a new record at the current file position, <F10> to change the program mode to entry mode, and <F11> to change the program mode to change mode.

Records may be entered successively while in entry mode. Enter the information in the fields, pressing the <ENTER> key after each record is complete. The record will be added to the end of the file.

After the record is added, a new screen will be displayed with the fields initialized to zero for a numeric field, blank for an alphanumeric field, or to an initial value for a field with a default value.

Press <F3> when you have added the required records to the file. This will cause the End Data Entry screen to be displayed. The operation of this screen is explained later in this chapter.

10.4.2 Changing Records in a File

Changing the program mode to change mode will allow you to change records in the file. Changing an indexed file will require you to enter a key value or relative record number, displaying the appropriate record. A sequential file will produce the records one after another from the current position in the file.

The DFU display is the same as in entry mode except the fields will contain information from the records in the file. You may enter new information into the fields and update the record by pressing the <ENTER> key.

A function key that is useful when changing records is the <F17> key, which will display accumulators. An extended definition of accumulation for a numeric field provides a running total of the field's contents to accumulate. These accumulators may be displayed or printed via the <F17> key. The following is an example of the Display Batch Accumulators screen (see Figure 10–13).

The <F21> key will display the current status of the DFU execution. The following example shows the Display Run Status Screen (see Figure 10–14).

This display shows the current program, data file and member, program mode, and other information concerning the status of the DFU program's execution.

10.4.3 Inserting Records

You may insert a new record by pressing the <F9> key. Inserting a record places the DFU program in entry mode and inserts the newly added record at the current file position.

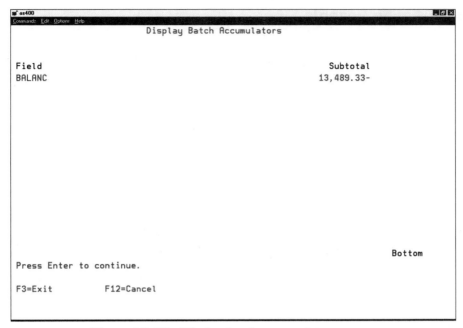

Figure 10–13: Display batch accumulators screen

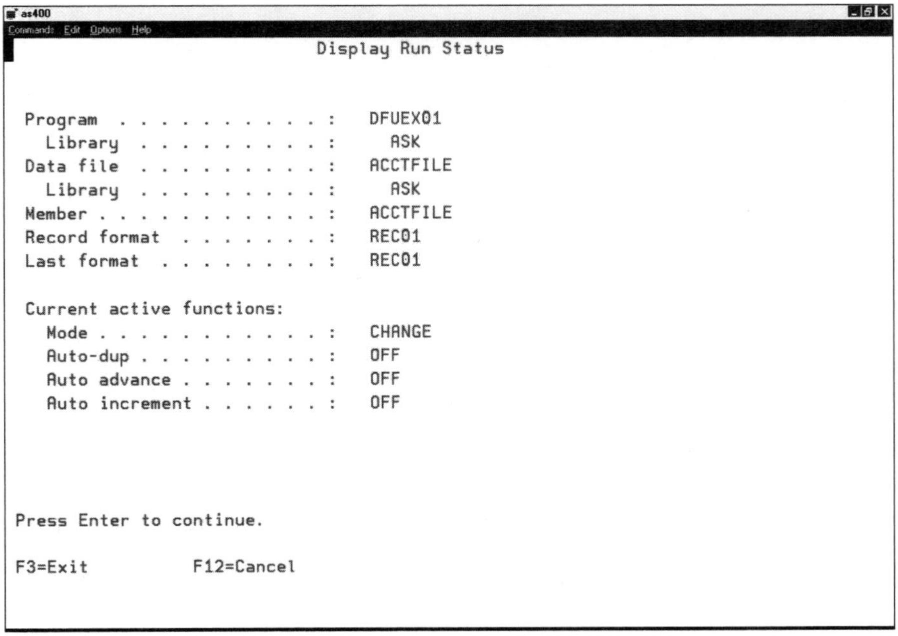

Figure 10–14: Display run status screen

10.4.4 Deleting Records

Records may be deleted from the data file with the DFU program. Pressing the <F23> key while in change mode will delete the current record. A message will appear at the bottom of the screen requesting you to press <F23> again to confirm the delete request. Pressing <F12> will cancel the delete request, while pressing <F23> again will delete the record from the data file.

10.5 SAVING YOUR WORK AND EXITING DFU

Pressing <F3> (while in entry or change mode) will display the End Data Entry display. This screen is shown here (see Figure 10–15):

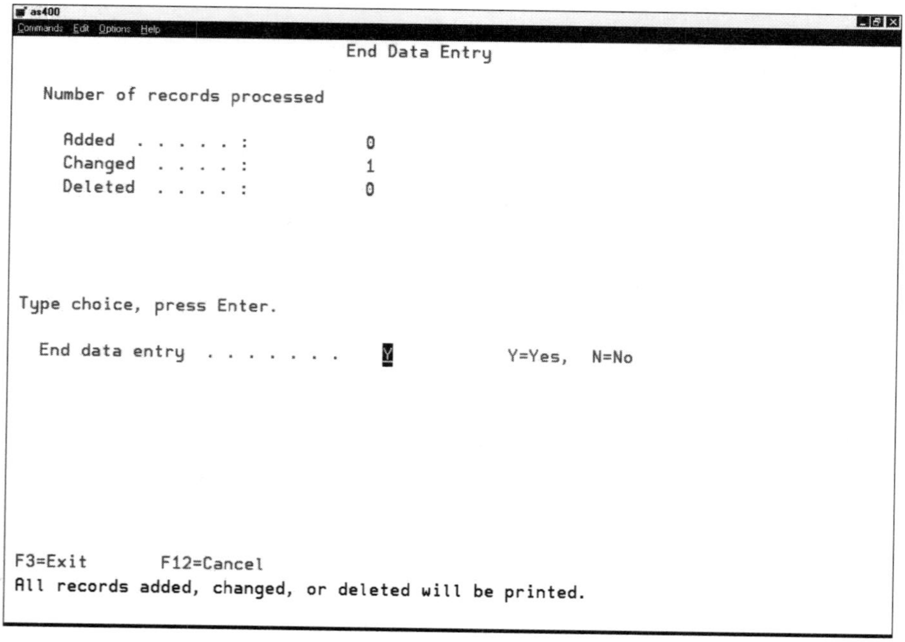

```
as400                                                                    _ 6 X
Commands  Edit  Options  Help
                                End Data Entry

    Number of records processed

        Added  . . . . . :        0
        Changed  . . . . :        1
        Deleted  . . . . :        0




    Type choice, press Enter.

        End data entry  . . . . . . .   Y          Y=Yes,   N=No








    F3=Exit        F12=Cancel
    All records added, changed, or deleted will be printed.
```

Figure 10–15: End data entry screen

The number of records processed will be shown, indicating the number of records added, changed, and deleted. A prompt, "End data entry," defaults to Y. You may respond with N to this prompt to return to the DFU program. Accepting the default of Y will end the DFU program. If an audit trail was selected (through the Define General Information screen), a message will appear at the bottom of the screen indicating that all records that were added, changed, or deleted will be printed. An example audit trail report is shown here (see Figure 10–16):

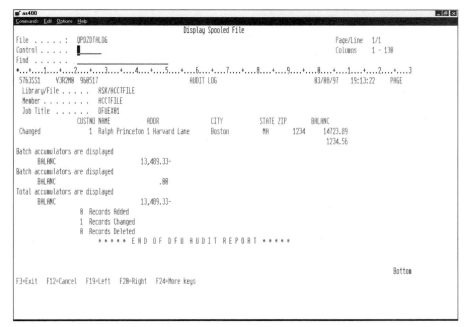

Figure 10–16: Example audit trail report

The next screen to be shown will be the Display Batch Accumulators screen if accumulators were defined in the DFU program. This is the same screen that is displayed when pressing <F17> during the execution of the DFU program. The Display Total Accumulators screen will also be shown.

10.6 CHANGING A DFU PROGRAM

The characteristics of a DFU program may be changed. These changes may reflect different processing needs, the desire for a different screen format, output editing changes, a different file to be processed, or other needs. Changing a DFU program is accomplished by selecting option 3 from the DFU main menu, which causes the Change a DFU Program screen to appear.

This screen is similar to the Create a DFU Program screen. Required entries include the name of the DFU program and library, and the name of the data file and library. Pressing <ENTER> will proceed to the Define General Information screen. Any of the information used to create a DFU program may be changed. This includes the general information, screen format, fields to be selected, and the extended field definitions. The process for changing a DFU program is the same as for creating a new DFU program.

The Exit from DFU Program Generation screen will be displayed when you press the <F3> key. You may wish to change the name of the DFU program at this time. This will create a new DFU program using the original DFU program as a base.

Points to consider when changing the file that the DFU program will access are: the file type (indexed or nonindexed) must remain the same, and the record format names and field names must be the same as in the original file. In addition, field attributes must be the same in both files.

10.7 DELETING A DFU PROGRAM

Deleting a DFU program will remove the program permanently from the system. You may wish to do this when there is no longer a need for the program, or when the data file that the program uses has been changed. You should delete DFU programs with this option as DFU actually uses two objects, a program and a display file. Using this option will delete both objects from the system.

Selecting option 4 from the DFU Main Menu will produce the Delete a DFU Program display. This display is shown here (see Figure 10–17):

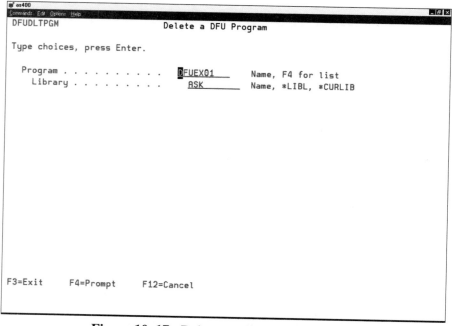

Figure 10–17: Delete a DFU program display

Specify the DFU "Program" name (and "Library" if needed). Note that you may produce a list of DFU programs within a specified library by pressing <F4> when the cursor is in the "Program" prompt area. Press the <ENTER> key to delete the program. A message will appear at the bottom of the screen requesting confirmation of the delete request. Press the <ENTER> key again to delete the DFU program.

10.8 CHANGING DATA WITH A TEMPORARY DFU PROGRAM

You may wish to create a DFU program to manipulate data without saving the program. The need for the data manipulation may be a special circumstance, such as correcting erroneous data in a file. DFU provides the capability to change data with a temporary program. Selecting option 5 from the DFU Main Menu will show the Update Data Using Temporary Program display. This display is shown here (see Figure 10–18):

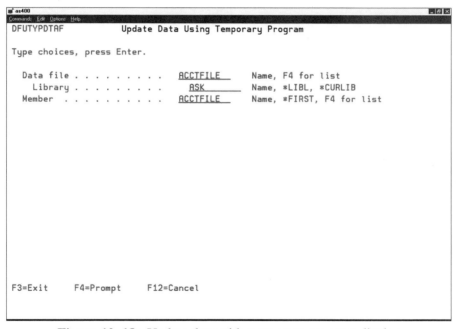

Figure 10–18: Update data with temporary program display

This screen requires the name of the "Data file," "Library," and "Member." Note that you may prompt for the name of the data file and the name of the member by pressing <F4> with the cursor in the appropriate prompt area.

The temporary DFU program will automatically select all record formats and all fields in the formats. In addition, the Define General Information screen prompts and the audit control prompts are all defaulted. The defaults will produce a multiple column display format with all added, changed, and deleted records printed at the end of the job.

The standard operations, such as adding records through entry mode and changing and deleting records through change mode, are available with a temporary program. The normal End Data Entry screen will be displayed when you press the <F3> key.

11

Screen Design Aid (SDA)

11.1 WHAT IS SDA?

The Screen Design Aid (SDA) is an IBM software product for creating, modifying, and testing display files and menus. SDA provides an interactive method for creating the Data Description Specifications (DDS) for a display file or menu. SDA enables the entry (into a display file) of field descriptions of fields contained within a database file. All attributes of display files, including attributes such as bold and mandatory entry, are available for selection through SDA.

OS/400 uses display files as the interface between a program and the user. Menus provide a method of choosing programs or commands to execute. Both display files and menus are described using DDS. The DDS are used to create a display file (a file with the DSPF attribute) or a menu (an object of type MNU).

A display file will contain at least one, (and perhaps multiple) record formats. Each record format may be an entire screen or a portion of a display. The record format will be named during the screen creation process during SDA. Each record format in a display file will contain fields and constants. The constants will be the text that is displayed on the screen. The fields in a display file may be input fields, output fields, or both input and output (update) fields.

A menu contains both the menu text and the commands to be executed as a result of choosing the menu option. The text and the list of commands are stored in two different objects. The objects are of type MNUDDS for the data description specifications for the menu, and of type MNUCMD for the list of commands for the menu. The SDA process creates both of these needed objects.

While DDS for display files and menus can be created or revised manually, SDA provides the capability to manipulate the DDS interactively. This interactive technique allows you to see the screen as it is being created or revised, and to move and position the fields and constants exactly as you wish them to be placed. In addition, the testing capability of SDA allows you to test the display file to ensure that the attributes and enhancements operate as you wish.

This chapter will explore the interactive capabilities of SDA, including the design screen process, selecting fields from a database file, creating menus, and testing the display files and menus.

11.2 STARTING SDA

SDA can be started directly by using the Start Screen Design Aid (STRSDA) command from the Programmer Menu (STRPGMMNU command) or the PROGRAM menu (GO PROGRAM). Chapter 6 ("Basic Editing with the SEU") contains a description of the Programmer Menu. The STRSDA command uses as defaults the information entered when you last used the command. The STRSDA command is shown here.

```
STRSDA SRCFILE(DEVELOP/QDDSSRC) OPTION(2).
```

The STRSDA command defaults to selecting *SELECT for the "SDA option" (OPTION), *PRV (for previous) for the "Source file" and "Library" (SRCFILE) parameter, *PRV for the "Member" (SRCMBR) parameter, and *STD (for standard AS/400 mode) for the "Mode" (MODE) parameter. Again, SDA defaults to the information entered when you last used SDA. Accept the defaults or enter the appropriate information for the "Source file," "Library," and "Member" that will contain the DDS statements. The member may contain multiple record formats.

You may also enter information for the name of the "Object Library" (OBJLIB) to contain the created display file, a "Job Description" (JOBD) to be used when creating the display file object, and a "Test file" and "Library" (TSTFILE) name if testing a display file. The "Mode" (MODE) parameter may contain values of *STD for AS/400 mode, *S38 for System/38 mode, and *S36 for System/36 mode. The mode options are ignored if the "SDA option" parameter has a value other than *SELECT. Press <ENTER> to begin SDA.

The following screen will be displayed if the "SDA option" parameter value was *SELECT. This display allows you to select the SDA option you wish (see Figure 11–1).

Option 1 is used to create and update display files. Option 2 is used to create and update menus. Option 3 is used to test display files that have already been created. This chapter will explain how to create and update display files.

11.3 DESIGNING SCREENS

When option 1, Design Screens, is selected, the following display (see Figure 11–2) will appear if member information was not entered with the STRSDA command.

This display requires the name of the "Source file," the "Library" containing the source file, and the name of the "Member" that contains or will contain the generated DDS. Enter the information required and press the <ENTER> key to proceed.

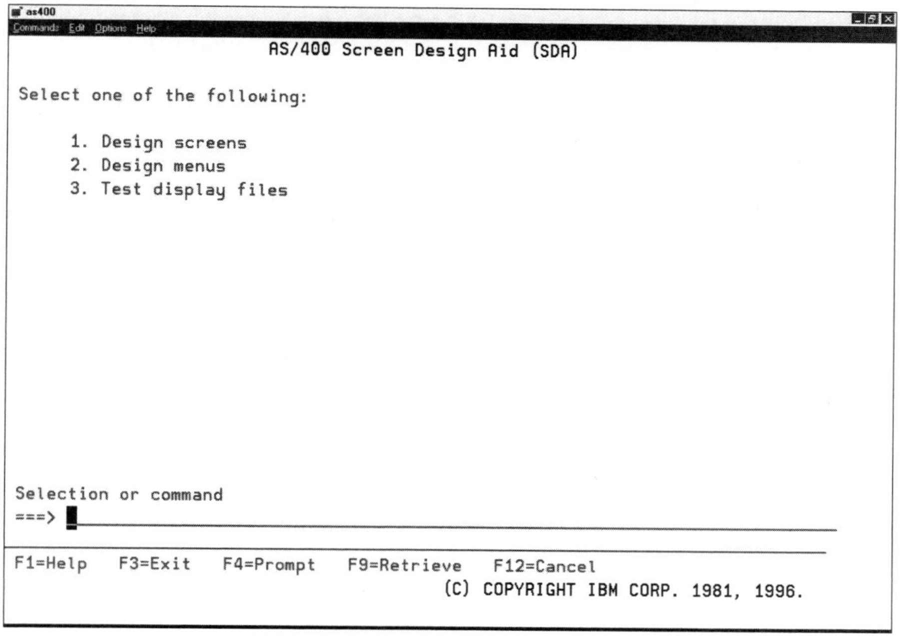

```
┌──────────────────────────────────────────────────────────────────────────┐
│ ■ as400                                                        _ ▢ ✕       │
│ Commands  Edit  Options  Help                                              │
│                     AS/400 Screen Design Aid (SDA)                         │
│                                                                            │
│  Select one of the following:                                             │
│                                                                            │
│       1. Design screens                                                   │
│       2. Design menus                                                     │
│       3. Test display files                                               │
│                                                                            │
│                                                                            │
│                                                                            │
│                                                                            │
│                                                                            │
│                                                                            │
│                                                                            │
│                                                                            │
│                                                                            │
│                                                                            │
│  Selection or command                                                     │
│  ===> █                                                                   │
│                                                                            │
│  ─────────────────────────────────────────────────────────               │
│  F1=Help    F3=Exit    F4=Prompt    F9=Retrieve   F12=Cancel              │
│                                (C) COPYRIGHT IBM CORP. 1981, 1996.         │
└──────────────────────────────────────────────────────────────────────────┘
```

Figure 11–1: SDA main menu options

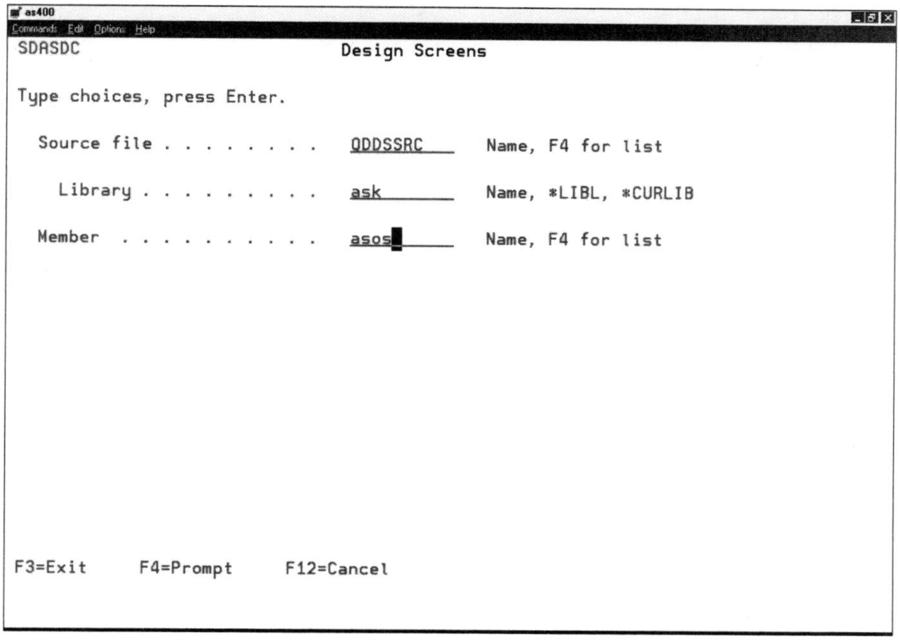

```
┌──────────────────────────────────────────────────────────────────────────┐
│ ■ as400                                                        _ ▢ ✕       │
│ Commands  Edit  Options  Help                                              │
│  SDASDC                      Design Screens                                │
│                                                                            │
│  Type choices, press Enter.                                               │
│                                                                            │
│    Source file . . . . . . . .   QDDSSRC     Name, F4 for list            │
│                                                                            │
│     Library . . . . . . . . .    ask         Name, *LIBL, *CURLIB         │
│                                                                            │
│    Member  . . . . . . . . . .   asos█       Name, F4 for list            │
│                                                                            │
│                                                                            │
│                                                                            │
│                                                                            │
│                                                                            │
│                                                                            │
│                                                                            │
│                                                                            │
│                                                                            │
│                                                                            │
│  F3=Exit     F4=Prompt     F12=Cancel                                     │
│                                                                            │
└──────────────────────────────────────────────────────────────────────────┘
```

Figure 11–2: Design screens display

The next screen shown is the "Work with Display Records" screen. This display shows the records that are already contained within the member. The following is an example of the Work with Display records screen (see Figure 11–3):

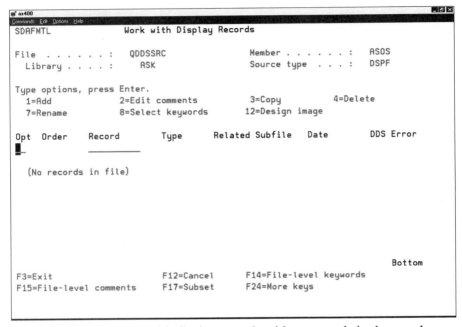

Figure 11–3: Work with display records with no records in the member

If no records are currently in the member (as shown in the example), a message will be displayed indicating "No records in file."

Available options with the Work with Display Records display include:

Option 1 (Add)—Allows you to add a new record. You may specify a name for the new record or press <ENTER>. Pressing <ENTER> will cause the Add New Record screen to be displayed.

Option 2 (Edit comments)—Invokes the Source Entry Utility (SEU) to enable you edit the comments that are associated with that record.

Option 3 (Copy)—Copies an existing display record to a new record name. The Copy Records screen will be displayed.

Option 4 (Remove)—Removes an existing display record from the member. You will be required to confirm the remove operation via the Confirm Remove of Records display.

Option 7 (Rename)—Renames an existing display record. The Rename Records display will be shown to allow you to change the name of the record.

Option 8 (Select keywords)—Allows you to change keyword selections for the display record. Selecting this option will produce the record-level keyword selection display.

Option 12 (Design image)—Allows you to change or update an existing display record. The design image screen will be displayed with the record format, allowing you to change the image of the record.

The headings on the record display are

Order—Refers to the order of the records within the member. You may wish to change the order of the most commonly used records to be near the top of the member as they will be accessed more quickly.

Record—The name of the display record in the member.

Record Type—The type of the record in the member. Valid record types are

RECORD—A display record.

USRDFN—A user-defined display record.

SFL—A subfile record. A subfile is a special record type that allows information to be arranged in a tabular or list format on the displayed screen.

SFLMSG—A subfile message record. These records are used for message passing from a program to the user.

SFLCTL—A subfile control record. This record type provides the control for a subfile.

Related subfile—A subfile control record will have subfile records with which it is associated. This heading lists the related subfile records.

Date—The creation date of the record.

DDS Error—This heading will indicate if any errors were found in the DDS statements for that record.

The function keys used on this display include the standards with the addition of

<F11> to display the text associated with the member.

<F14> to change the file level keywords for the member. The Select File keywords display will be shown.

<F15> for changing the file level comments through SEU.

<F17> to subset the list of display records. The Subset Records display will be shown where you may specify criteria of name or type to subset the record list.

Entering a 1 in the "Option" field and pressing <ENTER> will show the following display to add a new display record (see Figure 11–4):

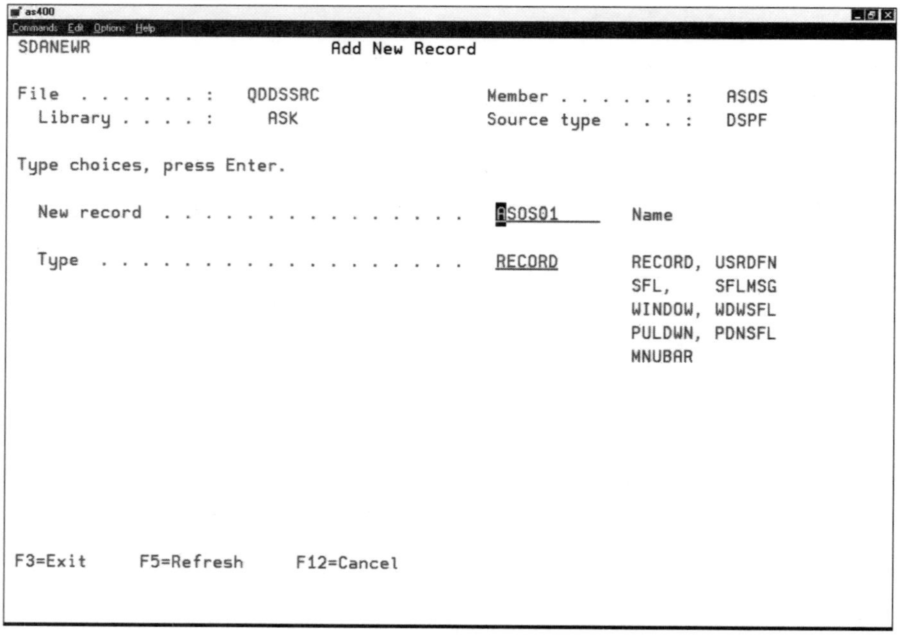

Figure 11–4: Add new record display

This display shows the "File," "Library," and "Member" names, as well as the "Source type." Specify values for the name of the "New record" and the "Type" of record. Press <ENTER> to create the record in the member.

11.3.1 Creating a Record Format

When creating a new record format, a blank screen will appear. This screen is a design area where you can lay out fields and constants, and assign attributes to them. The following (see Figure 11–5) is the blank create mode design screen.

The fields and constants that are specified on this screen will be used with different format characters to indicate the data type, size, display characteristics, and other information. This information will be converted into DDS by SDA.

Figure 11–5: SDA create mode screen

Fields and constants may be moved, sized, deleted, and copied, as well as having assigned attributes. These attributes include capabilities of bold, underline, mandatory entry, color, and many others.

The next section will provide an overview of the different format characters and how to maneuver in SDA. The process of revising an existing record are the same as for a new record.

As with most OS/400 displays, the help text is extensive. Press the <F1> key or the <HELP> key to view the help related to this display. In addition, SDA provides context-sensitive help. Place the cursor where you wish to receive help and press <F1> or the <HELP> key.

The function keys that are available when designing a screen include the following:

<F3> to end the screen design process. The Exit Design Image screen will be shown where you can save your work.

<F4> will show the Work with Fields display. You may enter attributes and other characteristics for the field from this display.

<F6> will show the Condition Work Screen display. This display allows you to specify indicators that will condition the display of records on the design screen.

<F9> will allow you to select additional records to be shown on the display. This is helpful when creating a new record that will be displayed with other records on the same screen.

<F10> will show the Select Database Files display. This display allows you to select a database file from which you may copy field definitions. This capability is described later in this chapter.

<F11> will display the list of database fields on the bottom row of the screen. This function key acts as a toggle; press <F11> again to remove the list.

<F12> will save your work and return you to the Work with Display Records display.

<F14> will display a horizontal and vertical ruler. The Ruler key is a toggle; press <F14> again to remove the ruler. Take care to not define any fields on the ruler as SDA may not be able to correctly place the field.

<F15> will prompt for subfile information and will only be available when a subfile exists on the screen.

<F17> will print the contents of the Design Image screen.

<F18> will move the cursor to the attribute position of the next field.

<F19> will move the cursor to the attribute position of the previous field.

<F20> will display the constants on the screen in reverse image. This may help you to determine the beginning and ending position of the constant.

<F21> will display additional selected records on the screen. This is a toggle key; pressing <F21> again will remove the additional records from the display. You may only make changes to the primary record, not to any of the additional records.

11.3.2 Adding and Deleting Fields and Constants

Fields and constants are added by specifying certain format and attribute codes on the display screen. Each field or constant must be separated by at least one blank space. No fields or constants may be placed in row 1, column 1 of a display file due to the leading attribute byte of the field or constant. A field may be placed directly after another field or constant (including the intervening space) by entering the format character over the last character position of the previous field or constant. Likewise, a constant may be entered by ending the constant with a double quotation mark (") and beginning the new constant or field.

A field may be added by entering a plus sign (+) followed by the format code for the field type desired. The format codes for different field types are

I   Input only field-alphanumeric

O   Output only field-alphanumeric

B   Both input and output (update) field-alphanumeric

3   Input only field-numeric

6   Output only field-numeric

9   Both input and output (update) field-numeric

A floating point field may be added by specifying the appropriate numeric format codes followed by an E for single precision or a D for double precision.

The length of a newly added field is determined in one of two ways: by specifying format characters for each character in the length of the field, or by specifying the format character followed by the length of the field in parentheses. Figure 11–6 shows the field type definitions and length specifications.

Constants are added to the display screen in a similar manner as fields. A constant is not added with the plus sign; it is simply typed onto the screen in the position desired. Constants are ended with a blank character. A constant that consists of several words may be defined as a single constant by placing single quotation marks (') around the group of words. You may also place quotation marks around several words that have already been added to the display screen to redefine them as one constant.

Special system-defined constants may be added to the display screen. These system-defined constants are

*DATE—Provides the system date

*TIME—Provides the system time

*USER—Provides the current user name

*SYSNAME—Provides the system name

These predefined constants may be placed in any valid location on the display screen.

Fields and constants may be deleted from the display screen in one of two ways: space over the entire field, including the immediately preceding position (the attribute byte), or place the character D in the position immediately preceding the field or constant and pressing the <ENTER> key.

The following example screen (see Figure 11–6) shows fields and constants being added to and deleted from the display screen.

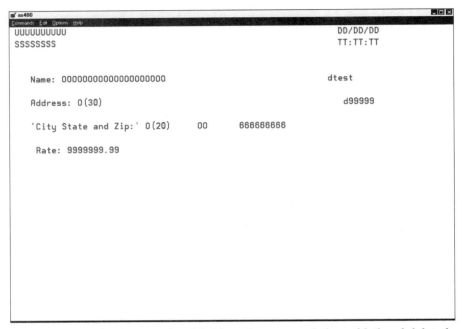

Figure 11–6: SDA example of fields and constants being added and deleted

11.3.3 Specifying Attributes and Color

Attributes may be manipulated for fields and constants. Color is an attribute that may be specified; of course, the workstation that will use the screen must be capable of supporting color. Attributes, including color, are placed in the attribute byte of the field or constant you are defining.

The attribute byte is the character position immediately preceding the field or constant. This is the reason a space must precede each field or constant on the display screen. You may press the <F18> key to position the cursor at the attribute byte of the previous field, and <F19> to position the cursor at the attribute byte of the next field. Multiple attributes may be selected by using multiple attribute codes. The following list shows the available attributes and colors:

B   Blink

H   High intensity

N   Nondisplay

R   Reverse image

S   Column separators

U   Underline

CB   Color blue

CG   Color green

CP   Color pink

CR   Color red

CT   Color turquoise

CW   Color white

You may remove an attribute or color by placing the attribute code prefaced with a minus (–) sign in the attribute position of the field or constant. Use –A to remove all attributes, and –CA to remove all colors.

The following screen shows examples of adding attributes and colors to fields and constants on the display screen (see Figure 11–7):

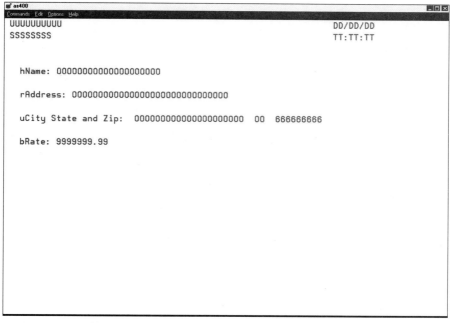

Figure 11–7: SDA example of adding attributes

You may also add attributes to a field or constant by placing an asterisk (*) in the attribute byte and pressing <ENTER>. This will show the Extended Field Definition display. This display will allow you to enter the attributes discussed above. A question mark (?) in the attribute position will show the field length, type, and field name. You may rename the field with this method.

11.3.4 Changing the Position of Fields and Constants

The position of fields and constants may be changed interactively through SDA. Fields and constants may be moved, copied, shifted, and centered through the use of special commands. These commands are placed in the attribute position of the field or constant. Pressing <ENTER> with position commands in place will change the position of the fields or constants; multiple fields or constants may be changed with one operation. Block positioning may also be used to position several fields and constants.

Use the AC command to center a field or constant in the same row. Moving a field or constant is done by specifying a – in the attribute byte of the field to be moved, and a = on the display to indicate the new position. A field may be copied by specifying a – in the attribute position of the field to be copied and == in the position where the field should be copied.

Blocks of fields and constants may be moved or copied by specifying a – in the upper left corner of the block and a – in the lower right corner of the block. Specify = (for a move) or == (for a copy) in the new position for the block.

Fields and constants may be shifted on the screen with the < and > characters. Shift a field or constant to the left by placing the < character in the attribute position. This will shift the field or constant to the left one character position. Placing a > in the position immediately following the field or constant will shift to the right one character position. Fields and constants may be shifted multiple positions by specifying multiple shift characters.

The following example screens (see Figure 11–8 and Figure 11–9) show the effects of moves, copies, centering, and shifting of fields and constants:

An error message will be displayed if an error is made when changing the position of fields and constants. This may happen when a field is moved or created over another field. SDA will display the message indicating an invalid operation. Press <ENTER> to clear the error message and to restore the design screen to the state it was in before the invalid operation.

11.3.5 Adding Fields from a Database File

Fields that are defined in a database file may be added to the SDA display through the Select Database Files display. SDA will select the fields from the database file and allow you to position the fields appropriately. The fields will have the same definition (data type, length, and so on) as the definition in the file. This display is accessed by pressing <F10> and is shown in Figure 11–10.

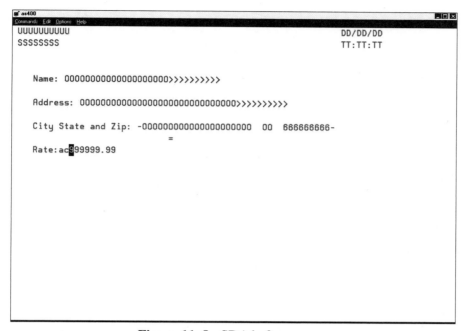

Figure 11–8: SDA before moves

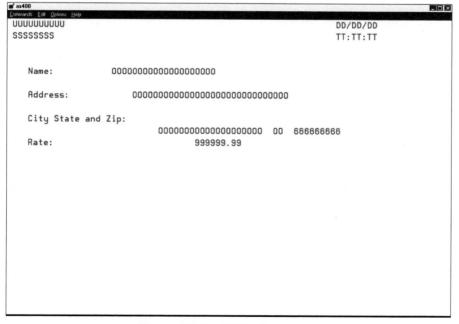

Figure 11–9: SDA after moves

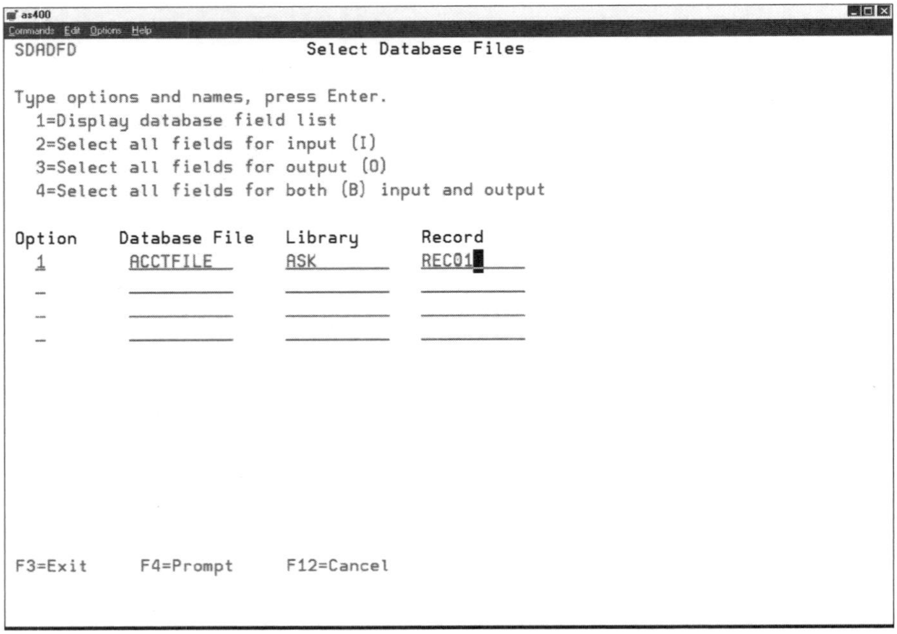

```
as400                                                               ■□区
Commands Edit Options Help
 SDADFD                        Select Database Files

 Type options and names, press Enter.
   1=Display database field list
   2=Select all fields for input (I)
   3=Select all fields for output (O)
   4=Select all fields for both (B) input and output


 Option    Database File   Library        Record
   1        ACCTFILE        ASK            REC01
   _        _____        _____       _____
   _        _____        _____       _____
   _        _____        _____       _____






 F3=Exit      F4=Prompt      F12=Cancel

```

Figure 11–10: Select database files display

Specify the "Database file" (and "Library" if needed). You may also specify the "Record" format name if the file has multiple records. Pressing <F4> will prompt you for missing values. There are four options for selecting fields: option 1 will provide a list of the fields in the database file, option 2 will select all the fields in the file as input fields, option 3 will select all fields as output fields, and option 4 will select all fields as input and output fields (both or update) fields.

Selecting option 1, Display database field list, will produce the following screen. This display (see Figure 11–11) is a list of the fields contained within the database file.

This display shows the fields from which you may select. The <ROLL UP> and <ROLL DOWN> keys are active to page through the field list. Specify a 1 for an extended description, 2 to select the field as an input field, 3 to select the field as an output field, or 4 to select the field as an input/output (update) field. You may select different fields as different types.

The selected fields will appear on the bottom of the design screen. You specify and position the fields with special characters. These characters are placed on the design screen at the position where the fields should be placed.

The ampersand (&) character is the special character for positioning. Other characters may be used to indicate if column headings (from the database file) should also be brought onto the screen. Since multiple fields may have been retrieved to the design screen, you may specify a number following the special character to indicate the correct field. The following list summarizes the special characters:

&	&n	Positions the database field but does not add the column heading.
&C	&nC	Positions the database field and centers the column heading above the field.
&L	&nL	Positions the database field and adds the column heading to the left of the field.
&R	&nR	Positions the database field and adds the column heading to the right of the field.
&P	&nP	Positions the column heading only.

The following example screens (see Figures 11–12 and 11–13) show the use of the positioning characters and the effect of the positioning after the <ENTER> key has been pressed.

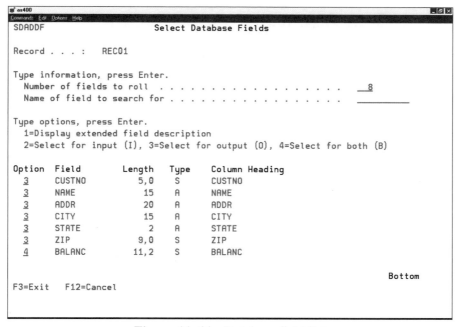

Figure 11–11: Database field list

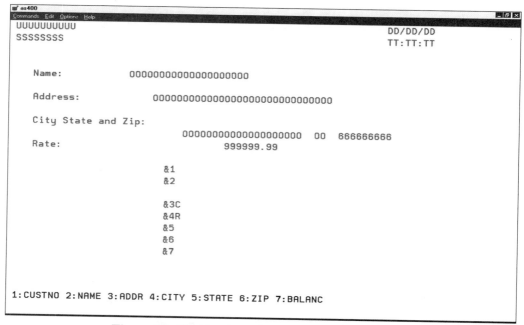

Figure 11–12: Database field positioning characters

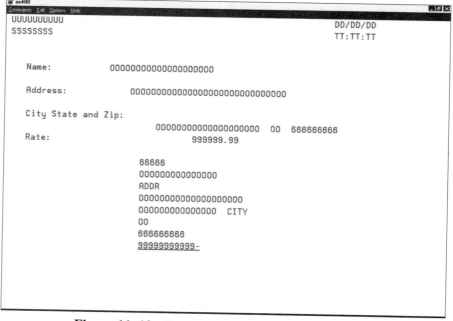

Figure 11–13: Database field positioning characters

11.4 SAVING YOUR WORK AND EXITING SDA

The <F12> Cancel key will save the record format with which you are currently working and return you to the Work with Display Records screen where you could choose a different record to manipulate.

The <F3> Exit key will display the Exit SDA Work Screen display shown below. Option 1 will save the work you have done since you last pressed <ENTER>. Option 2 will exit the design screen without saving the changes you have made. Options 1 and 2 will return to the Work with Display Records screen. Option 3 will return to the design screen (see Figure 11–14):

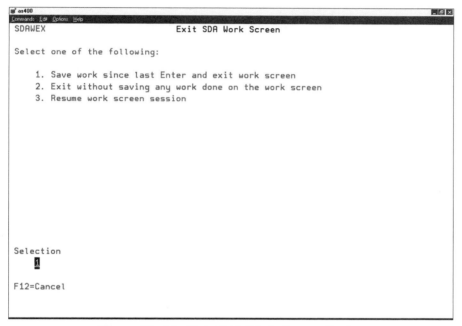

Figure 11–14: Exit SDA Work Screen display

After returning to the Work with Display Records screen you may create a new record, revise an existing record, or use the <F3> Exit or <F12> Cancel keys to exit the display. Either the Exit key or the Cancel key at this point will display the Save DDS–Create Display File screen shown below. The defaults are usually acceptable as they will save the DDS, submit a Create Display File (CRTDSPF) command in batch, and exit SDA (see Figure 11–15).

The first parameter, "Save DDS source," requires a response of Y or N. This parameter will default to Y if you have made any changes to the member. If you do not wish to save the changes made to the member, change this parameter to N.

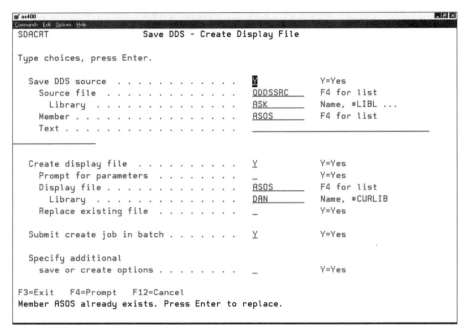

Figure 11–15: Save DDS-Create Display File screen

The next parameter specifies the name of the "Member," "Source file," and "Library" in which to save the member. If you wish to change the name of the member, overlay another member with this member, or change the library or file name, change the information associated with this prompt. Note that you may use the <F4> key to list file and member names.

The "Text" parameter is the optional fifty character text description that is to be associated with this member. It is a good practice to specify the "Text" description so you may more easily identify the member in a list of members.

The "Create display file" prompt determines if SDA should execute the CRTDSPF command to create a display file from the DDS. An entry of Y will create the display file while N will not create the display file.

"Prompt for parameters" prompts the CRTDSPF command and allows you to specify additional create options.

The "Display file" prompt defaults to the name of the member; you may change the name of the display file to be created and the "Library" in which the display file will be placed upon successful creation.

The "Replace existing file" prompt, if specified with an entry of Y, will delete and recreate the display file if it exists in the specified library. A response of N to this prompt will not delete an existing display file and will cause an error if the display file exists.

The "Submit create job in batch" prompt defaults to Y and indicates that SDA will create the display file by submitting the CRTDSPF command to a batch queue. A response of N will create the display file interactively. This usually slows other interactive processes, and also does not release your workstation for other work until the creation process completes.

The "Specify additional save or create options" will allow you to perform DDS related activities such as resequencing, and to specify a job description for the batch creation of the display file.

Enter the appropriate information and press the <ENTER> key to process the request and exit SDA.

11.5 CREATING A MENU

A menu is created in a similar fashion as a display file. A menu consists of a display screen, which contains the menu text (an object of type MNUDDS), and an associated command file, which contains the commands to be executed as a result of choosing menu options (an object of type MNUCMD). The menu display file may be named any valid name. The menu command file is named by SDA in the format *menuname*QQ.

Selecting option 2, Design Menus, from the SDA Main Menu produces the following screen (see Figure 11–16):

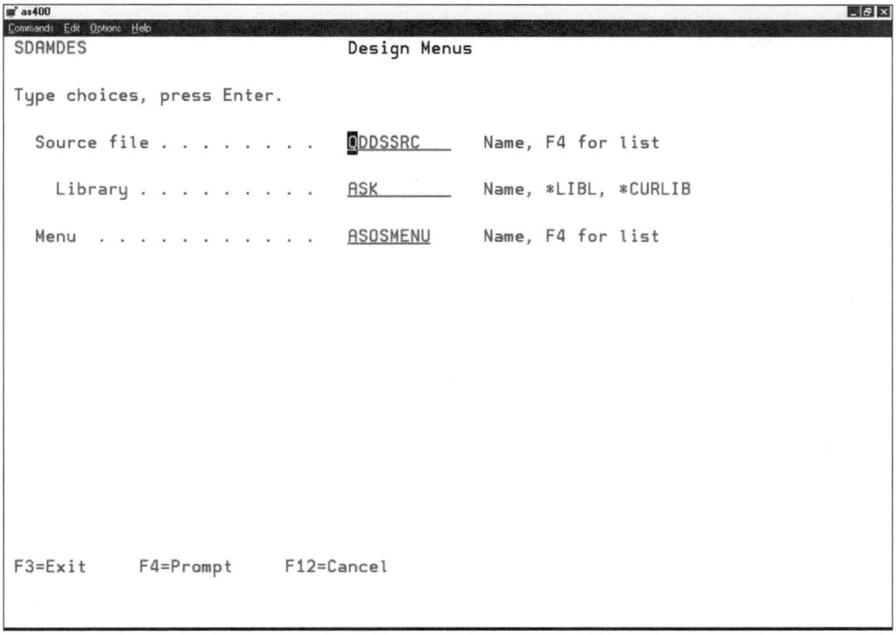

```
 as400                                                           _ 8 X
Commands  Edit  Options  Help
 SDAMDES                        Design Menus

 Type choices, press Enter.

    Source file . . . . . . . .  QDDSSRC      Name, F4 for list

       Library . . . . . . . . .  ASK         Name, *LIBL, *CURLIB

    Menu  . . . . . . . . . . .  ASOSMENU     Name, F4 for list












 F3=Exit      F4=Prompt     F12=Cancel

```

Figure 11–16: Design menus screen

This screen requires a "Source file" name (and "Library" name if needed) and the name of the "Menu." You may use the <F4> key to prompt for a list of source files and menus. Specify the appropriate values for the prompts and press <ENTER>. The Specify Menu Options screen will be shown (see Figure 11–17):

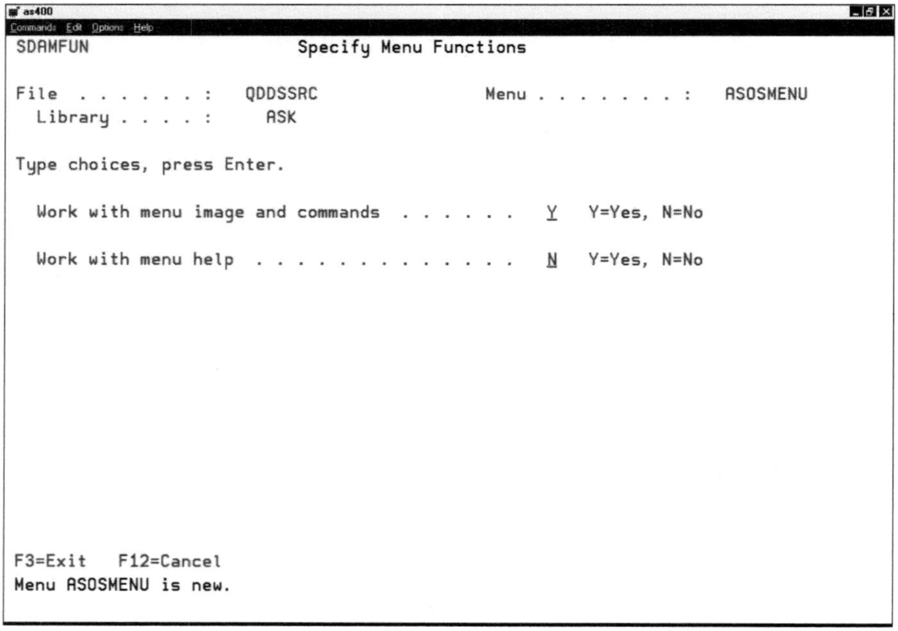

```
 as400                                                                    _ □ ×
Commands  Edit  Options  Help
SDAMFUN                        Specify Menu Functions

File  . . . . . . :    QDDSSRC             Menu . . . . . . . :    ASOSMENU
  Library . . . . :    ASK

Type choices, press Enter.

   Work with menu image and commands  . . . . . .   Y    Y=Yes, N=No

   Work with menu help  . . . . . . . . . . . . .   N    Y=Yes, N=No
















F3=Exit    F12=Cancel
Menu ASOSMENU is new.
```

Figure 11–17: Specify menu options screen

This menu initially defaults for a new menu to Y for the "Work with menu image and commands" prompt, and N to the "Work with menu help." This will allow you to specify the menu text and the menu commands for a menu.

Creating a new menu will cause the following screen to be displayed. Revising an existing menu will show the menu to be revised (see Figure 11–18).

The menu screen is displayed with option numbers. You may wish to use these option numbers (up to ninety-nine) and the format for the menu. You may also use any format you wish (known as "free format"), as long as option numbers in the range of one to ninety-nine are specified for each option.

Note that the menu name is already in the upper left corner of the screen, the "*menuname* Menu" title is centered over the menu options, and the subsequent lines (three to twenty) are for menu options. This is the default SDA uses, which you may change if you wish.

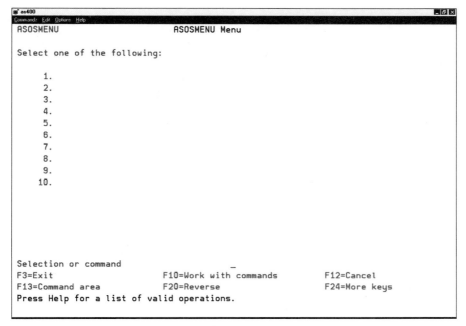

Figure 11–18: New menu screen

11.5.1 Entering Menu Text

Enter the command text as you would for designing a screen. The format characters, attribute codes, and method of changing the positions are the same. The items of menu text added are actually constants, the same as constants when designing a screen. Remember that a constant may consist of multiple words by surrounding the words with quotation marks.

The predefined constants discussed earlier (*DATE, *TIME, *USER, and *SYSNAME) when designing screens may also be used on a menu.

Attributes are added to constants as they are when designing a screen. The attribute codes are specified in the attribute byte position (the space immediately preceding the constant). An asterisk (*) may also be specified, which will display the Set Field Attributes display for the constant.

The following example screen (see Figure 11–19) is a menu with the text for several options completed:

<F13> allows you to work with the command area. This area of a menu at the bottom of the screen is where you enter the menu option and may also enter commands. The default text for the command line is "Selection or command." You may change this text by over-typing the text.

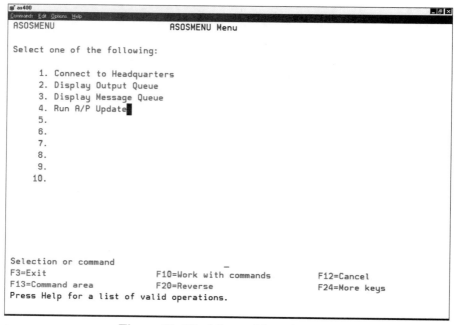

Figure 11–19: Menu with option text

You cannot assign or change the attributes of this constant in the same manner as with other constants. You must enter an asterisk (*) in row 21, column 43, to enter the Set Field Attributes display for this constant. SDA provides a one-character input field to enable you to enter the asterisk for this constant's attributes.

The location of the command line is determined by the Create Menu (CRTMNU) options you choose when you have completed designing the menu. The location of the command line and other command line choices will be discussed later in this chapter.

11.5.2 Entering Menu Commands

Pressing <F10> displays the Define Menu Commands screen. This display will contain the command that will be executed when you choose an option form the menu. Up to ninety-nine commands may be defined, each relating to a specific menu option. The following example screen (see Figure 11–20) shows the Define Menu Commands display.

The display shows the name of the menu being created or revised. The "Position to menu option" prompt allows you to position the list to a certain menu option to add or revise. You may enter a specific menu option number, a plus (+) sign to go to the next defined option, or a minus (–) sign to go to the previously defined option.

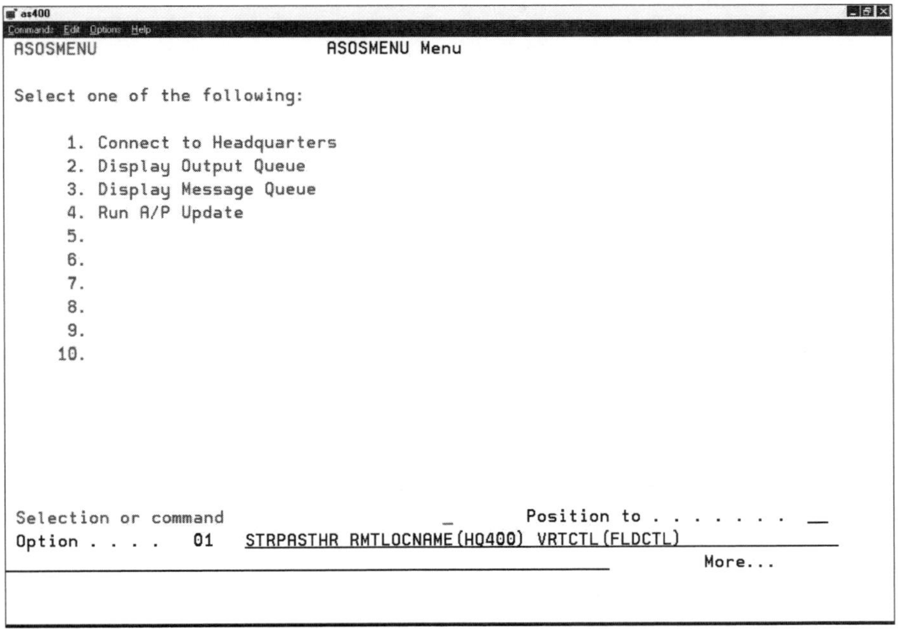

```
 as400                                                      _ ﾛ x
Commands  Edit  Options  Help
ASOSMENU                          ASOSMENU Menu

  Select one of the following:

       1. Connect to Headquarters
       2. Display Output Queue
       3. Display Message Queue
       4. Run A/P Update
       5.
       6.
       7.
       8.
       9.
      10.



  Selection or command                Position to . . . . . . . __
  Option . . . .  01   STRPASTHR RMTLOCNAME(HQ400) VRTCTL(FLDCTL)
                                                            More...

```

Figure 11–20: Define Menu Commands

Note the <F11> key. This key will display and allow you to manipulate only the menu options that you have already defined. This allows you to work with only the menu options that are specific for the menu.

Next to each option number (01, 02, and so on) is a "Command" line. You may enter any valid Command Language (CL) command, including CALL. Prompting with the <F4> key is allowed on this screen; enter the command name and press <F4>. The normal prompt for the command will appear, and you may enter the parameters that are appropriate for this usage of the command. When you press <ENTER> (after completing the parameters), the command with the appropriate parameters completed will be placed on the command line. The command may be a total of 115 characters in length.

You may also enter a question mark (?) in front of the command. When the user selects the menu option, the question mark will prompt the command.

Press <F3> to exit the Define Commands screen after the commands have been entered. The Menu Options screen will appear. Press <F3> again to proceed to the Exit SDA Menus screen. The following example screen (see Figure 11–21) shows the Exit SDA Menus display.

The "File" and "Library" are displayed, along with the name of the "DDS member" and the "Commands member." The "DDS member" contains the DDS statements for the menu, and the "Commands member" contains the commands for the menu options. Both members are created for the actual operational menu.

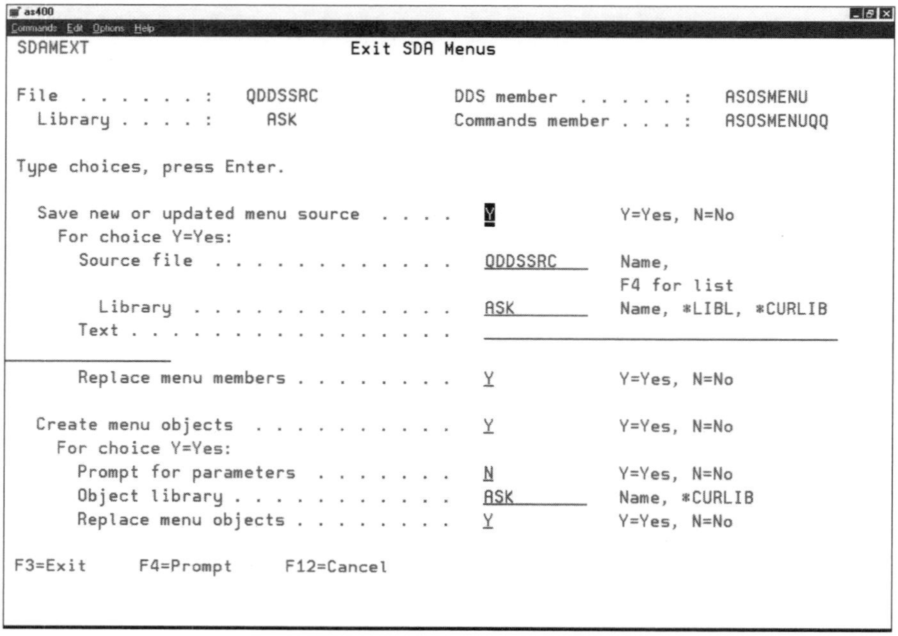

```
 as400                                                                    _ □ ×
Commands  Edit  Options  Help
 SDAMEXT                        Exit SDA Menus

 File  . . . . . . . :    QDDSSRC          DDS member  . . . . . :    ASOSMENU
   Library . . . . :    ASK              Commands member . . . :    ASOSMENUQQ

 Type choices, press Enter.

     Save new or updated menu source  . . . .  Y            Y=Yes, N=No
       For choice Y=Yes:
         Source file  . . . . . . . . . . .    QDDSSRC      Name,
                                                            F4 for list
           Library  . . . . . . . . . . . .    ASK          Name, *LIBL, *CURLIB
         Text . . . . . . . . . . . . . . .    _____

         Replace menu members . . . . . . . .  Y            Y=Yes, N=No

     Create menu objects  . . . . . . . . .    Y            Y=Yes, N=No
       For choice Y=Yes:
         Prompt for parameters  . . . . . . .  N            Y=Yes, N=No
         Object library . . . . . . . . . .    ASK          Name, *CURLIB
         Replace menu objects . . . . . . . .  Y            Y=Yes, N=No

 F3=Exit     F4=Prompt     F12=Cancel
```

Figure 11–21: Exit SDA Menus display

The first parameter, "Save new or updated menu source," requires a response of Y or N. This parameter will default to Y if you have made any changes to the member. If you do not wish to save the changes made to the member, change this parameter to N. A response of Y will require you to make entries for the "Source file" and "Library" in which to save the member. Note that you may use the <F4> key to list file names.

The "Text" parameter is the optional fifty-character text description that is to be associated with this member. It is a good practice to specify the "Text" description so you may more easily identify the member in a list of members.

The "Replace menu members" prompt defaults to Y if any changes have been made to the member. The menu members must be saved to create new menu objects.

The "Create menu objects" prompt defaults to Y if any changes have been made to the member. If the response is Y, then entries are required for the next three prompts. The "Prompt for parameters" prompt will display the prompted Create Menu (CRTMNU) command, allowing you to enter menu creation specific parameters. CRTMNU specific options that you may wish to enter are the CMDLINE and DSPKEYS parameters.

The CMDLINE parameter determines the type of command line the newly created menu will have. The DSPKEYS parameter determines if the newly created menu will show the function key legend at the bottom of the screen. The CMDLINE parameter may have one of three values: *LONG, meaning a command line that begins on line nineteen and is two lines long; *SHORT, a command line that begins on line twenty and is one line long;

and *NONE, meaning no command line. The DSPKEYS parameter may have one of two values: *YES, meaning display the function key legend; and *NO, meaning the function key legend will not be displayed.

The "Object library" prompt determines in which library the new menu objects will be placed. The last prompt, "Replace menu objects," will default to Y if the member is to be changed. A response of Y will replace an existing menu of the same name in the specified library. A response of N will not replace the menu objects; this will cause an error if the objects exist in the specified library.

Enter the appropriate parameters and press <ENTER> to create the menu. The menu will be created interactively and you will receive a message indicating the creation status of the menu.

11.6 TESTING MENUS AND DISPLAY FILES

SDA provides the capability to test the display files you create. Only display files that have been successfully created can be tested; display files with errors may not be tested. Attributes such as bolding, reverse image, and so on will be shown. Numeric fields will accept the <FIELD EXIT> and <FIELD MINUS> keys, while alphanumeric fields will not. In other words, the screen can be tested under the same conditions as would exist when actually placed in use.

Selecting option 3, "Test Display Files," from the SDA Main Menu will cause the following screen to be displayed (see Figure 11–22).

Required parameters are the "Display file" (and "Library" if required) to be tested and the "Record to be tested." You may also have "Additional records to display." These additional records will not be tested by SDA, but can appear on the screen to give you the full image as would be seen by the user of the screen. Enter the required information and press the <ENTER> key.

If a "Record to be tested" is not selected, or if <F4> was pressed for the prompt, the following screen will be displayed from which you may select records (see Figure 11–23).

Select the record to be tested with an entry of 1 in the "Option" field. Additional records may be selected to be displayed by entering the number 2, 3, or 4 in the "Option" field next to the record. Press <ENTER> after selecting the records.

The next screen, Set Test Output Data, is shown below. This display allows you to enter data into the fields of the record to be tested. This will show you how the data will be formatted and displayed when the screen is used. Enter the optional data for the fields and press <ENTER> (see Figure 11–24).

The display shown will contain the fields and constants defined for the record. Any input data you entered in the previous step will be displayed. Field and constant attributes will be displayed. Press <ENTER> after viewing the screen to continue (see Figure 11–25):

```
as400                                                              _ 5 X
Commands  Edit  Options  Help
 SDATDF                      Test Display File

 Type choices, press Enter.

     Display file . . . . . . . . . . . .   ASOS          Name, F4 for list
        Library  . . . . . . . . . . . . .  ASK           Name, *LIBL ...

     Record to be tested  . . . . . . . .   _____     Name, F4 for list

     Additional records to display  . . .   _____     Name, F4 for list
                                            _____
                                            _____




 F3=Exit     F4=Prompt     F12=Cancel
```

Figure 11–22: Test Display File screen

```
as400                                                              _ 5 X
Commands  Edit  Options  Help
 SDATFL                     Select Records for Test

 Display file . . . . . :   ASOS           Library . . . :   ASK

 Type information, press Enter.
   Number of records to roll . . . . . . . . . . . . . . .   10

 Type options, press Enter.
   1=Select for test   2,3,4=Display additional records

 Option   Record     Type      Related Subfile
   ▮      ASOS01     RECORD




                                                                Bottom
 F3=Exit   F12=Cancel
```

Figure 11–23: Select records for test screen

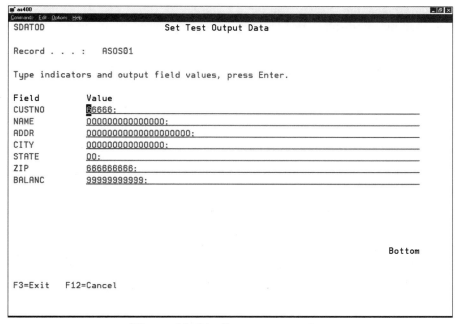

Figure 11–24: Set test output data

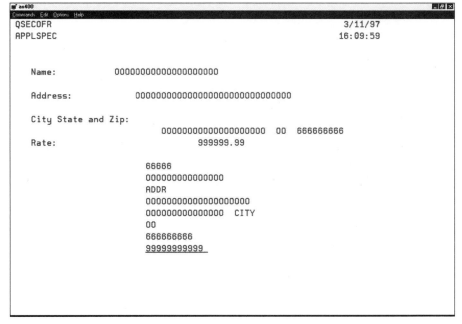

Figure 11–25: Tested SDA display

Another screen, the Display Test Input Data screen, shows the data in the fields after it is processed by the display file. This provides a visual check of the data so you may ensure the data entered is accurate. The <F14> key displays the input buffer. This may be helpful when writing the program that will use the display file, especially if the display file is described internally.

Press <F3> to exit the SDA testing feature and return to the SDA Main Menu.

12

Programming Development Manager (PDM)

12.1 WHAT IS PDM?

The Programming Development Manager (PDM) is an interface for working with different objects, including libraries and members in a file. PDM uses a list-oriented interface which provides lists of objects upon which you may perform operations.

PDM allows access to the Source Entry Utility (SEU), the Data File Utility (DFU), and the Screen Design Aid (SDA) through the list interface. PDM also provides a user-defined option mechanism where your own commands and IBM system commands may be used on the objects in the list. Operations that may be performed on objects in the list include copy, delete, and rename operations, object creation, and saving and restoring of objects.

PDM furnishes a grouping technique that allows you to subset a list of objects. PDM also uses a command structure that allows you to perform operations without needing to know the intricacies of the command. PDM uses information from the selected object (name, object type, and so on) to complete the command parameters.

PDM includes four main selections: working with libraries, working with objects, working with members, and user-defined options. The following sections will illustrate the use of each of these selections.

12.2 STARTING PDM

PDM may be started from the OS/400 Main Menu Programming option, or directly by using the Start PDM (STRPDM) command. The following screen (see Figure 12–1) will be displayed when the STRPDM command is executed.

Option 1 executes the Work with Libraries using PDM (WRKLIBPDM) command. Option 2 runs the Work with Objects using PDM (WRKOBJPDM) command. Option 3 executes the Work with Members using PDM (WRKMBRPDM) command. Option 9 allows you to change the user-defined options associated with PDM. Each of these selections will be explained in the following sections.

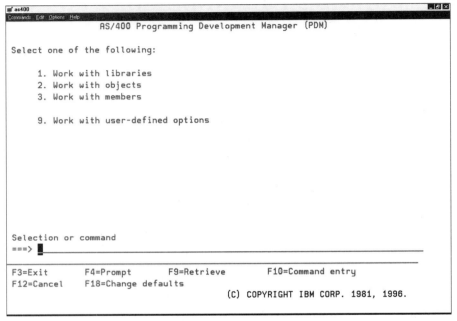

Figure 12–1: STRPDM screen

PDM provides common actions, functions, and a common interface across the four PDM selections. The common actions include the ability to create or delete objects, save or restore objects, and copy and rename objects. These actions are accessed through the use of options selected from the list-oriented interface. The common functions are accomplished through the use of standard function keys (those used with any OS/400 command) and with common function keys that are specific to PDM but accessible from any of the four PDM selections. The common interface is a list-oriented interface which displays the objects to be accessed in a list. This list-oriented interface is similar for each of the four PDM selections.

12.3 THE LIST-ORIENTED INTERFACE

The list-oriented interface of PDM provides a common method of accessing objects, whether the objects are libraries, files, programs, members, or others. This type of interface is important as it provides a common "look and feel" to all the PDM selections. This is one of the strengths of PDM. An example of this interface is shown here (see Figure 12–2):

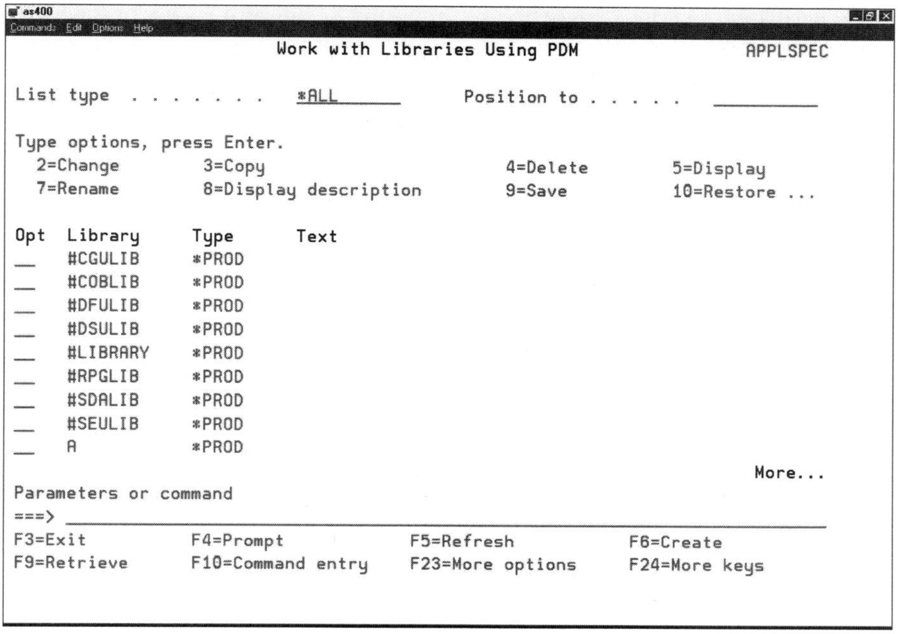

```
  as400                                                                _ 6 x
Commands  Edit  Options  Help
                        Work with Libraries Using PDM            APPLSPEC

    List type  . . . . . . .   *ALL____        Position to . . . . .  _____

    Type options, press Enter.
      2=Change         3=Copy                    4=Delete        5=Display
      7=Rename         8=Display description     9=Save          10=Restore ...

    Opt   Library    Type     Text
    __    #CGULIB    *PROD
    __    #COBLIB    *PROD
    __    #DFULIB    *PROD
    __    #DSULIB    *PROD
    __    #LIBRARY   *PROD
    __    #RPGLIB    *PROD
    __    #SDALIB    *PROD
    __    #SEULIB    *PROD
    __    A          *PROD
                                                                   More...
    Parameters or command
    ===> _____
    F3=Exit           F4=Prompt          F5=Refresh          F6=Create
    F9=Retrieve       F10=Command entry  F23=More options    F24=More keys
```

Figure 12–2: Example of list-oriented interface

Several common points exist in this interface, regardless of the type of object being accessed. The library containing the objects is shown, an entry field for positioning the list is provided, lists of the allowable options and function keys are shown, and the objects are displayed in a column with the type and text description of the object.

Next to each object displayed on the screen is an "Option" area. This option area allows you to specify the action you wish to perform upon the object. Multiple (and different) options may be selected for different objects in the list. The actions to be performed by the option selected will be performed on each object in sequence—from the top to the bottom of the list.

Several options are similar in effect across PDM. Since different object types are involved, the command executed by the use of the option may be different, but the action is the same. The sections which describe the four PDM selections will detail each of the actions available for that selection.

12.3.1 Subsetting a List

The <F17> key will allow you to subset the list of objects that are being displayed. Pressing <F17> will display a screen that, depending on the PDM selection with which you are currently working, will display selection criteria you may use to subset the list.

Any (or all) of the criteria may be used for a given subsetting selection which allows you to narrowly define the criteria desired for the subsetted list. The special value *ALL allows PDM to ignore (or in other words accept all) entries for that criterion.

The Work with Libraries using PDM (WRKLIBPDM) subsetting criteria are:

the name of the library, which may be a specific name, a generic name, or the special value *ALL.

the library type, which may be *TEST, *PROD, or the special value *ALL.

the text description, which may be specific or the special value *ALL.

The Work with Objects using PDM (WRKOBJPDM) subsetting criteria are:

The name of the object, which may be a specific name, a generic name, or the special value *ALL.

The object type, which may be a specific type (in the form *type), or the special value *ALL.

The object attribute, which may be a specific attribute name, a generic attribute name, the special value *ALL, or the special value *BLANK (meaning no attribute).

The text description, which may be specific or the special value *ALL.

The Work with Members using PDM (WRKMBRPDM) subsetting criteria are:

The name of the member, which may be a specific name, a generic name, or the special value *ALL.

The member type, which may be a specific type name, a generic type name, the special value *ALL, or the special value *BLANK (meaning no type).

The earliest date last modified to include (which defaults to 01/01/00).

The latest date last modified to include (which defaults to 12/31/99).

The text description, which may be specific or the special value *ALL.

12.4 FUNCTION KEYS

The function keys used within PDM may be divided into three types: standard function keys, common function keys, and specific function keys. The standard function keys are those which are used with most OS/400 commands. Common function keys are specific to PDM, but provide common functionality. Specific function keys are ones that are only appropriate for a specific PDM selection. The standard and common function keys are discussed below, while the keys that are specific to a given PDM selection are discussed in that section.

The standard function keys available from within PDM are

<F1> (or the <HELP> key)—provides general or context-sensitive help.

<F3>—exits PDM or stops a function with no action taken.

<F4>—prompts a command entered on the command line.

<F5>—refreshes the screen and rebuilds the list. This is helpful when you have removed objects from the list, or when you have changed the selection criteria. <F5> will restore the list to its original contents.

<F9>—retrieves a previously entered command from the command line.

<F12>—cancels the current function and returns to the previous display.

<F23>—displays the options that are not currently displayed on the screen.

<F24>—displays the function keys that are not currently displayed on the screen.

Function keys that are common to PDM selections include

<F4> to prompt. <F4> will prompt the command associated with the option and place any available information (from the list entry) in the appropriate keywords for the command.

<F6> to create a new object. Depending on the PDM selection, this function key may create an object (such as a library) or enter the Source Entry Utility (SEU) to create a member. This function key will also be explained in each of the PDM selection sections.

<F10> to display the Command Entry screen. This screen allows you to enter OS/400 commands. You may also use the <ROLL UP> and <ROLL DOWN> keys to position the screen to previously entered commands whereupon you may retrieve the command (with the <F9> Retrieve key) to reexecute the command.

<F11> is a toggle key that changes the information displayed in the list. Pressing <F11> will change the display to a multiple column display of object names only. Pressing <F11> again will return the display to its default setting of a single column list of names, types, and text descriptions.

<F13> will repeat the action performed from an option entered in a previous list entry. The action is performed for all the remaining entries in a list for which the option is valid. The action is performed for the list items that are further down the list from the entry where the option was initially selected. This may be used when several objects are to be manipulated, such as finding a text string or deleting objects. The cursor must be in an option field with an option entered in the field for the repeat function to execute.

<F16> allows you to work with the user-defined options. The Work with User-Defined Options screen will be displayed. This is the same screen that is displayed when you select Option 9 from the PDM Main Menu. This Work with User-Defined Options function of PDM is detailed later in this chapter.

<F17> will subset the list being displayed. This function was described in a previous section.

<F18> will change the defaults that are associated with your PDM session. This function is described in a following section.

<F21> will print the current list of objects. The spooled file will be located in the output queue that is associated with your interactive job.

12.5 CHANGING DEFAULTS

PDM uses default values for such functions as object creation and replacement, compilation options, and screen mode. These defaults are accessible through the use of function key <F18>. Pressing this function key will display the Change Defaults screen shown here (see Figure 12–3):

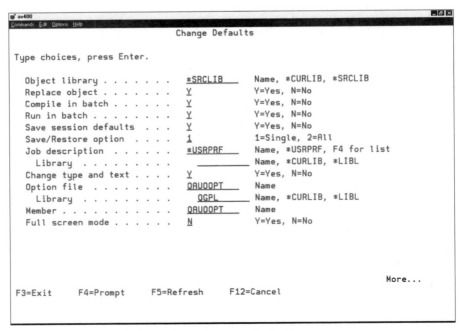

Figure 12–3: Change defaults screen

The first prompt, "Object library," determines the resulting location of a program that is compiled from within PDM (from the compile option on the WRKMBRPDM screen). This parameter may have one of three values: a specific library name, the special value *SRCLIB (which indicates that the compiled object should reside in the same library as the source module), and special value *CURLIB (which indicates that the compiled object should be placed in the current library). The default for this parameter is *SRCLIB.

The next prompt, "Replace object," will determine the action the compilation process will take if the object to be created already exists in the specified library. If the value for this parameter is N, then the object will not be replaced, and the compilation process will fail if the object already exists. If the value for this parameter is Y, then the object will be replaced if it already exists, and the compilation process will continue normally. No different action will be taken in either case if the object does not exist in the specified library.

The third prompt, "Compile in batch," has two possible values, Y and N. A value of Y (the default) indicates that the compilation process should be done in batch mode rather than interactively. A value of N indicates that the compile should be done interactively. This prompt refers to compiles initiated using option 14 from within PDM.

The next prompt, "Run in batch," determines if a process should be run in batch. The default for this parameter is N, meaning that the process should run interactively. The other value, Y, means that a process should run in batch. This prompt refers to programs executed using option 16 from within PDM.

The following prompt, "Job description," identifies the name of the job description that will be used to determine the characteristics of a job (compile or process) that is submitted to batch. The default for this parameter is job description QBATCH, which is usually located in library QGPL. You may specify a specific "Job description name" and the associated "Library" if needed, or use special value *USRPRF. Special value *USRPRF indicates that PDM should use the job description that is defined in your user profile.

The next prompt, "Change type and text," may have a value of Y or N. A value of Y (the default) indicates that the user may change the member type and text description entries when working on the Work with Members using PDM (WRKMBRPDM) display. A value of N means the user will not be able to change the type and text entries on the display.

The following prompt, "Option file," with the associated prompts "Library" and "Member," determine the user-defined option file that is to be used. The user-defined options are explained later in this chapter and contain options that are "shortcuts" for commands. This parameter defaults to option file QAUOOPT in library QGPL and member QAUOOPT. The options that are defined in this option file and member are the options that are currently active.

The last prompt, "Full screen mode," defaults to N, which means that PDM list displays are not shown in full screen mode. This allows the options and function key legends to be shown. The other value of Y will show more list entries, but will not display the options and function key legends.

The standard function keys of <F1> (or <HELP>) for help, <F3> to exit, <F4> to prompt (for the job description name), <F5> to refresh and set the screen to its initial values, and <F12> to cancel are supported.

12.6 GENERIC OBJECT SELECTION

Many objects may be accessed by a generic name selection in PDM. The objects include the entries in a list, job descriptions, object types, and others. Any parameter within PDM that allows a generic name selection (indicated by the *generic* legend) can use a generic value for the selection. This provides flexibility in that you may select like named objects with one generic value.

A generic name may be in any one of the forms that are shown in the following examples:

HOW*, where any object that begins with the characters "HOW" will be selected.

O, which will select any object with the character "O" in the object name.

*HOW, which will select any object where the object name ends in "HOW."

H*W, where any object whose name begins with "H" and ends with "W" will be selected.

12.7 WORKING WITH LIBRARIES

The first PDM main menu selection, Work with Libraries, invokes the WRKLIBPDM command. This command may also be executed directly from a command line. Choosing this option will display the Specify Libraries to Work With screen. An example of this display is shown in Figure 12–4.

The default for the "Library" prompt is *LIBL, meaning the libraries in your library list. Other possible values are special values, the name of a specific library, or a generic library name. The special values that may be specified for the "Library" prompt are *ALL, meaning all libraries that you have authority to access, *ALLUSR, indicating all the non-IBM (or user) libraries to which you have access, *USRLIBL, meaning the libraries in the user portion of your library list, and *CURLIB, which indicates your current library.

Specifying a special value such as *LIBL or *USRLIBL, or specifying a generic name will display a list of libraries. Enter the appropriate information for the parameters and press <ENTER> to display the list created for the Work with Libraries using PDM screen. This screen is shown in Figure 12–5.

This display contains the "List type" which shows the type of list criteria selected when the command was executed. The "List type" will contain the type of list if the selection criteria was a special value (such as *LIBL or *USRLIBL), a library name if a specific library name was selected, or *ALL if special value *ALL was chosen, or if a generic name was used.

```
as400                                                                    _ 6 x
Commands  Edit  Options  Help
                    Specify Libraries to Work With

 Type choice, press Enter.

     Library . . . . . . . . . .    *LIBL      *LIBL, name, *generic*, *ALL,
                                               *ALLUSR, *USRLIBL, *CURLIB

 F3=Exit      F5=Refresh     F12=Cancel
```

Figure 12–4: Specify libraries to work with screen

```
as400                                                                    _ 6 x
Commands  Edit  Options  Help
                    Work with Libraries Using PDM              APPLSPEC

 List type . . . . . . .    *LIBL

 Type options, press Enter.
    2=Change              3=Copy       5=Display     7=Rename
    8=Display description 9=Save       10=Restore    12=Work with ...

 Opt  Library   Type       Text
  __   QUSRSYS   *PROD-SYS
  __   QSYS      *PROD-SYS  System Library
  __   QSYS2     *PROD-SYS  System Library for CPI's
  __   QHLPSYS   *PROD-SYS
  __   QPDA      *PROD-PRD
  __   QTEMP     *TEST-USR
  __   TAATOOL   *PROD-USR  Library for QUSRTOOL tools
  __   TAATOOL2  *PROD-USR  Library for objects needed by user tools
  __   QUSRTOOL  *PROD-USR
                                                             More...
 Parameters or command
 ===> _____
 F3=Exit        F4=Prompt         F5=Refresh        F6=Add to list
 F9=Retrieve    F10=Command entry F23=More options  F24=More keys
```

Figure 12–5: Work with libraries using PDM

The "Position to" prompt allows you to specify a library name (or the beginning characters of a library name) to which the list of libraries will be positioned. You may also use special value *TOP to go to the top of the list, and special value *BOT to go to the bottom of the list.

Other information shown on this display is the name of the library, the type of the library, and the associated library text.

This display allows you to perform many different library functions by specifying an option before the library name in the "Opt" field. Multiple options may be chosen for different libraries, and the options need not be the same. You may delete a library, rename a library, copy a library, and perform other operations on multiple libraries.

The available library manipulation options are as follows:

Option 2 will allow you to change the text description or the type of a library. This option executes the Change Library (CHGLIB) command. A screen will be displayed where you can specify the new text description or library type.

Option 3 allows you to copy a library (or multiple libraries) to another library (or multiple libraries). A PDM screen will be displayed that shows the library to copy from, and places the same name in the field that specifies the name of the library to which you will copy. Change the name of the target library to contain the name of the receiving library. You will be prompted with an additional screen if the target library already exists and you will need to specify that the contents of the target library should be deleted in order to continue with the copy operation. The <F19> key will allow you to copy the library in batch mode rather than interactively.

Option 4 will delete the specified library. This option is only available when working with a specific or generic list of libraries, not when working with a library list. Using option 4 will remove the library from the system. A PDM screen will be shown and you will be prompted to confirm the deletion operation. The <F19> key will allow you to delete the library in batch mode rather than interactively.

Option 5 will display the name and types of the objects located within the library. This option calls the Display Library (DSPLIB) command. You will not be able to work with the objects; this is a display only option.

Option 7 will rename a library to a new name. Selecting option 7 will display a PDM screen that shows the old library name with the new library name defaulting to the old name. Change the entry for the new library name to the library name you want. The <F19> key will allow you to rename the library in batch mode rather than interactively.

Option 8 will display the description of a library. This option executes the Display Object Description (DSPOBJD) command with the *FULL option.

Option 9 will save a library (or multiple libraries) to diskette or tape. This option executes the Save Library (SAVLIB) command.

Option 10 will restore previously saved libraries from tape or diskette. Option 10 runs the Restore Library (RSTLIB) command.

Option 12 will allow you to work with the objects in a library. Selecting this option will execute the Work with Objects using PDM (WRKOBJPDM) command. The WRKOBJPDM command is explained later in this chapter.

Option 13 allows you to change the text description of a library. Option 13 executes the Change Object Description (CHGOBJD) command.

In addition to the options that are available for manipulating libraries, the standard, common, and specific function keys are also available. The specific function keys for the Work with Libraries using PDM (WRKLIBPDM) command are

<F6>—executes the Create Library (CRTLIB) command to create a new library if the "List type" specified on the Specify Libraries to Work With display is generic or *ALL.

<F6>—allows you to add an entry to a library list if you specified the "List type" on the Specify Libraries to Work With display to be *LIBL or *USRLIBL. This option executes the Add Library List Entry (ADDLIBLE) command.

12.7.1 Changing Your Library List

You may change your library list using the WRKLIBPDM function. When accessing the WRKLIBPDM function, specifying *LIBL (for library list) or *USRLIBL (for the user portion of the library list) for the "List type" parameter on the Specify Libraries to Work With screen will cause PDM to display the libraries that are in your library list.

The following options (20 through 23) are only available if the "List type" chosen on the Specify Libraries to Work With display is *LIBL or *USRLIBL.

Option 20 allows you to change the position of a library within your library list. As with the move and copy options with the Source Entry Utility (SEU), you must choose a target location in the list to move the specified library. The target options are explained below.

Option 21 specifies a target location for an option 20 move. Specifying option 21 will move the specified library before this target library in your library list.

Option 22 specifies a target location for an option 20 move. Specifying option 22 will move the specified library after this target library in your library list.

Option 23 will remove the specified library from your library list. This does not remove the library from the system, it only removes the library from your library list.

12.8 WORKING WITH OBJECTS

The second PDM main menu selection, Work with Objects, invokes the WRKOBJPDM command. This command may also be executed directly from a command line. Choosing this option will display the Specify Libraries to Work With screen. An example of this display is shown here (see Figure 12–6):

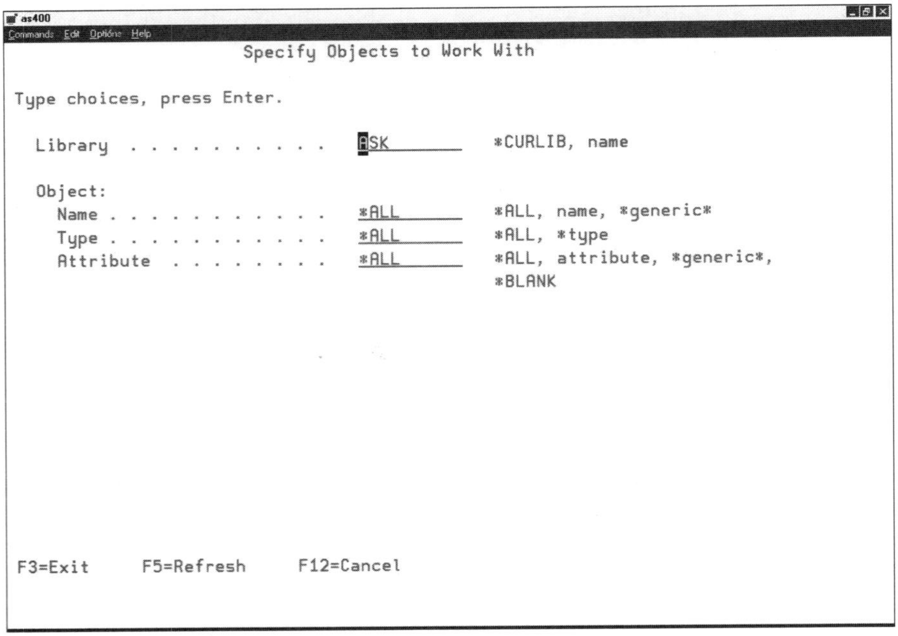

```
 as400                                                              _ 8 X
Commands  Edit  Options  Help
                        Specify Objects to Work With

Type choices, press Enter.

   Library . . . . . . . . .     SK            *CURLIB, name

   Object:
     Name . . . . . . . . . .    *ALL          *ALL, name, *generic*
     Type . . . . . . . . . .    *ALL          *ALL, *type
     Attribute . . . . . . .     *ALL          *ALL, attribute, *generic*,
                                               *BLANK

 F3=Exit     F5=Refresh     F12=Cancel
```

Figure 12–6: Specify objects to work with screen

The default for the "Library" parameter (in which the objects reside) is *CURLIB, meaning the current library. The other possible value is the name of a specific library.

The next group of parameters determine which "Objects" will be accessed. The "Name" parameter may be the special value *ALL (the default), a specific object name, or a generic object name. The "Type" parameter may be the special value *ALL (the default) or a specific type name. The following object types, shown in alphabetical order, are valid as a specific object type entry:

*ALRTBL, for alert table

*AUTL, for authorization list

*CFGL, for configuration list

*CHTFMT, for chart format

*CLD, for C locale description

*CLS, for class

*CMD, for command

*CNNL, for connection list

*COSD, for class of service definition

*CSI, for communication side information

*CSPMAP, for cross-system product map

*CSPTBL, for cross-system product table

*CTLD, for controller description

*DEVD, for device description

*DOC, for document

*DTAARA, for data area

*DTADCT, for data dictionary

*DTAQ, for data queue

*EDTD, for edit description

*FCT, for forms control table

*FILE, for file

*FLR, for folder

*FNTRSC, for font resource

*FORMDF, for form definition

*GSS, for graphic symbol set

*IGCDCT, for ideographic character dictionary

*IGCSRT, for ideographic character sort

*IGCTBL, for ideographic character table

*JOBD, for job description

*JOBQ, for job queue

*JRN, for journal

*JRNRCV, for journal receiver

*LIB, for library

*LIND, for line description

*MENU, for menu

*MODD, for mode description

*MSGF, for message file

*MSGQ, for message queue

*NWID, for network interface description

*OUTQ, for output queue

*OVL, for overlay

*PAGDFN, for page definition

*PAGSEG, for page segment

*PDG, for print descriptor

*PGM, for program

*PNLGRP, for panel group

*PRDAVL, for product availability

*PRDDFN, for product definition

*PRDFUN, for product function

*PRDLOD, for product load

*QMFORM, for Query manager form

*QMQRY, for Query manager query

*QRYDFN, for Query definition

*RCT, for remote control table

*SBSD, for subsystem description

*SCHIDX, for search index

*SPADCT, for spelling aid dictionary

*SSND, for session description

*S36, for System/36 objects

*TBL, for table

*USRIDX, for user index

*USRPRF, for user profile

*USRQ, for user queue

*USRSPC, for user space

The "Attribute" parameter may be the special value *ALL (the default), the name of a specific attribute name, a generic attribute name, or the special value *BLANK indicating objects with no attribute. The following object attributes, shown in alphabetical order, are valid as a specific or (when asterisks are used appropriately) as a generic object attribute entry:

BAS, for BASIC program

BAS36, for System/36 BASIC program

BAS38, for System/38 BASIC program

BSCF38, for System/38 Bisync communications file

C, for C program

CBL, for COBOL program

CBL36, for System/36 COBOL program

CBL38, for System/38 COBOL program

CLP, for Control Language program

CLP38, for System/38 Control Language program

CMD, for command

CMD38, for System/38 command

CMNF38, for System/38 communications file

CSPAE, for Cross-System Product application execution

DDMF, for Distributed Data Management file

DFU, for Data File Utility file

DFUEXEC, for Data File Utility executable file

DFUNOTEXC, for Data File Utility nonexecutable file

DKTF, for diskette file

DSPF, for display file

DSPF36, for System/36 display file

DSPF38, for System/38 display file

FTN, for FORTRAN program

ICFF, for Intersystem Communications Function file

LF, for logical file

LF38, for System/38 logical file

MXDF38, for System/38 mixed file

PAS, for Pascal program

PF-DTA, for physical file—data

PF-SRC, for physical file—source

PF38, for System/38 physical file

PLI, for PL/1 program

PLI38, for System/38 PL/1 program

PRTF, for printer file

PRTF38, for System/38 printer file

QRY38, for System/38 Query

RMC, for RM/COBOL program

RPG, for RPG program

RPG36, for System/36 RPG program

RPG38, for System/38 RPG program

RPT, for RPG auto report

RPT36, for System/36 RPG auto report

RPT38, for System/38 RPG auto report

SAVF, for save file

SPADCT, for spelling aid dictionary

SQLC, for Structured Query Language C program

SQLCBL, for Structured Query Language COBOL program

SQLFTN, for Structured Query Language FORTRAN program

SQLPLI, for Structured Query Language PL/1 program

SQLRPG, for Structured Query Language RPG program

TAPF, for tape file

TBL, for table

Enter the appropriate information for the parameters and press <ENTER> to display the list created for the Work with Objects using PDM screen. This screen is shown here (see Figure 12–7):

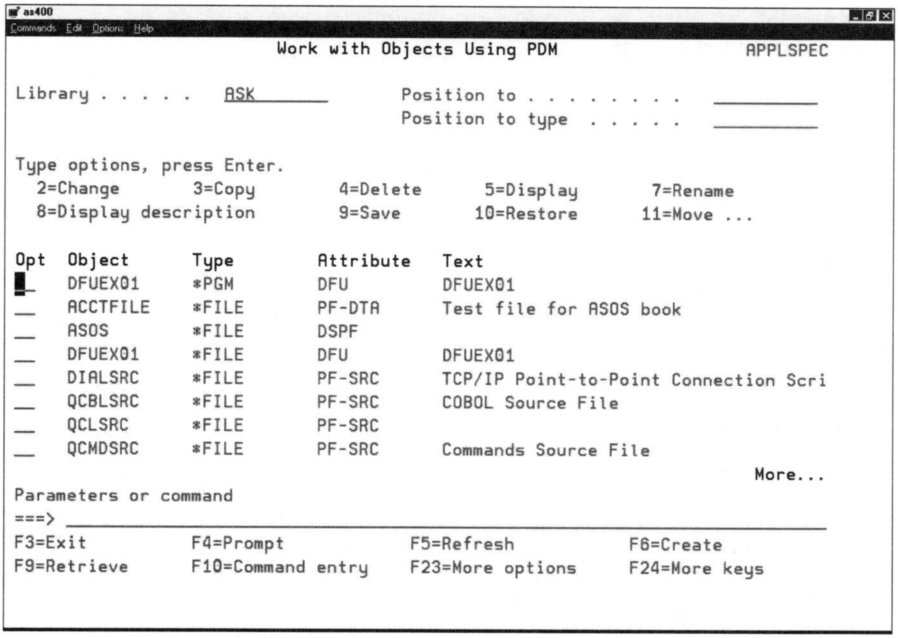

```
 as400                                                                  _ |&|×|
 Commands  Edit  Options  Help
                       Work with Objects Using PDM              APPLSPEC

  Library . . . . .    ASK          Position to . . . . . . .   _____
                                    Position to type  . . . . .  _____

 Type options, press Enter.
    2=Change        3=Copy        4=Delete      5=Display      7=Rename
    8=Display description          9=Save       10=Restore     11=Move ...

 Opt   Object     Type      Attribute    Text
 ▌     DFUEX01    *PGM      DFU          DFUEX01
 __    ACCTFILE   *FILE     PF-DTA       Test file for ASOS book
 __    ASOS       *FILE     DSPF
 __    DFUEX01    *FILE     DFU          DFUEX01
 __    DIALSRC    *FILE     PF-SRC       TCP/IP Point-to-Point Connection Scri
 __    QCBLSRC    *FILE     PF-SRC       COBOL Source File
 __    QCLSRC     *FILE     PF-SRC
 __    QCMDSRC    *FILE     PF-SRC       Commands Source File
                                                                More...
 Parameters or command
 ===> _____
 F3=Exit          F4=Prompt          F5=Refresh          F6=Create
 F9=Retrieve      F10=Command entry  F23=More options    F24=More keys
```

Figure 12–7: Work with objects using PDM

This display shows the "Library" where the objects reside. The "Position to" prompt allows you to specify an object name (or the beginning characters of an object name) to which the list of objects will be positioned. You may also use special value *TOP to go to the top of the list, and special value *BOT to go to the bottom of the list. The "Position to type" prompt allows you to specify an object type (or the beginning characters of an object type) to which the list of objects will be positioned.

Other information shown on this display is the name of the "Object," the "Type" of the object, the "Attribute" of the object, and the associated object "Text."

This display allows you to perform object manipulation functions by specifying an option before the object name in the "Opt" field. Multiple options may be selected for different objects, and the options need not be the same. You may delete an object, rename an object, change an object, move an object, and perform other operations on multiple objects.

The available object manipulation options are as follows:

Option 2 will allow you to change the text description or the type of an object. This option executes the Change object-type (CHGxxxx) command, where the "xxxx" is replaced by the correct object type qualifier. The command that is executed is object-dependent.

Option 3 will allow you to copy an object (or multiple objects) to another library (or multiple libraries). A PDM screen will be displayed that shows the object (and library) to copy from, and places the same name in the field that specifies the name of the object and library to which you will copy. Change the name of the target object or target library as appropriate. You will be prompted with an additional screen if the target object already exists in the specified library, and you will need to specify that the target object should be deleted in order to continue with the copy operation. The <F19> key will allow you to copy the object in batch mode rather than interactively.

Option 4 will delete the specified object. Using option 4 will remove the object from the system. A PDM screen will be shown where you will be prompted to confirm the deletion operation. The <F19> key will allow you to delete the object in batch mode rather than interactively.

Option 5 will display the object. This option calls the Display object-type (DSPxxxx) command, where the "xxxx" is replaced by the correct object-type qualifier. The command that is executed is object-dependent. You will not be able to work with the object; this is a display only option.

Option 7 will rename an object to a new name. Selecting option 7 will display a PDM screen that shows the old object name, with the new object name defaulting to the old name. Change the entry for the new object name to the object name you choose. The <F19> key will allow you to rename the object in batch mode rather than interactively.

Option 8 will display the description of an object. This option executes the Display Object Description (DSPOBJD) command with the OPTION(*FULL) parameter.

Option 9 will save an object (or multiple objects) to diskette or tape. This option executes the Save Object (SAVOBJ) command.

Option 10 will restore previously saved objects from tape or diskette. Option 10 runs the Restore Object (RSTOBJ) command.

Option 11 will move an object from one library to another. The move operation is a combination of copying the object to the new library and then deleting the object from the old library. A PDM screen will be shown where you will be prompted to specify the new library name. The <F19> key will allow you to move the object in batch mode rather than interactively.

Option 12 will allow you to work with the components in an object. Selecting this option with an object of type *FILE and attribute PF-DTA will execute the Work with Members using PDM (WRKMBRPDM) command. The WRKMBRPDM command is explained later in this chapter. Selecting an object of type *LIB will execute the Work with Objects using PDM (WRKOBJPDM) command. The command that is executed is object-dependent.

Option 13 will allow you to change the text description of an object. Option 13 executes the Change Object Description (CHGOBJD) command.

Option 15 will allow you to copy members from a file to another file. The object type must be *FILE for this command to execute. This option executes the Copy File (CPYF) command.

Option 16 will run the procedure contained within the object. The object type must be *CMD, *PGM, or some object type that is valid to be executed. The procedure will run interactively or in batch mode depending on the option selected on the Change Defaults screen.

Option 18 will allow you to change the object using the Data File Utility. The object type and object attribute must be a combination of FILE and PF-DTA, LF, or DDMF, or *PGM and DFU for this option to invoke DFU.

Option 25 will search members in files for a specific string. Only objects of type *FILE and attribute PF-DTA or PF-SRC are eligible for this option. Once the string is found, a PDM or user-defined option may be executed. In addition, the information found may be printed. A description of the Find String function may be found in the Work with Members using PDM (WRKMBRPDM) section.

In addition to the options that are available for manipulating objects, the standard, common, and specific function keys are also available. The specific function keys for the Work with Objects using PDM (WRKOBJPDM) command are

<F6>—displays the Create Commands menu (GO CMDCRT) to allow you to select the appropriate command for creating a new object.

<F14>—displays the size or the attribute of the object. <F14> is a toggle in that, if the sizes of the objects are displayed, pressing <F14> will display the object's attributes. Pressing <F14> again will display the object's sizes.

12.9 WORKING WITH MEMBERS

The third PDM main menu selection, Work with Members, invokes the WRKMBRPDM command. This command may also be executed directly from a command line. Choosing this option will display the Specify Members to Work With screen. An example of this display is shown here (see Figure 12–8):

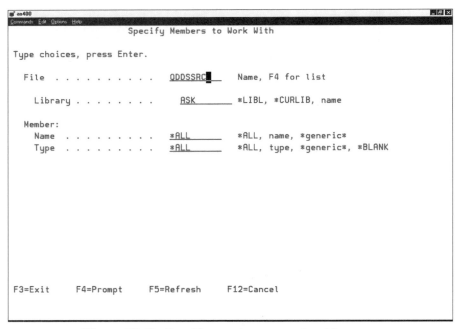

Figure 12–8: Specify members to work with screen

The first prompt, "File," indicates the file in which the members to be accessed reside. You may use the <F4> prompt key for a list of files. The default for the "Library" parameter (in which the file is located) is *LIBL, meaning your library list. You may also specify a specific library name, or special value *CURLIB, meaning the current library.

The next group of prompts determine which members will be accessed. The "Name" parameter may be the special value *ALL (the default), a specific member name, or a generic member name.

The "Type" parameter may be the special value *ALL (the default), a specific type name, a generic type name, or special value *BLANK, meaning a member with no type. The following member types, shown in alphabetical order, are valid as a specific member type entry. Note that they are similar, but not identical, to the object types that may be used for the WRKOBJPDM command.

BAS, for BASIC program

BAS36, for System/36 BASIC program

BAS38, for System/38 BASIC program

BASP, for BASIC procedure

BASP38, for System/38 BASIC procedure

C, for C program

CBL, for COBOL program

CBL36, for System/36 COBOL program

CBL38, for System/38 COBOL program

CLD, for C locale description

CLP, for Control Language program

CLP38, for System/38 Control Language program

CMD, for command

CMD38, for System/38 command

DSPF, for display file

DSPF36, for System/36 display file

DSPF38, for System/38 display file

FTN, for FORTRAN program

ICFF, for Intersystem Communications Function file

LF, for logical file

LF38, for System/38 logical file

MNU, for menu

MNUCMD, for menu command file

MNUDDS, for menu DDS

MNU36, for System/36 menu

MSGF36, for System/36 message file

OCL36, for System/36 Operator Control Language procedure

PAS, for Pascal program

PF, for physical file

PF38, for System/38 physical file

PLI, for PL/1 program

PLI38, for System/38 PL/1 program

PNLGRP, for panel group

PRTF, for printer file

PRTF38, for System/38 printer file

QRY38, for System/38 Query

REXX, for Restructured Extended Executor Language procedure

RMC, for RM/COBOL program

RPG, for RPG program

RPG36, for System/36 RPG program

RPG38, for System/38 RPG program

RPT, for RPG Auto Report program

RPT36, for system/36 RPG Auto Report program

RPT38, for system/38 RPG Auto Report program

SPADCT, for spelling aid dictionary

SQLC, for Structured Query Language C program

SQLCBL, for Structured Query Language COBOL program

SQLFTN, for Structured Query Language FORTRAN program

SQLPLI, for Structured Query Language PL/1 program

SQLRPG, for Structured Query Language RPG program

TBL, for table

TXT, for text

Enter the appropriate information for the parameters and press <ENTER> to display the list created for the Work with Members using PDM screen. This screen is shown here (see Figure 12–9):

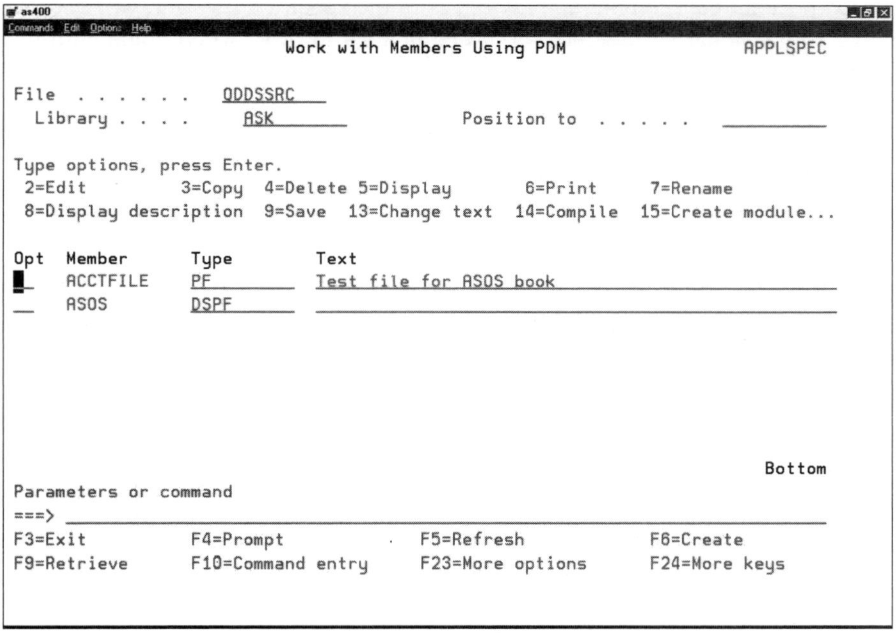

```
 as400                                                                _ 8 x
Commands  Edit  Options  Help
                       Work with Members Using PDM              APPLSPEC

 File  . . . . . .    QDDSSRC
    Library . . . .   ASK            Position to  . . . . .  _____

 Type options, press Enter.
   2=Edit         3=Copy  4=Delete 5=Display      6=Print     7=Rename
   8=Display description  9=Save  13=Change text  14=Compile  15=Create module...

 Opt  Member     Type      Text
 ▌    ACCTFILE   PF        Test file for ASOS book
 __   ASOS       DSPF      _____

                                                          Bottom
 Parameters or command
 ===> _____
 F3=Exit          F4=Prompt      .   F5=Refresh        F6=Create
 F9=Retrieve      F10=Command entry   F23=More options  F24=More keys

```

Figure 12–9: Work with members using PDM

This display shows the "File" and "Library" where the members are located. The "Position to" prompt allows you to specify a member name (or the beginning characters of a member name) to which the list of members will be positioned. You may also use special value *TOP to go to the top of the list, and special value *BOT to go to the bottom of the list.

Other information shown on this display is the name of the member, the type of the member, and the associated member text.

This display allows you to perform member manipulation functions by specifying an option before the member name in the "Opt" field. Multiple options may be selected for different members, and the options need not be the same. You may delete a member, rename a member, edit a member, change a member using the Screen Design Aid (SDA) or Report Layout Utility (RLU), and perform other operations on multiple members.

The available member manipulation options are as follows:

Option 2 will invoke the Source Entry Utility (SEU) to allow you to edit members.

Option 3 will allow you to copy a member (or multiple members) to another file (or multiple files). A PDM screen will be displayed that shows the member (and file) to copy from, and places the same name in the field that specifies the name of the member and file to which you will copy. Change the name of the target member or target file as appropriate. You will be prompted with an additional screen if the target member already exists in the specified file, and will need to specify that the target member should be deleted in order to continue with the copy operation. The <F19> key will allow you to copy the member in batch mode rather than interactively.

Option 4 will delete the specified member. Using option 4 will remove the member from the system. A PDM screen will be shown where you will be prompted to confirm the deletion operation. The <F19> key will allow you to delete the member in batch mode rather than interactively.

Option 5 will allow you to display the member. SEU will be invoked in Browse mode to display the member. You will not be able to work with the member; this is a display-only option.

Option 6 will print the member. PDM will invoke the Copy File (CPYF) command with the OUTPUT parameter set to a value of *PRINT. The spooled file will be located in the output queue that is associated with your interactive job.

Option 7 will rename a member to a new name. Selecting option 7 will display a PDM screen that shows the old member name, with the new member name defaulting to the old name. Change the entry for the new member name to the member name you want. The <F19> key will allow you to rename the member in batch mode rather than interactively.

Option 8 will display the description of a member. A PDM screen will be displayed that shows information about the member such as creation date, last changed date, size, number of records, and other information.

Option 9 will save a member (or multiple members) to diskette or tape. This option executes the Save Object (SAVOBJ) command.

Option 13 will allow you to change the text description of a member. This option calls the Change object-type (CHGxxxx) command, where the "xxxx" is replaced by the correct file object-type qualifier. The command that is executed is object-dependent.

Option 14 will compile selected members. The compilation process that is executed is determined by the type of the member. The compilation process will be executed interactively or in batch mode depending on the selection made on the Change Defaults display. The object library (where the successfully compiled object will be placed) is also determined from the Change Defaults display.

Option 16 executes the procedure contained within the source member. The member type must be BASP, BASP38, REXX, or OCL36. The procedure will run interactively or in batch mode depending on the option selected on the Change Defaults screen.

Option 17 will allow you to change the member using the Screen Design Aid (SDA). SDA will be invoked to work with a display if the member type is DSPF or DSPF38. SDA will be invoked to work with a menu if the member type is MNU, MNUDDS, or MNUCMD.

Option 18 will allow you to change the member using the Report Layout Utility (RLU).

Option 25 will search members in files for a specific string. Only objects of type *FILE and attribute PF-DTA or PF-SRC are eligible for this option. Once the string is found, a PDM or user-defined option may be executed. In addition, the information found may be printed. A description of the Find String function follows this section.

In addition to the options that are available for manipulating objects, the standard, common, and specific function keys are also available. The specific function keys for the Work with Members using PDM command are

<F6>—invokes the Source Entry Utility (SEU) to allow you to create a new source member.

<F14>—displays the date or the type of the member. <F14> is a toggle in that, if the date of the member is displayed, pressing <F14> will display the member's type. Pressing <F14> again will display the member's date.

<F15>—sorts the display by date or member name. <F15> is a toggle in that, if the display is sorted by date, pressing <F15> will sort the display by member name. Pressing <F15> again will sort the display by date.

12.10 USING THE FIND STRING FUNCTION

The Find String function is accessible through the use of option 25 from the WRKOBJPDM display or the WRKMBRPDM display. The Find String option is also available through the use of the Find String using PDM (FNDSTRPDM) command.

You can find character strings in source and data physical files using this function. When the character string is found in a member, a PDM option may be performed on the member. In addition, a list containing all occurrences of the character string may also be printed. Multiple members are often searched with Find String function.

The search is performed on the members in the order (from the top of the list to the bottom) that they are specified in the WRKMBRPDM or WRKOBJPDM display. The selected option (if any) is performed when a match is found in a member. The option is one that exists on the WRKMBRPDM or WRKOBJPDM displays, or may be a user-defined option. You may specify to be prompted before the option is performed. You may stop the Find String function by pressing <F3> to exit, or <F12> to cancel.

When option 25 is selected for a member (or for multiple members) from the WRKOBJPDM or the WRKMBRPDM screen, or when the FNDSTRPDM command is prompted, the following display is shown (see Figure 12–10):

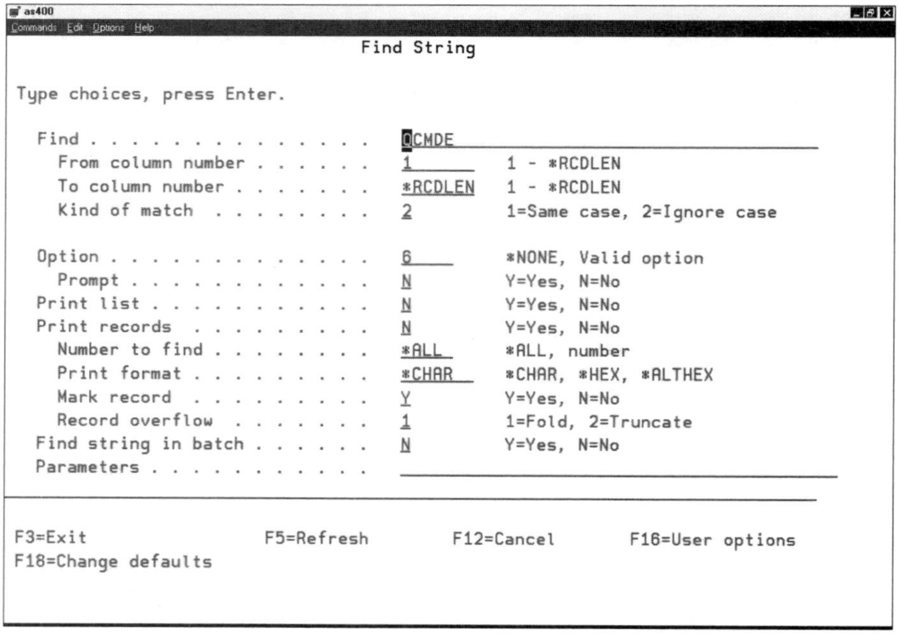

```
 as400                                                          _ 6 X
Commands  Edit  Options  Help
                            Find String

Type choices, press Enter.

    Find . . . . . . . . . . . .    QCMDE
      From column number . . . . . 1           1 - *RCDLEN
      To column number . . . . . . *RCDLEN     1 - *RCDLEN
      Kind of match  . . . . . . . 2           1=Same case, 2=Ignore case

    Option . . . . . . . . . . . . 6           *NONE, Valid option
      Prompt . . . . . . . . . . . N           Y=Yes, N=No
    Print list . . . . . . . . . . N           Y=Yes, N=No
    Print records  . . . . . . . . N           Y=Yes, N=No
      Number to find . . . . . . . *ALL        *ALL, number
      Print format . . . . . . . . *CHAR       *CHAR, *HEX, *ALTHEX
      Mark record  . . . . . . . . Y           Y=Yes, N=No
      Record overflow  . . . . . . 1           1=Fold, 2=Truncate
    Find string in batch . . . . . N           Y=Yes, N=No
    Parameters . . . . . . . . . .



 F3=Exit              F5=Refresh       F12=Cancel        F16=User options
 F18=Change defaults
```

Figure 12–10: Find string function screen

The first parameter, "Find," allows you to specify the character string that should be searched for in the selected members. A hexadecimal number search may be performed by enclosing the number in single quotation marks and prefacing the number with an x (for example, x'123f').

The associated parameters determine the scope of the search and the matching criteria. The "From column number" parameter defaults to 1 and indicates the starting point for the search within a record. The maximum value is indicated by the special value *RCDLEN, which means the length of the record.

The "To column number" parameter defaults to special value *RCDLEN and indicates the ending position for the search within a record. This ending position may be any value greater than or equal to the beginning position.

The "Kind of match" parameter determines whether a case-sensitive match should be performed. The default value of 2 means that the Find String function should ignore the case when searching. A value of 1 indicates that the case must be identical to the "Find" character string for a match to be successful.

The next parameter, "Option," determines what PDM option (if any) will be performed when a match is found. The special value *NONE means that no option will be performed. If the "Option" parameter has a value of *NONE, then the "Print list" or "Print records" (or both) parameters must have a value of Y.

The "Option" that is performed on the member operates in the same fashion as if the option was invoked directly. The type of "Option" that may be performed on the member when a match is found depends on whether the member is in a source physical file or a data physical file.

The allowable options for members in a source physical file are

2 to edit members using the Source Entry Utility (SEU).

3 to copy members to a new file.

4 to delete members from the file.

5 to display members using the Browse function of SEU.

6 to print members using SEU.

7 to rename members.

8 to display the description of the members.

9 to save members using the Save Object (SAVOBJ) command.

13 to change the text of the members.

14 to compile the members.

16 to run the procedure contained within the member.

17 to change the member using the Screen Design Aid (SDA).

19 to change the member using the Report Layout Utility (RLU).

The allowable options for members in a data physical file are

3 to copy members to a different file.

4 to delete members.

5 to display members.

7 to rename members.

8 to display the description of the members.

9 to save members using the Save Object (SAVOBJ) command.

13 to change the text of the members.

18 to change members using the Data File Utility (DFU).

The following parameter, "Prompt," indicates if PDM should prompt you to perform the function each time a match is found in a member. The default for this parameter is N, meaning that PDM should not prompt you when a match is found, and you should perform the action. A value of Y would cause PDM to prompt you to perform the operation each time a match is found.

The "Print list" parameter defaults to N, which indicates that PDM will not print a list of the members where a match was found. A value of Y will cause PDM to print the list. The spooled file will be placed in the output queue associated with your interactive job.

The "Print records" parameter defaults to N, meaning that records where a match was found will not be printed. A value of Y for this parameter indicates that PDM will print the records that contain a match (records in the member that do not match will not be printed).

The associated parameters indicate the type of print that will be performed if the "Print records" parameter is Y. The "Number to find" parameter defaults to special value *ALL, meaning all matching records should be printed. You may also specify a number in the range of one to 99,999.

The "Print format" may contain one of three special values. A value of *CHAR (the default) means that PDM will print the records in character format. A value of *HEX indicates that PDM will print the records in hexadecimal format. The character values will be printed beneath the hexadecimal values. Value *ALTHEX means that PDM will print the records in hexadecimal and character format in a side-by-side fashion.

The "Mark record" parameter defaults to Y, which means PDM will identify the portion of the record that contains the find string by printing the string above the position. A hexadecimal find string is denoted by a series of asterisks to mark the record. A value of N will not mark the records when matched.

The "Record overflow" parameter defaults to 1, which means fold the record. Multiple print lines will be used to print the entire record. The other value, 2, means to truncate the record. Only the first 100 characters will be printed in *CHAR or *HEX print formats, and the first 32 will be printed in *ALTHEX format.

The next parameter, "Find string in batch," defaults to N which indicates the find processing should be executed interactively. A value of Y means the find process will be executed in batch mode. You cannot execute any option that requires a display terminal if executing in batch mode.

The "Parameters" parameter defaults to blank. You may specify any parameters that are to be used by the option specified in the "Option" field.

The standard and common function keys are available with the Find String function. There are no specific function keys for this function.

12.11 WORKING WITH USER-DEFINED OPTIONS

The fourth PDM Main Menu selection, Work with User-Defined Options, allows you to manipulate the user-defined options. These options provide a mechanism allowing you to use options that you define in place of, or in addition to, the options that are provided by PDM. IBM provides a default file of user-defined commands to which you may add new options. In addition, you may have as many user-defined option files as needed. The user-defined option file that is active for your PDM session is specified on the Change Defaults screen.

The user-defined options are merely shortcut methods of accomplishing tasks. Each user-defined option will execute an IBM or user-written command. The structure of the user-defined option is unique as there is an interface provided through the use of substitution parameters to the information contained within the list entries. This allows you to obtain information from the list entry to execute the command. Special characters, prefaced with an ampersand (&), provide the interface as substitution parameters from the list entry to the command. These special characters are detailed later in this section.

After selecting the Work with User-Defined Options selection, the following screen will be displayed. This screen, the Specify Option File to Work With, determines the option file that contains the user-defined options. The initial default for this file is QUAOOPT in library QGPL with member QUAOOPT. This file contains the user-defined options as they are shipped from IBM. The Specify Option File to Work With screen is shown here in Figure 12–11.

The "File," "Library," and "Member" parameters will identify and provide access to the specified user-defined option file. Specify the appropriate information and press <ENTER> to access the option file. The next screen that will be shown is the Work with User-Defined Options display. An example of this display is shown in Figure 12–12.

This display shows the name of the file, library, and member that contains the user-defined options that are shown. The display also shows the "Option" and the "Command" that will be executed when the "Option" is selected.

This display allows you to manipulate the user-defined options by specifying an option before the user-defined option name in the "Opt" field. You may change a user-defined option, copy a user-defined option, delete a user-defined option, or display a user-defined option.

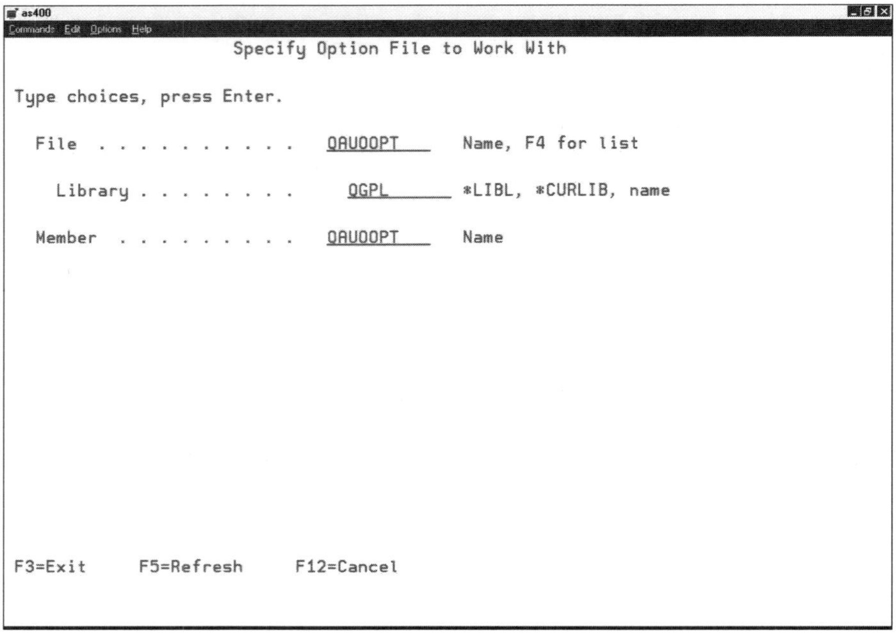

```
as400                                                                    _ 8 X
Commands  Edit  Options  Help
                        Specify Option File to Work With

Type choices, press Enter.

    File . . . . . . . . . .       QAUOOPT        Name, F4 for list

      Library . . . . . . . .        QGPL         *LIBL, *CURLIB, name

    Member  . . . . . . . .        QAUOOPT        Name













F3=Exit      F5=Refresh      F12=Cancel
```

Figure 12–11: Specify option file to work with screen

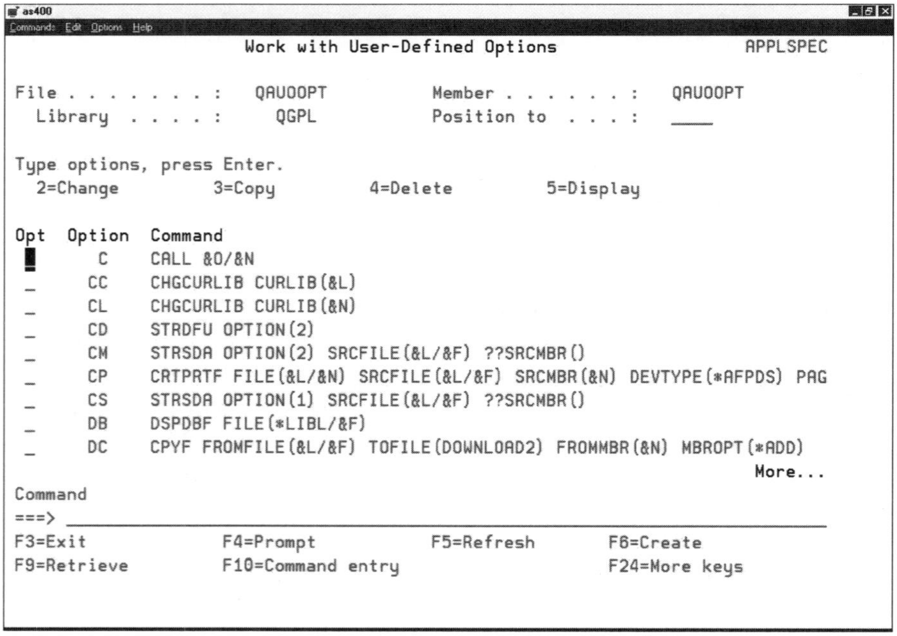

```
as400                                                                    _ 8 X
Commands  Edit  Options  Help
                      Work with User-Defined Options                 APPLSPEC

File . . . . . . . :    QAUOOPT         Member . . . . . . :    QAUOOPT
  Library . . . . :    QGPL             Position to . . . :    ____

Type options, press Enter.
  2=Change         3=Copy          4=Delete          5=Display

Opt   Option   Command
 ▮       C      CALL &O/&N
 _      CC      CHGCURLIB CURLIB(&L)
 _      CL      CHGCURLIB CURLIB(&N)
 _      CD      STRDFU OPTION(2)
 _      CM      STRSDA OPTION(2) SRCFILE(&L/&F) ??SRCMBR()
 _      CP      CRTPRTF FILE(&L/&N) SRCFILE(&L/&F) SRCMBR(&N) DEVTYPE(*AFPDS) PAG
 _      CS      STRSDA OPTION(1) SRCFILE(&L/&F) ??SRCMBR()
 _      DB      DSPDBF FILE(*LIBL/&F)
 _      DC      CPYF FROMFILE(&L/&F) TOFILE(DOWNLOAD2) FROMMBR(&N) MBROPT(*ADD)
                                                                       More...
Command
===> _____
F3=Exit             F4=Prompt         F5=Refresh         F6=Create
F9=Retrieve         F10=Command entry                    F24=More keys
```

Figure 12–12: Work with user-defined options screen

The available user-defined manipulation options are as follows:

Option 2 will allow you to change an existing user-defined option. The option code and the associated command will be displayed allowing you to change the option code and the command.

Option 3 will allow you to copy a user-defined option to a different user-defined option. A screen will be displayed where the target file, library, member, and option code default to the source information. Type over the target information to copy the information to a different option file.

Option 4 will delete a user-defined option. You will be prompted for confirmation of the deletion request.

Option 5 will allow you to display a user-defined option. This is a display-only option; you will not be able to change the option code or the associated command.

In addition to the options that are available for manipulating user-defined options, the standard, common, and specific function keys are also available. The specific function keys for the Work with User-Defined Options display are

<F6>—allows you to create a new user-defined option.

<F15>—allows you to exit the Work with User-Defined Options display without saving any changes you have made.

When changing an existing user-defined option, or when creating a new user-defined option, the following screen (see Figure 12–13) is displayed.

The "Option" parameter may be any character value (the parameter may not contain only numbers). Pick a value that describes the action that the option will take.

The "Command" parameter may be any command that you wish, and will be executed when the option is specified next to a list entry in the WRKLIBPDM, WRKOBJPDM, WRKMBRPDM, or when using the Find String function.

The commands may require no parameters, such as DSPJOBLOG, or may be more complex requiring parameters, such as Display File Description (DSPFD). PDM provides an interface between the list entry and the command through the use of special characters used as substitution parameters. The substitution parameters would then be used as arguments to the command that is to be executed. These special characters are detailed as follows:

&A—Object attribute. This parameter will be replaced by the object attribute from an entry in a list of objects or have the special value *NULL if not working with a list of objects.

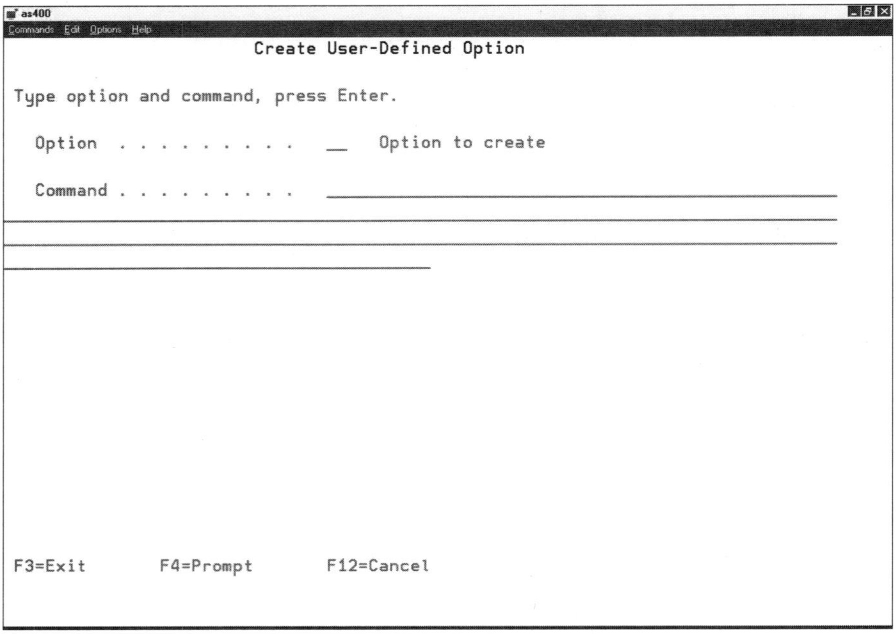

```
as400                                                              _|B|X
Commands  Edit  Options  Help
                        Create User-Defined Option

Type option and command, press Enter.

  Option . . . . . . . . .   _     Option to create

  Command . . . . . . . . .  _____
                             _____
                             _____
                             _____




















F3=Exit      F4=Prompt      F12=Cancel
```

Figure 12–13: Create user-defined option screen

&B—List type. This substitution parameter will have a value of L if you are working with a list of libraries, O if you are working with a list of objects, M if you are working with a list of members, and X if you are working with a library list.

&C—Option. This parameter is replaced by the user-defined option code.

&D—Date of last change to the member in the list of members. The date will be returned in the system date format. This value will be *NULL if you are not working with a list of members.

&E—Run in batch indication. This substitution parameter will be replaced by *YES if Y is specified on the Change Defaults screen for the "Run in batch" parameter, and *NO if N is specified for the "Run in batch" parameter.

&F—File name. This substitution parameter is replaced by the name of the file that contains the members if working with a list of members. This parameter will have a value of *NULL if you are not working with a list of members.

&G—Job description library. This parameter contains the name of the library associated with the "Job description" parameter from the Change Defaults screen.

&H—Job description name. This parameter contains the name of the "Job description" from the Change Defaults screen.

&J—Job description. This parameter contains the name of the "Job description" and the associated "Library" from the Change Defaults screen in the form of "library/jobd."

&L—Library name. This substitution parameter contains the name of the library that contains the objects or members with which you are working. This parameter will have the value QSYS if you are working with libraries.

&N—Name of the item. This parameter is replaced by the name of the item in the list.

&O—Object library. This parameter contains the name of the "Object library" from the Change Defaults screen.

&P—Compile in batch indication. This substitution parameter will be replaced by *YES if Y is specified on the Change Defaults screen for the "Compile in batch" parameter, and *NO if N is specified for the "Compile in batch" parameter.

&R—Replace object indication. This substitution parameter will be replaced by *YES if Y is specified on the Change Defaults screen for the "Replace object" parameter, and *NO if N is specified for the "Replace object" parameter.

&S—Item type without *. This parameter is replaced by LIB if you are working with libraries, by the object type (without the leading *) if you are working with objects, or the member type if you are working with members.

&T—Item type with *. This parameter is replaced by LIB if you are working with libraries, by the object type (with the leading *) if you are working with objects, or the member type if you are working with members.

&U—User-defined option file. This substitution parameter is replaced by the name of the active user-defined option file. The active user-defined option file is specified on the Change Defaults screen.

&V—User-defined option file library. This substitution parameter is replaced by the name of the library that contains the active user-defined option file. The active user-defined option file is specified on the Change Defaults screen.

&W—User-defined option file member. This substitution parameter is replaced by the name of the member that contains the active user-defined options. The active user-defined option file is specified on the Change Defaults screen.

&X—Item text. This parameter is replaced by the text associated with the list entry. The text is returned to the parameter enclosed in single quotation marks.

13

The System/36 Execution Environment

13.1 OVERVIEW

Because the AS/400 was created as the successor for the System/36 and the System/38, OS/400 includes user and operational environments for those different system types. Of course, the native AS/400 environment is the environment most commonly used; the native environment provides the greatest performance and efficiency. In addition, use of the native environment promotes greater productivity as all the tools and features of the AS/400 are available.

The architecture of the System/38 and the AS/400 are very similar, therefore the System/38 Environment is similar to the native AS/400 environment. The displays, commands, and interaction in the System/38 Environment are so alike that one may migrate from the System/38 to the AS/400 with minimal retraining. In fact, the major retraining effort is to "come up to speed" with the increased capabilities of the AS/400.

The System/36 (S/36), on the other hand, is a completely different system than the AS/400. Architecture, capabilities, and even the philosophy of the two systems are radically dissimilar. The System/36 Environment (S/36E) was developed to provide a relatively easy path for migrating from a System/36 to an AS/400. IBM has attempted (quite successfully) to give the "look and feel" of a System/36 the this emulation environment. The same commands (where appropriate) that are used on a System/36 may be used to accomplish the same function on the AS/400. Operator Control Language (OCL) commands used on a System/36 may be used to provide the interface to the system.

The S/36E emulates the same physical environment as well. Even though the AS/400 architecture is completely different from the architecture of the System/36, IBM has used an approach to make the physical environment seem the same as on the System/36. Through clever use of library lists, system tables, special libraries and files, and the translation of System/36 commands into the AS/400 equivalent, IBM has done a very thorough job of shielding the System/36 user from complexities of the AS/400 environment.

13.2 COMPONENTS OF THE SYSTEM/36 ENVIRONMENT

The heart of the S/36E lies in three libraries, #LIBRARY, QS36F, and QSSP. #LIBRARY provides the same function as #LIBRARY on a S/36; it contains the system procedures and other objects necessary for the S/36E operation. Library QSSP contains the object code required for the S/36E—the programs that emulate SSP, the S/36 operating system.

QS36F contains the data files (physical files in the native environment) and alternate indexes (logical files) used by applications in the S/36E. An important point to note is that, by default, all files used in the S/36E will be contained in QS36F. This default may be overridden with the Change S/36 Environment (CHGS36) command), but the majority of sites implementing the S/36E continue to use QS36F to contain files.

Storing the files in one library approximates the method used on a S/36. Files on a S/36 are stored separately on disk; an AS/400 stores files within libraries. By storing the files in one library, the S/36E can "see" the files as if they were on disk in the area on a System/36 that is reserved for files. Issuing the S/36E command CATALOG to obtain a listing of files and libraries on the system would produce a report similar to the System/36 CATALOG listing, showing the files that are contained in library QS36F and the libraries contained on the system.

Libraries are implemented in the S/36E in a manner similar to the implementation on a System/36. Libraries on a System/36 contain source and procedure members, screen formats, compiled programs, message members, and subroutine members. The implementation in the S/36E provides a relationship between the method of storage on the System/36 and the method of storage in the S/36E. The following table shows the location of information on a System/36 and the corresponding location on an AS/400 in the S/36E.

System/36 Item Location	AS/400 Object Location
Security information such as user ID, password, and so on	User Profile (*USRPRF)
#LIBRARY, operating system(SSP)	Libraries #LIBRARY and QSSP (*LIB)
Library	Library (*LIB)
Source member	Member in file QS36SRC
Procedure member	Member in file QS36PRC
Screen format	Source member in file QS36DDSSRC, screen in a display file (*FILE)
Message member	Message File (*MSGF)
Subroutine member	Member in files QS36LOD and QS36SBR
Compiled program	Program (*PGM)
Executable subroutine	Member in file QS36SBR
Executable load member	Member in file QS36LOD
Data file	Physical file (*PF) in library QS36F

System/36 Item Location	AS/400 Object Location
Alternate index	Logical file (*LF) in library QS36F
PC Support virtual disks	Shared folder
PC Support Folder	Folder (*FLR) in library QDOC
Folder documents	Documents in a folder in library QDOC
Communication descriptions, wrkstn communication configurations, line member information (ICF information)	Line descriptions (*LIND)
Remote system information	Controller descriptions (*CTLD)
Subsystem members	Device descriptions (*DEVD)

13.3 INVOKING THE S/36E

The S/36E may be invoked in a number of ways, depending if you wish to be placed in the environment automatically or if you wish to control entering the environment. You may be placed in the S/36E automatically by specifying the "Special Environment" (SPCENV) parameter in the User Profile to a value of *S36. This will cause you to enter the environment upon signing on to the system. An alternative method is to change system value QSPCENV to a value of *S36 and setting parameter SPCENV in your user profile to a value of *SYSVAL.

Another method of invoking the S/36E is the Start S/36 (STRS36) command. This command will place the user in the S/36E. Exiting the S/36E is done by signing off or with the End S/36 (ENDS36) command. An example of the STRS36 command is

```
STRS36 MENU(MKTMNU).
```

Optional parameters for the STRS36 command are the name of a "Menu" (MENU) to be displayed when the S/36E is started, the "Current library" (CURLIB) to be used while in the S/36E, and the "Program or procedure" (PRC) to be executed upon entering the S/36E. Entering the STRS36 command with no parameters will not cause a specific menu, procedure, or program to be invoked, but will put your session into the S/36E. One way of knowing that you are in the S/36E is that command line input will all be in capital letters.

13.4 SIMILARITIES AND DIFFERENCES

Your interaction in the S/36E will be very similar to working on an actual System/36. The vast majority of OCL commands will work successfully in the S/36E, with only the commands that are not applicable (due to the different architectures) unavailable.

However, the architectures of the different systems are different. Some of the System/36 OCL commands have no meaning in the S/36E. For instance, the CONDENSE and COMPRESS commands have no meaning on an AS/400. The native work management routines will manage the disk—user disk management is not required. These commands may still be part of the procedures; however, they will be ignored when encountered. A list of commands that are not supported in the S/36E is shown later in this chapter.

In addition, some methods and products used on a System/36 are not used on an AS/400. Nonsupported methods and products include the use of console and subconsole modes, the Work Station Utility (WSU), and user-written assembler routines.

The lack of console mode is addressed by taking advantage of the native AS/400 work management functions. WSU programs need to be rewritten in an AS/400 high level language (HLL). User-written assembler routines are not supported; there is no assembler language (though there is the MI language). While user-written assembler programs are not supported, the system assembler routines are still available.

The following list contains methods and techniques that are only available as a native function; there is no S/36E counterpart:

Data File Utility (DFU)

Source Entry Utility (SEU)

Screen Design Aid (SDA)

System Request Key

Security

Performance Tuning

Program Temporary Fix (PTF)

Blanks in numeric fields in a file are handled differently. The S/36E changes blanks in numeric fields in files to zeros (as did the System/36). A program accessing the file outside of the S/36E will fail with a decimal data error.

Date differentiated data files may be stored as separate members in a physical file on an AS/400 in the S/36E. Date differentiated files were stored as separate files on a System/36.

The System/36 procedure COPYPRT is used to copy a spooled file to a data file. This command exists in the S/36E; however, the format of the resulting file is different.

The equivalent of the System/36 HISTORY command is the AS/400 command Display Log (DSPLOG LOG(QHST)). While the functions of the commands are the same, the format of the output is different. Applications using the HISTORY log as input will need to be modified.

13.5 MANAGING THE S/36E

The S/36E is managed through the use of certain system tables and system values. This allows the performance and appearance of the S/36E to be monitored and modified. Other techniques exist to improve the performance in the S/36E. These techniques are discussed in the next section.

Different system values assist in the emulation of a System/36 on an AS/400. These system values include the following:

QAUTOCFG—Provides automatic configuration of devices on an AS/400 in the same manner as the automatic configuration on a S/36.

QPRTDEV—Identifies the system default printer. This is helpful as the System/36 could have a single queue for all printed output.

QCONSOLE—Specifies the name of the console. The console definition was an important concept on the System/36; the operator's console on the AS/400 may be any workstation.

QDEVNAMING—Determines the type of device naming that will be used for automatically created devices. Specifying a value of *S36 will cause newly created devices to be assigned a name in accordance with System/36 conventions.

A series of tables are used to define and manage the S/36E. These tables are accessible through the use of the Change S/36 Environment (CHGS36) command. This command allows you to change the values associated with the definition of the S/36E. Changing these values can change the appearance of the environment, and may also change the performance while in the environment.

The CHGS36 command (and the associated Display S/36 Environment (DSPS36) command) allows access to several configuration values. These values control the assignment of System/36 style device IDs for displays, printers, tapes, and the diskette device. In addition, the 3270 device emulation values and the S/36 Environment values may be manipulated. Each of these sets of values will be examined and explained.

Entering the CHGS36 command (there are no parameters with this command) will provide the following display (see Figure 13–1).

The first configuration value on the list is the "Display IDs" value. This value determines the name of a display device as it will be used in the S/36E. Accessing this value will produce the following display (see Figure 13–2).

This display shows all the display device names as defined to the AS/400 and the corresponding name for the workstation in the S/36E. In addition, the printer ID associated with the workstation is displayed. Since a System/36 uses a different naming convention than the AS/400, these configuration values allow you to assign and maintain the appropriate S/36E name for the workstation.

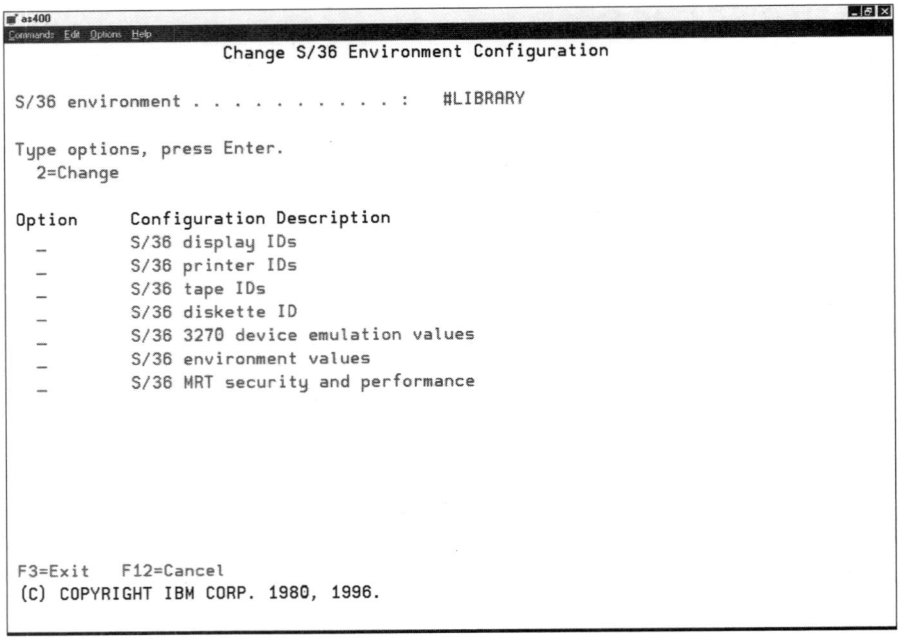

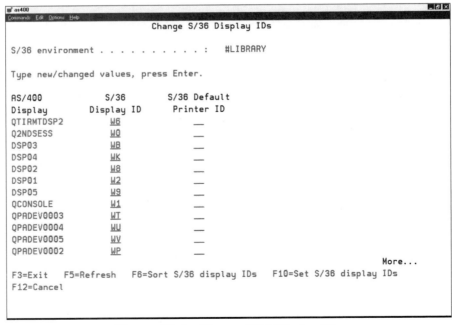

Figure 13–1: Change S/36 Environment Configuration

Figure 13–2: Change S/36 Display IDs

A workstation must have an S/36E ID to be able to be accessed in the S/36E, and that workstation will be identified by that S/36E ID (and not by the AS/400 device name). The S/36E name of the printer may be changed by typing over the existing name.

You may remove a display device from the S/36E by spacing over the name. This will disable use of the display device in the S/36E, but not in the native AS/400 environment. Note that default values may be assigned by pressing <F10>. This will assign a unique two character System/36 style identifier for each AS/400 display device name.

The next configuration value on the list is the "Printer IDs" value. This value determines the name of a printer device as it will be used in the S/36E. Accessing this value will produce the following display (see Figure 13–3):

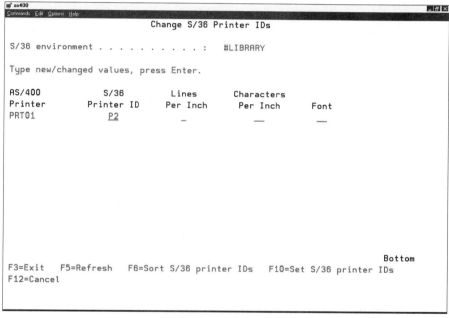

Figure 13–3: Change S/36 Printer IDs

This display shows all the printer device names as defined to the AS/400 and the corresponding name for the printer in the S/36E. Since a System/36 uses a different naming convention than the AS/400, these configuration values allow you to assign and maintain the appropriate S/36E name for the printer. Other information that may be specified for a printer is the number of lines per inch (LPI), characters per inch (CPI), and font. If a //PRINTER OCL statement is not used in an S/36E procedure, the LPI, CPI, and font values from this configuration table are used for the printer. If these values are blank for the requested printer, the information from the AS/400 printer device description are used.

A printer must have an S/36E ID to be able to be accessed in the S/36E, and that printer will be identified by that S/36E ID (and not by the AS/400 device name). The S/36E name of the printer may be changed by typing over the existing name.

You may remove a printer device from the S/36E by spacing over the name. This will disable use of the printer device in the S/36E, but not in the native AS/400 environment. Note that default values may be assigned by pressing <F10>. This will assign a unique two-character System/36 style identifier for each AS/400 printer device name.

The third configuration value on the list is the "Tape IDs" value. This value determines the name of a tape device as it will be used in the S/36E. Accessing this value will produce the following display (see Figure 13–4):

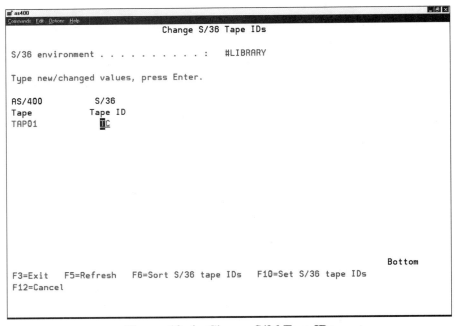

Figure 13–4: Change S/36 Tape IDs

This display shows the tape device names as defined to the AS/400 and the corresponding name for the tape device in the S/36E. Since a System/36 uses a different naming convention than the AS/400, these configuration values allow you to assign and maintain the appropriate S/36E name for the tape device.

A tape device must have an S/36E ID to be able to be accessed in the S/36E, and that tape device will be identified by that S/36E ID (and not by the AS/400 device name). The S/36E name of the tape device may be changed by typing over the existing name. Allowable names for S/36E tape IDs are T1, T2, or TC. Up to three tape devices may be defined for use in the S/36E.

You may remove a tape device from the S/36E by spacing over the name. This will disable use of the tape device in the S/36E, but not in the native AS/400 environment. Note that default values may be assigned by pressing <F10>. This will assign a unique two-character System/36 style identifier for each AS/400 tape device name.

The next configuration value on the list is the "Diskette ID" value. This value determines the name of the diskette device as it will be used in the S/36E. Accessing this value will produce the following display (see Figure 13–5):

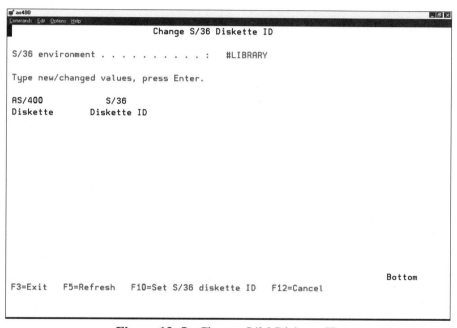

Figure 13–5: Change S/36 Diskette ID

This display shows the names of the diskette devices as defined to the AS/400 and the corresponding name for the diskette device in the S/36E. Since a System/36 uses a different naming convention than the AS/400, these configuration values allow you to assign and maintain the appropriate System/36 name for the diskette device.

A diskette device must have an S/36E ID to be able to be accessed in the S/36E, and that diskette device will be identified by that S/36E ID (and not by the AS/400 device name). The S/36E name of the diskette device may be changed by typing over the existing name. The only allowable name for S/36E diskette ID is I1. Only one diskette device may be defined for use in the S/36E.

You may remove a diskette device from the S/36E by spacing over the name. This will disable use of the diskette device in the S/36E, but not in the native AS/400 environment.

Note that a diskette device may be assigned by pressing <F10>. This will assign the S/36E diskette identifier for an AS/400 diskette device.

The next configuration value controls the "3270 device emulation" value. This value determines the characteristics of emulated 3270 devices in the S/36E. Accessing this value will produce the following display (see Figure 13–6):

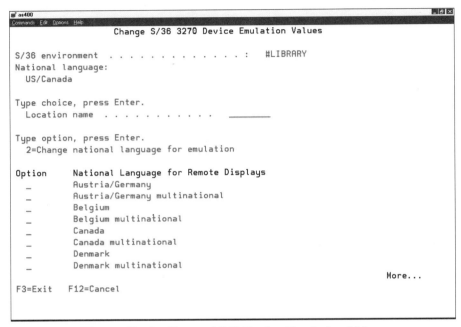

Figure 13–6: Change 3270 Device Emulation Values

The 3270 device emulation values that may be changed are the remote location, which the 3270 emulated device will access, and the national language to be used by the emulated device at the remote system. Change the remote location by typing over the eight-character name. Change the national language to be used by entering 2 before the name of the national language desired. Only one national language may be selected; this will be the national language used by all emulated devices.

The last parameter displayed in the list of configuration values is the "Change S/36 Environment Values" parameter. These values define several characteristics of the S/36E, including default libraries, file open techniques, and default printing options. Selecting this configuration parameter shows the following display (see Figure 13–7).

The first environment value, "S/36 default session library," determines the session library to be used by all users accessing the S/36E. #LIBRARY is used as the session library if no value is specified for this parameter.

```
as400                                                                    _ @ X
Commands  Edit  Options  Help
                      Change S/36 Environment Values

   S/36 environment  . . . . . . . . . . . . :    #LIBRARY

   Type choices, press Enter.

     S/36:
       Default session library . . . . . . . .   ▮
       Default files library . . . . . . . . .   QS36F
       Use library list for files  . . . . . .   N        Y=Yes, N=No
       Date differentiated files . . . . . . .   N        Y=Yes, N=No
       Shared opens of files . . . . . . . . .   Y        Y=Yes, N=No
       Record blocking when sharing files  . .   N        Y=Yes, N=No
       Store deleted files in cache  . . . . .   Y        Y=Yes, N=No
       Default lines per page  . . . . . . . .   066      1-112
       Default forms . . . . . . . . . . . . .   *STD
       Default message action  . . . . . . . .   *HALT     *CONTINUE, *IGNORE,
                                                           *HALT, *CANCEL

          Halt options  . . . . . . . . . . .    03

                                                               More...

   F3=Exit   F5=Refresh   F10=Set to default values   F12=Cancel
```

Figure 13–7: Change S/36 Environment Values

The next environment value, "S/36 default files library," identifies the name of the AS/400 library that contains the S/36E files. The default for this parameter is QS36F.

The "Use library list for S/36 files" parameter determines if the library list of the job should be used to find files referenced by jobs executing in the S/36E. The default for this parameter is N, meaning that the library list should not be used to locate files and that library QS36F contains the files to be accessed. If the value for this parameter is Y, then the library list associated with the job will be searched in the native OS/400 fashion to locate referenced files.

The next value, "S/36 date differentiated files," determines if date differentiated files may be used in the S/36E. Date differentiated files are files with the same name that are uniquely identified by the date that the file was created. The default for this parameter is N, which indicates that date differentiated files may not be used and that each file must have a unique name. A value of Y allows date differentiated files to be used.

The "S/36 shared opens of files" value determines how shared opens should be used. The default value of Y means that the S/36E will use shared opens. This will provide greater performance, but will also cause the application to function differently than on a System/36. A value of N will not allow shared opens of files.

The "S/36 record blocking when sharing files" value determines if record blocking should be used with sequential files that are shared with other jobs in the S/36E. The default value of N means that the S/36E will not use record blocking for shared files. This will allow the S/36E to be functionally identical to a System/36, but may degrade performance. A value of Y for this parameter will cause record blocking and will provide better performance.

"Store deleted files in cache" determines if deleted files should be stored in a cache area. This is useful when files are created and deleted multiple times. The default value of Y will cause deleted files to be stored in cache. A value of N will not allow OS/400 to store deleted files in cache.

The "S/36 default lines per page" value identifies the number of lines per page to be used by default for jobs in the S/36E. This value may be changed for a job by specifying the SET command, the //FORMS OCL statement, or the //PRINTER OCL statement. The default value is 66, with a range of valid values from one to 112.

The next value, "S/36 default forms," identifies the default form type to be used by jobs in the S/36E. This value may be specified with the SET command, the //FORMS OCL statement, or the //PRINTER OCL statement. The default value for this parameter is *STD.

The "Default message action" value determines the action that should be taken when an error occurs executing a CL command from within an S/36E procedure. Allowable values for this parameter are

*CONTINUE—The default replacement variable is set and processing continues with the next statement.

*IGNORE—The error is ignored. Processing continues with the statement following the statement in error.

*HALT—A halt message will be displayed.

*CANCEL—The procedure will be canceled.

The "Halt options" value determines what options are allowed when *HALT is specified for the "Default message action" value. This parameter may contain up to four digits (0, 1, 2, or 3). The default for this option is 03, which indicates that options 0 and 3 are allowable.

The "S/36 description" parameter specifies a description for the S/36E. The description may contain up to forty characters.

After changing any of the configuration parameters, the following screen will be shown when exiting. This display allows you to save and/or exit the individual configuration option change process. The following display is an example of exiting from changing S/36E printer IDs (see Figure 13–8).

The options on this display allow you to "Save and exit," "Exit without saving," or to "Resume" changing the configuration values. Select the appropriate option and press <ENTER> to continue.

Another display will be shown when exiting from the CHGS36 command (if changes have been made). This screen allows you to save and/or exit the S/36E configuration option change process. The following display is an example of exiting from changing the S/36 configuration (see Figure 13–9).

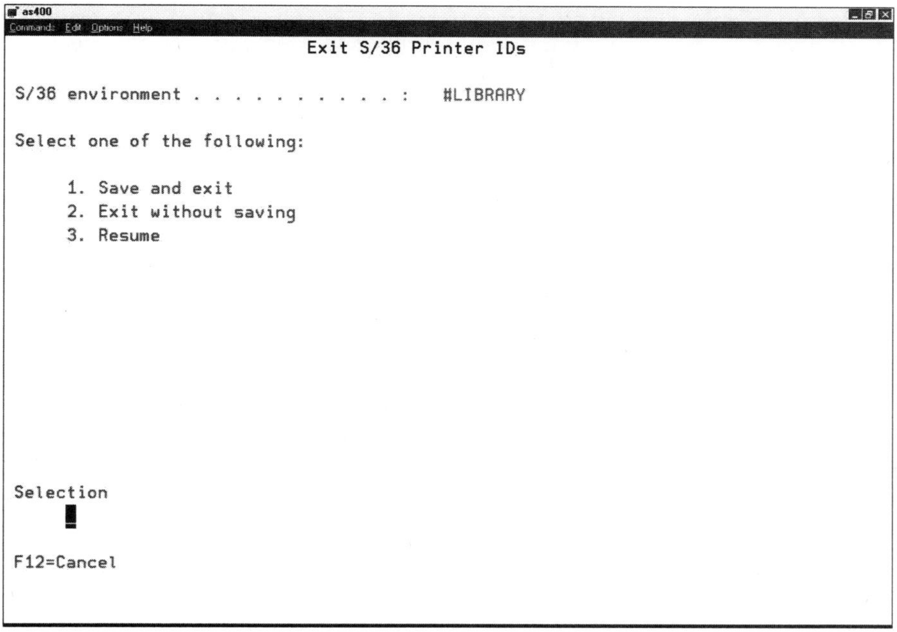

Figure 13–8: Exit S/36 Printer IDs

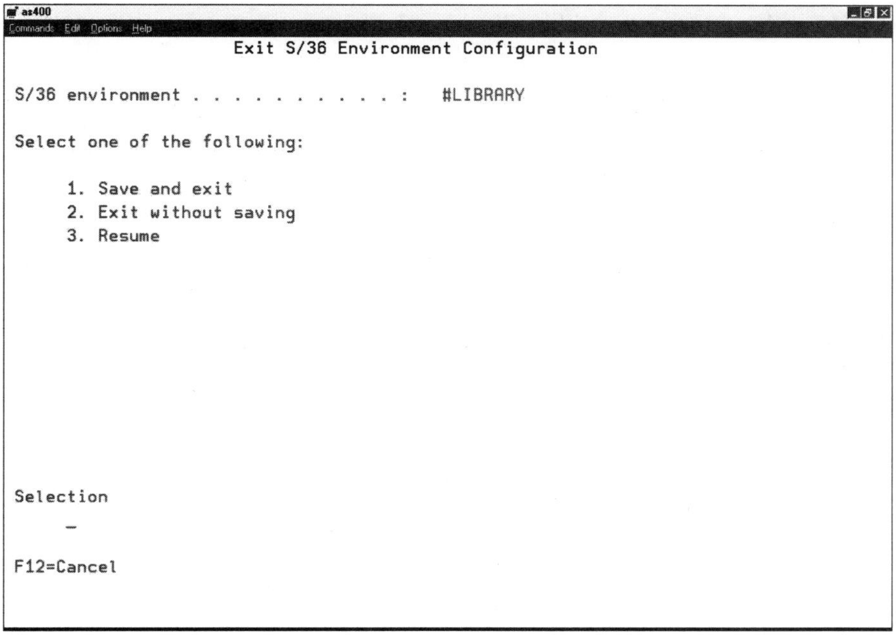

Figure 13–9: Exit S/36 Environment Configuration

The options on this display allow you to "Save and exit," "Exit without saving," or to "Resume" changing the configuration values. Select the appropriate option and press <ENTER> to continue.

13.6 COMMANDS USED IN THE S/36E

All the native OS/400 commands may be used in the S/36E, as well as commands and procedures that are only a part of the S/36E. In other words, any OS/400 command may be used in the S/36E, but System/36 commands may only be used in the S/36E. All the procedures and OCL statements used on a System/36 may be used with a few exceptions; these exceptions are discussed in the next section, "Improving performance in the S/36E."

The transparency of command invocation between a System/36 and the S/36E provides the capability for users experienced in the operation and use of a System/36 to be able to use the S/36E on the AS/400. While the commands used may execute different commands or provide different displays (see the "Similarities and differences" section) the same effect will be achieved.

An interesting point when working in the S/36E is that native OS/400 commands may be used in an S/36E procedure. The OS/400 command would be included in the procedure as if the command were being entered on a command line. The OS/400 command will be executed when it is encountered. Correspondingly, an S/36E procedure may be executed in a CL program through the use of the Start S/36 Procedure (STRS36PRC) command. This command is explained later in this section.

Most of the operator status commands used on a System/36 may also be used in the S/36E. Of course an equivalent native command may also be used. The operator status commands that are supported in the S/36E, and their native counterparts (where appropriate), are shown here.

D A   Not Supported

D C   Uses Work with Configuration Status (WRKCFGSTS)

D G   Uses Work with Writers (modified) (WRKWTR)

D H   Uses Work with Configuration Status (WRKCFGSTS)

D J   Uses Work with Job Queue (WRKJOBQ)

D L   Uses Work with Configuration Status (WRKCFGSTS)

D M   Uses Work with RJE Session (WRKRJESSN)

D P   Uses Work Spooled Files (modified) (WRKSPLF)

D S   Uses Display Job (Display Session Status) (DSPJOB)

D T   Not Supported

D U   Uses Work with User Jobs (WRKUSRJOB)

In addition to the OCL statements, procedures, and operator commands that may be used in the S/36E, other commands only have meaning to jobs or objects that are located in the S/36E. These native OS/400 commands perform a variety of functions. These functions include creating program and display file objects for the S/36E, changing the attributes of procedures and programs, executing S/36E procedures from within a native CL program, and saving and restoring information in the S/36E.

All native OS/400 commands are listed in Appendix A ("OS/400 Commands"). This section will show selected commands that would be used with jobs or objects in the S/36E. Note: In many cases, the command will have three forms: a CHG form to allow changes to the object, a DSP form to provide for view-only processing, and an EDT form that will retrieve the current values or attributes and allow them to be changed.

The Change S/36 Program Attributes (CHGS36PGMA) command allows you to change attributes of a program in the S/36E environment. The attributes would be changed to provide better performance. An example of this command is

```
CHGS36PGMA PGM(AP0002) MRTMAX(50).
```

Enter the name of the "Program" (PGM) which will have its attributes changed. The "Maximum number of multiple requester terminals" (MRTMAX) parameter allows you to change the number of terminals that may be attached to this program. The number selected must be in a range of 1-256, and cannot be greater than the current value for this parameter.

Another parameter, "Never-ending program" (NEP), may be changed to make this program never-ending. The possible values for this parameter are *YES and *NO, with YES making the program a never-ending program.

The Change S/36 Procedure Attributes (CHGS36PRCA) command provides a mechanism for you to change the attributes associated with a procedure in the S/36E. These attributes would be changed to provide better performance in the S/36E. An example of this command is

```
CHGS36PRCA MBR(AR0630) LOG(*NO).
```

The "Member" (MBR) parameter identifies the procedure member whose attributes are to be changed. The "File" (FILE) parameter may be specified to identify the file containing the procedure member; the default is *LIBL/QS36PRC.

A parameter that may be specified is the "Multiple requestor terminal" (MRT) parameter. This parameter (with allowable values of *YES or *NO) determines if the procedure is an MRT procedure.

Another parameter is "Log OCL statements" (LOG). This parameter specifies if OCL statements should be logged (copied) to the job log. A value of *YES will cause statements to be logged, a value of *NO will not log OCL statements. You may wish to set this parameter to *NO for performance considerations.

Other parameters include "MRT delay" (MRTDLY), which determines if the standard MRT invocation delay should be used, and "Program Data" (PGMDTA), which identifies whether the procedure will pass parameters or data to the program.

The Change S/36 Source Attributes (CHGS36SRCA) command allows you to change the attributes associated with a source member. The attributes may be changed to increase performance or to establish the type of a member. An example of this command is

```
CHGS36SRCA MBR(MKT714) FILE(WORKSRC) SRCTYPE(RPG36).
```

The "Member" (MBR) parameter identifies the source member whose attributes are to be changed. The "File" (FILE) parameter may be specified to identify the file containing the source member; the default is *LIBL/QS36SRC.

A parameter that may be specified is the "Source type" (SRCTYPE) parameter. This parameter establishes the type of the member. Many allowable values exist for this parameter; some of the more common are RPG36 for RPG source, CBL36 for COBOL source, DFU36 for DFU source, and UNS36 for unspecified.

Another parameter is "Defer write" (DFRWRT). This parameter accepts values of *YES or *NO. A value of *YES indicates that writing of data to the display file will be deferred until a read operation is requested. This may improve performance in the S/36E.

The Start S/36 Procedure (STRS36PRC) command allows you to execute a S/36E procedure (and the corresponding S/36E program) from a native CL program. An example of this command is

```
STRS36PRC PRC(GENLED) PARM('01/01/93').
```

The "Procedure" (PRC) parameter identifies the name of the S/36E procedure to be executed. The procedure must exist in a source physical file named QS36PRC. The search order for finding the appropriate source file is the current library, #LIBRARY, and the library list.

The "Current library" (CURLIB) parameter defines the current library in which the procedure will be located. This allows you to designate a specific library to obtain the procedure. The default for the current library is #LIBRARY.

Another parameter, "Procedure parameters" (PARM), allows you to pass parameters to the specified procedure.

13.7 SAVING AND RESTORING INFORMATION

Commands exist to save and restore information. Of course, native OS/400 commands provide a multitude of different save and restore functions; the commands that provide these functions are discussed in Chapter 8 ("Operations"). In addition, System/36 commands such as SAVE, RESTORE, SAVELIBR, and RESTLIBR are also included. Note that not all the System/36 save and restore commands may be used in the S/36E—some of the commands are not supported and a native OS/400 command must be used.

A critical point when examining the capabilities of saving and restoring information in the S/36E lies in the fact that the System/36 was file-oriented, while the AS/400 uses the single-level storage concept. A complete system save on the System/36 consisted of saving the files and libraries contained on disk. A complete system save on an AS/400 consists of saving the system (with the SAVSYS command) and the libraries on the system [with the SAVLIB LIB(*NONSYS) command]. Native save commands **MUST** be used to provide the complete system save required in the event of disaster recovery. The S/36E commands for saving information will only save files and libraries; the commands will not save the system.

Several native OS/400 commands will process save and restore operations in a format that is compatible with a System/36. This allows information to be transferred between systems by saving the information on one system and restoring the information on another system. This section will discuss the save and restore commands that are compatible with a System/36.

The Save S/36 File (SAVS36F) command allows you to save information in a format that is compatible with the System/36. Information saved with this command may be restored to a System/36 with the RESTORE procedure or with the $COPY utility. The SAVS36F can save a single physical or logical file, or a group of physical or logical files in a save set.

The Save S/36 Library Member (SAVS36LIBM) command is used to save members from a source file. This command will create a record-mode file (in the format of a System/36 LIBRFILE) as if it was created with the FROMLIBR procedure. The information saved using the SAVS36LIBM command may be restored onto a System/36 with the TOLIBR procedure or the $MAINT utility. Both source (*SRC) and procedure (*PRC) members may be saved.

The Restore S/36 File (RSTS36F) command will restore a file onto the AS/400. The file to be restored must have been saved on a System/36 with the SAVE procedure (or with $COPY) or on an AS/400 with the SAVS36F command. Individual files or save sets may be restored.

The Restore S/36 Folder (RSTS36FLR) command will restore a folder to the AS/400. The folder must have been saved on a System/36 using the SAVEFLDR command. Two types of System/36 folders may be restored—document folders and IDDU folders. Document folders will be restored to a document folder on the AS/400. IDDU folders will be restored to a data dictionary (*DTADCT) on the AS/400.

The Restore S/36 Library Member (RSTS36LIBM) command will restore a library member that was saved from either a System/36 with the FROMLIBR or SAVELIBR procedures, or from an AS/400 with the SAVS36F command.

13.8 IMPROVING PERFORMANCE IN THE S/36E

IBM has made great strides in improving the efficiency of the S/36E with each new release of OS/400. Although the performance has increased, emulating an environment will never be as efficient as the actual environment. The following are some techniques to increase performance and efficiency in the S/36E.

Reduce the number of signons and signoffs. Each interactive session on an AS/400 is a job, requiring system resources. Job initiation on an AS/400 is slower than on an S/36. Reducing the number (as much as practical) can help improve performance.

Using EVOKE and JOBQ in S/36E procedures will cause a job to be initiated. Since the AS/400 will execute more quickly than an S/36, some of these job initiations could be changed to be completed interactively. Change //EVOKE commands to //INCLUDE commands.

Multiple Requester Terminal (MRT) processes use a large amount of overhead when invoking the procedure. The Change S/36 (CHGS36) procedure can be used to change timing and performance parameters for MRT procedures. An MRT procedure could also be changed to an MRT-Never Ending Program. This would reduce the overhead associated with job initiation. Programs may be changed with the Change S/36 Program Attributes (CHGS36PGMA) command. Procedures may be changed with the Change S/36 Procedure Attributes (CHGS36PRCA) command. Another method is to use the //ATTR NEP-Y statement in the procedure.

Nesting commands (entering a command on the command line of a previously entered command) increase the size of the Process Action Group (PAG), which causes more system resources to be used. Avoid entering a command from another command's command line; instead exit the previous command before entering another command.

Use of the DBLOCK parameter in OCL may improve performance by accessing disk in blocks. Choosing a better blocking size for sequentially accessed files will improve performance.

Keeping files open throughout the procedure will improve performance. Files open and close slower on the AS/400 than on an S/36. Specifying JOB-YES on the //FILE statement will keep the file open until the procedure completes. Another method of reducing file opens is to have a "controlling" CL program that would open the files needed for a job and then close the files after the job has completed.

Reducing the use of temporary files helps increase performance as a new file does not need to be created each time the procedure executes. Disk access for open and closes (creates and deletes) is slower on an AS/400 than on an S/36. Clear the physical file (using CLRPFM) rather than deleting and recreating the file.

Change sorts to using alternate indexes or logical files. A sort should only be used if more than 25 percent of the record keys have been changed. Use the Build Index (BLDINDEX) procedure to create an alternate index, or the Create Logical File (CRTLF) command to create a logical file.

Turn off procedure logging to reduce system overhead.

Enter the S/36E at signon by specifying the environment in the user profile rather than by using the Start S/36 (STRS36) command.

Remove OCL that is no longer needed in a procedure. Since OCL is interpreted (rather than executed directly as in a compiled CL program), OS/400 needs to examine each statement. Remove the statements that are no longer required. Procedures and OCL statements not used in the S/36E are:

ALOCFLDR

ALOCLIBR

ASM

ASMLOAD

BALPRINT

CACHE

COMPRESS

CONDENSE

DFA

DOCCNV

ICFVERIFY

IDDURBLD

KEYSORT

MAINTX25

MOVEFLDR

OLINK

PATCH

REQUESTX

TEXTCONV

WSU

// REGION

// RESERVE

14

AS/400 Communications

The AS/400 is one of the most capable data communications platforms found in the industry. The AS/400 supports many different physical and network protocols and both Local Area Networking (LAN) and Wide Area Networking (WAN) communications. The AS/400, especially with the latest releases of OS/400, can also play in the biggest network around—the Internet.

A full, in-depth analysis of AS/400 supported data communications and networking topics would require several books. The IBM manuals are always a good reference, and the data communications and networking books are well represented in the IBM manual set. The IBM "Red Books" are also a great source of information, especially for newer topics.

This chapter will cover several communications related topics. You will be exposed to

- Initiating a pass-through session
- AS/400 communication links
- Workstation connectivity
- The relationship between APPC and APPN in the midrange environment
- The purpose and use of TCP/IP, including the new V3R2/V3R7 features

14.1 DISPLAY STATION PASS-THROUGH

The display station pass-through facility provides a means of accessing another AS/400 (or System/36, or System/38) system from the AS/400 to which you are currently connected. Once you initiate a pass-through session, you may perform workstation operations as if you were directly connected to a workstation. You can also use the System Request menu to jump back and forth between your native AS/400 (termed the "source" system), and the other AS/400 (the "target" system) to which you have passed through. In many instances, initiating a display station pass-through command is performed by entering

```
STRPASTHR <target system name> [<virtual controller>].
```

In this example, the <target system name> defines the network name of the system to which you want to connect. The <virtual controller> may be used to select a particular virtual workstation controller on the target system (the virtual workstation controller is used by the target system to identify the capabilities of your workstation). For example, if you wanted to connect to a target system named "AS400B" using the virtual workstation controller named "REMOTEVWS" you would enter the command

```
STRPASTHR AS400B REMOTEVWS.
```

The STRPASTHR command can be prompted through the use of the <F4> key; additional parameters are available after prompting through the <F10> key. As you will see, a number of parameters and options are available for the STRPASTHR command. The particular parameters you will use in conjunction with the STRPASTHR command are dependent on your communications network. The example shown is fairly typical, but your network may require the use of additional parameters with the command.

The standard Sign On menu is sent to the workstation by the target system after a pass-through session has been successfully initiated. As noted, you can sign on that system and perform operations as if you were directly attached to a workstation. You may also access your source AS/400 through the System Request menu. When you press <SYSRQ>, you will receive a variation of the standard System Request menu (see Figure 14–1):

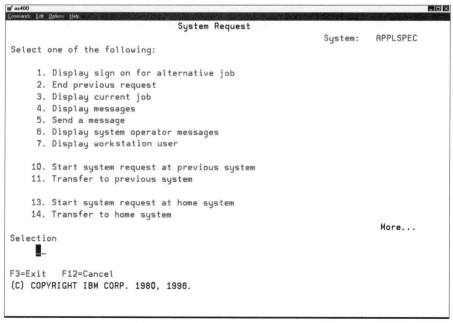

Figure 14–1: System Request from DSPT session

This System Request menu generated from the target system for the display station pass-through session has two additional options

10. (Start system request at source system)—takes you to a System Request menu generated and controlled by the source AS/400.

11. (Transfer to source system)—transfers back to the source AS/400. The first time you use this option, you will receive the Sign On menu from the source system and be required to sign on again. A new session is required because your original source session is "busy" handling the pass-through activity.

If you return to the source AS/400 and you want to switch back to the target AS/400, simply access the System Request menu and specify option 11. This option is available on both the source and target System Request menus, so it allows you to switch back and forth between your two sessions regardless of which system you are on at the moment.

When you complete your pass-through activity and want to disconnect your link with the target system, use the ENDPASTHR command instead of the SIGNOFF command. The ENDPASTHR command terminates pass-through activity and returns you to your original source session. If you initiated a second source session while you were accessing the target system, that session remains available as a normal alternate session accessible through the System Request menu.

NOTE: The SIGNOFF command can be modified to automatically perform an END-PASTHR command. If this is the case, you do not have to use the ENDPASTHR command.

14.2 COMMUNICATION LINKS

The AS/400 is well versed in the areas of networking and communication. The hardware architecture of the AS/400 includes independent processors for input and output activities. In terms of software, OS/400 includes a number of utilities to facilitate communication with other AS/400s. Additional packages are available for communication with mainframes and other types of systems and devices.

In the most general sense, AS/400 communications may be broken into two categories

1. SNA-compliant communications links that are capable of transporting SNA Logical Unit 6.2 (LU 6.2) traffic. This category of links includes SDLC, X.25, ISDN, Ethernet/802.3, and IBM token-ring/802.5.

2. Noncompliant communications links that are useful for specific instances or to interface with certain types of equipment. This category of links includes BSC, asynchronous, and twinaxial connections.

The most important distinction between the two categories is the services they can offer. These services, grouped by SNA-compliance, are as follows:

SNA-based services (LU 6.2)

Distributed Data Management (DDM)—allows an AS/400 to access files on another AS/400.

Display Station Pass-Through—This utility permits a workstation attached to one AS/400 to access another AS/400.

SNA Distribution System (SNADS)—used to distribute jobs, files, documents, and mail among other midrange and mainframe systems.

Non-SNA services

Intersystem Communications Function (ICF)—This function allows a program resident on an AS/400 to communicate with a program resident on another AS/400 or mainframe.

Interactive Terminal Facility (ITF)—This facility allows an AS/400 workstation to access interactive, ASCII-based hosts. ITF is only available over asynchronous links.

File Transfer Support (FTS)—FTS is a set of callable routines that may be used to develop programs which perform file transfers between midrange systems.

Transmission Control Protocol/Internet Protocol (TCP/IP)—This set of services can be used to facilitate a broad range of communication services with other midrange systems, mainframe systems, and non-IBM systems. TCP/IP is available over LAN (Token-Ring or Ethernet) links or WAN links (SLIP—Serial Line Internet Protocol or X.25). Please see the *TCP/IP* section in this chapter for more information.

In general, communication links that are SNA-capable can sponsor any of the available services. Those links that are not SNA-compliant, however, can only offer non-SNA services. The exceptions to both of these guidelines are where services are tied to specific types of links (for example, ITF and TCP/IP).

The next sections discuss additional aspects of the available AS/400 communications links.

14.2.1 Synchronous Links (BSC and SDLC)

Synchronous communication normally involves analog or digital phone links (although under unusual circumstances synchronous communications can be accomplished by direct connection). The speed that synchronous links can operate at is totally dependent on the type of link. Analog phone links can operate at speeds up to 19,200 bps. Digital links (DDS, fractional T1, T1, and so on) can offer speeds up to 64 Kbps.

Under synchronous communications, extra characters (sync characters) are inserted into to data stream at regular intervals to insure that data is delivered intact. Sync characters are inserted by the transmitting equipment (modem or CSU/DSU) and expected by the receiving equipment—if sync characters aren't detected in regular intervals, the receiver regards the transmission as flawed. Once the information arrives correctly, sync characters are eliminated.

In the AS/400 environment, two different style of synchronous communications are often used.

Binary Synchronous Communication (BSC)—This is an "old" byte-oriented style of communication pervasively used by IBM prior to the introduction of its Systems Network Architecture (SNA). A BSC link may be dedicated to different types of traffic, such as Remote Job Entry (RJE), 3270 workstation, document exchange, and others. For midrange-to-midrange traffic, BSC may be used with the ICF and FTS facilities. BSC usage remains prevalent in both mainframe and midrange environments.

Synchronous Data Link Control (SDLC)—SDLC was introduced as part of IBM's global SNA architecture. SDLC is bit-oriented and, like BSC, can be used to carry several types of traffic (3270, RJE, document exchange, and so on). More importantly, because SDLC is part of the SNA suite, it can carry PU 2.1/LU 6.2 traffic, which is used for midrange-to-midrange services like DDM, Display Station Pass-Through, Object Distribution, and Document Distribution. This makes SDLC the mainstay for wide area communication links. Finally, an SDLC link is often used to communicate with remote PCs (running PC Support) and remote workstation controllers. Please see the *Workstation Connectivity* section of this chapter for more information.

In general, an SDLC link is more efficient and more versatile than a BSC link; given a choice, SDLC should always be selected over BSC.

Both BSC and SDLC support the RS232 and V.24 physical interfaces for communications up to 19.200 bps, and the V.35 interface for communications up to 64 Kbps (although BSC can only run up to 56 Kbps). SDLC also supports the X.21 interface for communications up to 64 Kbps.

14.2.2 Asynchronous Links

Asynchronous communications can be performed over analog phone lines or through direct connections, and in both cases can operate at speeds up to 19,200 bps. Direct connect asynchronous links can use simple unshielded twisted pair (UTP) cable, which can be run up to one hundred feet without requiring any additional devices.

The foundation of asynchronous communications is the addition of extra bits to each 8-bit character being transferred. A bit termed the "start" bit is transmitted before the first actual bit in the character and one or more "stop" bits are added to the end of the 8-bit character. Thus, each 8-bit character actually ends up being transmitted over the communications link as at least a 10-bit group. The purpose of the start bit is to alert the receiving equipment that a character is coming, and the stop bit serves to delineate the end of the character. If the receiver does not detect both a start and stop bit, the transmission is rejected.

Like the synchronous BSC implementation, asynchronous communication is not SNA-compliant, therefore it cannot be used to carry PU 2.1/LU 6.2 traffic. Despite this limitation, asynchronous communication has a number of uses.

ASCII workstation attachment—The AS/400 supports an integrated workstation controller that allows ASCII workstations and PCs running PC Support to be attached via local or remote (modem) asynchronous lines. Supported ASCII workstation models include the IBM 3151, 3161, the DEC VT100, VT220, and others. Each integrated controller may support six or eighteen attachments.

ASCII workstation converter—An optional external protocol converter (model 5308) can be used to interface non-IBM ASCII workstations. The 5308 comes in two models: a 2-port model that includes two 28.8 modems, and a 7-port model with no internal modems. The 5208 attaches to the workstations using asynchronous links, and to the AS/400 using a twinaxial link. The workstations can be attached directly or may be attached remotely using modems. The 5308 allows the AS/400 to "see" the attached workstations as native twinax-attached devices.

Remote system dial—The Interactive Terminal Facility may be used to initiate an asynchronous ASCII connection with a foreign system (for example, a electronic mail or bulletin board service).

X.25 network access—An asynchronous link may be used for dialed access into a Packet Switching Data Network (PSDN). This capability is supported by the addition of a Packet Assembly/Disassembly (PAD) unit. Also refer to the description under the heading *X.25 Links*.

An asynchronous link may be used with the ICF and FTS facilities in a midrange-to-midrange environment over a direct or dialed connection. Asynchronous communications supports the RS232 and V.24 physical interfaces.

14.2.3 X.25 Links

In addition to the X.25 interface provided by the asynchronous link, the AS/400 supports a direct interface to a Packet-Switched Data Network (often called an "X.25 network"). This attachment allows the AS/400 to connect using a leased analog or digital phone line so, unlike the asynchronous counterpart, the connection to the network remains established at all times.

A Packet-Switched Data Network provides an economical way for a geographically diverse set of computers and workstations to achieve connectivity with one another. In a packed-switched network, computer systems and workstations interface to the nearest packet-switching node. Computer systems normally interface directly using the X.25 protocol, while workstations normally interface through a Packet Assembly/Disassembly (PAD) device, that, in turn, interfaces to the nearest packet-switching node.

Information destined for the packet-switched network is broken down into small "packets" by the computer system or the PAD. Once a packet arrives in the network, it is forwarded from one packet-switching node to another until it reaches its destination. Each packet takes the best possible route available at that time, so it is normal for packets from the same message to take different routes to the destination. When all the packets arrive at the destination (in order of transmission or not), they are assembled back into the original message.

X.25 is part of the SNA suite so, like SDLC, it is capable of carrying the full range of midrange services. X.25 supports the RS232 and V.24 physical interfaces for communications up to 19.200 bps, and the X.21 and V.35 for communications up to 64 Kbps. TCP/IP is also supported over X.25 links. Please note, however, that even though an AS/400 may interface to a packet-switched network at 64 Kbps, there is no guarantee that the packets will race through the network at the same speed.

14.2.4 ISDN Links

The Integrated Services Digital Network (ISDN) is a digital-based network for voice and data transmission. Like X.25, ISDN serves a broad base of geographically dispersed equipment. In fact, ISDN was designed to be international in nature—one ISDN network for the globe. Unfortunately, ISDN has not achieved that goal.

ISDN offers high speed connections, much higher than the internal rates used by X.25 networks. Two interfaces are available to bring computer systems into the ISDN environment.

Basic Rate Interface (BRI)—The BRI attachment is composed of two 64-Kbps digital links (called the "B" channels) and one 16-Kbps link (called the "D" channel).

Primary Rate Interface (PRI)—The PRI attachment features twenty-three B channels (each at 64 Kbps) and an single "D" channel also operating at 64 Kbps.

In addition to the performance offered by ISDN over the "B" channels, the "D" channel can be used for special application functions. For example, the "D" channel can carry the network management protocol associated with the data transmitted on the "B" channel. Or the "D" channel may carry a customer identification transmitted by a PBX using one of the "D" channels for voice so the answering PBX can display the customer identifier when the phone starts ringing. In short, the "D" channel has applicability to both data and voice applications.

The AS/400 supports the BRI for ISDN connectivity.

14.2.5 Twinaxial Links

Twinaxial links are a special type of attachment used to connect 5250 workstations, print-ers, and PCs to a workstation controller. The workstation controller may be integrated in the AS/400, or it may be a separate external device. A workstation controller normally supports up to forty workstations and printers. These devices are usually distributed over eight twinaxial links, with each link supporting up to seven devices.

A twinaxial link, sometimes referred to as a Twinaxial Data Link Control (TDLC) link, is composed of two strands of cable carried in a protective sheath. Twinax links offer a speed of 1 Mbps, and attachment is made by chaining devices together using T-shaped connectors. Finally, note that the twinaxial system is different from and incompatible with the coaxial system used for IBM 3270 equipment.

14.2.6 LAN Links

LAN connectivity allows an AS/400 to communicate with other AS/400s, PCs, worksta-tions, other IBM systems, and even with non-IBM systems. The LAN environment pro-vides transmission speeds far above all of the other types of communications links. For example, even one "low-speed" token-ring LAN operating at 4 Mbps is faster than fifty 64 Kbps digital lines running in parallel.

The AS/400 supports two major groups of LANs, Ethernet/802.3 and IBM token-ring/802.5.

> Ethernet/802.3—Ethernet and 802.3 are actually different types of LANs, but they share so many similarities that they can be implemented on the same phys-ical network without interfering with one another. Both LANs provide operation at 10 Mbps, and both use a Carrier Sense, Multiple Access with Collision Detect (CSMA/CD) access discipline. In a nutshell, a device using CSMA/CD access "listens" to the LAN when it wants to transmit. If no activity is detected, it goes ahead and transmits. In the event that two devices transmit at the same time, both devices detect a data collision and attempt to retransmit.
>
> Ethernet was originally developed by the Xerox Corporation, but was subse-quently revised by Xerox, Intel Corporation, and Digital Equipment Corpora-tion in 1980. This later revision is sometimes referred to as Ethernet Version 2. The 802.3 standard was also developed in 1980 by the Institute of Electrical and Electronics Engineers (IEEE) as part of its 802 series of LAN standards. The

ability for Ethernet and 802.3 to co-exist on the same physical network was not the result of an accident.

IBM token-ring/802.5—IBM supports the official IEEE version of the 802.5 token-passing ring LAN and its own variation of that LAN. Both LANs support operation at 4 or 16 Mbps using a token-passing access discipline. Under the token-passing ring methodology, devices are connected in a logical ring and a special message, termed a "token," is passed from one device to another. The device that possesses the token can transmit a message. When that device then receives a positive or negative acknowledgment to the message, it relinquishes the token to the next logical device.

IBM has been a long-term user of token-ring technology and was a major contributor to the 1980 IEEE 802.5 standard. IBM does, however, occasionally enhance its own implementation of token-ring to include features that have been submitted to the IEEE for approval, but have not yet been incorporated into a formal revision of the 802.5 standard. In a very real sense, IBM is simply a step ahead in offering features (such as larger frame sizes or the use of multiple tokens) planned for future revisions of the standard. The use of these features is completely optional.

The advantage of token-ring over Ethernet/802.3 is that each device is guaranteed an opportunity to transmit; in an Ethernet/802.3 network, repeated collisions can delay and sometimes prevent transmissions. The disadvantage of token-ring, however, is that each device must wait for the opportunity to transmit, even if only one device has messages to send; in a lightly loaded Ethernet/802.3 network, the devices that need to send can dominate the network.

In terms of choosing a LAN for IBM AS/400-to-AS/400 or AS/400-to-mainframe connectivity, a 16-Mbps token-ring offers clear performance advantages over Ethernet/802.3. If system-to-system connectivity is not an issue, each type of LAN should be considered in its own right.

Finally, note that all supported LANs are included in the SNA suite, so they are capable of supporting the full range of AS/400 services. TCP/IP is also supported on all LANs, allowing an AS/400 to communicate with a wide variety of IBM and non-IBM equipment, as further discussed in the *TCP/IP* section of this chapter.

14.2.7 Communications Hierarchy

To configure an AS/400 for communications, you must provide descriptions for lines, controllers, and devices. Although some lines may have multiple controllers and some controllers may have multiple devices, each communication link must have at least one line, one controller, and one device description. The purpose of each of these three communications objects is as follows:

Line—A line description defines the operational characteristics for an external interface pertaining to a communications adapter housed in the AS/400. In particular, the line description sets the protocol, line speed, and physical interface for the line. If the adapter supports multiple connections (multiple lines), then a separate description is required for each connection.

Controller—A controller description defines a point of contact on a line. Normally, this point of contact is another computer, a workstation controller, or some other type of intelligent equipment. The controller-level definitions widely vary from one type of connection to another, but in general terms, the controller description defines timing, flow control, and data size characteristics. In many cases, multiple controllers can be defined for the same line, and all controllers can be used at once. This is particularly relevant to LANs where multiple controllers (multiple systems) share the same physical LAN.

Device—A device description defines the physical or logical devices associated with a controller. In some cases, a controller may have only one device associated with it; in other cases, multiple devices may be defined. For example, a device might be a workstation or a printer attached to a controller. Or, on the other extreme, a device might be a logical point of contact in another computer system. The device description defines the characteristics of the device relevant to the purpose of the communication. The device description may define, for example, the specific model number of a workstation or printer to the AS/400 so it can correctly format transmitted information (see Diagram 14–1).

If APPC or APPN communication links are used, additional communication objects are required.

Mode—A mode description, used for both APPC and APPN links, controls the number of sessions that can operate over a communication link. A session may be a workstation session, a program-to-program conversation, a remote file access request, or some other system-to-system service. A mode is associated with a device, and each device can sponsor multiple modes. Using multiple modes for one device is frequently used to set different levels for different types of services; in this scenario, workstation sessions would use one mode definition, and remote file access requests would use another mode.

Class-of-service—A class-of-service description is only used for APPN links. A class-of-service description is associated with every mode and defines, among other things, a transmission priority for the session traffic. This priority is used in an APPN network to determine the route that session traffic takes. This insures that high priority traffic does not have to compete with low priority traffic if multiple communication paths are available.

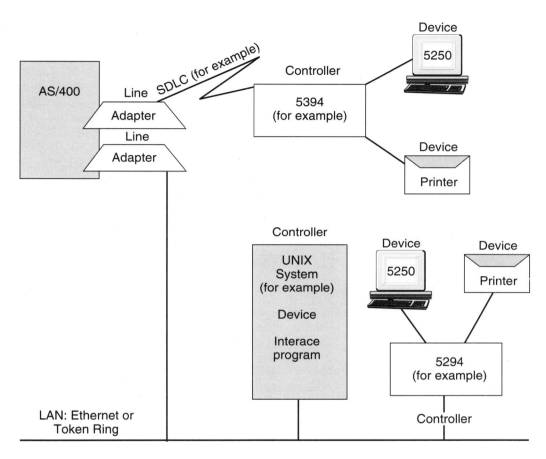

Diagram 14–1: Configuration for lines, controllers, and devices

If a TCP/IP communication link is used, the network controller and network device are usually automatically configured by the system. In addition, several other configuration steps must be taken. These additional steps are accessed from the Configure TCP/IP menu by issuing the GO CFGTCP command.

Other types of definitions may be appropriate for a communications network, depending on the mix of links and services. The communications configuration of an AS/400 can be easily changed—with the exception of adding or modifying internal hardware adapters, no system-level restart is required when line, controller, device, mode, or class-of-service descriptions are deleted or changed.

14.3 WORKSTATION CONNECTIVITY

In the AS/400 environment, a workstation or printer is attached to a controller, which, in turn, interfaces with an AS/400 system. The workstation controller may be a totally separate unit (for example, the 5294 and 5394 controllers), or the controller may be integrated into a communications adapter which is housed inside the AS/400 itself. In both cases, a controller supports a number of ports to accommodate workstation connectivity (see Diagram 14–2):

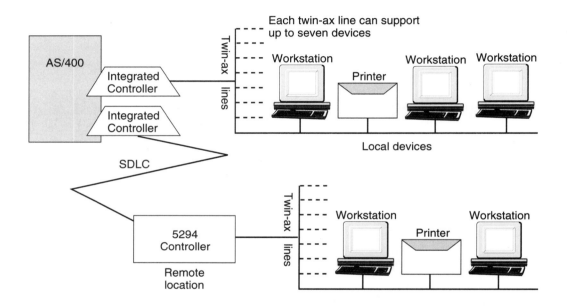

Diagram 14–2: Workstation connectivity

An external controller is normally used to accommodate workstations that are remotely located from the main AS/400 system. The connection between the external controller and the AS/400 is typically an SDLC link that can operate over local wiring, over analog phone lines, or over high-speed digital links. This architecture provides efficient, hierarchical connectivity for workstations dispersed over a wide geographical area.

The connection between a workstation and a controller can be an asynchronous link or, more commonly, a twinaxial link. When an asynchronous link is used, each workstation or printer consumes one port on the controller. When a twinaxial link is used, up to seven workstations or printers share a common twinax connection to one port.

14.4 APPN VERSUS APPC

Advanced Program-to-Program Communication (APPC) and Advanced Peer-to-Peer Networking (APPN) are terms used frequently to discuss two aspects of IBM's SNA. Specifically, APPC refers to the ability for application programs to communicate with one another using the SNA Logical Unit 6.2 (LU 6.2) format for communications. APPN, on the other hand, refers to the ability for Physical Unit 2.1 (PU 2.1) devices, such as an AS/400, to route messages to other systems in the network—with APPN, a system can communicate with systems to which it is not physically connected.

In the AS/400 environment, the terms APPC and APPN are also used to describe a communications link. In particular

APPC describes a communications link where an AS/400 may communicate with other AS/400s (or other PU 2.1 devices) provided there is a direct link. The LU 6.2 format is used for communications over the link.

APPN describes a communications link where AS/400s (or other PU 2.1 devices) are handling message routing functions. For example, AS/400 "A" can send a message intended for AS/400 "C" to AS/400 "B," and AS/400 "B" will forward that message to AS/400 "C." APPN links support APPC communications, therefore, APPN is a superset of APPC.

As noted, both APPC and APPN rely on the PU 2.1 and LU 6.2 structures within SNA. The primary distinction between the two approaches is that APPN makes use of the routing capability available to PU 2.1 devices.

Only SNA-capable links may be described as APPC or APPN links. In terms of the AS/400, this means that SDLC, X.25, ISDN, Ethernet/802.3, and IBM token-ring/802.5 communications may be used for APPC and APPN links.

14.5 TCP/IP

The Transmission Control Protocol/Internet Protocol (TCP/IP) is often used to interconnect seemingly incompatible devices. The roots of TCP/IP extend into the United States Government's Department of Defense, which needed to implement a wide area network in the early 1970s to allow its vendors and research organizations to exchange information with one another. The resulting network, Arpanet, interconnected computer systems of all shapes, sizes, and manufacturers, and is still in use today.

Over time, TCP/IP has became the de facto network for UNIX systems and for those operating systems which are derivatives of UNIX (IBM AIX, HP-UX, DEC Ultrix, Sun Microsystems Solaris, OSF's DCE, to name a few). As the popularity of UNIX has grown, so has the popularity of TCP/IP. Furthermore, the fact that so many different systems (both

UNIX and non-UNIX) support TCP/IP make it an attractive candidate for solving interoperability problems.

TCP/IP itself is a set of protocols that can be applied to both local and wide area networks. The "TCP" part of TCP/IP controls operations in a single logical network while the "IP" part controls the flow of information between multiple logical networks. In addition to these core functions, TCP/IP implementations normally include four additional services, listed here.

> TELNET—TELNET allows a workstation on one system to access another system interactively. The type and sophistication of workstation emulation is dependent on the TELNET implementation. For example, IBM's implementation allows IBM workstations to emulate DEC VT 220 terminals during TELNET sessions. Similarly, third-party software is available on other systems (Unix, PCs, and so on) to allow terminals to emulate IBM 5250 workstations when accessing an AS/400 through TELNET. IBM 3270 workstation emulation, and many other types of terminal emulation are available in the market. TN5250 is a TELNET-based protocol that implements the 5250 data stream while using TELNET. This is the best TELNET choice when accessing AS/400 systems.

> File Transfer Protocol (FTP)—FTP facilitates the movement of files between systems in the TCP/IP network. FTP is normally implemented as an interactive program where you send and receive explicit files, however, some third-party implementations allow FTP to be used for batch-style file transfer. In addition, a CL program technique of overriding the standard input to FTP allows file transfers to take place in batch mode. FTP is a transfer facility and not a real-time file access facility (like DDM), so programs may not use FTP to open a remote file for read or write access. FTP is also not a "store and forward" mechanism like SNA Distribution Services (SNADS), so two systems using FTP to transfer files must both be operational and connected.

> Simple Mail Transfer Protocol (SMTP)—SMTP delivers electronic mail between devices participating in a TCP/IP network. In the context of the AS/400, Office/400 can use SMTP to send and receive mail with other IBM and non-IBM systems. SMTP may also be used without Office/400. This would be done when the AS/400 is implemented as an Internet mail server. The mail would be retrieved (and sent) from the Internet using SMTP, with POP3 (discussed below) used to provide mail access for client systems (usually PCs).

> Program-to-program connections (sockets)—TCP/IP allows programs to establish unique identities (normally numbers) for themselves on a system. This program identity is then combined with the system's network address to create a "socket." Once a program has made itself available as a socket, programs on other systems may request attachment to that socket and communicate with the associated program.

The IBM AS/400 supports TCP/IP with TELNET, FTP, SMTP, and program-to-program services on Token-Ring or Ethernet LANs, or serial or X.25 WAN links.

The newest versions of OS/400 (V3R2 for CISC machines, V3R7 for RISC machines) also support the ability to access the Internet or a private intranet with TCP/IP-based services. The AS/400 also can serve as an Internet or intranet server with these capabilities. The new TCP/IP functions are described below.

14.5.1 HyperText Transport Protocol (HTTP) Server

The HTTP Server enables the AS/400 to host World Wide Web (WWW) pages. Web pages constructed with HyperText Markup Language (HTML) may be placed in an AS/400 file system. A WWW browser, such as Netscape Navigator or Microsoft Internet Explorer, can then access the Web page. A full implementation of HTTP serving is provided by OS/400, with HTML document serving, clickable maps, CGI-Bin application support, and user and error logging all available as standard functions.

The HTML pages would be developed on a PC or Unix system with any of the standard tools, such as SoftQuad's HoT MetaL, Sausage Software's Hot Dog Pro, or Microsoft's Front Page. These tools have no knowledge of an AS/400; they simply create the HTML pages that can be served from any HTTP server. This is the important message about the AS/400's Web server capability: It is the same server capability that exists on traditional Unix-based or Windows NT systems.

The file system being used for HTTP serving bears discussion. While almost any of the file systems may be used, certain file systems have characteristics which help or hinder Web serving. For instance, the fastest Web serving file system is the Root (/) file system. Storing the Web pages in their native ASCII format, and retrieving the pages with a Web browser, is the highest speed transfer scenario. No translation (from EBCDIC to ASCII) is needed, and the structure of the file system also is the same as a PC or Unix system that was probably used to create the Web pages. Web developers will find that property most helpful. The QDLS file system, used for folders on the AS/400 (including Client Access shared folders), is the next best choice for a storage area for Web pages. The QDLS file system is rated at approximately 75 percent of the speed of the Root file system. An advantage of the QDLS file system is the ease of integration with Client Access, especially the mapping of a folder in the QDLS file system with a drive on a PC. Another file system that may be used is the traditional QSYS.LIB file system. This is the system used to accommodate the library/file/member structure in use on all AS/400 systems. A drawback with using this file system is that the pages are stored in EBCDIC. This requires a translation of the Web page *every* time the page is accessed. Unneeded overhead is required on the AS/400 to accommodate the translation. The QSYS.LIB file system functions at approximately 45 percent of the speed of the Root file system.

The configuration of the HTTP server is not difficult, but a knowledge of HTTP server directives is helpful in the case of advanced configuration. The directives needed for basic Web page access are simple. IBM ships a default configuration file that contains the directives needed for most operations. The directives will need to be "uncommented" to be used for HTTP serving. The OS/400 command to configure the HTTP server is Work with HTTP Configuration (WRKHTTPCFG). Issuing this command will produce the following screen (see Figure 14–2):

```
as400                                                                    _ □ ×
Commands Edit Options Help
                        Work with HTTP Configuration
                                                     System:   APPLSPEC
Type options, press Enter.
   1=Add    2=Change   3=Copy    4=Remove    5=Display    13=Insert

        Sequence
Opt     Number     Entry

   _     00010     # * * * * * * * * * * * * * * * * * * * * * * * * * *   >
   _     00020     # HTTP DEFAULT CONFIGURATION                            >
   _     00030     # * * * * * * * * * * * * * * * * * * * * * * * * * *   >
   _     00040     #                                                       >
   _     00050     #                                                       >
   _     00060     HostName                applspec.com
   _     00070     #                                                       >
   _     00080     #  The default port for HTTP is 80;  Should specify por >
   _     00090     #  if port 80 is not used.                              >
   _     00100     Port                       80
   _     00110     #                                                       >
   _     00120     Enable                     GET
                                                              More...
F3=Exit   F5=Refresh   F6=Print List   F12=Cancel   F17=Top   F18=Bottom
F19=Edit Sequence
```

Figure 14–2: WRKHTTPCFG display

The WRKHTTPCFG provides a list of server directives that may be modified to allow or prohibit access, describe the Welcome (or initial) Web page, and to identify CGI programs.

This HTTP server capability makes the AS/400 a full-function Web server. The HTTP server allows Common Gateway Interface (CGI) programs to interact with an HTML form. The CGI programs can be written in any ILE language with Application Programming Interfaces (API) used to access the HTML form data. Another aspect of the HTTP server capability on the AS/400 is the Net.Data or DB2WWW function. The Net.Data function (known as DB2WWW in an earlier release of the product) joins the use of HTML form entry (as described above) with the power of the DB2/400 in a simple, easy-to-implement method. While CGI processing allows complete access to any information and processing on the AS/400 (of course subject to security restrictions), programming in CGI is more difficult than using Net.Data since high-level language programs must be written using APIs. Net.Data uses HTML forms and macros to enable queries of the DB2/400 data. The actual queries are implemented as Structured Query Language statements that are executed against the database. The process works as follows:

- An HTML form is displayed on the browser screen.
- The user enters data into the form.
- The data is entered (by Net.Data) into an SQL call.
- The SQL call is executed against the database.
- The query result is returned to the browser as a report form.

With the World Wide Web being the most popularly used innovation on the Internet, the capabilities of the HTTP server function on the AS/400 provide the ability for all AS/400 installations to immediately provide a presence on the Internet.

14.5.2 5250 HTML Workstation Gateway

The Workstation Gateway (WSG) enables a Web browser to access familiar AS/400 "green screen" applications. This means that a user could have only one software application (a Web browser) to access both the Internet and AS/400 programs. No modification is needed to the AS/400 applications; the WSG will translate the 5250 data stream to a HyperText Markup Language (HTML) data stream automatically. Fields, constants, and attributes contained in the 5250 data stream are changed to corresponding HTML tag equivalents.

An example of the standard sign on screen when accessed with traditional methods is shown in Figure 14–3.

The same screen, but accessed through the 5250 HTML WSG, is shown in Figure 14–4.

Here is the HTML output produced by the 5250 HTML WSG to display the sign on screen (see Figure 14–5).

While existing display files do not need to be changed, a new DDS keyword, HTML, can be used to place HTML tag language in the display file, and consequently in the data stream presented to a Web browser. This allows any HTML tag to be presented, including images. The HTML tags are ignored if the data stream is sent to a nonbrowser device.

Currently, the Web browser is not attached to the WSG process on the AS/400. This means that use of the "Back" or "Forward" keys on the Web browser (or other navigation keys) do not change the state of the AS/400 application. For example, when accessing an AS/400 application, the user will press CF03 to exit an application. A Web browser user may press the "Back" key to access the previously displayed page. This will also work with the WSG but with unexpected and probably undesired results. While the Web browser will show the previously displayed page, nothing changes on the AS/400. The application on the AS/400 still thinks that the current page is being displayed. Entering information on a previously displayed page in this fashion will cause the WSG to issue an error message such as "Not the active 5250/HTML WSG panel." This indicates that the displayed page is not the current page. Another aspect of this "nonattachment" is that the function keys on the keyboard cannot be used for AS/400 applications. The WSG provides the ability to enter function keys from a list, but the user cannot press a function key and have the application realize that a key has been pressed. This can be changed with Java applications executing within the Web browser; Java applets for 5250 emulation will resolve this problem.

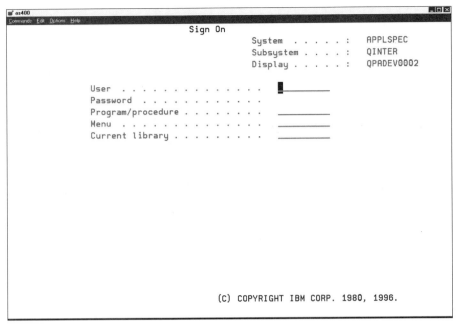

Figure 14–3: Traditional green screen sign on display

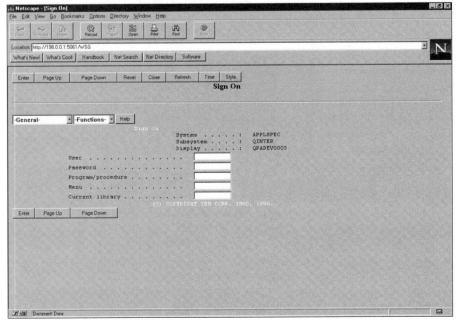

Figure 14–4: WSG sign on display

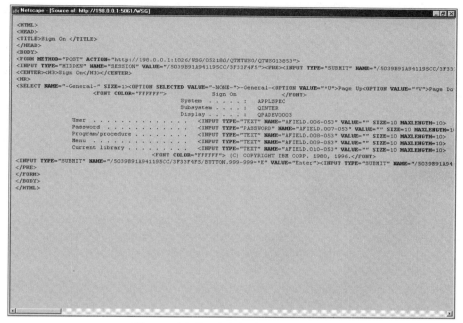

Figure 14–5: WSG sign on source

14.5.3 POP3 Mail Serving

The Post Office Protocol 3 (POP3) support on the AS/400 provides the capability for POP3 compliant mail software clients to access mail stored on the AS/400. POP3, which is an acronym for Post Office Protocol 3, is a popular mail protocol and is used by Netscape, Eudora, and many other mail software products. The configuration is simple on the AS/400, and when combined with the Simple Mail Transport Protocol (SMTP) support already available with OS/400, the AS/400 can be a mail server for Internet mail.

14.5.4 TCP/IP Security

The new TCP/IP capabilities and services open the AS/400 to the Internet, and all the exciting possibilities for business and interaction that exist within. However, openness can also cause problems. The traditional role of an AS/400 was as a departmental or company system that interoperated with other known systems. Security could be handled within an organization, and the system or systems would have the appropriate security levels to accommodate the needs of the organization.

The AS/400 has a well-designed architecture. All OS/400 programs, files, and other constructs are implemented as objects. This object orientation means that a virus cannot be introduced into AS/400 programs from the Internet (without actually transferring an AS/400 object). In addition, the resource security of the AS/400 is embedded within the objects, meaning that security is an integral part of the object that cannot easily be compromised. Another security benefit is that AS/400 systems are not well known in the hacker or cracker communities. Be assured that this will change as more AS/400 systems are connected to the Internet.

However, the new TCP/IP capabilities create security exposures that many AS/400 installations have not had to face. Connecting to the Internet exposes the AS/400 to security problems that must be dealt with, or violations may occur. IBM provides the Security Toolkit, which is a no-cost Request for Price Quotation (RPQ) at OS/400 levels V3R1 and earlier and V3R6. This security capability is part of OS/400 V3R2 and V3R7; use the GO SECTOOLS command to access the security toolkit. This RPQ or command will analyze default passwords, work with user profiles, and allow activation or expiration of user ids based on a schedule. Consider using the Security Toolkit and ensure your AS/400 is at least at Level 30 security before attaching to the Internet.

14.6 CLIENT ACCESS/400

14.6.1 The Evolution of Client/Server Computing

In the early 1980s, personal computers (PCs) were deployed as stand-alone units for specific desktop applications. Software for PCs was limited at that time; therefore, PCs were relegated to isolated areas. However, as the number of mainstream business applications increased (for example, spreadsheets, word processing, database, and graphics), the number of PCs in company departments increased as well.

The rollout of PCs to end-user desktops create two significant problems in corporate mainframe or midrange computer environments. First, PC users who needed access to corporate applications found they needed two devices on their desktops—a terminal for corporate application access and a PC for desktop applications. Secondly, PC users wanted the information stored on the corporate computer to also be available on their local PCs. This raised additional issues regarding data duplication and centralized information control.

In short order, PC-oriented hardware and software manufacturers came up with solutions to both of these problems. To address the issue of desktop real estate, terminal emulation software and hardware was introduced into PCs. Using these products, a PC could be attached to the corporate computer and function as a traditional terminal unit. This eliminated the need for both a terminal and a PC on the desktop.

To solve the issue of information access, file-transfer capabilities were introduced to the PC. Thus, an accounting user could, for example, extract information from a corporate database, download it to a local PC, and manipulate the data using a spreadsheet program. If information needed to go back to the corporate computer, it could be uploaded into a separate file and then processed as batch input to the database. This two-step approach protected the integrity of the corporate databases.

These solutions were effective, but they only addressed the pressing and obvious needs of terminal access and file transfer between desktop PCs and corporate computers. As PCs and PC software grew more powerful, the end-user community expressed need for new capabilities—they wanted to share information between PCs, share printers, and even share applications.

In the mid–1980s companies such as Novell, Davong, and 3Com responded to these needs by bringing the concept of peer-to-peer networking to the PC community. These companies offered PC solutions that allowed PC users in a small, local geographical area to share files, printers, and programs, as well as other PC-oriented resources.

With the advent of these peer-oriented PC LAN solutions, terminal and file-transfer access to the corporate computer seemed, by comparison, to be pretty crude and ineffective. In a PC LAN environment, if a file needed to move from one user to another, the standard DOS COPY command could do the job quickly and efficiently. Similarly, if access to a special application was required, a user just had to access the logical disk drive containing it and run the application. The PC LAN solution provided a nearly seamless interface between resource sharing and the normal DOS environment.

Access to the corporate computer, however, involved entirely different procedures, procedures that required separate user names, passwords, access rights, and other technical considerations. As a general rule, the terminal and file transfer interfaces were cruder and more difficult to use than any of the PC LAN tools. Users that needed to access PC LAN resources and corporate computer resources had to learn to live by two sets of rules and procedures.

As PC LANs grew bigger, and as the applications that could run in the LAN environment became more sophisticated, the power of the distributed PC environment started to affect the corporate computer world. Budgets for point-to-point terminal lines were reallocated for LAN connectivity. Corporate computer applications were forced to import and export data in formats compatible with PC applications. And, in many cases, traditional corporate computer-based applications were abandoned in favor of PC LAN software.

The growth of PC LANs forced the computer manufacturing and data processing community to take serious notice of PC LAN technology. Computer manufacturers, such as IBM and Digital Equipment, responded by developing products that offered new levels of cooperation and synergy between PC LANs and corporate computers. This is where client/server computing got a foothold in corporate computing environments; and more importantly this is where Client Access/400 got its start.

14.6.2 The Client Access/400 Solution

The AS/400 implementation of CA/400 is an attempt to find a middle ground between centralized computing functions performed on an AS/400 and distributed computing functions performed in a PC LAN environment. In the broader spectrum that encompasses all computer platforms, CA/400 is not unique. For example, Digital Equipment Corporation offers a PC product named "Pathworks" and Sun Microsystems sells a PC product named "PC-NFS," both of which offer functionality similar to CA/400.

The CA/400 family of products grew and matured alongside the AS/400. When the AS/400 was introduced in the late 1980s, the product was termed "PC Support," a name borrowed from a PC System/36 integration product that offered similar functions. The PC Support name remained in place until 1994 when IBM decided to catch the wave of the client/server mania that was sweeping the industry. Therefore, IBM reintroduced PC Support as "Client Access/400" (CA/400) in 1994.

CA/400, Pathworks, PC-NFS, and other similar products provide a high degree of integration between the PC LAN environment and the corporate computer environment. CA/400 provides this integration through the use of both PC-resident and AS/400-resident software, although the majority of CA/400 software resides on the PC. This software allows CA/400 to provide a broad range of integration functions.

For example, CA/400 terminal-access and file-transfer functions address the traditional corporate computing model where the AS/400 is the central source for information. In terms of terminal access, CA/400 includes software that emulates IBM 5250 terminals. CA/400 allows a single PC to initiate multiple terminal sessions with one or more AS/400 systems. This aspect of CA/400 is used to access traditional "green-screen" AS/400-resident applications.

For file transfer, CA/400 includes a program that facilitates the movement of files or file members between a PC and an AS/400 host. This CA/400 facility can transfer all records within a member or it can transfer record subsets (that is, particular fields within a file). Rudimentary reformatting capabilities are provided to deliver AS/400 information in a usable format on the PC.

CA/400 also includes more advanced distributed and client/server capabilities that take advantage of the capabilities of a PC LAN. These capabilities include

- File sharing—CA/400 allows one or more libraries on an AS/400 disk to be allocated for use by CA/400 workstations as network drives. These network drives can be used to share information among CA/400 users (analogous to file sharing on a PC LAN), or to exchange information between CA/400 workstations and the AS/400 acting as the file server.

- Printer sharing—CA/400 enables a PC to use an AS/400-attached printer as if it were a direct-attached printer. Similarly, a printer directly attached to a CA/400 workstation can be used by an AS/400 as a system printer.

- Client/server programming—CA/400 includes Application Program Interfaces (APIs) that allow PC-resident programs to access AS/400-resident system resources, including AS/400 applications. This technology allows CA/400 programs to communicate with AS/400 programs using either a client/server or peer-oriented architecture to implement highly integrated, distributed computing solutions.

CA/400 provides additional functions, such as the ability to submit commands to an AS/400 from the PC environment, the ability to access AS/400 message queues, as well as other utilities.

CA/400 runs in a number of communications environments. For example, CA/400 can run in a Token-Ring or an Ethernet LAN environment, much like other PC LAN solutions. However, unlike PC LAN solutions, CA/400 can also operate over other types of communications connections, such as twinaxial, asynchronous, and synchronous links. Support for nonLAN connections means that CA/400 can be used to implement many of the advantages of a PC LAN solution without actually installing a LAN.

In the case where the PCs are already functioning in a LAN environment, CA/400 can operate alongside other PC LAN products, such as Novell NetWare, Banyan VINES, IBM LAN Server, or Microsoft's LAN Manager, Windows for Workgroups, Windows 95, or Windows NT. The combined solution of CA/400 and another PC LAN product offers the best of all worlds—you get the centralized and client/server functions of CA/400 and the distributed functions of the PC LAN product.

14.6.3 CA/400 Operating Environments

In today's market, there is no single PC operating system that dominates the entire market. As a result, versions of CA/400 are available to address the following operating system environments:

- Standard ("basic") DOS—Any PC running MS-DOS/PC-DOS Version 3.3 (or later).
- Extended DOS—A PC with an 80286, 80386, 80486, or Pentium processor running MS-DOS/PC-DOS Version 3.3 (or later). The base system must included at least 384 KB of extended memory (memory above 640 KB).
- OS/2—A PC or PS/2 computer with an 80386, 80486, or Pentium processor running IBM's OS/2 multitasking operating system version 1.3 (or later).
- Windows—A PC with an 80386, 80486, or Pentium processor running Windows 3.10, Windows 3.11, Windows for Workgroups 3.10, or Windows for Workgroups 3.11.
- Windows 95—A PC with an 80386, 80486, or Pentium processor running Windows 95.
- Windows NT—A PC with an 80486, or Pentium processor running Windows NT Workstation 4.0 (or later).

Although the CA/400 implementations for these environments offer similar capabilities, they do not offer identical capabilities. For example, the Standard DOS implementation of CA/400 does not support access to AS/400 data queues (for program-to-program communication); however, the other implementations do.

Similarly, CA/400 for Windows also includes a number of features not available in CA/400 for Standard DOS or Extended DOS. This includes the ability to function over a Transmission Control Protocol/Internet Protocol (TCP/IP) link (via SNA tunneling), support for Open DataBase Connectivity (ODBC), additional Windows-related Application Program Interfaces (APIs), and more.

One final but very significant difference is the network protocols supported by the Windows 95 and Windows NT versions of CA/400. These CA/400 implementations can operate over SNA, native TCP/IP (no tunneling), or IPX. The other implementations are currently restricted to SNA and SNA tunneling through TCP/IP. (IBM is planning on addressing these limitations in future CA/400 releases.) Version 3.1 or later of OS/400 is required to support native TCP/IP and IPX CA400 attachments.

14.6.4 CA/400 Components

The specific modules and module names for the components that make up CA/400 vary from one CA/400 implementation to the next. However, the significant components found in most of the CA/400 implementations are as follows:

- CA/400 Router—The router component provides the core SNA communications functions for all the CA/400 components and is also responsible for handling many of the Application Program Interfaces (APIs) available to PC-based user application programs. In brief, the router provides a high-level interface (LU 6.2) that isolates the PC-based programs from the characteristics of the physical communications attachment (twinax, SDLC, LAN, and so on).

- CA/400 Connections—In the Windows 95 and Windows NT implementations of CA/400, an additional communications component, the AS/400 Connections component, supervises CA/400 communication over SNA, TCP/IP, and IPX. In the case of SNA, the Connections component routes data through the CA/400 router, as previously described. For TCP/IP and IPX, the AS/400 Connections component routes the data through the standard Windows 95/NT TCP/IP or IPX interface.

- Workstation/Printer Emulation—5250 workstation emulation and printer emulation (to receive print originating from an AS/400) are handled by the same component. Over the history of CA/400, a variety of modules have been used for this purpose; the DOS implementation uses a character-mode workstation/printer emulation program and the Windows implementation included two different workstation/printer emulation programs (Rumba and PC5250). The Windows 95/NT implementation includes just PC5250 for workstation/printer emulation; however, printer emulation is not supported over the native TCP/IP or IPX protocols. In all CA/400 implementations, each PC client can host multiple workstation and printer emulation sessions.

NOTE: All of the Windows-based CA/400 implementations include a separate GUI-based workstation emulator. This provides a more intuitive look and feel, but it does not support printer emulation.

- Shared Folders (Network Drives)—The shared folders facility allows that AS/400 to act as a network file server. In addition to providing a means for sharing files between PCs, the shared folders facility also allows files to be shared between PCs and AS/400 applications. A DOS or Windows PC using shared folders simply assigns a folder to a network drive letter (for example, I:). A Windows 95 or Windows NT PC opens it as a desktop folder via the Network Neighborhood facility. In all cases, once the connection is in place, the PC can read and write to that drive/folder as if it were a local resource.

- Virtual Printer—The virtual printer component enables print routing from a PC to an AS/400-attached printer. When this feature is enabled, PC programs can send output to a local printer definition and CA/400 will redirect that output to an AS/400 output queue.

- Data Transfer—The data transfer component provides a controlled and structured means for transferring information between the PC and the AS/400 CA/400 server. Entire files may be transferred, or information can be filtered based on field-level values. A variety of different modules have been used to provide this function in the various CA/400 implementations, however, they all support both interactive and batch operation, and they all support conversion into and out of several PC file formats.

- Message Access—Message access allows the PC to send and receive information to and from AS/400 message queues. This facility is normally used as a means by which you can send and receive messages to and from other AS/400 users.

- Submit Remote Command—The submit remote command component can be used to send either a single AS/400 CL command or a file containing a series of CL commands. The AS/400 response to each CL command is returned to the CA/400 workstation for display.

- CA/400 ODBC—All of the Windows implementations (but none of the DOS implementations) contain the necessary drivers and supporting routines to enable ODBC access to AS/400 files. ODBC can be used to connect existing business applications (for example, Word, Excel, Access) to AS/400 information without new or custom programming.

- CA/400 Update—The update component is used to examine the CA/400 files on the PC to ensure they are at the same levels (for example, the most recent versions) as the files contained in a control folder on the AS/400 server. If files are not the same, the update function automatically copies the more current versions from the AS/400 to the PC. The update component can also be applied to user-specified file sets.

- Programming Interfaces—CA/400 supports a variety of APIs to enable program-to-program or client/server communications between PC-based programs. Some of the

APIs, such as the Enhanced High-Level Language API (EHLLAPI), allow PC-based programs to appear as workstations to the AS/400, while others, such as data queues, provide an asynchronous means of sending and receiving messages. The exact programming interfaces are very dependent on the CA/400 implementation and on the network protocol in use.

In addition to these core components, all of the CA/400 implementations contain comprehensive help and configuration functions. Furthermore, the DOS implementations of CA/400 also contain components to provide better integration between the DOS and AS/400 working environments. Those components include

- Session Manager—The Session Manager is a memory-resident module that arranges terminal/printer emulation sessions and DOS sessions into character-oriented windows on the PC screen. These windows may be moved and resized as desired by the operator. The active window can be selected through the use of a hot-key sequence or via a mouse. Session Manager allows the CA/400 operator to have a glimpse of the activity in each session without having to hot-key through multiple, full-screen sessions.
- PC Organizer—The PC Organizer module is a memory-resident module that works in conjunction with the workstation emulation component. The organizer allows both PC and AS/400 host applications to be launched from a common terminal session menu.
- CA/400 Menu—This foreground program provides a menu-driven method for accessing CA/400 configuration and interactive usage modules.

14.6.5 CA/400 and Physical Networks

As previously mentioned, CA/400 can operate in a LAN environment like conventional PC LAN solutions do, or it can function over conventional communications links. The specific connections supported by CA/400 include

- 4 Mbps or 16 Mbps Token-Ring/802.5 LAN
- 10 Mbps Ethernet/802.3 LAN
- 1 Mbps twinaxial link
- SDLC link (at rates up to 64 Kbps)
- Remote workstation controller attachment
- Asynchronous link (at rates up to 19.2 Kbps)

Although many features of CA/400 may not be unique within the computer industry, no other PC integration product offers such a range of connectivity options. From a broad perspective, CA/00 connections can be broken into the following two categories:

1. Local connections—If the CA/400 workstations are in the same physical location as the AS/400 server, then the ideal connection is either a Token-Ring or Ethernet LAN. Both of these LAN environments provide performance and expandability that ranges above and beyond all the other types of connections. In the absence of a LAN, twinaxial links offer the next best compromise for performance and number of connections.

2. Remote connections—When CA/400 workstations are not located near the AS/400 server, the options are different. Point-to-point leased or dial-in connections can be made using either asynchronous or SDLC links. If the CA/400 workstations are colocated with other terminals, or if there are multiple CA/400 workstations at one location, a remote workstation controller can be used to interface a number of CA/400 workstations over a single SDLC link or X.25 connection back to the AS/400 server.

Also note that each type of connection has a matching hardware component in the AS/400 server. For example, asynchronous connections require ports on an ASCII workstation controller or third-party protocol converter, SDLC connections require unused SDLC ports, LAN connections require LAN adapters, and twinax connections require a twinaxial workstation controller.

14.6.6 CA/400 and PC LAN Products

The PC LAN environment that exists today is primarily the result of the development efforts of Novell, IBM, Microsoft, and 3Com. Of these four manufacturers, IBM, Microsoft, and 3Com all traveled similar paths in the development of PC LAN technology and created two popular LAN "protocols": NETBIOS and Server Message Block (SMB).

Together NETBIOS and SMB provide the interface between PC-based applications and network services: NETBIOS provides the protocol services required to communicate with a server or with other PCs in the LAN. SMB provides the interface for remote file and print access. IBM and Microsoft developed their own implementations of the NETBIOS and SMB protocols; however, these implementations are compatible with one another and live on today as part of IBM's PC LAN and OS/2 LAN Server products and Microsoft's LAN Manager, Windows for Workgroups, Windows 95, and Windows NT products.

Novell followed a different technical path to arrive at NetWare; therefore, NetWare does not conform to the NETBIOS/SMB model (although NetWare can emulate the NETBIOS protocol when necessary). Under the NetWare scheme, the Novell IPX protocol provides services that are equivalent to both the NETBIOS and SMB protocol.

Both styles of PC LANs, NetWare and SMB/NETBIOS, offer services similar to CA/400. For example, they facilitate file sharing, printer sharing, and program-to-program communications in a LAN environment. But despite these similarities, CA/400 and PC LAN implementations have significant differences.

One of the biggest differences is in the area of performance. Because the file services for CA/400 are processing within an AS/400, they must compete with OS/400 operating system services and application programs for processor and memory resources. This means that performance of network services can be less than ideal when an AS/400 is heavily loaded. In contrast, PC LAN implementations generally use a server that is solely dedicated to providing network services.

Another key difference is the level of AS/400 integration. The degree of integration between a PC and an AS/400 system that CA/400 provides cannot be achieved through a PC LAN solution. In this respect, CA/400 does it all—terminal emulation, file sharing, file transfer, printer sharing, program-to-program communications, and more. To try to build a similar solution around a PC LAN implementation would require the addition of a number of products (such as terminal emulators and file transfer utilities) and often deployment of a gateway to facilitate the physical connection.

Clearly, both CA/400 and PC LAN implementations have their own distinct advantages. Fortunately, one choice does not exclude the other—implementing CA/400 does not lock out the possible implementation of a PC LAN (and vice versa). Both types of products can be implemented in the same PC and on the same LAN.

15

Advanced Topics

The AS/400 contains a large number of features oriented toward advanced users. Information about many of these topics may be obtained through the on-line help and education facilities explained in Chapter 1 ("Getting Started"). Additional material can be found in the documentation provided by IBM.

Several advanced topics, however, are worth discussing in the context of this book. This chapter will familiarize you with: the System Request menu; initiating an alternate session; system values; AS/400 Systems Query Language (SQL) implementation; IBM Systems Application Architecture (SAA) concepts; and the RISC AS/400 systems.

15.1 THE SYSTEM REQUEST MENU

The System Request menu serves several purposes: it can be used to display information about your working environment; to access message queues; and to launch and manage alternate AS/400 sessions. Access to the System Request menu is gained through the <SYSRQ> key or key sequence (<SHIFT> and <SYSRQ> on a 122-key workstation). The <SYSRQ> key is unusual because it can be used even if your workstation is inhibited for input.

Once the key is pressed, a data entry line appears on the bottom of the screen. If you know in advance which System Request menu option you want to invoke, you can enter the menu number on this line and press <ENTER>. If, however, you want to access the menu, simply press <ENTER> when the data entry line appears.

NOTE: The System Request function may be disabled by the system administrator (see Figure 15–1).

The System Request menu contains the following options:

1. (Display sign-on for alternative job)—allows you to start a new (alternate) session while retaining your current session. In effect, this allows you to have two active sessions through one workstation address. Please see the *Alternate Sign On* section of this chapter for more information. Note that the current session will be suspended until it is terminated or resumed.

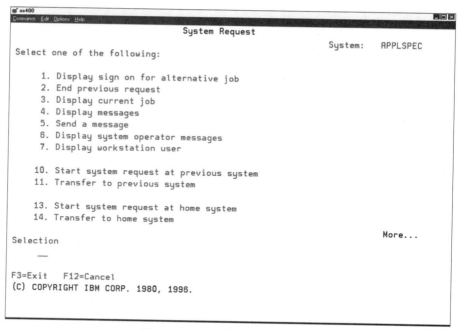

Figure 15–1: System Request

2. (End previous request)—terminates the program you are accessing. When this option is invoked, all files associated with the program are closed normally, and any data you may have input is retained. In practical terms, this option may be used if you have initiated a command or procedure that will take more time to process than you have patience for—for example, if you inadvertently requested a list of all files on disk. Since the <SYSRQ> key is available even if your workstation is inhibited from input, you can go to the System Request menu and cancel the request.

3. (Display current job)—brings up another menu allowing you to select specific job information to view. From this menu you can obtain information about job attributes, spooled files, open files, and other aspects of the job environment.

4. (Display messages)—shows messages logged for your user and workstation. This is equivalent to performing a DSPMSG command on your user and workstation queues. The advantage of performing this operation from the System Request menu is that it allows you to display these messages without having to exit from your current program.

5. (Send messages)—allows you to place messages in user or workstation queues. The most common use for this option is to send short messages to the system operator (QSYSOPR) or other users.

6. (Display system operator messages)—shows messages logged for the system operator (QSYSOPR). This is the equivalent of performing a DSPMSG command for the QSYSOPR user. The advantage of performing this operation from the System Request menu is that it allows you to display these messages without having to exit from your current program.

7. (Display workstation user)—shows information about your current session, including your user name, workstation name, and current interactive jobs. This option is also useful for determining who is signed on an unattended workstation.

20. (Set inquiry condition for S/36 programs)—If you are operating in the System/36 environment (normally used for compatibility), this option may be used to set an inquiry flag used by programs also operating in the System/36 environment.

80. (Disconnect job)—suspends activity on the primary and alternate sessions and places the sign-on menu on your workstation. When you sign back in, your activities are resumed. This option allows you to "park" your workstation activity while you pursue other matters, and then return to them at a later time.

90. (Sign-off)—signs you off the current session. You are asked to confirm the sign-off operation by pressing the <ENTER> key.

While at the System Request menu, you may use either <F3> or <F12> to exit from the menu. If you have two sessions active, you will be returned to the session which was active when you pressed the <SYSRQ> key.

15.2 ALTERNATE SIGN-ON

Option 1 (Display sign-on for alternative job) from the System Request menu allows you to initiate a second session from the same workstation. After you select 1, you will receive the standard Sign-On menu, allowing you to start your alternate session. For example, from the User Support and Education menu, you could press <SYSRQ>, select option 1, and you would receive a Sign-On menu (see Figures 15–2 through 15–4).

After you complete your alternate sign-on, you can transfer back and forth between the two sessions by using the <SYSRQ> key and specifying option 1 (Transfer to alternate job) on the System Request menu. Note that options 1 and 90 have slightly altered meanings when an alternate session is established (see Figure 15–5).

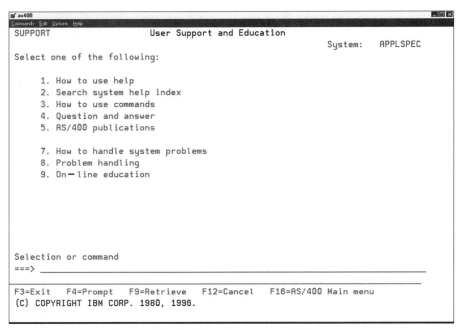

Figure 15–2: User Support and Education

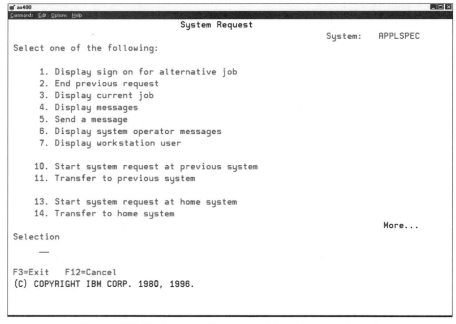

Figure 15–3: System Request with option 1 selected

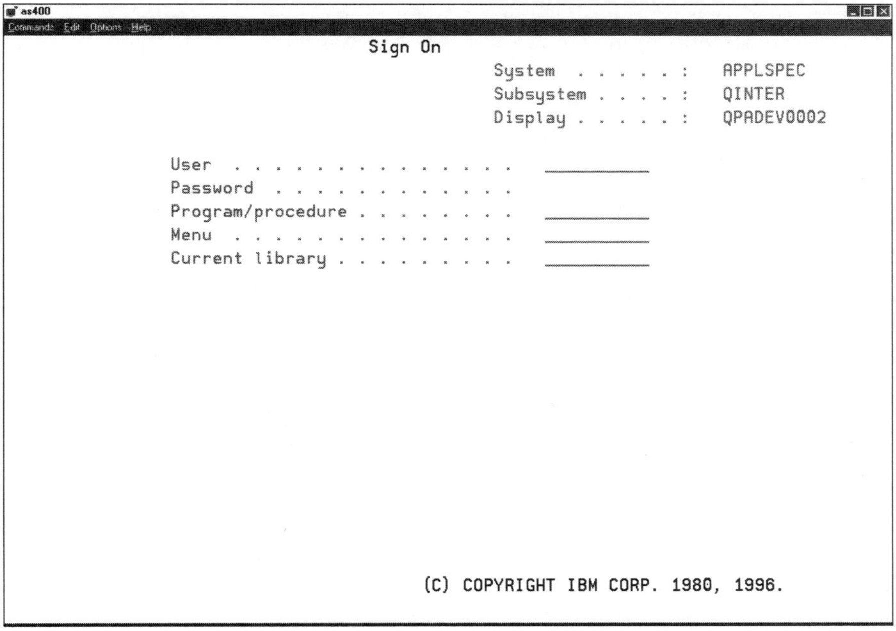

```
as400                                                               _ □ ×
Commands  Edit  Options  Help
                              Sign On
                                       System  . . . . . :    APPLSPEC
                                       Subsystem . . . . :    QINTER
                                       Display . . . . . :    QPADEV0002

          User  . . . . . . . . . . . . . .      _____
          Password  . . . . . . . . . . . .      _____
          Program/procedure . . . . . . . .      _____
          Menu  . . . . . . . . . . . . . .      _____
          Current library . . . . . . . . .      _____
```

```
                              (C) COPYRIGHT IBM CORP. 1980, 1996.
```

Figure 15–4: Sign On

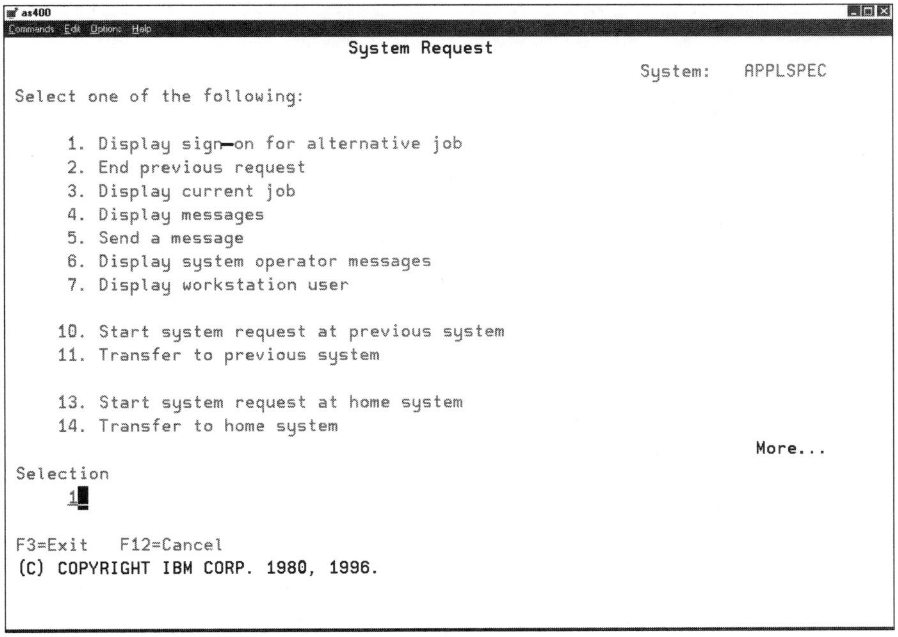

```
as400                                                               _ □ ×
Commands  Edit  Options  Help
                           System Request
                                              System:   APPLSPEC
     Select one of the following:

          1. Display sign-on for alternative job
          2. End previous request
          3. Display current job
          4. Display messages
          5. Send a message
          6. Display system operator messages
          7. Display workstation user

         10. Start system request at previous system
         11. Transfer to previous system

         13. Start system request at home system
         14. Transfer to home system
                                                         More...
     Selection
         1_

     F3=Exit   F12=Cancel
     (C) COPYRIGHT IBM CORP. 1980, 1996.
```

Figure 15–5: System Request for alternate session

Your alternate session is terminated when you sign off using the SIGN-OFF command, or if you select option 90 (Sign off and transfer to alternate job) from the System Request menu. After signing off, you are automatically placed in the other session.

15.3 SYSTEM VALUES

System values control many of the actions that take place within OS/400. These system values may only be accessed by the system administrator, but an understanding of the concept is important to understanding the working environment of OS/400.

System values provide default actions for many commands. A command parameter with an allowable value of *SYSVAL indicates that a system value may be used for the parameter. This provides a consistent action for users executing commands.

System values also contain information such as the current date and time which are often retrieved into CL programs. Other system values control the environment in which users will execute commands, the security level of the system, new and changed password rules, default message queues, and many other system characteristics.

The system values are divided into categories based on the type of operation they control. A category can be selected with the Work with System Value (WRKSYSVAL) command to subset the list of system values with which you wish to work. The categories of system values are

*ALC—The Allocation system values control the amount of disk or memory that may be allocated.

*DATTIM—The Date and Time system values contain the current date (month, day, and year) and the time.

*EDT—The Editing values determine the editing used on command displays for currency amounts and date/time separators.

*LIBL—The Library List system values contain the system and user library list values.

*MSG—The Message and Logging values set the level and type of messages and logging that will be done throughout the system.

*SEC—The Security system values determine the level of system security, password rules, and the action to be taken for unauthorized attempts to access the system.

*STG—The Storage values determine the default amount of initial storage used for new objects.

*SYSCTL—The System Control system values control the default response for many command parameters that are used for user interaction with the system.

The commands to display and manipulate the system values are

CHGSYSVAL—allows you to change a specific system value.

DSPSYSVAL—displays a specific system value.

RTVSYSVAL—used only in CL programs and will retrieve a system value into a CL program variable.

WRKSYSVAL—allows you to work with multiple system values.

15.4 STRUCTURED QUERY LANGUAGE (SQL)

The Structured Query Language (SQL) was developed by IBM and subsequently adopted by the American National Standards Institute (ANSI) as a system-independent mechanism for accessing information stored in files or databases. SQL is not, however, a programming language itself, rather it is an interface available for programming languages (RPG, C, COBOL, and others) and for interactive users.

In the AS/400 environment, SQL interfaces with physical and logical files; in essence, SQL is layered on top of the standard AS/400 file system, described in Chapter 3 ("Libraries, Files, and Members"). SQL also introduces several new information constructs to the topic of accessing data. They are as follows:

Tables—A table is an AS/400 physical file that will be read from or written to during SQL access. The information contained in a table is then further broken down into rows and columns.

Rows—Each record within the physical file associated with the table is referred to as a "row." This is conceptually similar to a spreadsheet where a row contains different types of information.

Columns—The occurrence of a single field in multiple records is referred to as a "column." Again, this is conceptually similar to a spreadsheet where a column contains different values for the same type of data.

Views—A view is an AS/400 logical file that can access one or more tables (physical files). All read and write accesses to information in tables is funneled through a view structure. The view is the object through which programs and interactive users see and change SQL-based information.

Indexes—An index is an AS/400 keyed logical file that arranges columns in tables in ascending or descending order. Indexes may be applied to tables to provide structured or faster paths to information. The information itself is accessed through the view structure.

Interactive SQL and precompiled SQL programs may interact with AS/400 database files without further complications. Using SQL interactively allows you to query information contained in database files and view the information on your screen (or redirect the results elsewhere).

Access to the interactive SQL handler is accomplished through the STRSQL command. Once the command is issued, you are presented with the Enter SQL Statements menu (see Figure 15–6):

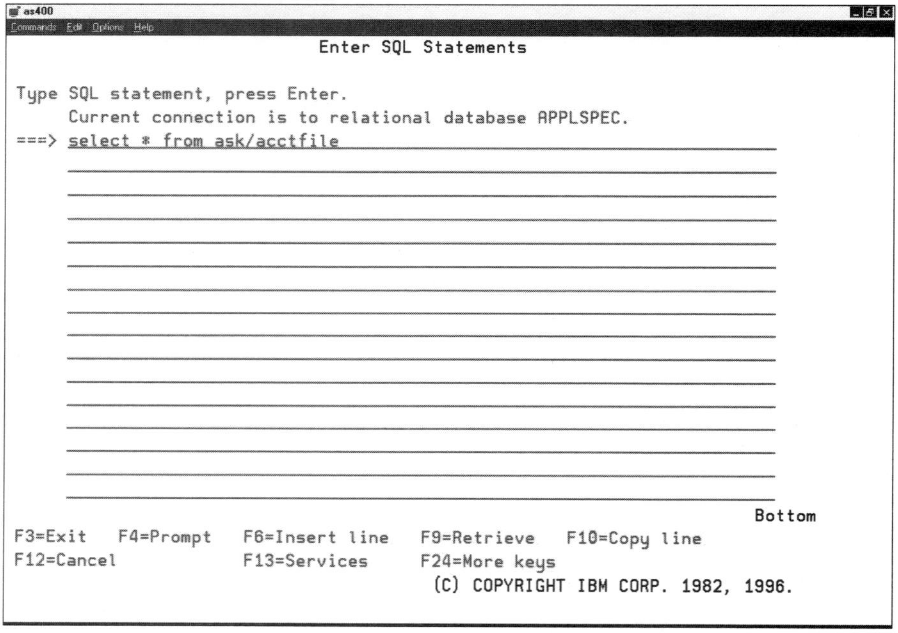

```
 as400                                                                    _ 6 X
Commands  Edit  Options  Help
                            Enter SQL Statements

Type SQL statement, press Enter.
      Current connection is to relational database APPLSPEC.
 ===> select * from ask/acctfile
 _____
 _____
 _____
 _____
 _____
 _____
 _____
 _____
 _____
 _____
 _____
 _____
 _____
 _____
 _____
                                                                      Bottom
 F3=Exit   F4=Prompt   F6=Insert line   F9=Retrieve   F10=Copy line
 F12=Cancel             F13=Services     F24=More keys
                                   (C) COPYRIGHT IBM CORP. 1982, 1996.
```

Figure 15–6: SQL display with SELECT command

With interactive SQL you can perform queries on existing physical files by using standard SQL commands. For example, you can use the SQL command SELECT* to select all fields in a file, then use a WHERE clause to define your selection criteria. When you transmit your SQL directives, the resulting SQL view is presented on your screen (see Figure 15–7).

When developing SQL programs, however, the programming environment requires additional constructs to manage resources associated with SQL access. These constructs include

> Collections—A collection contains SQL tables, views, indexes, and programs that interrelate to one another. A collection also contains a journal, a journal receiver, a catalog, and a data dictionary. A collection is conceptually similar to a library.

Journals and journal receivers—These structures are used to record changes to the information being accessed. Journals and journal receivers allow the program to post and recover information updates.

Data dictionaries—A data dictionary defines the structures of the tables in the collection.

Catalogs—A catalog maintains the associations between the views, tables, and indexes in the collection.

SQL is integrated into the OS/400 operating system and is a component in the Systems Applications Architecture (SAA). SQL access is available to local programs, remote programs, and interactive users. Support for remote access allows SQL to be an important component in developing distributed applications.

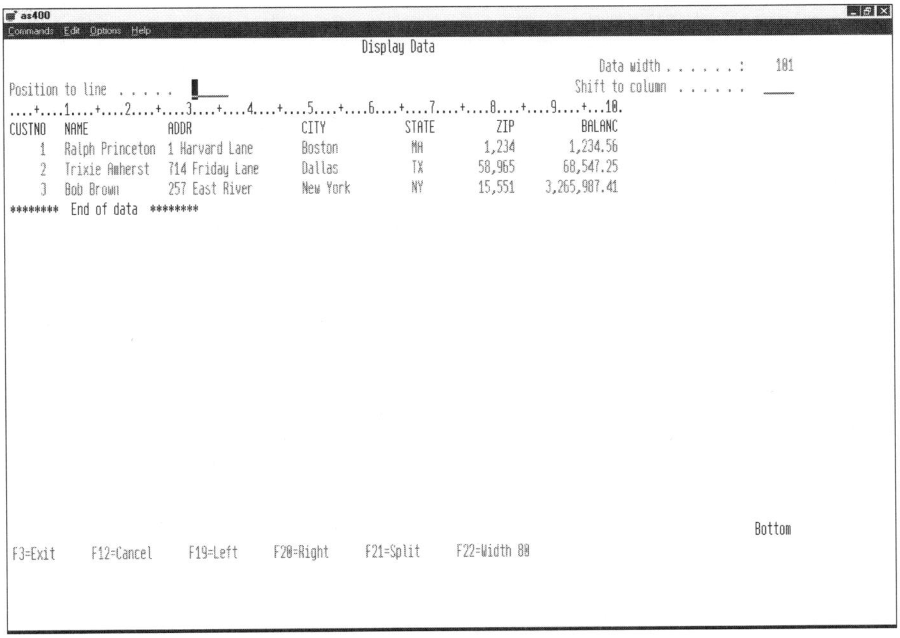

Figure 15–7: SQL view

15.5 SYSTEMS APPLICATION ARCHITECTURE (SAA)

IBM's Systems Application Architecture (SAA) defines characteristics and interfaces used to develop application programs. The primary purpose of SAA is to allow applications to be developed without a high degree of dependability on the specifics of the system on which they will operate. This independence allows SAA programs to be easily ported from one system to another; for example, an application can be moved from an AS/400 to a mainframe. A secondary goal of SAA is to provide the user community with a common interface and predictable behavior for application programs. Although each application can serve a different purpose, the screen appearance and use of keys for standard functions (for example, "exit," "files," "help," and so on) remains consistent between applications.

Finally, in addition to portability and predictability, applications developed under SAA may communicate with one another. This allows SAA to sponsor cooperative or client/server relationships between applications running on different systems.

SAA is composed of four key elements. They are

Common User Access (CUA)— Describes the characteristics of the screen presentation and keyboard/mouse interactions for both text-based and graphics-oriented application displays. The CUA interface is one of the best known aspects of SAA because application programs often advertise their conformance to this specification.

Common Programming Interface (CPI)—Defines the mechanisms used by SAA applications to access files, other programs, or data communications devices. For example, SQL is a recommended mechanism for database access.

Common Applications—These are applications that use SAA interfaces and conform to SAA behavioral standards.

Common Communications Support (CCS)—Specifies data formats and protocols that can be used to move information around in an SAA environment. For example, SNA Distribution Services (SNADS) is a supported SAA protocol, and the Document Content Architecture (DCA) is a supported SAA data format.

To facilitate SAA, each system has a set of routines that translate SAA-level activities into the specific operations required to perform that activity on that system. Again, this allows the application program to be isolated from many of the technical details of the host system.

15.6 THE RISC REVOLUTION

IBM announced the Reduced Instruction Set Computing (RISC) AS/400 systems in May of 1995. These new systems, known as the AS/400 Advanced Series, use the new PowerPC AS processors. While other computer companies have also made a move to RISC technology, the AS/400, due to its unique architecture, enables these system migrations to be conducted with minimal impact on business processes. The application programs are translated automatically and the system downtime is manageable.

This section will discuss the characteristics of the RISC systems, provide an overview of the migration process, and identify the key architectural aspects of the AS/400 that enable such a major transition to be accomplished.

15.7 RISC SYSTEM CHARACTERISTICS

The characteristics of a RISC system are fundamentally different than those of a Complex Instruction Set Computing (CISC) system. All AS/400 systems, until the advent of the RISC systems, were CISC systems. The difference between these two types of systems lie in the instruction set supported. A CISC system has a robust instruction set that contains many instructions, many of which will expand to many additional instructions. Another term for the CISC architecture implementation on the AS/400 is the Internal Microprogrammed Interface, or IMPI.

A RISC system contains fewer instructions, with the instructions being atomic, or not able to be decomposed into other instructions. Why would this difference provide an advantage for computing? The advantage lies in the fact that compilers—the system programs that translate source code written in a programming language to an executable program—are so highly developed that functions that had to be implemented at the microprocessor level can now be implemented in software.

To explain this a bit further, a CISC instruction set had instructions at the machine level that closely matched the high level language instructions. While this meant that there would be fewer of the lower level instructions, it also meant that more microprogramming had to be performed by the AS/400 developers. This increase in microprogramming meant more system overhead (leading to less performance) and that even simple instructions would be slow due to the need for the microprogramming at the processor level. However, a RISC instruction set is much simpler, and the complex, compound instructions in the CISC instruction set are not found in the pure implementation of a RISC processor. A compiler on a RISC system will generate the simple, low-level instructions from the complex and compound instructions of the programming language. RISC programs are typically faster and less expensive than corresponding CISC programs. RISC programs are also larger, since many atomic instructions must be used rather than the fewer, more complex CISC instructions.

15.8 THE POWERPC AS PROCESSOR

The idea for a processor used in the AS/400 RISC implementation was born in Rochester, Minnesota and developed in Austin, Texas. The Power in PowerPC does not stand for powerful (although it is); it is an acronym for Power Optimization for Enhanced RISC. The RISC/6000 (and IBM Unix system) processor was being developed in Austin while the Rochester people (home of the AS/400) were deciding that a RISC implementation was needed for the AS/400. Initially, the two groups were marching along separate but similar paths.

The Rochester team felt that a separate RISC implementation was needed because of the unique needs for the community supported by the AS/400. An AS/400 system is a transactional-based interactive system. A typical RISC implementation (until the AS/400) was for an engineering system. These two models are very different in their needs for a processor. The transaction-based system moves information in and out of memory, but does little modification of the information. An engineering system will operate on smaller amounts of information, but will perform many more computations. A transaction-based system will usually perform many more input and output operations than an engineering system, while an engineering system will perform more looping and branching.

In 1991 the decision was made to combine the processing capabilities of the engineering-based microprocessor developed in Austin with the needs of the transaction-oriented system based in Rochester. The two different orientations were brought together in a single microprocessor.

Characteristics of the AS/400 PowerPC implementation include RISC standards such as use of registers, fixed length instructions, simple addressing, and register-to-register operations. These are standard RISC characteristics. The AS/400 implementation expands on these basic strengths to provide the processing capability needed for transaction-based processing. The 64-bit architecture implemented on the PowerPC AS chip enables the AS/400 to accommodate the unique transaction-oriented needs of a commercial system.

15.8.1 RISC Performance

The performance of CISC systems have been eclipsed by the sheer horsepower of a cost-equivalent RISC system. The performance gains are impressive, but come with a cost. Since RISC systems create programs with more but smaller instructions, the program sizes are larger. This requires more main storage in an AS/400 to achieve acceptable performance levels. Rules of thumb when upgrading from CISC to RISC are

If the CISC memory is 96 Mbytes or less, double the memory for RISC and add 16 Mbytes.

If the CISC memory is greater than 96 Mbytes, double the memory for RISC.

As you can see, the memory requirements are much larger than for CISC. IBM provides more memory on the processor board, and memory prices for RISC are tailored to accommodate the greater need for memory.

The disk storage requirements are also greater. A CISC system uses disk allocation units that are 512 bytes in size. Disk allocation units for a RISC system are 4 Kbytes (4096). This means that a small object (less than 4 Kbytes in size) will still require a 4-Kbyte allocation unit, meaning that some space may be wasted. Disk files become larger when transitioning from CISC to RISC.

While memory and disk requirements increase, the performance gain obtained by moving to RISC outweigh the increased requirements. The performance of AS/400 systems is based on a Relative Performance Rating, or RPR. The RPR is a measure of system performance, with the B10 AS/400 rated at 1 RPR. The following table shows the Relative Performance Ratings of AS/400 Advanced Series systems:

15.8.2 Relative Performance Ratings of AS/400 Advanced Series systems

9402 Model 400 systems

Processor	RPR
2130	13.8
2131	20.6
2132	27.0
2133	33.3

9406 Model 500 systems

Processor	RPR
2140	21.4
2141	30.7
2142	43.9

9406 Model 510 systems

Processor	RPR
2143	77.7
2144	104.2

9406 Model 530 systems

Processor	RPR
2150	131.1
2151	162.7
2152	278.8
2153	450.3
2162	509.9

Contrasting these RPR values with Advanced Series CISC models shows the increase in performance:

9406 Model 300 systems

Processor	RPR
2040	11.6
2041	16.8
2042	21.1

9406 Model 310 systems

Processor	RPR
2043	33.8
2044	56.5

9406 Model 320 systems

Processor	RPR
2050	67.5
2051	120.3
2052	177.4

Note that the highest RPR rating for an AS/400 prior to the Advanced Series was 177.4 for a 9406-F97.

Performance capabilities have increased tremendously with the advent of RISC, and IBM has committed to a 40 percent performance growth rate across the entire AS/400 product line, with a 70 percent growth rate for the high-end systems. Clearly, the RISC product line should be chosen for any new AS/400 systems and is the upgrade path wherever growth is expected.

15.9 WHY UPGRADE?

The performance increases, the cost-effectiveness, and the growth potential of RISC systems are certainly strong reasons to make the move to RISC. Another important reason is IBM's position on future AS/400 systems. IBM has stated that the current shipping release of OS/400 for CISC systems, V3R2, is the last release that will be developed. However, development for the RISC versions of OS/400 will continue, and new features will continue to be developed and included in the operating system.

This is the single biggest reason to move to RISC. With no new development, CISC systems are essentially frozen with the features and capabilities that currently exist in that version of the operating system. While this may be acceptable to a site that has no growth plans or needs for additional functionality, the vast majority of AS/400 sites will continue to grow as the business they support grows.

The upgrade process from CISC to RISC is unique for the AS/400. Never before in the history of the AS/400 product line have both the hardware and the software changed at the same time. The traditional method for an upgrade was to upgrade the software (or hardware) over one weekend and monitor the changes for a few weeks. Once the comfort level reached a certain point, the other component would be changed. However, the RISC operating systems (V3R6 and V3R7) will not run on a CISC system, and the CISC operating systems (V3R2 and earlier) are not compatible with the RISC systems. Of course, the RISC microprocessor and associated hardware are completely different than in the CISC version. This requires a complete change of both operating system and microprocessor.

15.10 THE UPGRADE PROCESS

This process sounds a bit scary, but take heart! IBM has developed a roadmap to take you from CISC to RISC. This section will discuss the steps needed to migrate your system to the new technology. This is not an exhaustive guide for the CISC to RISC transition, and the IBM roadmap should be used to develop and implement the migration plan. The IBM roadmap is titled "AS/400 Roadmap for Changing to PowerPC Technology," publication number SA41-4150. (Be certain you have the latest version of the roadmap as IBM changes the roadmap when new techniques are developed.)

IBM recommendations for a migration path are divided into four main areas. The first is the planning stage, where you will analyze the existing system, determine the hardware and software requirements for the RISC system, specify the configuration, and order the new AS/400. The second stage is preparation, where you will prepare your existing system for the change. The Upgrade Assistant procedure will also be used in this phase. The third stage is the upgrade procedure, where you will install or upgrade the new hardware and operating system. The fourth stage is the postupgrade phase, where you restore the data, convert the applications, and test the application systems on the new system.

Consulting services, either from IBM or a Business Partner, should be considered. The transition from CISC to RISC is straightforward, and IBM has done an excellent job in providing information and a step-by-step checklist (contained in the roadmap) for the migration effort. However, the checklist is involved, quite long (usually around 150 separate steps), and the potential exposure is large. You may find that using IBM or a Business Partner as the overall project manager will make the effort as smooth as possible.

15.10.1 Plan for the Upgrade

The first step in the planning stage is to analyze your existing system. The analysis must identify your current performance level, and the software and hardware products contained within your current system. Some software and hardware features are not supported under RISC, and steps must be taken to either replace the nonsupported features with RISC-supported features, or to develop a workaround where the nonsupported features are no longer needed.

Performance analysis is performed using the Performance Tools for OS/400. The complete Performance Tools package is a licensed program product from IBM. If you do not have Performance Tools installed on your system, consider obtaining the product from IBM or have a consulting service use the Performance Tools on your system to identify the current system performance. PTFs are available to model system performance (using BEST/1, a part of Performance Tools) that will indicate the proper RISC system to use.

Nonsupported features, either hardware or software, can be identified using Upgrade Assistant, a no-cost RPQ (Request for Programming Quotation) that contains programs and menus to allow cleanup of the system, estimating disk capacity required, and will save system information prior to the upgrade. Upgrade Assistant will be used in the planning, preparation, and upgrade phases of the project.

The system should be "cleaned up." The amount of disk that must be ordered for the new RISC system will be identified through the use of the Upgrade Assistant, but an accurate estimate can only be made if the existing system is using the proper amount of disk. Users and system managers should delete objects that are no longer needed, and spooled files that are not needed should be deleted or printed. The Reclaim Storage (RCLSTG) command should be executed to remove lost or damaged objects on the system. Run the Reorganize Document Library Objects (RGZDLO) command to reduce the amount of disk storage used by folders and documents.

The software on the existing system should be analyzed to ensure that the software will operate on a RISC system. The Upgrade Assistant will identify any IBM-licensed program products that are not RISC compatible, but the Upgrade Assistant will also identify user-written programs that cannot transition to RISC. This is a critical aspect of the migration. The internal structure of OS/400 programs is very complex, and would require a chapter to simply describe the contents of a program object. However, to concentrate on the program conversion issue, you should know that an OS/400 program object contains a template. The template holds a variety of information regarding the actual executable instructions contained within the object. Some of the information in the program template allows a program to be translated from the object code to program source. This information, known as observeability, also enables debugging of the program object. The observeability of a program may be removed for one of two reasons: to save storage space and to disable the source code retrieval capability. Programs that have had the observeability removed CANNOT be translated from CISC to RISC!

OS/400 uses the observeability information in the program object template to translate the instructions (in the CISC instructions set) to corresponding RISC instructions. The Upgrade Assistant can analyze the existing programs on a system and determine if observeability exists. If a program object does not have observeability, then the program must be recompiled. Note that observeability must be explicitly removed; all programs are compiled with observeability, with the observeability removed with the Change Program (CHGPGM) command.

The above holds true for user-written programs as well as vendor-supplied programs. The vendor for any supplied programs or systems should be contacted to determine if they have a "RISC-ready" replacement. This will reduce the time needed for the transition.

The Upgrade Assistant will identify many of the issues discussed above. The Upgrade Assistant main menu is shown here (see Figure 15–8).

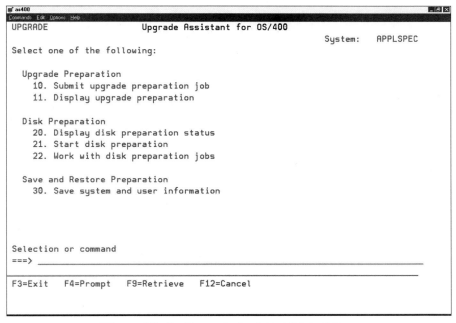

Figure 15–8: Upgrade Assistant Main Menu

Option 10 (Submit upgrade preparation job)—submits an upgrade preparation job to gather information regarding the user objects on the system. This information is collected to be used for option 11, Display Upgrade Preparation.

Option 11 (Display upgrade preparation)—displays the results collected from Option 10. This option will identify unsupported program objects, unsupported hardware, and increased disk storage requirements due to the increased size of the disk allocation units, the growth of OS/400 and the licensed program products, and the potential increased size of objects due to conversion.

Option 20 (Display disk preparation status)—used when the Replace-a-Release upgrade method is used. This option identifies the amount of disk preparation that has been completed, the amount of time remaining to complete the disk preparation, and the last date a disk preparation job was executed.

Option 21 (Start disk preparation)—submits a disk preparation job.

Option 22 (Work with disk preparation jobs)—allows changes to scheduled disk preparation jobs.

Option 30 (Save system and user information)—used when the Unload/Reload method of transition is used. This option will save the information needed to be restored on the CISC system.

15.10.2 Prepare for the Upgrade

The most important decision point in upgrade preparation is to determine which upgrade method should be used. Three methods exist: the Unload/Reload method (with or without the Staged Upgrade offering), the Replace-a-Release method (with or without the Staged Upgrade offering), and the Side-by-Side method. This section will explain the three methods. Regardless of the method chosen, the hardware and software (OS/400 and licensed program products) will be replaced.

The Unload/Reload method saves all user information to tape (the unload portion). Note that OS/400 and licensed program products do not need to be saved as they will be replaced by the new RISC objects. The user information is then restored to the upgraded RISC machine (the reload). The Unload (or save) portion of the user information is accomplished through the use of Upgrade Assistant. The Unload/Reload method may be used for both an upgrade to an existing system and for a new replacement system.

The Replace-a-Release method actually replaces OS/400 and the licensed program products after the hardware change has been made. User information does not need to be saved and restored. The disk preparation task available through the Upgrade Assistant changes the disk allocation units from 512 bytes to 4096 bytes. Note that this is a long running job and should be scheduled around system availability. The Replace-a-Release method may only be used with upgrades.

The Side-by-Side method requires a new system to be installed. Existing applications would be saved and restored on the RISC system. The ported applications could be tested without impacting the production CISC system. After the testing has been completed, the software and possibly the hardware would be migrated to the new RISC system. The Side-by-Side method may only be used with a new system order.

A variant on the upgrade methods is the Staged Upgrade offering. The Staged Upgrade is somewhat similar to the Side-by-Side method. The Staged Upgrade offering takes advantage of the fact that an upgrade to RISC requires that most of the hardware for the new RISC system be shipped with the upgrade. In other words, an almost complete AS/400 system is available on which the IBM Customer Engineer will perform the upgrade. The Staged Upgrade offering provides enough hardware with the upgrade order to have a functioning system, and any additional disk that you order for your new system can be added to the temporary system. In addition, other hardware, such as tape drives, can be rented for the purpose of testing on the RISC system. The application software and user information can be ported to the temporary system. This reduces the amount of downtime required to actually convert the applications. System values, user profiles, object security, and other system-related issues can be explored and resolved prior to the migration. The temporary machine may be used for twenty-one days and may not be used for production work. Note that the Staged Upgrade offering is a separate offering from IBM and requires an additional charge.

15.10.3 The Upgrade Process

The IBM Customer Engineer will remove hardware from the existing system and install the hardware on the upgraded system with any upgrade. The existing system will be powered down and the hardware swap will be made. Depending on the type of upgrade, you may need to convert your programs from CISC technology to RISC technology. The operating system and licensed program products may or may not be present on the new system. Remember that the method of upgrade used (Unload/Reload, Replace-a-Release, or Side-by-Side) will determine the amount of downtime that may be expected. Use of the Staged Upgrade offering will also dramatically affect downtime. Actual downtime information can be calculated based on the type of processor, the amount of disk available, and the amount of information that must be converted.

One of the longest running processes in the overall transition to RISC is the conversion of application programs. Remember that IBM will ship new RISC-ready copies of the operating system and licensed program products so these will not need to be converted. However, the application programs will need to be converted to the new 64-bit RISC model. This conversion can be very time-consuming and is dependent on the number of programs to be converted. One method for decreasing the program conversion time is to convert the applications on a RISC system prior to your conversion. This can be done with the Staged Upgrade offering, or through a Business Partner, consulting firm, or on another RISC system within your enterprise.

Note that there are many steps in the actual upgrade. The hardware and several of the software steps will be conducted by IBM. An average conversion requires 100 to 150 separate steps for the conversion. The IBM Roadmap for Changing to PowerPC Technology details these steps and provides checklists that should be followed precisely.

15.10.4 The Post-Upgrade Process

Several steps are required after the upgrade. Some of the most important are

- restoring authority.
- restoring and setting system values.
- ensuring the system has been initialized after the installation of the operating system.
- performing an Initial Program Load.

- creating configuration lists and reply list entries if used in your organization.
- updating subsystem descriptions.
- recreating the journaling used on your system.
- migrating to a new version of Client Access.

Objects that are migrated from a CISC system to a RISC system must be converted. The object may be converted when they are restored or at a later time. Converting objects when they are restored from tape can be time-consuming as the conversion process is limited by the fairly slow tape drive. Another method is to restore the objects without conversion. They can then be converted later with the STROBJCNV (Start Object Conversion) command. This uses subsystem QSYSNOMAX and will multithread jobs through the subsystem. The conversion should take less time overall. Another conversion method is known as "first touch." This method requires that the objects are restored to the RISC system and not immediately converted. The object will be converted when it is first accessed or "touched." This decreases the time needed for the restoration of objects to the system, but increases the time spent when the object is first accessed. This may be acceptable for seldom-used objects.

Testing is critical to the transition effort. While IBM has produced a remarkable effort in making this migration to be as painless as possible, a responsible systems person will ensure that the new system performs correctly and efficiently. A formal test plan should be developed that will allow complete testing of all applications. Verify system operations in terms of the test plan. Remember that a successful migration requires planning and execution of the upgrade with the results of the upgrade tested and verified.

A

OS/400 Commands

The OS/400 environment includes literally hundreds of commands that can be initiated by workstation operators. In addition to the operator-oriented commands are a set of commands that can only be used within CL programs; these commands are described in Appendix E "CL Programming Operators."

This appendix presents the operator-oriented commands as follows:

Section 1 lists all operator-oriented commands in ascending order of action (the first three characters of the command).

Section 2 lists the same set of commands shown in Section 1; however, in Section 2 they are presented in ascending order of object (the fourth and subsequent characters of the command).

A.1 SECTION 1: COMMANDS SORTED BY ACTION (FIRST THREE CHARACTERS)

ADDACC	Add Access Code
ADDAJE	Add Autostart Job Entry
ADDALRD	Add Alert Description
ADDAUTLE	Add Authorization List Entry
ADDBKP	Add Breakpoint
ADDCFGLE	Add Configuration List Entries
ADDCMNE	Add Communications Entry
ADDCNNLE	Add Connection List Entry
ADDDIRE	Add Directory Entry
ADDDLOAUT	Add Document Library Object Authority
ADDDSTLE	Add Distribution List Entry
ADDDTADFN	Add Data Definition
ADDICFDEVE	Add Intersystem Communications Function Program Device Entry
ADDJOBQE	Add Job Queue Entry

ADDLFM	Add Logical File Member
ADDLIBLE	Add Library List Entry
ADDMSGD	Add Message Description
ADDNETJOBE	Add Network Job Entry
ADDPFM	Add Physical File Member
ADDPFRCOL	Add Performance Collection
ADDPGM	Add Program
ADDPJE	Add Prestart Job Entry
ADDREXBUF	Add REXX Buffer
ADDRPYLE	Add Reply List Entry
ADDRTGE	Add Routing Entry
ADDSCHIDXE	Add Search Index Entry
ADDSOCE	Add Sphere of Control Entry
ADDTRAINF	Add TRLAN Adapter Information
ADDTRC	Add Trace
ADDWSE	Add Workstation Entry
ALCOBJ	Allocate Object
ANSLIN	Answer Line
ANSQST	Answer Questions
ANZPRB	Analyze Problem
ANZQRY	Analyze Query
APYJRNCHG	Apply Journaled Changes
APYPTF	Apply Program Temporary Fix
ASKQST	Ask Question
BCHJOB	Batch Job
CALL	Call Program
CFGDSTSRV	Configure Distribution Services
CFGRPDS	Configure VM/MVS Bridge
CHGACGCDE	Change Accounting Code
CHGAJE	Change Autostart Job Entry
CHGALRD	Change Alert Description
CHGALRTBL	Change Alert Table
CHGAUTLE	Change Authorization List Entry
CHGCFGL	Change Configuration List
CHGCLNUP	Change Cleanup
CHGCLS	Change Class
CHGCMD	Change Command
CHGCMDDFT	Change Command Default
CHGCMNE	Change Communications Entry
CHGCNNL	Change Connection List
CHGCNNLE	Change Connection List Entry
CHGCOSD	Change Class-of-Service Description

CHGCSI	Change Communications Side Information
CHGCSPPGM	Change CSP/AE Program
CHGCTLAPPC	Change Controller Description (APPC)
CHGCTLASC	Change Controller Description (Async)
CHGCTLBSC	Change Controller Description (BSC)
CHGCTLFNC	Change Controller Description (Finance)
CHGCTLHOST	Change Controller Description (SNA Host)
CHGCTLLWS	Change Controller Description (Local Workstation)
CHGCTLNET	Change Controller Description (Network)
CHGCTLRTL	Change Controller Description (Retail)
CHGCTLRWS	Change Controller Description (Remote Workstation)
CHGCTLTAP	Change Controller Description (TAPE)
CHGCTLVWS	Change Controller Description (Virtual Workstation)
CHGCURLIB	Change Current Library
CHGDBG	Change Debug
CHGDDMF	Change Distributed Data Management File
CHGDEVAPPC	Change Device Description (APPC)
CHGDEVASC	Change Device Description (Async)
CHGDEVBSC	Change Device Description (BSC)
CHGDEVDKT	Change Device Description (Diskette)
CHGDEVDSP	Change Device Description (Display)
CHGDEVFNC	Change Device Description (Finance)
CHGDEVHOST	Change Device Description (SNA Host)
CHGDEVINTR	Change Device Description (Intrasystem)
CHGDEVNET	Change Device Description (Network)
CHGDEVPRT	Change Device Description (Printer)
CHGDEVRTL	Change Device Description (Retail)
CHGDEVSNUF	Change Device Description (SNUF)
CHGDEVTAP	Change Device Description (Tape)
CHGDIRE	Change Directory Entry
CHGDKTF	Change Diskette File
CHGDLOAUT	Change Document Library Object Authority
CHGDLOOWN	Change Document Library Object Owner
CHGDOCD	Change Document Description
CHGDSPF	Change Display File
CHGDSTD	Change Distribution Description
CHGDSTPWD	Change Dedicated Service Tools Password
CHGDTA	Change Data
CHGDTAARA	Change Data Area
CHGGRPA	Change Group Attributes
CHGHLLPTR	Change High-Level Language Pointer
CHGICFDEVE	Change ICF Program Device Entry

CHGICFF	Change Intersystem Communications Function File
CHGJOB	Change Job
CHGJOBD	Change Job Description
CHGJOBQE	Change Job Queue Entry
CHGJRN	Change Journal
CHGKBDMAP	Change Keyboard Map
CHGLF	Change Logical File
CHGLFM	Change Logical File Member
CHGLIB	Change Library
CHGLIBL	Change Library List
CHGLINASC	Change Line Description (Async)
CHGLINBSC	Change Line Description (BSC)
CHGLINETH	Change Line Description (Ethernet)
CHGLINIDLC	Change Line Description for IDLC
CHGLINSDLC	Change Line Description (SDLC)
CHGLINTDLC	Change Line Description (TDLC)
CHGLINTRN	Change Line Description (Token-Ring Network)
CHGLINX25	Change Line Description (X.25)
CHGMNU	Change Menu
CHGMODD	Change Mode Description
CHGMSGD	Change Message Description
CHGMSGQ	Change Message Queue
CHGNETA	Change Network Attributes
CHGNETJOBE	Change Network Job Entry
CHGNWIISDN	Change Network Interface Description for ISDN
CHGOBJD	Change Object Description
CHGOBJOWN	Change Object Owner
CHGOUTQ	Change Output Queue
CHGPDGPRF	Change Print Descriptor Group Profile
CHGPF	Change Physical File
CHGPFM	Change Physical File Member
CHGPFRCOL	Change Performance Collection
CHGPGM	Change Program
CHGPGMVAR	Change Program Variable
CHGPJ	Change Prestart Job
CHGPJE	Change Prestart Job Entry
CHGPRB	Change Problem
CHGPRF	Change Profile
CHGPRTF	Change Printer File
CHGPTR	Change Pointer
CHGPWD	Change Password
CHGPWRSCD	Change Power On/Off Schedule

CHGPWRSCDE	Change Power On/Off Schedule Entry
CHGQSTDB	Change Question-and-Answer Database
CHGRPYLE	Change Reply List Entry
CHGRTGE	Change Routing Entry
CHGS36	Change System/36
CHGS36MSGL	Change System/36 Message List
CHGS36PGMA	Change System/36 Program Attributes
CHGS36PRCA	Change System/36 Procedure Attributes
CHGS36SRCA	Change System/36 Source Attributes
CHGSAVF	Change Save File
CHGSBSD	Change Subsystem Description
CHGSCHIDX	Change Search Index
CHGSHRPOOL	Change Shared Storage Pool
CHGSPLFA	Change Spooled File Attributes
CHGSRCPF	Change Source Physical File
CHGSSNMAX	Change Session Maximum
CHGSYSLIBL	Change System Library List
CHGSYSVAL	Change System Value
CHGTAPF	Change Tape File
CHGTRAINF	Change TRLAN Adapter Information
CHGUSRPRF	Change User Profile
CHGWSE	Change Workstation Entry
CHGWTR	Change Writer
CHKDKT	Check Diskette
CHKDLO	Check Document Library Object
CHKIGCTBL	Check DBCS Font Table
CHKOBJ	Check Object
CHKPWD	Check Password
CHKRCDLCK	Check Record Locks
CHKTAP	Check Tape
CLOF	Close File
CLRDKT	Clear Diskette
CLRJOBQ	Clear Job Queue
CLRLIB	Clear Library
CLRMSGQ	Clear Message Queue
CLROUTQ	Clear Output Queue
CLRPFM	Clear Physical File Member
CLRSAVF	Clear Save File
CLRTRCDTA	Clear Trace Data
CMPJRNIMG	Compare Journal Images
COMMIT	Commit
CPROBJ	Compress Object

CPYCFGL	Copy Configuration List
CPYDOC	Copy Document
CPYF	Copy File
CPYFRMDKT	Copy from Diskette
CPYFRMQRYF	Copy from Query File
CPYFRMTAP	Copy from Tape
CPYIGCSRT	Copy IGC Sort
CPYIGCTBL	Copy DBCS Font Table
CPYLIB	Copy Library
CPYPTF	Copy Program Temporary Fix
CPYSPLF	Copy Spooled File
CPYSRCF	Copy Source File
CPYTODKT	Copy to Diskette
CPYTOTAP	Copy to Tape
CRTALRTBL	Create Alert Table
CRTAPAR	Create Authorized Program Analysis Report
CRTAUTHLR	Create Authority Holder
CRTAUTL	Create Authorization List
CRTCFGL	Create Configuration List
CRTCLPGM	Create Control Language Program
CRTCLS	Create Class
CRTCMD	Create Command
CRTCNNL	Create Connection List
CRTCOSD	Create Class-of-Service Description
CRTCSI	Create Communications Side Information
CRTCSPAPP	Create CSP/AE Application Objects
CRTCSPMSGF	Create CSP/AE User Message File
CRTCTLAPPC	Create Controller Description (APPC)
CRTCTLASC	Create Controller Description (Async)
CRTCTLBSC	Create Controller Description (BSC)
CRTCTLFNC	Create Controller Description (Finance)
CRTCTLHOST	Create Controller Description (SNA Host)
CRTCTLLWS	Create Controller Description (Local Workstation)
CRTCTLNET	Create Controller Description (Network)
CRTCTLRTL	Create Controller Description (Retail)
CRTCTLRWS	Create Controller Description (Remote Workstation)
CRTCTLTAP	Create Controller Description (Tape)
CRTCTLVWS	Create Controller Description (Virtual Workstation)
CRTDDMF	Create Distributed Data Management File
CRTDEVAPPC	Create Device Description (APPC)
CRTDEVASC	Create Device Description (Async)
CRTDEVBSC	Create Device Description (BSC)

CRTDEVDKT	Create Device Description (Diskette)
CRTDEVDSP	Create Device Description (Display)
CRTDEVFNC	Create Device Description (Finance)
CRTDEVHOST	Create Device Description (SNA Host)
CRTDEVINTR	Create Device Description (Intrasystem)
CRTDEVNET	Create Device Description (Network)
CRTDEVPRT	Create Device Description (Printer)
CRTDEVRTL	Create Device Description (Retail)
CRTDEVSNUF	Create Device Description (SNUF)
CRTDEVTAP	Create Device Description (Tape)
CRTDKTF	Create Diskette File
CRTDOC	Create Document
CRTDSPF	Create Display File
CRTDSTL	Create Distribution List
CRTDTAARA	Create Data Area
CRTDTADCT	Create a Data Dictionary
CRTDTAQ	Create Data Queue
CRTDUPOBJ	Create Duplicate Object
CRTEDTD	Create Edit Description
CRTFLR	Create Folder
CRTFNTRSC	Create Font Resources
CRTFORMDF	Create Form Definition
CRTGSS	Create Graphics Symbol Set
CRTICFF	Create Intersystem Communications Function File
CRTIGCDCT	Create DBCS Conversion Dictionary
CRTJOBD	Create Job Description
CRTJOBQ	Create Job Queue
CRTJRN	Create Journal
CRTJRNRCV	Create Journal Receiver
CRTLF	Create Logical File
CRTLIB	Create Library
CRTLINASC	Create Line Description (Async)
CRTLINBSC	Create Line Description (BSC)
CRTLINETH	Create Line Description (Ethernet)
CRTLINIDLC	Create Line Description for IDLC
CRTLINSDLC	Create Line Description (SDLC)
CRTLINTDLC	Create Line Description (TDLC)
CRTLINTRN	Create Line Description (Token-Ring Network)
CRTLINX25	Create Line Description (X.25)
CRTMNU	Create Menu
CRTMODD	Create Mode Description
CRTMSGF	Create Message File

CRTMSGFMNU	Create Message File Menu
CRTMSGQ	Create Message Queue
CRTNWIISDN	Create Network Interface for ISDN
CRTOUTQ	Create Output Queue
CRTOVL	Create Overlay
CRTPAGDFN	Create Page Definition
CRTPAGSEG	Create Page Segment
CRTPASPGM	Create Pascal Program
CRTPDG	Create Print Descriptor Group
CRTPF	Create Physical File
CRTPNLGRP	Create Panel Group
CRTPRTF	Create Printer File
CRTQMFORM	Create Query Management Form
CRTQMQRY	Create Query Management Query
CRTQSTDB	Create Question-and-Answer Database
CRTQSTLOD	Create Question-and-Answer Load
CRTS36DSPF	Create System/36 Display File
CRTS36MNU	Create System/36 Menu
CRTS36MSGF	Create System/36 Message File
CRTSAVF	Create Save File
CRTSBSD	Create Subsystem Description
CRTSCHIDX	Create Search Index
CRTSPADCT	Create Spelling Aid Dictionary
CRTSRCPF	Create Source Physical File
CRTTAPF	Create Tape File
CRTTBL	Create Table
CRTUSRPRF	Create User Profile
CVTCLSRC	Convert CL Source
CVTEDU	Convert Education
CVTPFRDTA	Convert Performance Data
CVTTOFLR	Convert to Folder
DCPOBJ	Decompress Object
DLCOBJ	Deallocate Object
DLTALR	Delete Alert
DLTALRTBL	Delete Alert Table
DLTAUTHLR	Delete Authority Holder
DLTAUTL	Delete Authorization List
DLTCFGL	Delete Configuration List
DLTCLS	Delete Class
DLTCMD	Delete Command
DLTCNNL	Delete Connection List
DLTCOSD	Delete Class-of Service Description

DLTCSI	Delete Communications Side Information
DLTCSPMAP	Delete CSP/AE Map Group
DLTCSPTBL	Delete CSP/AE Table
DLTCTLD	Delete Controller Description
DLTDEVD	Delete Device Description
DLTDKTLBL	Delete Diskette Label
DLTDLO	Delete Document Library Object
DLTDOCL	Delete Document List
DLTDST	Delete Distribution
DLTDSTL	Delete Distribution List
DLTDTAARA	Delete Data Area
DLTDTADCT	Delete Data Dictionary
DLTDTAQ	Delete Data Queue
DLTEDTD	Delete Edit Description
DLTF	Delete File
DLTFNTRSC	Delete Font Resources
DLTFORMDF	Delete Form Definition
DLTGSS	Delete Graphics Symbol Set
DLTIGCDCT	Delete DBCS Conversion Dictionary
DLTIGCSRT	Delete IGC Sort
DLTIGCTBL	Delete DBCS Font Table
DLTJOBD	Delete Job Description
DLTJOBQ	Delete Job Queue
DLTJRN	Delete Journal
DLTJRNRCV	Delete Journal Receiver
DLTLIB	Delete Library
DLTLICPGM	Delete Licensed Program
DLTLIND	Delete Line Description
DLTMNU	Delete Menu
DLTMODD	Delete Mode Description
DLTMSGF	Delete Message File
DLTMSGQ	Delete Message Queue
DLTNETF	Delete Network File
DLTNWID	Delete Network Interface Description
DLTOUTQ	Delete Output Queue
DLTOVL	Delete Overlay
DLTOVR	Delete Override
DLTOVRDEVE	Delete Override Device Entry
DLTPAGDFN	Delete Page Definition
DLTPAGSEG	Delete Page Segment
DLTPDG	Delete Print Descriptor Group
DLTPGM	Delete Program

DLTPNLGRP	Delete Panel Group
DLTPRB	Delete Problem
DLTQMFORM	Delete Query Management Form
DLTQMQRY	Delete Query Management Query
DLTQRY	Delete Query
DLTQST	Delete Question
DLTQSTDB	Delete Question-and-Answer Database
DLTSBSD	Delete Subsystem Description
DLTSCHIDX	Delete Search Index
DLTSPADCT	Delete Spelling Aid Dictionary
DLTSPLF	Delete Spooled File
DLTTBL	Delete Table
DLTUSRIDX	Delete User Index
DLTUSRPRF	Delete User Profile
DLTUSRQ	Delete User Queue
DLTUSRSPC	Delete User Space
DLYJOB	Delay Job
DMPDLO	Dump Document Library Object
DMPJOB	Dump Job
DMPJOBINT	Dump Job Internal
DMPOBJ	Dump Object
DMPSYSOBJ	Dump System Object
DMPTAP	Dump Tape
DMPTRC	Dump Trace
DSCJOB	Disconnect Job
DSPACC	Display Access Code
DSPACCAUT	Display Access Code Authority
DSPACTPJ	Display Active Prestart Jobs
DSPAPPNINF	Display APPN Information
DSPAUTHLR	Display Authority Holder
DSPAUTL	Display Authorization List
DSPAUTLDLO	Display Authorization List Document Library Objects
DSPAUTLOBJ	Display Authorization List Objects
DSPAUTUSR	Display Authorized Users
DSPBKP	Display Breakpoints
DSPCFGL	Display Configuration List
DSPCLS	Display Class
DSPCMD	Display Command
DSPCNNL	Display Connection List
DSPCNNSTS	Display Connection Status
DSPCOSD	Display Class-of-Service Description
DSPCSI	Display Communications Side Information

DSPCSPOBJ	Display CSP/AE Object
DSPCTLD	Display Controller Description
DSPDBG	Display Debug
DSPDBR	Display Database Relations
DSPDDMF	Display Distributed Data Management File
DSPDEVD	Display Device Description
DSPDIR	Display Directory
DSPDKT	Display Diskette
DSPDLOAUT	Display Document Library Object Authority
DSPDOC	Display Document
DSPDSTL	Display Distribution List
DSPDSTLOG	Display Distribution Log
DSPDSTSRV	Display Distribution Services
DSPDTA	Display Data
DSPDTAARA	Display Data Area
DSPDTADCT	Display Data Dictionary
DSPEDTD	Display Edit Description
DSPFD	Display File Description
DSPFFD	Display File Field Description
DSPFLR	Display Folder
DSPHDWRSC	Display Hardware Resources
DSPHFS	Display Hierarchical File Systems
DSPHLPDOC	Display Help Document
DSPIGCDCT	Display DBCS Conversion Dictionary
DSPJOB	Display Job
DSPJOBD	Display Job Description
DSPJOBLOG	Display Job Log
DSPJRN	Display Journal
DSPJRNRCVA	Display Journal Receiver Attributes
DSPKBDMAP	Display Keyboard Map
DSPLCLHDW	Display Local Hardware
DSPLIB	Display Library
DSPLIBD	Display Library Description
DSPLIBL	Display Library List
DSPLIND	Display Line Description
DSPLOG	Display Log
DSPMNUA	Display Menu Attributes
DSPMODD	Display Mode Description
DSPMODSTS	Display Mode Status
DSPMSG	Display Messages
DSPMSGD	Display Message Descriptions
DSPNETA	Display Network Attributes

DSPNWID	Display Network Interface Description
DSPOBJAUT	Display Object Authority
DSPOBJD	Display Object Description
DSPOVR	Display Override
DSPPDGPRF	Display Print Descriptor Group Profile
DSPPFM	Display Physical File Member
DSPPGM	Display Program
DSPPGMADP	Display Program Adopt
DSPPGMREF	Display Program References
DSPPGMVAR	Display Program Variable
DSPPRB	Display Problem
DSPPTF	Display Program Temporary Fix
DSPPWRSCD	Display Power On/Off Schedule
DSPRCDLCK	Display Record Locks
DSPS36	Display System/36
DSPSAVF	Display Save File
DSPSBSD	Display Subsystem Description
DSPSFWRSC	Display Software Resources
DSPSOCSTS	Display Sphere of Control Status
DSPSPLF	Display Spooled File
DSPSRVSTS	Display Service Status
DSPSYSVAL	Display System Value
DSPTAP	Display Tape
DSPTRAPRF	Display TRLAN Adapter Profile
DSPTRC	Display Trace
DSPTRCDTA	Display Trace Data
DSPTRNSTS	Display TRN Status
DSPUSRPMN	Display User Permission
DSPUSRPRF	Display User Profile
DSPWSUSR	Display Workstation User
DUPDKT	Duplicate Diskette
DUPTAP	Duplicate Tape
EDTAUTL	Edit Authorization List
EDTDEVRSC	Edit Device Resources
EDTDLOAUT	Edit Document Library Object Authority
EDTDOC	Edit Document
EDTIGCDCT	Edit DBCS Conversion Dictionary
EDTIGCTBL	Edit DBCS Table
EDTLIBL	Edit Library List
EDTOBJAUT	Edit Object Authority
EDTQST	Edit Questions and Answers
EDTRBDAP	Edit Rebuild Of Access Paths

EDTS36PGMA	Edit System/36 Program Attributes
EDTS36PRCA	Edit System/36 Procedure Attributes
EDTS36SRCA	Edit System/36 Source Attributes
EJTEMLOUT	Eject Emulation Output
EMLPRTKEY	Emulate Printer Key
ENDBCHJOB	End Batch Job
ENDCLNUP	End Cleanup
ENDCMTCTL	End Commitment Control
ENDCPYSCN	End Copy Screen
ENDCTLRCY	End Controller Recovery
ENDDBG	End Debug
ENDDEVRCY	End Device Recovery
ENDGRPJOB	End Group Job
ENDINP	End Input
ENDJOB	End Job
ENDJOBABN	End Job Abnormal
ENDJRNAP	End Journal Access Path
ENDJRNPF	End Journal Physical File Changes
ENDLINRCY	End Line Recovery
ENDMOD	End Mode
ENDNWIRCY	End Network Interface Recovery
ENDPASTHR	End Pass-Through
ENDPFRMON	End Performance Monitor
ENDPJ	End Prestart Jobs
ENDPRTEML	End Printer Emulation
ENDRDR	End Reader
ENDRMTSPT	End Remote Support
ENDRQS	End Request
ENDS36	End System/36
ENDSBS	End Subsystem
ENDSRVJOB	End Service Job
ENDSYS	End System
ENDTIESSN	End Technical Information Exchange Session
ENDWTR	End Writer
FILDOC	File Document
FMTDTA	Format Data
GO	Go to Menu
GRTACCAUT	Grant Access Code Authority
GRTOBJAUT	Grant Object Authority
GRTUSRAUT	Grant User Authority
GRTUSRPMN	Grant User Permission
HLDCMNDEV	Hold Communications Device

HLDDSTQ   Hold Distribution Queue
HLDJOB   Hold Job
HLDJOBQ   Hold Job Queue
HLDOUTQ   Hold Output Queue
HLDRDR   Hold Reader
HLDSPLF   Hold Spooled File
HLDWTR   Hold Writer
INZDKT   Initialize Diskette
INZPFM   Initialize Physical File Member
INZSYS   Initialize System
INZTAP   Initialize Tape
LNKDTADFN   Link Data Definition
LODPTF   Load Program Temporary Fix
LODQSTDB   Load Question-and-Answer Database
MOVDOC   Move Document
MOVOBJ   Move Object
MRGFORMD   Merge Form Description
MRGMSGF   Merge Message File
OPNDBF   Open Database File
OPNQRYF   Open Query File
OVRDBF   Override with Database File
OVRDKTF   Override with Diskette File
OVRDSPF   Override with Display File
OVRICFDEVE   Override Intersystem Communications Function Program
               Device Entry
OVRICFF   Override with Intersystem Communications Function File
OVRMSGF   Override with Message File
OVRPRTF   Override with Printer File
OVRSAVF   Override Save File
OVRTAPF   Override with Tape File
POSDBF   Position Database File
PRTAFPDTA   Print Advanced Function Printer Data
PRTCMDUSG   Print Command Usage
PRTCSPAPP   Print CSP/AE Application
PRTDEVADR   Print Device Addresses
PRTDOC   Print Document
PRTERRLOG   Print Error Log
PRTINTDTA   Print Internal Data
PWRDWNSYS   Power Down System
QRYDOCLIB   Query Document Library
QRYDST   Query Distribution
QRYTIEF   Query Technical Information Exchange File

RCLDDMCNV	Reclaim Distributed Data Management Conversations
RCLDLO	Reclaim Document Library Object
RCLRSC	Reclaim Resources
RCLSPLSTG	Reclaim Spool Storage
RCLSTG	Reclaim Storage
RCLTMPSTG	Reclaim Temporary Storage
RCVDST	Receive Distribution
RCVJRNE	Receive Journal Entry
RCVNETF	Receive Network File
RCVTIEF	Receive Technical Information Exchange File
RETURN	Return
RGZDLO	Reorganize Document Library Object
RGZPFM	Reorganize Physical File Member
RLSCMNDEV	Release Communications Device
RLSDSTQ	Release Distribution Queue
RLSJOB	Release Job
RLSJOBQ	Release Job Queue
RLSOUTQ	Release Output Queue
RLSRDR	Release Reader
RLSRMTPHS	Release Remote Phase
RLSSPLF	Release Spooled File
RLSWTR	Release Writer
RMVACC	Remove Access Code
RMVAJE	Remove Autostart Job Entry
RMVALRD	Remove Alert Description
RMVAUTLE	Remove Authorization List Entry
RMVBKP	Remove Breakpoint
RMVCFGLE	Remove Configuration List Entries
RMVCMNE	Remove Communications Entry
RMVCNNLE	Remove Connection List Entry
RMVDIRE	Remove Directory Entry
RMVDLOAUT	Remove Document Library Object Authority
RMVDSTLE	Remove Distribution List Entry
RMVICFDEVE	Remove Intersystem Communications Function Program Device Entry
RMVJOBQE	Remove Job Queue Entry
RMVJRNCHG	Remove Journaled Changes
RMVLIBLE	Remove Library List Entry
RMVM	Remove Member
RMVMSG	Remove Message
RMVMSGD	Remove Message Description
RMVNETJOBE	Remove Network Job Entry

RMVPGM	Remove Program
RMVPJE	Remove Prestart Job Entry
RMVPTF	Remove Program Temporary Fix
RMVREXBUF	Remove REXX Buffer
RMVRPYLE	Remove Reply List Entry
RMVRTGE	Remove Routing Entry
RMVSCHIDXE	Remove Search Index Entry
RMVSOCE	Remove Sphere of Control Entry
RMVTRA	Remove TRLAN Adapter
RMVTRAINF	Remove TRLAN Adapter Information
RMVTRC	Remove Trace
RMVWSE	Remove Workstation Entry
RNMCNNLE	Rename Connection List Entry
RNMDKT	Rename Diskette
RNMDLO	Rename Document Library Object
RNMM	Rename Member
RNMOBJ	Rename Object
ROLLBACK	Rollback
RPLDOC	Replace Document
RRTJOB	Reroute Job
RSMBKP	Resume Breakpoint
RSMCTLRCY	Resume Controller Recovery
RSMDEVRCY	Resume Device Recovery
RSMLINRCY	Resume Line Recovery
RSMNWIRCY	Resume Network Interface Recovery
RSTAUT	Restore Authority
RSTCFG	Restore Configuration
RSTDLO	Restore Document Library Object
RSTLIB	Restore Library
RSTLICPGM	Restore Licensed Program
RSTOBJ	Restore Object
RSTS36F	Restore System/36 File
RSTS36FLR	Restore System/36 Folder
RSTS36LIBM	Restore System/36 Library Members
RSTUSRPRF	Restore User Profiles
RTVAUTLE	Retrieve Authorization List Entry
RTVCFGSRC	Retrieve Configuration Source
RTVCFGSTS	Retrieve Configuration Status
RTVCLDSRC	Retrieve C Locale Description Source
RTVCLNUP	Retrieve Cleanup
RTVCLSRC	Retrieve CL Source
RTVDOC	Retrieve Document

RTVGRPA	Retrieve Group Attributes
RTVJRNE	Retrieve Journal Entry
RTVLIBD	Retrieve Library Description
RTVMBRD	Retrieve Member Description
RTVMSG	Retrieve Message
RTVOBJD	Retrieve Object Description
RTVPDGPRF	Retrieve Print Descriptor Group Profile
RTVPWRSCDE	Retrieve Power On/Off Schedule Entry
RTVQMFORM	Retrieve Query Management Form
RTVQMQRY	Retrieve Query Management Query
RTVSYSVAL	Retrieve System Value
RTVUSRPRF	Retrieve User Profile
RUNQRY	Run Query
RVKACCAUT	Revoke Access Code Authority
RVKOBJAUT	Revoke Object Authority
RVKUSRPMN	Revoke User Permission
SAVCHGOBJ	Save Changed Object
SAVDLO	Save Document Library Object
SAVLIB	Save Library
SAVLICPGM	Save Licensed Program
SAVOBJ	Save Object
SAVS36F	Save System/36 File
SAVS36LIBM	Save System/36 Library Members
SAVSAVFDTA	Save Save File Data
SAVSECDTA	Save Security Data
SAVSTG	Save Storage
SAVSYS	Save System
SBMDBJOB	Submit Database Jobs
SBMDKTJOB	Submit Diskette Jobs
SBMFNCJOB	Submit Finance Job
SBMJOB	Submit Job
SBMNETJOB	Submit Network Job
SBMRMTCMD	Submit Remote Command
SETATNPGM	Set Attention Program
SETKBDMAP	Set Keyboard Map
SIGNOFF	Sign Off
SLTCMD	Select Command
SNDBRKMSG	Send Break Message
SNDDST	Send Distribution
SNDDSTQ	Send Distribution Queue
SNDEMLIGC	Send DBCS 3270PC Emulation Code
SNDFNCIMG	Send Finance Diskette Image

SNDJRNE	Send Journal Entry
SNDMSG	Send Message
SNDNETF	Send Network File
SNDNETMSG	Send Network Message
SNDNETSPLF	Send Network Spooled File
SNDPTFORD	Send Program Temporary Fix Order
SNDRPY	Send Reply
SNDSRVRQS	Send Service Request
SNDTIEF	Send Technical Information Exchange File
STRCLNUP	Start Cleanup
STRCMTCTL	Start Commitment Control
STRCPYSCN	Start Copy Screen
STRCSP	Start CSP/AE Utilities
STRDBG	Start Debug
STRDBRDR	Start Database Reader
STRDKTRDR	Start Diskette Reader
STRDKTWTR	Start Diskette Writer
STREDU	Start Education
STREML3270	Start 3270 Display Emulation
STRFMA	Start Font Management Aid
STRIDD	Start Interactive Data Definition Utility
STRIDXSCH	Start Index Search
STRITF	Start Interactive Terminal Facility
STRJRNAP	Start Journal Access Path
STRJRNPF	Start Journal Physical File
STRMOD	Start Mode
STRPASTHR	Start Pass-Through
STRPFRMON	Start Performance Monitor
STRPGMMNU	Start Programmer Menu
STRPJ	Start Prestart Jobs
STRPRTEML	Start Printer Emulation
STRPRTWTR	Start Printer Writer
STRQMPRC	Start Query Management Procedure
STRQMQRY	Start Query Management Query
STRQRY	Start Query
STRQST	Start Question and Answer
STRREXPRC	Start REXX Procedure
STRRMTSPT	Start Remote Support
STRS36	Start System/36
STRS36PRC	Start System/36 Procedure
STRSBS	Start Subsystem
STRSCHIDX	Start Search Index

STRSPTN	Start Support Network
STRSRVJOB	Start Service Job
STRSST	Start System Service Tools
STRTIESSN	Start Technical Information Exchange Session
TFRBCHJOB	Transfer Batch Job
TFRGRPJOB	Transfer to Group Job
TFRJOB	Transfer Job
TFRPASTHR	Transfer Pass-Through
TFRSECJOB	Transfer Secondary Job
TRCCSP	Trace CSP/AE Application
TRCICF	Trace ICF
TRCINT	Trace Internal
TRCJOB	Trace Job
TRCREX	Trace REXX
UPDDTA	Update Data
VFYCMN	Verify Communications
VFYLNKLPDA	Verify Link Supporting LPDA-2
VFYPRT	Verify Printer
VFYTAP	Verify Tape
VRYCFG	Vary Configuration
WRKACTJOB	Work with Active Jobs
WRKALR	Work with Alerts
WRKALRD	Work with Alert Descriptions
WRKALRTBL	Work with Alert Tables
WRKAUTL	Work with Authorization Lists
WRKCFGL	Work with Configuration Lists
WRKCFGSTS	Work with Configuration Status
WRKCHTFMT	Work with Chart Formats
WRKCLS	Work with Classes
WRKCMD	Work with Commands
WRKCNNL	Work with Connection Lists
WRKCNNLE	Work with Connection List Entries
WRKCNTINF	Work with Contact Information
WRKCOSD	Work with Class-of-Service Descriptions
WRKCSI	Work with Communications Side Information
WRKCTLD	Work with Controller Descriptions
WRKDBFIDD	Work with DB Files Using IDDU
WRKDDMF	Work with Distributed Data Management Files
WRKDEVD	Work with Device Descriptions
WRKDEVTBL	Work with Device Tables
WRKDIR	Work with Directory
WRKDOC	Work with Documents

WRKDOCLIB	Work with Document Libraries
WRKDOCPRTQ	Work with Document Print Queue
WRKDPCQ	Work with DSNX/PC Distribution Queues
WRKDSKSTS	Work with Disk Status
WRKDSTL	Work with Distribution Lists
WRKDSTQ	Work with Distribution Queue
WRKDTAARA	Work with Data Areas
WRKDTADCT	Work with Data Dictionaries
WRKDTADFN	Work with Data Definitions
WRKDTAQ	Work with Data Queues
WRKEDTD	Work with Edit Descriptions
WRKF	Work with Files
WRKFLR	Work with Folders
WRKFNTRSC	Work with Font Resources
WRKFORMDF	Work with Form Definitions
WRKGSS	Work with Graphics Symbol Sets
WRKHDWPRD	Work with Hardware Products
WRKHDWRSC	Work with Hardware Resources
WRKJOB	Work with Job
WRKJOBD	Work with Job Descriptions
WRKJOBQ	Work with Job Queue
WRKJRN	Work with Journal
WRKJRNA	Work with Journal Attributes
WRKJRNRCV	Work with Journal Receivers
WRKLIB	Work with Libraries
WRKLIND	Work with Line Descriptions
WRKMNU	Work with Menus
WRKMODD	Work with Mode Descriptions
WRKMSG	Work with Messages
WRKMSGD	Work with Message Descriptions
WRKMSGF	Work with Message Files
WRKMSGQ	Work with Message Queues
WRKNETF	Work with Network Files
WRKNETJOBE	Work with Network Job Entries
WRKNWID	Work with Network Interface Description Command
WRKOBJ	Work with Objects
WRKOBJCSP	Work with Objects for CSP/AE
WRKOBJLCK	Work with Object Locks
WRKOBJOWN	Work with Objects by Owner
WRKORDINF	Work with Order Information
WRKOUTQ	Work with Output Queue
WRKOUTQD	Work with Output Queue Description

WRKOVL	Work with Overlays
WRKPAGDFN	Work with Page Definitions
WRKPAGSEG	Work with Page Segments
WRKPFRCOL	Work with Performance Collection
WRKPGM	Work with Programs
WRKPGMTBL	Work with Program Tables
WRKPNLGRP	Work with Panel Groups
WRKPRB	Work with Problem
WRKPRDINF	Work with Product Information
WRKPRTSTS	Work with Printing Status
WRKQMFORM	Work with Query Management Form
WRKQMQRY	Work with Query Management Query
WRKQST	Work with Questions
WRKRDR	Work with Readers
WRKRPYLE	Work with System Reply List Entries
WRKSBMJOB	Work with Submitted Jobs
WRKSBS	Work with Subsystems
WRKSBSD	Work with Subsystem Descriptions
WRKSBSJOB	Work with Subsystem Jobs
WRKSCHIDX	Work with Search Indexes
WRKSCHIDXE	Work with Search Index Entries
WRKSHRPOOL	Work with Shared Storage Pools
WRKSOC	Work with Sphere of Control
WRKSPADCT	Work with Spelling Aid Dictionaries
WRKSPLF	Work with Spooled Files
WRKSPLFA	Work with Spooled File Attributes
WRKSRVPVD	Work with Service Providers
WRKSYSSTS	Work with System Status
WRKSYSVAL	Work with System Values
WRKTBL	Work with Tables
WRKTIE	Work with Technical Information Exchange
WRKTRA	Work with TRLAN Adapters
WRKUSRJOB	Work with User Jobs
WRKUSRPRF	Work with User Profiles
WRKUSRTBL	Work with User Tables
WRKWTR	Work with Writers

A.2 SECTION 2: COMMANDS SORTED BY OBJECT

GO	Go to Menu
ADDACC	Add Access Code

RMVACC	Remove Access Code
DSPACC	Display Access Code
RVKACCAUT	Revoke Access Code Authority
GRTACCAUT	Grant Access Code Authority
DSPACCAUT	Display Access Code Authority
CHGACGCDE	Change Accounting Code
WRKACTJOB	Work with Active Jobs
DSPACTPJ	Display Active Prestart Jobs
PRTAFPDTA	Print Advanced Function Printer Data
CHGAJE	Change Autostart Job Entry
ADDAJE	Add Autostart Job Entry
RMVAJE	Remove Autostart Job Entry
DLTALR	Delete Alert
WRKALR	Work with Alerts
CHGALRD	Change Alert Description
ADDALRD	Add Alert Description
RMVALRD	Remove Alert Description
WRKALRD	Work with Alert Descriptions
CRTALRTBL	Create Alert Table
DLTALRTBL	Delete Alert Table
CHGALRTBL	Change Alert Table
WRKALRTBL	Work with Alert Tables
CRTAPAR	Create Authorized Program Analysis Report
DSPAPPNINF	Display APPN Information
SETATNPGM	Set Attention Program
RSTAUT	Restore Authority
DSPAUTHLR	Display Authority Holder
CRTAUTHLR	Create Authority Holder
DLTAUTHLR	Delete Authority Holder
DSPAUTL	Display Authorization List
CRTAUTL	Create Authorization List
DLTAUTL	Delete Authorization List
EDTAUTL	Edit Authorization List
WRKAUTL	Work with Authorization Lists
DSPAUTLDLO	Display Authorization List Document Library Objects
CHGAUTLE	Change Authorization List Entry
ADDAUTLE	Add Authorization List Entry
RMVAUTLE	Remove Authorization List Entry
RTVAUTLE	Retrieve Authorization List Entry
DSPAUTLOBJ	Display Authorization List Objects
DSPAUTUSR	Display Authorized Users
ENDBCHJOB	End Batch Job

TFRBCHJOB	Transfer Batch Job
DSPBKP	Display Breakpoints
RMVBKP	Remove Breakpoint
ADDBKP	Add Breakpoint
RSMBKP	Resume Breakpoint
SNDBRKMSG	Send Break Message
RSTCFG	Restore Configuration
VRYCFG	Vary Configuration
DLTCFGL	Delete Configuration List
DSPCFGL	Display Configuration List
CRTCFGL	Create Configuration List
CHGCFGL	Change Configuration List
CPYCFGL	Copy Configuration List
WRKCFGL	Work with Configuration Lists
ADDCFGLE	Add Configuration List Entries
RMVCFGLE	Remove Configuration List Entries
RTVCFGSRC	Retrieve Configuration Source
RTVCFGSTS	Retrieve Configuration Status
WRKCFGSTS	Work with Configuration Status
SAVCHGOBJ	Save Changed Object
WRKCHTFMT	Work with Chart Formats
RTVCLDSRC	Retrieve C Locale Description Source
CHGCLNUP	Change Cleanup
ENDCLNUP	End Cleanup
RTVCLNUP	Retrieve Cleanup
STRCLNUP	Start Cleanup
CRTCLPGM	Create Control Language Program
CRTCLS	Create Class
CHGCLS	Change Class
DSPCLS	Display Class
DLTCLS	Delete Class
WRKCLS	Work with Classes
CVTCLSRC	Convert CL Source
RTVCLSRC	Retrieve CL Source
DSPCMD	Display Command
CHGCMD	Change Command
DLTCMD	Delete Command
CRTCMD	Create Command
SLTCMD	Select Command
WRKCMD	Work with Commands
CHGCMDDFT	Change Command Default
PRTCMDUSG	Print Command Usage

VFYCMN	Verify Communications
RLSCMNDEV	Release Communications Device
HLDCMNDEV	Hold Communications Device
CHGCMNE	Change Communications Entry
RMVCMNE	Remove Communications Entry
ADDCMNE	Add Communications Entry
ENDCMTCTL	End Commitment Control
STRCMTCTL	Start Commitment Control
DLTCNNL	Delete Connection List
CRTCNNL	Create Connection List
DSPCNNL	Display Connection List
CHGCNNL	Change Connection List
WRKCNNL	Work with Connection Lists
CHGCNNLE	Change Connection List Entry
ADDCNNLE	Add Connection List Entry
RNMCNNLE	Rename Connection List Entry
RMVCNNLE	Remove Connection List Entry
WRKCNNLE	Work with Connection List Entries
DSPCNNSTS	Display Connection Status
WRKCNTINF	Work with Contact Information
CRTCOSD	Create Class-of-Service Description
DSPCOSD	Display Class-of-Service Description
DLTCOSD	Delete Class-of Service Description
CHGCOSD	Change Class-of-Service Description
WRKCOSD	Work with Class-of-Service Descriptions
ENDCPYSCN	End Copy Screen
STRCPYSCN	Start Copy Screen
CHGCSI	Change Communications Side Information
DSPCSI	Display Communications Side Information
DLTCSI	Delete Communications Side Information
CRTCSI	Create Communications Side Information
WRKCSI	Work with Communications Side Information
STRCSP	Start CSP/AE Utilities
TRCCSP	Trace CSP/AE Application
CRTCSPAPP	Create CSP/AE Application Objects
PRTCSPAPP	Print CSP/AE Application
DLTCSPMAP	Delete CSP/AE Map Group
CRTCSPMSGF	Create CSP/AE User Message File
DSPCSPOBJ	Display CSP/AE Object
CHGCSPPGM	Change CSP/AE Program
DLTCSPTBL	Delete CSP/AE Table
CRTCTLAPPC	Create Controller Description (APPC)

CHGCTLAPPC	Change Controller Description (APPC)
CHGCTLASC	Change Controller Description (Async)
CRTCTLASC	Create Controller Description (Async)
CHGCTLBSC	Change Controller Description (BSC)
CRTCTLBSC	Create Controller Description (BSC)
DSPCTLD	Display Controller Description
DLTCTLD	Delete Controller Description
WRKCTLD	Work with Controller Descriptions
CHGCTLFNC	Change Controller Description (Finance)
CRTCTLFNC	Create Controller Description (Finance)
CHGCTLHOST	Change Controller Description (SNA Host)
CRTCTLHOST	Create Controller Description (SNA Host)
CRTCTLLWS	Create Controller Description (Local Workstation)
CHGCTLLWS	Change Controller Description (Local Workstation)
CRTCTLNET	Create Controller Description (Network)
CHGCTLNET	Change Controller Description (Network)
ENDCTLRCY	End Controller Recovery
RSMCTLRCY	Resume Controller Recovery
CRTCTLRTL	Create Controller Description (Retail)
CHGCTLRTL	Change Controller Description (Retail)
CRTCTLRWS	Create Controller Description (Remote Workstation)
CHGCTLRWS	Change Controller Description (Remote Workstation)
CHGCTLTAP	Change Controller Description (TAPE)
CRTCTLTAP	Create Controller Description (Tape)
CRTCTLVWS	Create Controller Description (Virtual Workstation)
CHGCTLVWS	Change Controller Description (Virtual Workstation)
CHGCURLIB	Change Current Library
OVRDBF	Override with Database File
OPNDBF	Open Database File
POSDBF	Position Database File
WRKDBFIDD	Work with DB Files Using IDDU
ENDDBG	End Debug
CHGDBG	Change Debug
DSPDBG	Display Debug
STRDBG	Start Debug
SBMDBJOB	Submit Database Jobs
DSPDBR	Display Database Relations
STRDBRDR	Start Database Reader
RCLDDMCNV	Reclaim Distributed Data Management Conversations
DSPDDMF	Display Distributed Data Management File
CRTDDMF	Create Distributed Data Management File
CHGDDMF	Change Distributed Data Management File

WRKDDMF	Work with Distributed Data Management Files
PRTDEVADR	Print Device Addresses
CHGDEVAPPC	Change Device Description (APPC)
CRTDEVAPPC	Create Device Description (APPC)
CHGDEVASC	Change Device Description (Async)
CRTDEVASC	Create Device Description (Async)
CHGDEVBSC	Change Device Description (BSC)
CRTDEVBSC	Create Device Description (BSC)
DSPDEVD	Display Device Description
DLTDEVD	Delete Device Description
WRKDEVD	Work with Device Descriptions
CRTDEVDKT	Create Device Description (Diskette)
CHGDEVDKT	Change Device Description (Diskette)
CRTDEVDSP	Create Device Description (Display)
CHGDEVDSP	Change Device Description (Display)
CHGDEVFNC	Change Device Description (Finance)
CRTDEVFNC	Create Device Description (Finance)
CHGDEVHOST	Change Device Description (SNA Host)
CRTDEVHOST	Create Device Description (SNA Host)
CRTDEVINTR	Create Device Description (Intrasystem)
CHGDEVINTR	Change Device Description (Intrasystem)
CRTDEVNET	Create Device Description (Network)
CHGDEVNET	Change Device Description (Network)
CHGDEVPRT	Change Device Description (Printer)
CRTDEVPRT	Create Device Description (Printer)
RSMDEVRCY	Resume Device Recovery
ENDDEVRCY	End Device Recovery
EDTDEVRSC	Edit Device Resources
CHGDEVRTL	Change Device Description (Retail)
CRTDEVRTL	Create Device Description (Retail)
CHGDEVSNUF	Change Device Description (SNUF)
CRTDEVSNUF	Create Device Description (SNUF)
CHGDEVTAP	Change Device Description (Tape)
CRTDEVTAP	Create Device Description (Tape)
WRKDEVTBL	Work with Device Tables
DSPDIR	Display Directory
WRKDIR	Work with Directory
ADDDIRE	Add Directory Entry
RMVDIRE	Remove Directory Entry
CHGDIRE	Change Directory Entry
INZDKT	Initialize Diskette
DSPDKT	Display Diskette

CLRDKT	Clear Diskette
RNMDKT	Rename Diskette
CHKDKT	Check Diskette
DUPDKT	Duplicate Diskette
CHGDKTF	Change Diskette File
OVRDKTF	Override with Diskette File
CRTDKTF	Create Diskette File
SBMDKTJOB	Submit Diskette Jobs
DLTDKTLBL	Delete Diskette Label
STRDKTRDR	Start Diskette Reader
STRDKTWTR	Start Diskette Writer
CHKDLO	Check Document Library Object
DLTDLO	Delete Document Library Object
SAVDLO	Save Document Library Object
RSTDLO	Restore Document Library Object
DMPDLO	Dump Document Library Object
RCLDLO	Reclaim Document Library Object
RGZDLO	Reorganize Document Library Object
RNMDLO	Rename Document Library Object
CHGDLOAUT	Change Document Library Object Authority
ADDDLOAUT	Add Document Library Object Authority
RMVDLOAUT	Remove Document Library Object Authority
DSPDLOAUT	Display Document Library Object Authority
EDTDLOAUT	Edit Document Library Object Authority
CHGDLOOWN	Change Document Library Object Owner
CPYDOC	Copy Document
PRTDOC	Print Document
RPLDOC	Replace Document
RTVDOC	Retrieve Document
DSPDOC	Display Document
MOVDOC	Move Document
FILDOC	File Document
CRTDOC	Create Document
EDTDOC	Edit Document
WRKDOC	Work with Documents
CHGDOCD	Change Document Description
DLTDOCL	Delete Document List
QRYDOCLIB	Query Document Library
WRKDOCLIB	Work with Document Libraries
WRKDOCPRTQ	Work with Document Print Queue
WRKDPCQ	Work with DSNX/PC Distribution Queues
WRKDSKSTS	Work with Disk Status

CHGDSPF	Change Display File
OVRDSPF	Override with Display File
CRTDSPF	Create Display File
DLTDST	Delete Distribution
RCVDST	Receive Distribution
QRYDST	Query Distribution
SNDDST	Send Distribution
CHGDSTD	Change Distribution Description
CRTDSTL	Create Distribution List
DSPDSTL	Display Distribution List
DLTDSTL	Delete Distribution List
WRKDSTL	Work with Distribution Lists
RMVDSTLE	Remove Distribution List Entry
ADDDSTLE	Add Distribution List Entry
DSPDSTLOG	Display Distribution Log
CHGDSTPWD	Change Dedicated Service Tools Password
SNDDSTQ	Send Distribution Queue
HLDDSTQ	Hold Distribution Queue
RLSDSTQ	Release Distribution Queue
WRKDSTQ	Work with Distribution Queue
CFGDSTSRV	Configure Distribution Services
DSPDSTSRV	Display Distribution Services
CHGDTA	Change Data
DSPDTA	Display Data
FMTDTA	Format Data
UPDDTA	Update Data
DSPDTAARA	Display Data Area
CHGDTAARA	Change Data Area
DLTDTAARA	Delete Data Area
CRTDTAARA	Create Data Area
WRKDTAARA	Work with Data Areas
CRTDTADCT	Create a Data Dictionary
DLTDTADCT	Delete Data Dictionary
DSPDTADCT	Display Data Dictionary
WRKDTADCT	Work with Data Dictionaries
LNKDTADFN	Link Data Definition
ADDDTADFN	Add Data Definition
WRKDTADFN	Work with Data Definitions
CRTDTAQ	Create Data Queue
DLTDTAQ	Delete Data Queue
WRKDTAQ	Work with Data Queues
CRTDUPOBJ	Create Duplicate Object

PWRDWNSYS	Power Down System
DLTEDTD	Delete Edit Description
DSPEDTD	Display Edit Description
CRTEDTD	Create Edit Description
WRKEDTD	Work with Edit Descriptions
CVTEDU	Convert Education
STREDU	Start Education
STREML3270	Start 3270 Display Emulation
SNDEMLIGC	Send DBCS 3270PC Emulation Code
EJTEMLOUT	Eject Emulation Output
PRTERRLOG	Print Error Log
CLOF	Close File
DLTF	Delete File
CPYF	Copy File
WRKF	Work with Files
DSPFD	Display File Description
DSPFFD	Display File Field Description
CRTFLR	Create Folder
DSPFLR	Display Folder
WRKFLR	Work with Folders
STRFMA	Start Font Management Aid
SNDFNCIMG	Send Finance Diskette Image
SBMFNCJOB	Submit Finance Job
CRTFNTRSC	Create Font Resources
DLTFNTRSC	Delete Font Resources
WRKFNTRSC	Work with Font Resources
MRGFORMD	Merge Form Description
CRTFORMDF	Create Form Definition
DLTFORMDF	Delete Form Definition
WRKFORMDF	Work with Form Definitions
CPYFRMDKT	Copy from Diskette
CPYFRMQRYF	Copy from Query File
CPYFRMTAP	Copy from Tape
CHGGRPA	Change Group Attributes
RTVGRPA	Retrieve Group Attributes
ENDGRPJOB	End Group Job
TFRGRPJOB	Transfer to Group Job
CRTGSS	Create Graphics Symbol Set
DLTGSS	Delete Graphics Symbol Set
WRKGSS	Work with Graphics Symbol Sets
WRKHDWPRD	Work with Hardware Products
DSPHDWRSC	Display Hardware Resources

WRKHDWRSC	Work with Hardware Resources
DSPHFS	Display Hierarchical File Systems
CHGHLLPTR	Change High-Level Language Pointer
DSPHLPDOC	Display Help Document
TRCICF	Trace ICF
ADDICFDEVE	Add Intersystem Communications Function Program Device Entry
OVRICFDEVE	Override Intersystem Communications Function Program Device Entry
CHGICFDEVE	Change ICF Program Device Entry
RMVICFDEVE	Remove Intersystem Communications Function Program Device Entry
CHGICFF	Change Intersystem Communications Function File
CRTICFF	Create Intersystem Communications Function File
OVRICFF	Override with Intersystem Communications Function File
STRIDD	Start Interactive Data Definition Utility
STRIDXSCH	Start Index Search
CRTIGCDCT	Create DBCS Conversion Dictionary
DSPIGCDCT	Display DBCS Conversion Dictionary
DLTIGCDCT	Delete DBCS Conversion Dictionary
EDTIGCDCT	Edit DBCS Conversion Dictionary
DLTIGCSRT	Delete IGC Sort
CPYIGCSRT	Copy IGC Sort
CPYIGCTBL	Copy DBCS Font Table
EDTIGCTBL	Edit DBCS Table
DLTIGCTBL	Delete DBCS Font Table
CHKIGCTBL	Check DBCS Font Table
ENDINP	End Input
TRCINT	Trace Internal
PRTINTDTA	Print Internal Data
STRITF	Start Interactive Terminal Facility
DSCJOB	Disconnect Job
DLYJOB	Delay Job
ENDJOB	End Job
SBMJOB	Submit Job
HLDJOB	Hold Job
CHGJOB	Change Job
RLSJOB	Release Job
DSPJOB	Display Job
RRTJOB	Reroute Job
DMPJOB	Dump Job
BCHJOB	Batch Job
TRCJOB	Trace Job

TFRJOB	Transfer Job
WRKJOB	Work with Job
ENDJOBABN	End Job Abnormal
DLTJOBD	Delete Job Description
CHGJOBD	Change Job Description
CRTJOBD	Create Job Description
DSPJOBD	Display Job Description
WRKJOBD	Work with Job Descriptions
DMPJOBINT	Dump Job Internal
DSPJOBLOG	Display Job Log
RLSJOBQ	Release Job Queue
CLRJOBQ	Clear Job Queue
CRTJOBQ	Create Job Queue
DLTJOBQ	Delete Job Queue
HLDJOBQ	Hold Job Queue
WRKJOBQ	Work with Job Queue
CHGJOBQE	Change Job Queue Entry
ADDJOBQE	Add Job Queue Entry
RMVJOBQE	Remove Job Queue Entry
DSPJRN	Display Journal
CHGJRN	Change Journal
DLTJRN	Delete Journal
CRTJRN	Create Journal
WRKJRN	Work with Journal
WRKJRNA	Work with Journal Attributes
ENDJRNAP	End Journal Access Path
STRJRNAP	Start Journal Access Path
RMVJRNCHG	Remove Journaled Changes
APYJRNCHG	Apply Journaled Changes
RTVJRNE	Retrieve Journal Entry
RCVJRNE	Receive Journal Entry
SNDJRNE	Send Journal Entry
CMPJRNIMG	Compare Journal Images
ENDJRNPF	End Journal Physical File Changes
STRJRNPF	Start Journal Physical File
CRTJRNRCV	Create Journal Receiver
DLTJRNRCV	Delete Journal Receiver
WRKJRNRCV	Work with Journal Receivers
DSPJRNRCVA	Display Journal Receiver Attributes
CHGKBDMAP	Change Keyboard Map
SETKBDMAP	Set Keyboard Map
DSPKBDMAP	Display Keyboard Map

CALL	Call Program
ROLLBACK	Rollback
DSPLCLHDW	Display Local Hardware
CHGLF	Change Logical File
CRTLF	Create Logical File
ADDLFM	Add Logical File Member
CHGLFM	Change Logical File Member
RSTLIB	Restore Library
CRTLIB	Create Library
CPYLIB	Copy Library
CHGLIB	Change Library
SAVLIB	Save Library
DSPLIB	Display Library
CLRLIB	Clear Library
DLTLIB	Delete Library
WRKLIB	Work with Libraries
DSPLIBD	Display Library Description
RTVLIBD	Retrieve Library Description
EDTLIBL	Edit Library List
DSPLIBL	Display Library List
CHGLIBL	Change Library List
ADDLIBLE	Add Library List Entry
RMVLIBLE	Remove Library List Entry
DLTLICPGM	Delete Licensed Program
SAVLICPGM	Save Licensed Program
RSTLICPGM	Restore Licensed Program
ANSLIN	Answer Line
CRTLINASC	Create Line Description (Async)
CHGLINASC	Change Line Description (Async)
CHGLINBSC	Change Line Description (BSC)
CRTLINBSC	Create Line Description (BSC)
DLTLIND	Delete Line Description
DSPLIND	Display Line Description
WRKLIND	Work with Line Descriptions
CHGLINETH	Change Line Description (Ethernet)
CRTLINETH	Create Line Description (Ethernet)
CRTLINIDLC	Create Line Description for IDLC
CHGLINIDLC	Change Line Description for IDLC
RSMLINRCY	Resume Line Recovery
ENDLINRCY	End Line Recovery
CHGLINSDLC	Change Line Description (SDLC)
CRTLINSDLC	Create Line Description (SDLC)

CRTLINTDLC	Create Line Description (TDLC)
CHGLINTDLC	Change Line Description (TDLC)
CHGLINTRN	Change Line Description (Token-Ring Network)
CRTLINTRN	Create Line Description (Token-Ring Network)
CHGLINX25	Change Line Description (X.25)
CRTLINX25	Create Line Description (X.25)
VFYLNKLPDA	Verify Link supporting LPDA-2
DSPLOG	Display Log
RNMM	Rename Member
RMVM	Remove Member
RTVMBRD	Retrieve Member Description
COMMIT	Commit
CRTMNU	Create Menu
CHGMNU	Change Menu
DLTMNU	Delete Menu
WRKMNU	Work with Menus
DSPMNUA	Display Menu Attributes
ENDMOD	End Mode
STRMOD	Start Mode
CHGMODD	Change Mode Description
DLTMODD	Delete Mode Description
CRTMODD	Create Mode Description
DSPMODD	Display Mode Description
WRKMODD	Work with Mode Descriptions
DSPMODSTS	Display Mode Status
RTVMSG	Retrieve Message
RMVMSG	Remove Message
DSPMSG	Display Messages
WRKMSG	Work with Messages
SNDMSG	Send Message
RMVMSGD	Remove Message Description
ADDMSGD	Add Message Description
CHGMSGD	Change Message Description
DSPMSGD	Display Message Descriptions
WRKMSGD	Work with Message Descriptions
DLTMSGF	Delete Message File
OVRMSGF	Override with Message File
CRTMSGF	Create Message File
MRGMSGF	Merge Message File
WRKMSGF	Work with Message Files
CRTMSGFMNU	Create Message File Menu
DLTMSGQ	Delete Message Queue

CLRMSGQ	Clear Message Queue
CHGMSGQ	Change Message Queue
CRTMSGQ	Create Message Queue
WRKMSGQ	Work with Message Queues
DSPNETA	Display Network Attributes
CHGNETA	Change Network Attributes
RCVNETF	Receive Network File
DLTNETF	Delete Network File
SNDNETF	Send Network File
WRKNETF	Work with Network Files
SBMNETJOB	Submit Network Job
ADDNETJOBE	Add Network Job Entry
RMVNETJOBE	Remove Network Job Entry
CHGNETJOBE	Change Network Job Entry
WRKNETJOBE	Work with Network Job Entries
SNDNETMSG	Send Network Message
SNDNETSPLF	Send Network Spooled File
SIGNOFF	Sign Off
DLTNWID	Delete Network Interface Description
DSPNWID	Display Network Interface Description
WRKNWID	Work with Network Interface Description Command
CHGNWIISDN	Change Network Interface Description for ISDN
CRTNWIISDN	Create Network Interface for ISDN
RSMNWIRCY	Resume Network Interface Recovery
ENDNWIRCY	End Network Interface Recovery
ALCOBJ	Allocate Object
DCPOBJ	Decompress Object
CPROBJ	Compress Object
DLCOBJ	Deallocate Object
SAVOBJ	Save Object
DMPOBJ	Dump Object
RSTOBJ	Restore Object
RNMOBJ	Rename Object
CHKOBJ	Check Object
MOVOBJ	Move Object
WRKOBJ	Work with Objects
DSPOBJAUT	Display Object Authority
RVKOBJAUT	Revoke Object Authority
GRTOBJAUT	Grant Object Authority
EDTOBJAUT	Edit Object Authority
WRKOBJCSP	Work with Objects for CSP/AE
CHGOBJD	Change Object Description

RTVOBJD	Retrieve Object Description
DSPOBJD	Display Object Description
WRKOBJLCK	Work with Object Locks
CHGOBJOWN	Change Object Owner
WRKOBJOWN	Work with Objects by Owner
WRKORDINF	Work with Order Information
CRTOUTQ	Create Output Queue
DLTOUTQ	Delete Output Queue
CHGOUTQ	Change Output Queue
CLROUTQ	Clear Output Queue
HLDOUTQ	Hold Output Queue
RLSOUTQ	Release Output Queue
WRKOUTQ	Work with Output Queue
WRKOUTQD	Work with Output Queue Description
CRTOVL	Create Overlay
DLTOVL	Delete Overlay
WRKOVL	Work with Overlays
DLTOVR	Delete Override
DSPOVR	Display Override
DLTOVRDEVE	Delete Override Device Entry
DLTPAGDFN	Delete Page Definition
CRTPAGDFN	Create Page Definition
WRKPAGDFN	Work with Page Definitions
DLTPAGSEG	Delete Page Segment
CRTPAGSEG	Create Page Segment
WRKPAGSEG	Work with Page Segments
CRTPASPGM	Create Pascal Program
ENDPASTHR	End Pass-Through
STRPASTHR	Start Pass-Through
TFRPASTHR	Transfer Pass-Through
CRTPDG	Create Print Descriptor Group
DLTPDG	Delete Print Descriptor Group
CHGPDGPRF	Change Print Descriptor Group Profile
RTVPDGPRF	Retrieve Print Descriptor Group Profile
DSPPDGPRF	Display Print Descriptor Group Profile
CRTPF	Create Physical File
CHGPF	Change Physical File
CLRPFM	Clear Physical File Member
RGZPFM	Reorganize Physical File Member
ADDPFM	Add Physical File Member
CHGPFM	Change Physical File Member
INZPFM	Initialize Physical File Member

DSPPFM	Display Physical File Member
ADDPFRCOL	Add Performance Collection
CHGPFRCOL	Change Performance Collection
WRKPFRCOL	Work with Performance Collection
CVTPFRDTA	Convert Performance Data
ENDPFRMON	End Performance Monitor
STRPFRMON	Start Performance Monitor
DSPPGM	Display Program
RMVPGM	Remove Program
ADDPGM	Add Program
CHGPGM	Change Program
DLTPGM	Delete Program
WRKPGM	Work with Programs
DSPPGMADP	Display Program Adopt
STRPGMMNU	Start Programmer Menu
DSPPGMREF	Display Program References
WRKPGMTBL	Work with Program Tables
DSPPGMVAR	Display Program Variable
CHGPGMVAR	Change Program Variable
ENDPJ	End Prestart Jobs
CHGPJ	Change Prestart Job
STRPJ	Start Prestart Jobs
ADDPJE	Add Prestart Job Entry
CHGPJE	Change Prestart Job Entry
RMVPJE	Remove Prestart Job Entry
DLTPNLGRP	Delete Panel Group
CRTPNLGRP	Create Panel Group
WRKPNLGRP	Work with Panel Groups
ANZPRB	Analyze Problem
CHGPRB	Change Problem
DSPPRB	Display Problem
DLTPRB	Delete Problem
WRKPRB	Work with Problem
WRKPRDINF	Work with Product Information
CHGPRF	Change Profile
VFYPRT	Verify Printer
ENDPRTEML	End Printer Emulation
STRPRTEML	Start Printer Emulation
CRTPRTF	Create Printer File
OVRPRTF	Override with Printer File
CHGPRTF	Change Printer File
EMLPRTKEY	Emulate Printer Key

WRKPRTSTS	Work with Printing Status
STRPRTWTR	Start Printer Writer
LODPTF	Load Program Temporary Fix
RMVPTF	Remove Program Temporary Fix
APYPTF	Apply Program Temporary Fix
CPYPTF	Copy Program Temporary Fix
DSPPTF	Display Program Temporary Fix
SNDPTFORD	Send Program Temporary Fix Order
CHGPTR	Change Pointer
CHGPWD	Change Password
CHKPWD	Check Password
CHGPWRSCD	Change Power On/Off Schedule
DSPPWRSCD	Display Power On/Off Schedule
RTVPWRSCDE	Retrieve Power On/Off Schedule Entry
CHGPWRSCDE	Change Power On/Off Schedule Entry
RTVQMFORM	Retrieve Query Management Form
DLTQMFORM	Delete Query Management Form
CRTQMFORM	Create Query Management Form
WRKQMFORM	Work with Query Management Form
STRQMPRC	Start Query Management Procedure
DLTQMQRY	Delete Query Management Query
CRTQMQRY	Create Query Management Query
RTVQMQRY	Retrieve Query Management Query
WRKQMQRY	Work with Query Management Query
STRQMQRY	Start Query Management Query
DLTQRY	Delete Query
ANZQRY	Analyze Query
RUNQRY	Run Query
STRQRY	Start Query
OPNQRYF	Open Query File
DLTQST	Delete Question
ANSQST	Answer Questions
ASKQST	Ask Question
EDTQST	Edit Questions and Answers
WRKQST	Work with Questions
STRQST	Start Question and Answer
CRTQSTDB	Create Question-and-Answer Database
DLTQSTDB	Delete Question-and-Answer Database
CHGQSTDB	Change Question-and-Answer Database
LODQSTDB	Load Question-and-Answer Database
CRTQSTLOD	Create Question-and-Answer Load
EDTRBDAP	Edit Rebuild Of Access Paths

DSPRCDLCK	Display Record Locks
CHKRCDLCK	Check Record Locks
HLDRDR	Hold Reader
RLSRDR	Release Reader
ENDRDR	End Reader
WRKRDR	Work with Readers
TRCREX	Trace REXX
RMVREXBUF	Remove REXX Buffer
ADDREXBUF	Add REXX Buffer
STRREXPRC	Start REXX Procedure
SBMRMTCMD	Submit Remote Command
RLSRMTPHS	Release Remote Phase
ENDRMTSPT	End Remote Support
STRRMTSPT	Start Remote Support
CFGRPDS	Configure VM/MVS Bridge
SNDRPY	Send Reply
CHGRPYLE	Change Reply List Entry
RMVRPYLE	Remove Reply List Entry
ADDRPYLE	Add Reply List Entry
WRKRPYLE	Work with System Reply List Entries
ENDRQS	End Request
RCLRSC	Reclaim Resources
CHGRTGE	Change Routing Entry
RMVRTGE	Remove Routing Entry
ADDRTGE	Add Routing Entry
CHGS36	Change System/36
ENDS36	End System/36
DSPS36	Display System/36
STRS36	Start System/36
CRTS36DSPF	Create System/36 Display File
RSTS36F	Restore System/36 File
SAVS36F	Save System/36 File
RSTS36FLR	Restore System/36 Folder
RSTS36LIBM	Restore System/36 Library Members
SAVS36LIBM	Save System/36 Library Members
CRTS36MNU	Create System/36 Menu
CRTS36MSGF	Create System/36 Message File
CHGS36MSGL	Change System/36 Message List
CHGS36PGMA	Change System/36 Program Attributes
EDTS36PGMA	Edit System/36 Program Attributes
STRS36PRC	Start System/36 Procedure
EDTS36PRCA	Edit System/36 Procedure Attributes

CHGS36PRCA	Change System/36 Procedure Attributes
EDTS36SRCA	Edit System/36 Source Attributes
CHGS36SRCA	Change System/36 Source Attributes
CLRSAVF	Clear Save File
OVRSAVF	Override Save File
DSPSAVF	Display Save File
CRTSAVF	Create Save File
CHGSAVF	Change Save File
SAVSAVFDTA	Save Save File Data
WRKSBMJOB	Work with Submitted Jobs
ENDSBS	End Subsystem
STRSBS	Start Subsystem
WRKSBS	Work with Subsystems
CRTSBSD	Create Subsystem Description
DSPSBSD	Display Subsystem Description
DLTSBSD	Delete Subsystem Description
CHGSBSD	Change Subsystem Description
WRKSBSD	Work with Subsystem Descriptions
WRKSBSJOB	Work with Subsystem Jobs
CRTSCHIDX	Create Search Index
CHGSCHIDX	Change Search Index
DLTSCHIDX	Delete Search Index
WRKSCHIDX	Work with Search Indexes
STRSCHIDX	Start Search Index
RMVSCHIDXE	Remove Search Index Entry
ADDSCHIDXE	Add Search Index Entry
WRKSCHIDXE	Work with Search Index Entries
SAVSECDTA	Save Security Data
TFRSECJOB	Transfer Secondary Job
DSPSFWRSC	Display Software Resources
CHGSHRPOOL	Change Shared Storage Pool
WRKSHRPOOL	Work with Shared Storage Pools
WRKSOC	Work with Sphere of Control
RMVSOCE	Remove Sphere of Control Entry
ADDSOCE	Add Sphere of Control Entry
DSPSOCSTS	Display Sphere of Control Status
DLTSPADCT	Delete Spelling Aid Dictionary
CRTSPADCT	Create Spelling Aid Dictionary
WRKSPADCT	Work with Spelling Aid Dictionaries
HLDSPLF	Hold Spooled File
CPYSPLF	Copy Spooled File
RLSSPLF	Release Spooled File

DSPSPLF	Display Spooled File
DLTSPLF	Delete Spooled File
WRKSPLF	Work with Spooled Files
CHGSPLFA	Change Spooled File Attributes
WRKSPLFA	Work with Spooled File Attributes
RCLSPLSTG	Reclaim Spool Storage
STRSPTN	Start Support Network
CPYSRCF	Copy Source File
CRTSRCPF	Create Source Physical File
CHGSRCPF	Change Source Physical File
ENDSRVJOB	End Service Job
STRSRVJOB	Start Service Job
WRKSRVPVD	Work with Service Providers
SNDSRVRQS	Send Service Request
DSPSRVSTS	Display Service Status
CHGSSNMAX	Change Session Maximum
STRSST	Start System Service Tools
RCLSTG	Reclaim Storage
SAVSTG	Save Storage
INZSYS	Initialize System
ENDSYS	End System
SAVSYS	Save System
CHGSYSLIBL	Change System Library List
DMPSYSOBJ	Dump System Object
WRKSYSSTS	Work with System Status
RTVSYSVAL	Retrieve System Value
CHGSYSVAL	Change System Value
DSPSYSVAL	Display System Value
WRKSYSVAL	Work with System Values
DSPTAP	Display Tape
DMPTAP	Dump Tape
DUPTAP	Duplicate Tape
CHKTAP	Check Tape
INZTAP	Initialize Tape
VFYTAP	Verify Tape
OVRTAPF	Override with Tape File
CHGTAPF	Change Tape File
CRTTAPF	Create Tape File
CRTTBL	Create Table
DLTTBL	Delete Table
WRKTBL	Work with Tables
WRKTIE	Work with Technical Information Exchange

QRYTIEF	Query Technical Information Exchange File
RCVTIEF	Receive Technical Information Exchange File
SNDTIEF	Send Technical Information Exchange File
ENDTIESSN	End Technical Information Exchange Session
STRTIESSN	Start Technical Information Exchange Session
RCLTMPSTG	Reclaim Temporary Storage
CPYTODKT	Copy to Diskette
CVTTOFLR	Convert to Folder
CPYTOTAP	Copy to Tape
RMVTRA	Remove TRLAN Adapter
WRKTRA	Work with TRLAN Adapters
RMVTRAINF	Remove TRLAN Adapter Information
CHGTRAINF	Change TRLAN Adapter Information
ADDTRAINF	Add TRLAN Adapter Information
DSPTRAPRF	Display TRLAN Adapter Profile
ADDTRC	Add Trace
RMVTRC	Remove Trace
DSPTRC	Display Trace
DMPTRC	Dump Trace
DSPTRCDTA	Display Trace Data
CLRTRCDTA	Clear Trace Data
DSPTRNSTS	Display TRN Status
RETURN	Return
GRTUSRAUT	Grant User Authority
DLTUSRIDX	Delete User Index
WRKUSRJOB	Work with User Jobs
GRTUSRPMN	Grant User Permission
RVKUSRPMN	Revoke User Permission
DSPUSRPMN	Display User Permission
DSPUSRPRF	Display User Profile
RSTUSRPRF	Restore User Profiles
CRTUSRPRF	Create User Profile
DLTUSRPRF	Delete User Profile
RTVUSRPRF	Retrieve User Profile
CHGUSRPRF	Change User Profile
WRKUSRPRF	Work with User Profiles
DLTUSRQ	Delete User Queue
DLTUSRSPC	Delete User Space
WRKUSRTBL	Work with User Tables
ADDWSE	Add Workstation Entry
CHGWSE	Change Workstation Entry
RMVWSE	Remove Workstation Entry

DSPWSUSR	Display Workstation User
CHGWTR	Change Writer
ENDWTR	End Writer
HLDWTR	Hold Writer
RLSWTR	Release Writer
WRKWTR	Work with Writers

B

Types of Objects

Objects on the AS/400 are organized into "types," as shown in this appendix. All object types are predefined and may be referenced using the object type keywords listed (for example, *CLD, *DOC, and so on). Attributes are then applied to object types for further clarity (for example, a *FILE object type may be qualified as a physical file, a source file, or a logical file).

Object Type	Description
*ALRTBL	Alert table
*AUTL	Authorization list
*BNDDIR	Binding Directory
*CLD	C locale description
*CHTFMT	Chart format
*CLS	Class
*COSD	Class-of-service description
*CMD	Command
*CNNL	Connection list
*CFGL	Configuration list
*CTLD	Controller description
*CSPMAP	Cross-system product map
*CSI	Communications side information
*CSPTBL	Cross-system product table
*DTAARA	Data area
*DTADCT	Data dictionary
*DTAQ	Data queue
*DEVD	Device description
*DOC	Document
*EDTD	Edit description
*FNTRSC	Font resource
*FCT	Forms control table
*FILE	File
*FLR	Folder
*FORMDF	Form definition

Object Type	Description
*GSS	Graphics symbol set
*IGCSRT	Double-byte character set sort table
*IGCTBL	Double-byte character set font table
*IGCDCT	Double-byte character set conversion dictionary
*JOBD	Job description
*JOBQ	Job queue
*JRN	Journal
*JRNRCV	Journal receiver
*LIB	Library
*LIND	Line description
*MENU	Menu
*MODD	Mode description
*MODULE	Module
*MSGF	Message file
*MSGQ	Message queue
*NWID	Network identifier
*OUTQ	Output queue
*OVL	Overlay
*PAGDFN	Page definition
*PAGSEG	Page segment
*PDG	Print descriptor group
*PNLGRP	Panel group
*PRDAVL	Product availability
*PRDDFN	Product definition
*PRDLOD	Product load
*PGM	Program
*QRYDFN	Query definition
*QMFORM	Query management form
*QMQRY	Query management query
*RCT	Reference code translate table
*S36	System/36 machine description
*SBSD	Subsystem description
*SCHIDX	Information search index
*SPADCT	Spelling aid dictionary
*SQLPKG	Structured query language package
*SRVPGM	Service Program
*SSND	Session description
*TBL	Table
*USRIDX	User index
*USRPRF	User profile
*USRQ	User queue
*USRSPC	User space

All objects reside in libraries and occupy physical space. Objects that are of type *AUTL, *COSD, *CTLD, DEVD, *LIB, *LIND, *MODD, and *USRPRF appear in the QSYS library. Objects that are type *DOC and *FLR appear in the QDOC library. All other objects can be assigned to libraries when you create them.

Information on what object types are assigned to specific objects can be obtained through the WRKOBJ command.

C

5250 Keys

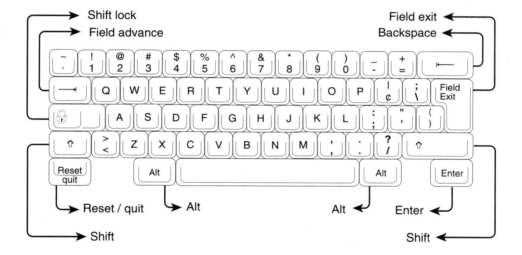

Figure C–1: Keyboard layout

The following standard 5250 keys perform the listed function. For more information, please refer to Chapter 1 ("Getting Started").

<SYSRQ>—Produces a data entry line on the bottom of the screen. If you then press <ENTER>, the System Request menu will appear.

<ATTN>—Suspends the current operation and activates the default attention program defined in your user profile.

<CLEAR>—Erases all input fields in the current screen and relocates the cursor to the first field on the display.

<ERASE INPUT>—Erases the current input field and moves the cursor to the beginning of that same field.

<PRINT>—Sends a copy of the current screen to the default print output queue for your current session.

<HELP>—Brings up information about the current screen or the current field.

<HEX>—Generates an input character from a specified two-digit hexadecimal value.

<PLAY>—Allows you to play keystrokes that have been associated with function keys through the <RECRD> key.

<TEST>—Used for advanced diagnostics. It has no value for normal operations.

<SETUP>—Allows you to define some of the operating characteristics for your workstation.

<PRTSET>—Allows you to define the attributes for a printer directly attached to your workstation.

<RECRD>—Allows you to associate keystrokes with function keys. These keystrokes are then activated through the <PLAY> key.

<PAUSE>—Used with the <RECRD> key to insert a pause into a keystroke sequence.

<FIELD ADVANCE>—Moves the cursor from the current field to the next field.

<SHIFT LOCK>—Locks the alphanumeric keys into their shifted states. Cleared by pressing the <SHIFT> key.

<SHIFT>—Used in conjunction with other alphanumeric keys to generate their shifted values.

<RESET>—Clears the workstation of error conditions and terminates the Help, Insert, and System Request functions.

<QUIT>—Used in conjunction with the Record and Play functions.

<ALT>—Used in conjunction with other keys to select functions shown on the front of key caps.

<ENTER>—Transmits the information contained in the data entry fields to the AS/400 program.

<FIELD EXIT>—Used in alphanumeric fields to erase information in the current field that is behind and to the right of the cursor, and then advance the cursor to the next field. Also used in numeric fields to right-justify the field contents and clear the sign position of the field.

<BACKSPACE>—Performs a destructive backspace and eliminates the character to the left of the cursor.

<FIELD BACK>—Moves the cursor to the beginning of the current field, or to the beginning of the previous field.

<DUP>—Requests the application program to use the data from the last record entered in the current field.

<JUMP>—Accesses the activity for the alternate workstation address.

<NEW LINE>—Moves the cursor to the beginning of the first input field on the next line of the display.

<INS>—Allows you to enter new characters at the cursor position. Insert remains in effect until you press the <RESET> key.

<DEL>—Deletes the character at the current cursor location.

<CURSOR UP>—Moves the cursor up one row.

<CURSOR DOWN>—Moves the cursor down one row.

<CURSOR LEFT>—Moves the cursor left one character position.

<CURSOR RIGHT>—Moves the cursor right one character position.

<ROLL UP>—Requests the next screen in a multiscreen series.

<ROLL DOWN>—Requests the previous screen in a multiscreen series.

<HOME>—Moves the cursor to the beginning of the first input field on the screen.

<RULE>—Turns the ruler on or off.

<FIELD+>—Right-justifies a number in a numeric field and clears the sign position.

<FIELD->—Right-justifies a number in a numeric field and sets the sign position.

The following function keys have the indicated meanings while processing menus driven by standard AS/400 Command Language (CL) commands. Note that the full set of keys is not necessarily available for every command. For more information, please refer to Chapter 2 ("Command Language").

<F1>—Shows help information for the command. The <HELP> key can also be used for the same purpose.

<F3>—Exits the current command and returns to the last major screen.

<F5>—Refreshes the current screen.

<F9>—Shows all possible parameters associated with the current command.

<F10>—Prompts for additional relevant parameters associated with the current command.

<F11>—Shows keyword names available for the command.

<F12>—Cancels the current command and returns to the previous screen.

<F13>—Displays the standard IBM command help text.

<F14>—Shows the command string that will be constructed as passed to OS/400 based on the supplied parameters.

<F15>—Displays the error message if a command error occurs. You can then position the cursor on the message and press the <HELP> key for further information.

<F16>—Suppresses the display of any additional screens associated with a command and executes it immediately.

<F18>—Provides Double Byte Character Set (DBCS) conversion.

<F24>—Shows additional function keys associated with the command.

The following function keys are available at the command line for working with commands. For more information, please refer to Chapter 2 ("Command Language").

<F4>—Invokes parameter prompting for the command.

<F9>—Recalls the previous command.

The following function keys have the associated meanings while using the workstation setup function (accessed through the <SETUP> key). For more information, please refer to Chapter 1 ("Getting Started").

<F2>—Selects the ruler style.

<F3>—Sets the automatic dim interval.

<F4>—Controls the alarm volume.

<F5>—Sets the clicker (key click) volume.

<F6>—Turns the clicker on or off.

<F7>—Toggles cursor blink on and off.

<F8>—Switches between block and underline cursor.

<F10>—Enables or disables extended code display.

<F11>—Turns the row/column indicators on or off.

<F12>—Toggles limited color mode on and off.

D

AS/400 Device Names

The AS/400 provides device names for any devices created with automatic configuration (system value QAUTOCFG set to 1). The device-naming convention is controlled by system value QDEVNAMING. This system value may have one of the following three values:

*NORMAL—indicates that the normal AS/400 device-naming convention should be used,

*S36—indicates that the System/36 style of device-naming conventions should be used,

*DEVADR—indicates that the address of the automatically created device should be part of the device name.

Examples of these naming conventions for the different values of QDEVNAMING are as follows, with an "x" indicating a number in sequence:

QDEVNAMING Value	Device Type	Name Format	Example Name
*NORMAL	Controllers	CTLxx	(CTL01)
	Workstations	DSPxx	(DSP01)
	Printers	PRTxx	(PRT02)
	Tape	TAPxx	(TAP03)
	Diskette	DKTxx	(DKT04)
*S36	Controllers	CTLxx	(CTL01)
	Workstations	Wx	(W1)
	Printers	Px	(P2)
	Tape	Tx	(T3)
	Diskette	Ix	(I4)
*DEVADR	Controllers	CTLxx	(CTL01)
	Workstations	DSPxxxxxx	(DSP010203)
	Printers	PRTxxxxxx	(PRT020304)
	Tape	TAPxx	(TAP03)
	Diskette	DKTxx	(DKT04)

E

CL Programming Operators

The use of commands as an interface to OS/400 functions provides a simple method of constructing programs using Control Language (CL). These programs can perform almost every function under program control that can be executed by a user sitting at a workstation. In addition, several commands are available only from within a CL program. This appendix will describe the CL program-only commands and statements, functions, operators, and special-purpose programs available in CL programming.

E.1 CL PROGRAM-ONLY COMMANDS AND STATEMENTS

CHGVAR—Changes the contents of a variable used in a CL program.

CVTDAT—Converts the format of a date.

DATA—Indicates the beginning of an inline data file used in batch processing.

DCL—Declares a variable used in a CL program.

DCLF—Declares a file to be used for processing within a CL program.

DMPCLPGM—Dumps (displays) all variables used in a CL program and all messages on the program message queue to a spooled file.

DO—Executes a series of commands (a DO group) based on a comparison.

ELSE—Provides an alternate course of action based on a comparison. Used with the IF statement.

ENDPGM—Ending statement for a CL program.

ENDDO—Provides the end to a DO group. Used with the DO command.

ENDRCV—Ends a request for input. Used with the SNDF, RCVF, and SNDRCVF commands.

GOTO—Transfers control to a label within the CL program.

IF—Provides a comparison using CL logical, mathematical, or relational operators.

MONMSG—Monitors for messages within a CL program. This command provides error trapping and recovery functions.

PGM—Beginning statement for a CL program. May optionally include the PARM keyword for parameter passing.

RCVF—Receives information from a database file or a display file.

RCVMSG—Receives a message from a message queue into CL program variables. Used for interprocess communications.

RMVMSG—Removes a message from a message queue.

RTVDTAARA—Retrieves the contents of the Local Data Area or of a named data area into CL program variables.

RTVJOBA—Retrieves the attributes of a job into CL program variables.

RTVMBRD—Retrieves the member description of a member of a database file into a file.

RTVMSG—Retrieves a message from a message file into CL program variables.

RTVNETA—Retrieves the network attributes in CL program variables.

RTVSYSVAL—Retrieves a system value into a CL program variable.

RTVUSRPRF—Retrieves attributes contained in a user profile into CL program variables.

SNDF—Sends information to a display file.

SNDRCVF—Sends information to a display file and then retrieves information from the display file.

SNDPGMMSG—Sends a message under program control to a message queue.

SNDUSRMSG—Sends a message under program control to a user message queue.

SNDRPY—Sends a reply to an inquiry message.

TRFCTL—Transfers control to a program.

WAIT—Waits for information to be received from a database file or a display file. Used with the SNDF, RCVF, or SNDRCVF commands.

E.2 CL FUNCTIONS

%SUBSTRING—This built-in function will extract a substring from a character variable. This function may also be abbreviated as %SST. The syntax for this function is

```
%SUBSTRING(char-var start-pos length)
```

where char-var is the character variable from which the substring will be extracted, start-pos is the starting position in the character to begin the extraction, and length is the number of characters to be extracted.

The result of a %SUBSTRING operation may be placed into a different character variable.

%SWITCH—This built-in function will compare the settings of external switches with a mask. The external switches would be set using the SWS parameter on Submit Job (SBMJOB), Change Job (CHGJOB), or Job (JOB) commands. The default or initial value for the external switches is defined in the Job Description (JOBD) associated with the batch job. The syntax for the %SWITCH function is

```
%SWITCH(mask)
```

where mask is a series of eight characters with possible values of 1, 0, or X. The characters in the mask correspond to the switch that occupies that position in the mask (1 through 8). A value of 0 indicates that the switch in that position is to be tested for a value of 0 (off), a 1 indicates that the corresponding switch should be tested for a value of 1 (on), and an X indicates that the switch in the corresponding position should not be tested.

A value of 1 will be returned from the %SWITCH function if all values in the mask match the corresponding values of the external switches. A value of 0 will be returned if any of the external switches do not match the value in the mask.

E.3 CL PROGRAMMING OPERATORS

Logical Operators

*AND—Provides a logical AND function between two conditional statements. Both of the conditional statements must evaluate to true for the overall conditional statement to be true.

*OR—Provides a logical OR function between two conditional statements. Either of the conditional statements may be true for the overall conditional statement to be true.

*NOT—Proves a logical NOT function. Negates the value of a statement.

Relational Operators

>	or	*GT—Greater Than
<	or	*LT—Less Than
=	or	*EQ—Equal To
>=	or	*GE—Greater Than or Equal To
<=	or	*LE—Less Than or Equal To
<>	or	*NE—Not Equal To

Mathematical Operators

+ —addition
– —subtraction
* —multiplication
/ —division

String Operators

*CAT—Concatenates two string variables together with no intervening spaces.

*BCAT—Concatenates two string variables together with one blank space between the variables.

*TCAT—Concatenates two string variables together and trims any trailing spaces from the first variable.

E.4 SPECIAL PURPOSE PROGRAMS

QCMDEXC—Executes a single command from within a CL program. The name of the program to be executed is contained in a variable and does not need to be known to the program at run time.

QCMDCHK—Checks the syntax of a single command and optionally prompts the command. Often used in conjunction with QCMDEXC to ensure a syntactically valid command is passed to the command processor for execution.

QCLSCAN—Scans a string of characters to determine if a specified substring exists. A "wild card" character may be used to allow any character to match.

QDCXLATE—Provides translation between different character codes. A user created translation table may be used, or one of the following IBM supplied tables:

QASCII and QEBCDIC for ASCII and EBCDIC translations.

QSYSTRNTBL and QCASE256 for upper- and lowercase translations.

Index

A